GOOSE FAT AND GARLIC
Country Recipes
from South-West France

Jeanne Strang's interest in food and cooking
took a professional turn when she was loaned
by the Consumer's Association, for whom she
worked, to Raymond Postgate to help with the
first publication under their auspices of his
Good Food Guide. She is co-author of *The
Good Food Guide Dinner Party Book* and *The
Good Cook's Guide* and has contributed
articles to various wine and food publications.

She and her husband, Paul, bought a house
in South-West France nearly forty years ago
and they have been researching home
cooking throughout the region ever since.
Their knowledge of the country recipes and of
the wines is unsurpassed.

GOOSE FAT
AND GARLIC

Country Recipes
from South-West France

JEANNE STRANG

ILLUSTRATIONS BY TONY GREGSON

KYLE CATHIE LIMITED

First published 1991 in Great Britain by
Kyle Cathie Limited
122 Arlington Road
London NW1 7HP
general.enquiries@kyle-cathie.com
www.kylecathie.com

Published in paperback 1993
Reprinted 1998

This revised edition published 2003
Reprinted 2005

ISBN 1 85626 536 6

A Cataloguing in Publication record for this title is
available from the British Library.

Typeset by DP Photosetting, Aylesbury, Bucks and Mick Hodson Associates
Printed in Great Britain by Biddles Ltd, King's Lynn, Norfolk

FOR
PAUL

All spoon measurements are for level spoonfuls.

Conversions to imperial weights and measures are rounded up or down where more practicable. Obviously it would be unwise to mix the two systems.

The glossary on page 326 contains explanations of some less familiar or local French terms used in the text.

ACKNOWLEDGEMENTS

TO THE memory of Jane Redon and to all our countless friends in South-West France who gave us the idea of writing this book, I owe its dedication. I am profoundly grateful to them for handing on to me their own skills and recipes and their family traditions.

I am also most grateful to Kyle Cathie who has been more than a publisher, an enthusiastic and constructive editor as well.

Finally I would like to acknowledge the assistance of the following publishers and authors who have allowed me to quote from their works: Editions du Seuil and Fernande Costes for *Bonaguil ou le château fou*; Editions Duculot for *Les Mangeurs de Rouergue* by A. Merlin & A.Y. Beaujour; Scolar Press for *Montaillou* by Emmanuel Le Roy Ladurie and Mainstream Publishing and Gordon Golding for *The Cévennes Journal* by Robert Louis Stevenson.

CONTENTS

AUTHOR'S PREFACE
TO THE THIRD EDITION

It is now twelve years since *Goosefat and Garlic* was first published, during which time many more English-speaking francophiles have discovered the South-West. Whether they come as holiday makers or decide to buy properties and settle in the region, they cannot help being drawn to the way of life described in this book.

They and other visitors have undoubtedly been a stimulus in the expansion of the tourist industry and also in the development of artisanal trades promoting the local cuisine for this new market. Some of the traditional recipes were in danger of disappearing, but these have been given a new lease of life.

This third edition contains a number of improvements in the writing of some recipes, also alterations in the text where updating has been necessary, but the recipes remain the same.

I am happy to think that *Goosefat and Garlic* has been of interest and instruction and I hope that it will continue to help many more to develop the same deep affection for South-West France as I have over the last forty years.

JEANNE STRANG
April 2003

LE GRAND SUD-OUEST

J ANE RAN THE most colourful bar in our local village. That was in 1961 when we had just bought our abandoned farmhouse in the Aveyron, which is still one of the least discovered parts of South-West France. The area was then nearly unknown, though our village was listed in Green Michelin as 'worth a detour' and boasted in Red Michelin a small hotel where one could eat well for ten shillings, wine and service included. Indeed it was that Michelin accolade for good food at a reasonable price which first attracted us to the district.

Jane's bar was always crowded after Mass on Sunday mornings, her customers – all men – gossiping and enjoying their aperitifs while their wives went home to put the finishing touches to Sunday lunch. On weekdays, the café was usually quiet and it was then, during a hot June, that we got to know Jane and she began to introduce us to local life and customs.

Each visit to France, while sometimes posing problems quite novel for us, opened new vistas and yielded fresh experiences, especially in eating. We remember vividly one morning spent in our local town, shopping at the open-air market in the central square where, once a week, the farmers' wives arrived to sell their produce and livestock. We saw a vegetable new to us: peas in their pods but looking as if they had been picked too soon since the pods were quite flat. They were, we were told, *mangetout* peas since you ate them whole. On our way home we called at Chez Jane for further information. The bar was the front room of a house, with a few tables, a quantity of straggly potted plants and a counter behind which Jane presided – as often as not barefoot. She was a farmer's wife and her name really was Jane; large, red-haired and with a voice like a Valkyrie, she had a southern accent and a temperament to match the hair. There were no other customers except one old boy so we had a more or less free hand to consult her about how to cook this vegetable which we had bought. Almost before we had opened our mouths, the other occupant of the bar cut in: 'First you must have one or two pigeons . . .' he began, only to be fiercely put in his place by Jane. A noisy debate ensued, too difficult for us to follow, in the strong local accent which we were still struggling to interpret. Having won the battle, Jane then gave us her own simple but quite delicious recipe which is on page 171.

Jane ruled her establishment with a rod of iron but had a soft spot for us because in those days English residents were rare enough to be regarded as acceptable eccentrics, not dangerous foreigners. She explained to us the mysteries of buying *foie gras* at Christmas time, though we had neither money nor opportunity to follow her advice just then. She described to us many of the traditions of country life, and we learned how different was the world of South-West France from that of our own experience, or more importantly, from even the rest of France. We learned of the poverty and struggles of the inhabitants of the hill country compared with the comfortable lifestyles of those living in the valleys or on the plains; of the violent swings of climate in winter and summer, about hailstones that could ruin a year's work and impoverish whole villages; about those lucky enough to find and be able to market truffles at thirty pounds a pound; and about the young people in the countryside unable to find a job, even in the booming French economy.

Jane told us of the mystique of '*midi*': how everything and everybody stops for two hours in the middle of the day, even if it is only to enjoy a bowl of soup, that national institution which is so embedded in farmhouse life but rarely finds its way on to bourgeois restaurant menus. She showed us the marvellous jars of preserves stored away in her cupboards; *pâtés*, of course, but also whole joints of duck and goose preserved in their own fat; pieces of wild boar in a rich wine sauce; parcels of lamb's trotters wrapped in a thin piece of tripe and cooked in a spicy tomato sauce; or the famous *cassoulet*: preserved goose or duck pieces and sausage cooked with white beans, plenty of wine and garlic and destined for a final overcoat of crispy breadcrumbs dotted with goose fat.

We started to search out local produce, we ordered local dishes wherever we could so as to find out what to buy and how to cook the local ingredients. After all, there was little point in trying to cook *à l'anglaise*; the cuts of meat were different, the vegetables were different. What to do with *cèpes*, *chanterelles*, salsify, was at that time a mystery to us. We would ask for details from the owners of tiny country restaurants where they saw few English people in the '60s. Often it was *grand'maman* in the kitchen and she never hesitated to explain charmingly and lovingly the dishes she had prepared. Almost unwittingly, we built up a collection of recipes. We found ourselves fascinated by the origins and development of the real country cooking of the South-West. We are not the only ones: the old days of the *haute cuisine* with its wearisome formalities, heavy sauces and obsolete complications have been succeeded by its aesthetic opposite – *nouvelle cuisine*, which has been wittily and accurately described as 'children's portions arranged by interior decorators'. Now at last there seems to be a real interest in getting back to basics. France has rediscovered the greatness of its regional cookery, and the South-West is deservedly top of the class. '*Là-bas, on mange bien*' they will say to you all over France.

The mention of South-West France to most Anglo-Saxons produces a slightly glazed look in the eye. The South of France or Normandy, yes, most of us could pick them out on a map, but even those who have motored from the Channel towards Spain will probably have driven too fast to have registered much of a picture. That is, apart from those who discovered the Dordogne from the 1950s onwards, who fell in love with that valley and who returned year after year, or even bought property and settled there.

But as seen from Jane's bar, the South-West is not just the Dordogne valley, lovely as it is. The French call this country of the goose, the duck and the pig *le grand sud-ouest*. Its area exceeds that of all England south of the Wash. Look at the map and you will see that all the tributaries of the river Gironde have risen in an amphitheatre of mountains and hills swinging from the Limousin in the north eastwards to the mountains of Cantal and the western Auvergne, then on to the Cévennes, southwards towards the Black Mountain, the hills of Corbières and finally the Pyrenees. The waters from these mountains sometimes flow through narrow gorges between barren limestone plateaux – *causses* – and then into wide fertile valleys and out between the vineyards of Bordeaux into the Atlantic.

Until the coming of modern communications, not only was the South-West cut off from the rest of France but its fertile river valleys and plains were cut off from each other. Conditions have changed today but there is still a vivid contrast between the small-holdings on the *causses* and the huge fruit farms in the lower river valleys. In the hill country there persists the same attachment to a tiny local neighbourhood, the same awe of travelling any further than the local market town, even in an emergency like going into hospital. We buy our wine from a *vigneron* whose farm is half an hour's drive away but he and his family have never been to our village. It is almost unheard of for the older generation to take a holiday and they smile uncomprehendingly when you speak of your own. We employed a roofer who had moved into the area from Lyon and he was described locally as *un étranger*. Once we made ratatouille when our neighbours were coming for lunch, and they regarded it with amazement. In the earliest days we made the even greater mistake of offering them *gazpacho* – a *cold* soup – and this they simply could not face.

Variety of landscape is the keynote to the complete culinary repertoire. On the lush rolling hills of the Limousin in the north, handsome brown cattle are grazed for beef, but on the rich mountain pastures of the Cantal (the lower western slopes of the Massif Central) or in the Pyrenees, they are grazed for their milk, made principally into a variety of lovely cheeses. Below the treeline the sweet chestnut tree finds its perfect environment – hot sunshine but also rain to swell the fruit – and there are chestnut woods everywhere. Chestnuts used to be one of the most important staple foods, pre-dating the potato by many centuries; if the crop failed, a disastrous famine was inevitable. In these mountains of the Auvergne, in the old days, the poverty was sometimes almost impossible for us to imagine. Pork was the only animal meat consumed by most people – the pig is easily fed and it adores chestnuts – and we shall see the variety of ways in which practically every part of the animal enters into the cuisine.

On the quick-draining limestone *causses* it is difficult to make things grow and in the past the farmers eked out a precarious living. Those who lived near enough to the mountain pastures sent their cattle and sheep up there to graze because there was not enough water at home. Nowadays more and more farms are deserted and those remaining are among the poorest in the South-West. You can come across a farmer with a *troupeau* of sheep or goats but in summer it is hard for him to find enough water for even such unthirsty animals. As the great rivers flow further west into the old counties of Périgord and Quercy the *causses* become less wild and inhospitable. Honeysuckle, wild sweet pea, dog roses and poppies grow in profusion, as does a particularly puny kind of oak tree which plays host to one of the gastronomic wonders of the region – the truffle.

The uplands between the rivers Lot and Tarn are underpinned with solid granite, which is covered with a top soil of more or less red earth – hence its old name of *le Rouergue*, literally meaning red earth. Nowadays it is the modern department of Aveyron and this is Jane's and our home county. The soil used to be acid and waterlogged and nothing much would grow except a rather feeble rye crop. This land used to be desolate and was known as *le Ségala*, deriving from *seigle*, the French for rye. Now fertilization has changed the soil structure; potatoes and cereals grow well and the region has been transformed. But traditional recipes we have found here obviously date from former times.

Where there are woods, beneath their canopies another harvest may lie. The same mushrooms are as common or rare in the northern province of the Limousin as they are in the Pyrenees – *girolles*, *coulemelles* and the most prized of all – *cèpes*.

The old county of Périgord, which has given its name to many of the finest regional dishes, covers some of the most varied and beautiful landscapes, each providing the raw materials for these dishes. The geese and ducks which have made the *pâtés* of the Périgord world-famous are reared on every farm. In the north there are lush meadows interlaced with chestnut woods, then comes the higher ground to either side of the river Dordogne where the truffles grow. The valley of the Dordogne seems to be one continuous orchard, while everywhere there are the elegant walnut trees, one of the most important of local crops, supplying half the demand in France.

Just to the south is the old province of Quercy – the name deriving from *quercus*, the Latin name for the oak tree. Quercy stretches from the Dordogne down to and beyond the river Lot as far as the north banks of the rivers Tarn and Garonne. It has much in common with the Périgord; rich valleys growing cereals, fruit and nuts alternating with barren plateaux producing truffles of competing renown.

The south of this county is known locally as the Bas-Quercy or Quercy Blanc and the countryside becomes richer and more fertile as you go down to the wide Garonne valley. The gentleness of the climate allows melons, peaches, apricots and nectarines to grow. There are orchards of plums, too, many of which are dried when fully ripe and marketed as *les pruneaux d'Agen*, claimed to be the best in the world. You are now well on the way to Toulouse, the centre of a wonderfully rich agricultural area, and which in many ways can be regarded as the 'capital' of the region. Toulouse, rather than Paris, is the Mecca for the young people of the South-West who cannot find employment in their local towns and villages. This vibrant southern city has also given its name to the giant goose which is almost the symbol of the South-West.

Wine used to be made over nearly the whole region, but after the devastating phylloxera epidemic a hundred years ago, only the better areas had the resources to replant with new vines. Many peasants still grow their own grapes and make their own wine, while at the other end of the quality scale the South-West makes the greatest wines in the world – the clarets of Bordeaux.

Beyond Bordeaux and the great rivers lies the heartland of Gascony, the armagnac country, a rolling landscape almost Italian in style, where appetites are gargantuan and of whose gourmand inhabitants the whole South-West is respectful. The finest poultry in France comes from here and from the adjoining area called Les Landes. Even Jane, fiercely proud *aveyronnaise* that she was, would concede that. She would also agree that the *foie gras* from Gascony is among the finest in France. And as for the brandy, well . . .

Jane's first real lesson was that the local cuisine was based on poultry and pork fat. We soon found that this was true of the whole of the South-West, except for a few pockets – the Languedoc coast, the Basque country and the coastal area north of the Gironde. Pork and poultry fats give to cooking a quite distinct character and are healthier than either butter or beef fat. However their use is determined largely by the climate. The summers are too dry for rearing cattle on a large scale, except in the higher mountains, and the winters can be too cold for the olive tree. So the South-West was compelled to develop its own cooking medium.

During July and August it can be fiercely hot and dry but during the rest of the year the climate is just as unpredictable as Britain's. Rain, wind and cold, either singly or in any combination, can reach a ferocity difficult to imagine at that latitude. In spring and autumn the rainfall can be Welsh in wetness, and the wind which blows up from the south-east (*le vent d'autan*), gathering strength and heat as it crosses the southern arm of the Cévennes, is reputedly capable of driving the locals out of their minds.

In summer there is always the risk of storms which can demolish the results of a year's careful and painstaking husbandry with five minutes' hail. In winter the cold can be severe enough to keep the population indoors round their fires, though it comes generally in short, sharp snaps. Much of the winter can be, by our standards, spring-like.

Jane explained to us how these vagaries of weather have taught farmers the wisdom of polyculture. If her husband concentrated on one crop he might easily find that he had lost his entire income through the ravages of one storm. He therefore spread his risks and grew a little bit of everything. The typical farmer was fiercely independent. His basic aim was to supply himself as far as he could, and to produce enough by way of surplus to pay for his clothes, electricity, petrol and the very few commodities which his own land could not provide. More often than not he would keep a pig or two, a few cattle (Jane's husband was always down at the river with his cows) while his wife or the older generation made themselves responsible for the chickens, ducks, geese and rabbits. They grew whatever was required to feed the animals – maize, beet, Jerusalem artichokes as well as hay. In the country every home has its kitchen garden which supplies practically the entire demand for vegetables all the year round, and there are usually vines and fruit and nut trees on the property.

We asked Jane in our best French whether such a system was inefficient. Did farming on such a small scale not prevent investment in modern machinery, and so deprive them of the benefits of big crop production enjoyed elsewhere in France? Her reply was that the excellence of the produce in the South-West derives from the painstaking labour and surveillance which only polyculture allows. What substitute is there for home-grown vegetables and fruit or for free-range, corn-fed chickens and ducks? Mass production would no doubt increase the prosperity of the local farmers but many would not even today put up with the resulting fall in standards. Jane's generation is scornful of convenience foods; it has taken many years for the freezer to become accepted. This is surprising in a country which pioneered refrigeration, until one remembers that the household refrigerator, unlike the freezer, does not modify the texture or consistency of the food.

Jane's important gift to us was an appreciation of the dignity of the peasant and his way of life. It took a long time for us to understand the fundamental contrasts between country life in South-West France and the bourgeois concept of 'living in the country' as it is understood in other countries. In English the word 'peasant' has a pejorative ring, suggesting a refusal to better one's condition and to participate fully in the modern world. In France, and above all in the South-West, it means none of these things and we do not hesitate to use the word in Jane's sense, connoting a whole way of life attached to the soil and lived according to the seasons, involving a constant love-hate relationship with nature and the elements, rooted in the necessity to provide for oneself with one's own hands from one's own land. The peasant is as little reliant on others outside the family as possible, proud and perhaps a little obstinate but always dignified and with no sense of inferiority to any other class or group. So we use the word in this book in its factual, descriptive sense and always as a compliment.

For the peasant, the basic family unit has always been the farmhouse as represented by those living within its walls. This is not quite the same as our concept of 'family' because to the peasant there is an almost mystical link between the human beings living under the same roof, whether related or not, and the physical reality of the house. This enlarged concept of home is called in the South-West *l'oustal*. The family and the farm are one and the same. Jane would have endorsed this description of peasant life in the Middle Ages as still largely valid today:

> The main effort (of a farming family) is directed towards more or less satisfactory subsistence rather than towards the creation of accumulated surpluses. The aim is not so much the extended reproduction of agricultural capital as the production of usable values such as food and clothing. Abundance is not asked for, but want can be avoided or dealt with. People are not necessarily lazy, but . . . there are no inordinate incentives to work. The peasant family, when it is large enough, with sons and daughters old enough to work, as well as adults, functions below its capacity . . . This refusal to over-exert oneself is reflected in all the naps taken, the time spent sitting in the sun.
>
> *Montaillou*, Emmanuel Le Roy Ladurie (Penguin, 1980 pp 354–5)

What is difficult to imagine is the extent of the privations of Jane's parents and grandparents a hundred years ago when poverty and starvation were commonplace. The South-West happens to provide the gourmets of the world with at least two of the most luxurious foods: *foie gras* and truffles. Perhaps this is why Parisians like to pretend that the peasants are really rolling in money, with gold bars and sacks of *Napoléons* under the bed. Paradoxically, until modern times the country people have been very poor by any standards, and up to the end of the last century real famines were frequent and tragic in their effect upon whole areas of countryside.

> The house where I was born was built on high ground, with views to the blue line of the horizon. My grandmother used to tell me how, further off, there was a very large plain through which flowed a river – *le bas-*

pays – rich and highly cultivated. She had been in service before she was married and came to live in our hilly part of the world . . . She had the eyes of a real gourmand when she conjured up the food which could be grown on that miracle soil. My grandmother was extrovert and highly strung and she was always hungry. I felt she must often have suffered the pangs of hunger without being able to enjoy any of these treasures. I would go with her to watch over the sheep and I would sit on her lap, listening to the throbbing of her hunger as she evoked memories of the *bas-pays* and her bitterness towards her rich and tyrannical employers. If I wanted to throw a crust of bread to the dog, her patois became threatening. It was amazing how hunger, even at that age, struck me in my relationship with my parents, 'Eat up your soup or you'll get nothing else.' How it continued to govern my ties with my mother and how typical she was of the end of the last century when poverty was total.

Bonaguil ou le château fou, Fernande Costes (Seuil, 1976, pp 7–8)

From a gastronomic point of view family life in the *oustal* was based at the central fireplace which is known in patois as *lou cantou*. The principal fireplace in our farmhouse has a mantel or hood eight feet wide. It was striking enough visually as soon as we walked in for the first time but only over the years have we come to appreciate its significance in a peasant farm. We know now that every house had at least one room in which there was a large chimney where the fire served to keep the family warm and where all the food was prepared. The fireplace was always constructed on such a scale that it could house a number of people and keep them away from the draughts. The French still have a phobia about draughts but on the poorer farms this was not surprising since the doors and floors were often ill-fitting and families needed every insulation they could get. Indeed the cattle were often housed next to, or underneath, the living room to provide some added warmth. After dark during both winter and summer and after a supper which would have been prepared at the fire, the household would gather round the hearth. Sometimes this would be to complete such farm chores as shelling the new crop of walnuts. Or neighbours would be asked in to help with stripping the leaves off the maize cobs; they would be fed in lieu of payment before going home. On long winter evenings chestnuts might be roasted and old, familiar stories told and re-told over a glass of wine.

Our *cantou* is typical. Behind our wood fire, built on the ground beneath a wide chimney opening, we have a large iron fireback, about three feet square, studded with nails, which prevents the fire's heat from eating into the thick stone wall of the house. One or two small hollowed-out squares in this wall serve as dry places to store kindling or spices. At the fireside is a *coffre à sel*, a wooden box, made of carved chestnut wood, originally used for keeping the salt dry and doubling as a settle. A large, cast-iron firedog – *un chenet* – stands at either side of the fire to support the logs and also serves to hold a roasting spit. The top of each firedog is cup-shaped so that a soup bowl can be warmed in it. Close to the fireplace is an oblong wooden table, flanked by wooden benches, and containing a large, deep drawer in which the huge loaves of country bread can be stored. Numerous hooks are fixed to the thick oak beams across the ceiling, from which hams and sausages can be hung to dry. Shelves for the storage of bread or pots of conserves are also slung from these beams because the thickness of the stone walls makes driving in a nail virtually impossible. An important piece of furniture is *le pétrin*, the wooden, lidded trough in which the bread dough is mixed and left to rise.

Next to this room is another which used to house two or three sleeping quarters, built along one wall in alcoves. Each would have contained a straw mattress and a feather eiderdown and could be curtained off for privacy or warmth. (Many of these features can be seen at Sailles near Saint-Nectaire where a typical Auvergnat house and its contents have been preserved as a museum.)

Food is prepared and the dishes washed up in a small scullery leading off the main room. This is known in the region as *la souillarde*, a narrow, stone-floored, vaulted room lined with stone shelves – often solid sheets of granite – for storing food and cooking utensils. At the end a huge slab of stone forms the sink – *l'évier* – hollowed out and sloping towards the wall where a small outlet hole allows the water to drain outside. At one time running water indoors could only be had if you possessed *une fontaine*. This was a copper, brass or earthenware tank, which hung on the wall and was filled from the outside well. A tap at the bottom of the tank released the water and below it a matching bowl held any overflow. *Fontaines* were often beautifully crafted; nowadays they are preserved as valuable ornaments in local homes or antique shops. Our house used to be lit by wall-mounted brass oil lamps known as *les calels*. More simple forms of lighting were home-made resin or beeswax candles, or even, in poorer homes in the very south, resin-wood twigs stuck to a piece of slate.

The use of an open fire as the sole place for cooking does mean that the number of different processes and utensils is somewhat limited. In the old days the all-purpose saucepan was a kind of cauldron – *l'oule* –

often with small feet. It could either be suspended over the fire by means of an adjustable hook called *une crémaillère* or it could stand on a trivet beside the fire or even sit in the ashes. (The charming French phrase for giving a house-warming party is *pendre la crémaillère*.) A neighbour of ours tells us that in his childhood the family *oule* could hold as much as 50 litres and so contain a good supply of constant hot water or a week's supply of stock. Obviously it was difficult to manage many pots at once so there gradually evolved a repertoire of composite stews and braised dishes, or even a succession of dishes all of which could be cooked simultaneously in the same utensil. *La garbure* or *la poule au pot* are recipes where the cooking liquid is first eaten as a soup and the meat and vegetables cooked in it are then the subsequent main course. In this way the solids flavour and enrich the *bouillon*, thereby providing two courses from the one set of basic ingredients.

The other principal cooking vessel was roughly the equivalent of our frying pan – *la poêle*. It usually had an extra long handle – an asset if frying meant the cook had to be close to the hot fire. Or it could be fixed by its handle to a hook in the chimney.

It is not surprising that within this setting meals acquired something of a ritual significance, at once shaping and underlining social attitudes within the household. Until quite recently, for example, it was quite common for only the men to sit at the dining table, the women taking their food as they could, standing in another part of the room or house. When we have been invited into a home for an aperitif or glass of wine, the women rarely take anything, and often stand somewhat in the background while we sit at the table with our host. The men, working extremely hard all day, needed and expected sustenance, so took their meals and mealtimes seriously.

For the women life was equally hard, perhaps harder. Cooking for a large household was the responsibility of the wife, but she was also expected to work outside – in the fields, in the kitchen garden, and to feed the poultry – and raise the children. So it is easy to see how a composite style of cooking was not only the result of the primitive facilities but of the demands put on the cook. This is demonstrated by the variety and importance of soups in the repertoire and so the most appropriate starting point for our culinary journey. *Allez-y et bon appétit!*

LA SOUPE

THE FIRST SOUP we ever tasted in South-West France was a chicken *bouillon* with vermicelli. This is one of the few soups you see on restaurant menus and we call it 'Maz soup' because it was made so well by our local *aubergiste*, Louis Mazières. He managed to produce such a densely flavoured stock – not like the usual watery stuff of which this sort of soup is made elsewhere.

An old farmer just across the valley from us, who sent his grandchildren over to our field to graze his few cows, explained that real soup had been the staple diet of all peasant families for hundreds of years. Taken at breakfast time, at midday and again in the evening, it not only served as standard fare but as the starting point from which other more luxurious dishes were conceived. Peasants do not speak of lunchtime or suppertime but of *l'heure de la soupe*. One does not talk of cooking: *vous faîtes la soupe*. When it is time to go home to eat, *vous allez à la soupe*. *La soupe* is a meal in itself.

Le potage, on the other hand, is something quite different: a first course intended to line the stomach so that the diner can better appreciate what is to follow. There are borderline cases, of course, but generally *la soupe is trempée* – that is to say, pieces of stale bread (nothing ever being wasted) are put in the bottom of the bowl or the tureen and the hot soup poured over them. The 'soaked' bread gives a serious and solid character. The bread makes the soup. According to an old timer in our district:

> It was market day so my father would go and tend the animals, and while he changed his farm trousers and put on some clean ones for the

market, my mother would prepare this meal which never changed: a *torril* and fried egg. *Torril* is a quickly made soup: you fry small slices of onion and cover them with water. You boil them for a little while and then pour the whole lot over the slices of bread. Oh, and the egg too, a fried egg, which you turned over and seasoned with vinegar.

Les Mangeurs de Rouergue, A. Merlin & A.Y. Beaujour (Duculot, 1978, p 84)

This is nearly the same soup as *le tourin* on page 24, *torril* being the equivalent in patois.

In its fuller and more elaborate forms, *la soupe* is both food and drink, hardly surprising since it can combine just about every available ingredient. From the basic formula many regional varieties have emerged, making use of the different farm products available in each district; *la garbure* from Les Landes incorporates preserved goose or duck, *la potée* from the Auvergne is pork-based, *le mourtairol* from the Rouergue is founded on chicken or veal stock, *le sobronade* from the Périgord substitutes haricot beans for bread, and so on. What remains constant is the fundamental principle: pork or poultry cooked with vegetables in water or stock, the solids then either wholly or partially removed and eaten as a second instalment or main dish.

We were initially puzzled as to why there were so many postcards illustrating peasants in berets drinking their soup from the bowl without a spoon. A gourmet dentist whom we met in Périgueux explained why. The last few mouthfuls of hot broth are diluted with a little wine, the warmth developing the alcohol into what was believed to be a fortifying tonic. The custom is called *faire le chabrol*, and is also said to aid the digestion.

> *Après le potage un coup de vin*
> *vole un écu au médecin.*
> (After the soup, a glass of wine
> robs the doctor of a fee.)

is an old saw from the Ariège. To some palates the *chabrol* is a custom which can safely be left to other people: it certainly cools down the *bouillon* although it must be emphasized that the French do not take their soup as hot as we do. Our French friends insist that too much heat detracts from the flavour and takes away the appetite.

The country people have a much fattier diet than we do. The rules of bourgeois cuisine require that as much fat as possible is removed from any stock or soup but this would be unthinkable in, for instance, the

Cantal or the Rouergue. Chicken *bouillon* in particular is often served with quite a lot of the fat left in it and the bread, or sometimes nowadays the pasta, seems to absorb the surplus well enough. The older generation will nevertheless complain that soup is no longer what it was and that the young don't like fat in it. And according to one of our friendliest neighbours, now in his seventies: '*Avant la guerre on mangeait davantage de graisse que maintenant; les gens n'étaient jamais malades.*' (Before the war we ate more fat than nowadays; then, people were never ill.) He also recounted to us with relish how, as a special treat, he was sometimes given a lump of pork fat to eat with his bread at breakfast. Although this might seem highly unhealthy to the diet-conscious, it has to be related to an everyday diet which did not provide butter on the bread, nor any manufactured fat-containing foods like cakes or biscuits, so what fat was eaten was that surrounding the small quantities of meat when these appeared at table, or that used in cooking.

LA GARBURE
Rich soup with vegetables and preserved meats

This is a typical meal-on-its-own from Southern Gascony, where in the pine forests of Les Landes – François Mauriac country – and the foothills of the Pyrenees, a hearty soup is needed to fight the winter fogs and rains. The vegetables will vary from season to season and in the old days the meat would have depended on what was to hand, even if it was only a small piece of salt belly of pork. The Sunday-best version is made with *lou trebuc*, pieces of *confit* of goose or duck – those luscious joints of poultry conserved in their own fat which are described on page 36. The soup must be thick which means you must use either potatoes or white haricot beans. When the pot is put on the table, the ladle should stand up in it on its own! The pieces of meat are taken out and kept warm, to be served afterwards, with either gherkins or salad.

It is important that the vegetables are as fresh as possible. In England we tend to think that soup can be made with even the stalest materials but the French rightly insist that they must be absolutely fresh, even if not the finest specimens. In many cases they will have come straight from the kitchen garden to the soup pot.

Here is perhaps the most traditional version of *la garbure* with all the trimmings; adapt it to your own requirements as you wish. This is the first of many recipes which use salt belly of pork. You can either prepare this yourself (page 83) or buy it ready salted at a *charcuterie*. The *jambon de campagne* is described fully on pages 79–83 and can also be readily bought.

Serves 6

2 small leeks
250 g (½ lb) potatoes
125 g (4 oz) celery
125 g (4 oz) white turnips
1 large onion
4 cloves garlic, peeled
250 g (½ lb) white haricot beans
  (previously soaked if dried)
175 g (6 oz) *jambon de campagne*

250 g (½ lb) salt belly of pork
1.75 litres (3 pt) water
bouquet garni
salt, pepper
1 Savoy cabbage
6 small pieces *confit d'oie* or *confit de canard*
12 small slices stale country bread
  (to line soup bowls)

You are supposed to use an earthenware pot but an enamelled *marmite* – one of those tall, bright red or orange ones which all French ironmongers seem to sell – will do just as well.

Chop fairly roughly all the vegetables except the cabbage, and dice the ham and salt pork. Cover these with water, bring the pot to the boil, skim, and add the bouquet and seasoning. The amount of salt will depend on what meats you are using. Simmer over a low heat, or better still, over a wood fire, for two hours at least. At the end of this time, either coarsely shred the cabbage, or if it is small divide it into segments, and add it to the pot, together with the pieces of *confit*, and continue the cooking for another half an hour. Your *confit* will come with some fat attached, whether you get it out of your preserving jar, or out of a tin or if it has come from the *charcutier*. Do not be too fussy about removing every scrap of fat; a little left on the joints of meat will help the soup no end and the potatoes and beans will absorb it.

Just before serving, line the soup bowls with the slices of bread, take the meats out of the pot if you are going to serve them as a separate course, and serve the rest of the soup.

———— • ————

An extra, authentic touch can be added with the help of a fireside utensil called a *capucin* or in patois *flambadou*. This is a conical piece of iron shaped like a Franciscan friar's hood, pierced at the point and fitted to the end of a long handle. It is mainly used for basting a joint which is being roasted in front of the fire. The cone is placed in the embers of the fire until it becomes red hot. Then a piece of solid fat – back pork fat – is put into the cone, catches fire and drips flaming fat on to the joint through the small hole at the point. You can improve your *garbure* in almost the same way by trickling a thin coating of melted goose or duck fat on top of the soup, and leaving it to cook for a final ten minutes.

Dishes of the same character as *la garbure* are to be found all over the South-West. In Béarn they add red peppers. If meats are not to hand, there may well be a ham bone available, and if it is a little rancid, it is said to add a richness to the soup. If a little salt belly of pork is the only meat to be included, it is chopped up to make a *hachis* (see page 18). This too gives added richness and body. Towards the end of winter, when so many vegetables run to seed, their shoots are not spurned, particularly those of cabbages and turnips. Cut into 15 cm (6 in) lengths, they are incorporated into the soup and are then eaten either with the broth or separately with a vinaigrette. In winter chestnuts often replace the white haricots or potatoes.

Closely related to *garbures* are the *potées* of the South-West. The beautiful pink city of Albi has a particularly successful version called *la potée albigeoise*. This uses shin of beef instead of pork, adding some *saucisse sèche* (thin dried country sausage) and carrots instead of turnips and potatoes. Otherwise the cooking method is similar.

The cabbage is ubiquitous, but it grows particularly well in the Auvergne. Here is a basic recipe for their cabbage soup, to be found no doubt in as many different versions as there are farmers' wives.

La Soupe aux Choux Auvergnate
Cabbage soup from the Auvergne

Serves 6

500 g (1 lb) salt belly of pork, soaked overnight
1 ham bone or salt pork knuckle, soaked overnight
bouquet garni
250 g (½ lb) *saucisse sèche*
250 g (½ lb) carrots

500 g (1 lb) potatoes
1 large onion, sliced
3 leeks, cut into 2.5-cm (1-inch) lengths
2 small green Savoy cabbages
slices of rye or wholemeal bread

Put the pork and bones in a large *marmite* or soup pan with the bouquet garni, cover with plenty of cold water and bring slowly to the boil; skim thoroughly and leave to simmer very gently for at least an hour before adding the sausage and carrots, followed shortly by the potatoes, onion, leeks and the quartered cabbages. Simmer for a further hour. Check the seasoning.

Serve the *bouillon* over the slices of bread, followed by the meat and sausage and then the vegetables. The meat can be accompanied by gherkins.

———— • ————

The fondness of the Auvergnats for stuffed cabbage, a dish which seems somehow more east European in style than French, is well known and a recipe for the full version appears on page 155. Cabbage leaves are also used as the wrapping for *le farci* (page 19), the embellishment for many soups of the region. Sometimes each diner has his own little stuffed *chou* which is baked in a little pork fat for an hour before being transferred to the soup tureen.

Here from further south is a delightful variation on the same idea where the stuffed cabbage is optimistically referred to as a 'green chicken'.

La Potée Landaise 'Poule Verte'
A soup of cabbage dressed as chicken

Serves 6

For the *potée*:
750 g (1½ lb) salt belly of pork, soaked overnight
1 green cabbage
4 or 5 carrots
3 leeks
1 onion stuck with a clove
a few peppercorns

for the *poule verte*:
several large cabbage leaves
1 slice *jambon de campagne*
250 g (½ lb) fresh belly of pork
1 onion
3 or 4 cloves garlic, peeled
1 egg

Put the pork into a soup pan, cover it with plenty of cold water and bring slowly to the boil. Skim, then add the vegetables, cover and simmer gently for 2 hours.

Meanwhile prepare the *poule verte*. Briefly blanch and then refresh the cabbage leaves. Drain them and spread out flat on a board. Chop up the ham and belly of pork together with the onion and garlic. Bind these with the beaten egg. If the mixture is too wet, you can if you like add some breadcrumbs. Wrap the stuffing in the cabbage leaves in the shape of a chicken and tie up securely with string. Put into the soup pot to cook gently for an hour.

Serve the *bouillon* first on slices of bread. Lift the meat, stuffed cabbage and the other vegetables out of the remaining stock, drain them and arrange on a heated platter. Gherkins or mustard are traditional accompaniments.

———— ● ————

The peasants often thicken their soup particularly in the Périgord and the Quercy with a mixture known as *la fricassée*, especially if the meat or vegetables are to be removed and served afterwards on their own. If in winter the soup has to be made with dried pulses, then a simpler method called *le hachis* is used.

LA FRICASSÉE
To give body to a soup

2–3 tablespoons sliced vegetables	2 tablespoons flour
1 tablespoon goose or duck fat	stock from the soup

A *fricassée* is often made with the same vegetables as are being used in the soup; you can either extract some from the soup half way through the cooking or start with raw ones. Do not include potato or dried pulses, or tender vegetables like peas or beans, but keep to onions, carrots, turnips, leeks or tomatoes which all colour well.

Chop the onion and slice the other vegetables thinly and fry them in the fat until they are golden. Stir in the flour and colour it lightly, then gradually add several spoonfuls of *bouillon* from the soup until you have the consistency of a thinnish sauce. Simmer this for a few minutes before tipping it back into the soup.

LE HACHIS
To give body, where there are no vegetables

60 g (2 oz) salt belly of pork	1 tablespoon goose or duck fat
2 cloves garlic, peeled	stock from the soup
2 tablespoons chopped parsley or chopped onion	

Le hachis is also added to the soup half-way through the cooking. Chop the pork finely. If you use a crescent-shaped chopper – *un hachoir* – heat it first over a flame as this makes it easier to chop finely.

Melt the fat in a heavy frying pan and fry the pork for 10 minutes or so quite gently to extract the fat. Then add the chopped garlic and parsley or onion, raise the heat a little and cook for long enough to colour the contents before mixing in enough of the stock to make a thinnish sauce. Stir back into the soup.

———— ● ————

An *hachis* is also used in winter to give taste and aroma to ragoûts of dried pulses like lentils or haricot beans. An old cook from the Périgord once said that without a *fricassée* 'the ragoût would only be pap and the soup like washing-up water'.

Another way in which extra weight is given to a soup is by adding *le farci*. This ball of savoury stuffing is either cooked inside a chicken in the pot or is wrapped up in cabbage leaves before being popped into the soup. This 'treat', as it often was, was really a way of stretching a small quantity of meat. The amount would vary according to availability, though on poorer farms the stuffing would contain none at all.

It used to be the custom that the master of the house carved the *farci* into slices and distributed them to the rest of the family. As with our own tradition of father carving the joint, this was symbolic of his authority. Not long ago we were invited to an evening meal and the father of the household was unexpectedly held up on his way home. The chicken came to table and the mother was just about to send one of the children with it out in the pouring rain and pitch dark to ask a neighbour to carve it. She would not carve herself, and felt it was wrong to ask us to do so.

LE FARCI PÉRIGOURDIN OU LE FARCI DE GASCOGNE
Savoury stuffing

125 g (4 oz) fresh breadcrumbs
125-150 g (4-5 oz) chopped pork or
   jambon de campagne
2 tablespoons chopped parsley
1 clove garlic, peeled and chopped

1 shallot, chopped
2 egg yolks
salt, pepper
2 or 3 large cabbage leaves

Soak the breadcrumbs in stock or milk for a short while, then drain off any excess moisture. Add all the other ingredients and bind together with the beaten egg yolks.

Blanch the cabbage leaves in boiling water for a few minutes to make them supple. Drain them and wrap them round the ball of stuffing, then tie it round with string to keep the leaves in position.

Have the vegetable soup or meat broth at simmering point, and gently lower the ball into it. Bring back to simmering point and cook gently for half an hour. At the end of the cooking, remove the *farci*, cut off the string and sort out who shall cut it into slices. Put these into the soup plates and ladle soup over.

———•———

In poorer areas, a good filling soup can still be made if the farmer's wife has some chicken stock, plenty of bread and a little saffron. This spice was brought to South-West France during the Moorish invasions in the eighth century and for a time it was cultivated widely in the region. This soup, still to be found in Quercy, the Rouergue and the Auvergne, is one of the few surviving recipes which uses it. Then it disappeared but attempts have recently begun in the Quercy to restart its cultivation. Without the saffron, this soup is sometimes called *soupe rouergate*.

We first tasted it at a restaurant near us in a village which boasts the title, *capitale mondiale du motocross*. We arrived the evening before an important scrambling event; a team of Yugoslav competitors had put up at the local hotel and this was their first taste of French food. It is hard to say whether they or we were the more amazed at this simple filling soup – nor do we know whether it enabled them to win their event the following day! Since then we have often met this soup on the midday menu of local restaurants mainly frequented by farmworkers, lorry drivers and other *ouvriers*. It makes a soothing but solid start to a meal.

The word *mourtairol* is a dialect name for bread with *bouillon*, thought to be connected with the French word *mortier*, connoting perhaps the idea of pounded bread.

LE MOURTAIROL
Bread melted in chicken *bouillon*

Serves 4

175 g (6 oz) country bread, cut in thin slices
1 litre (1¾ pt) well-flavoured chicken stock

1 pinch saffron
salt, pepper

Put the slices of bread in a casserole in layers and press them down with the hand. Pour over the very hot chicken stock in which you have dissolved the saffron. The bread should absorb all the liquid so that there is none swimming above it.

Put the casserole into a preheated oven at 150°C, 300°F, Gas Mark 2, covered, and leave to cook for half an hour. From time to time check in case the soup is becoming too dried up. If so, put in a very little more stock or hot water but do not overdo it as the finished soup should be of a thick, creamy texture with practically no superfluous liquid.

———— ● ————

For special occasions there is *le mourtairol des fêtes* which is a rather grand sort of *pot-au-feu* to which is added a small ham and a boiling fowl as well as the usual beef and vegetables. The meat and vegetables are served as the main course while the broth is strained and thickened with a bread *panade* to which saffron has been added. This dish is not seen much nowadays but had quite a vogue among better-off farmers early last century and was apparently a favourite of the monks of Conques.

Bread can also be combined with other flavourings. The Périgord has a *soupe des vendangeurs* which includes layers of cheese between the bread, while further south in the *département* of the Tarn, an even more de-luxe version is named after the town of Cordes.

Cordes is a beautiful 13th-century hilltop town which has survived religious wars and revolutions with little sign of damage. The grand buildings in the square at the top of the town – once the homes of the local ruler's falconer and his master of hounds – still have their beautiful Gothic windows. The town's ramparts and fortified gateways also still stand. In later centuries Cordes has enjoyed several periods of prosperity; manufacturing linen, then turning to leather tanning, followed by some of the earliest machine embroidery. Nowadays it is having a fourth renaissance with many of its houses carefully restored and converted into studios for artists and craftsmen. Cordes sits on its pinnacle overlooking the valley of the Cérou, encircled by hills. Truffles once grew on the limestone plateaux above the valley, so the *cordais* added these to their bread and cheese soup, making it a very sumptuous one.

LA POTÉE GRATINÉE CORDAISE
Chicken *bouillon* enriched with cheese and truffles

Serves 4

1 tablespoon goose or duck fat	1 truffle, preferably fresh (optional)
slices of bread	1 litre (1¾ pt) strong chicken stock,
300 ml (½ pt) milk	well-seasoned
150-175 g (5-6 oz) grated Gruyère	1 tablespoon *eau-de-vie de prunes*
cheese	

The exact amount of bread is difficult to specify – it will depend on the size of the loaf and the thickness of the crust. Use crusty white bread or *pain de campagne*.

Grease a tall, round *marmite* or ovenproof casserole. Soak the bread in the milk and then arrange a layer of bread in the pot. Sprinkle some grated cheese on top and several thin slices of truffle. Cover this with a second layer of soaked bread and on top of that more cheese and slices of truffle. Continue forming the layers until the required height in the pot is reached, then pour the stock over gently. Sprinkle a final covering of cheese and the *eau-de-vie* on top.

Cook gently, uncovered, in a warm oven (150°C, 300°F, Gas Mark 2) for 3 hours, and until the top is nicely browned. Serve hot.

———— ● ————

We shall see in a later chapter that when the specially fattened geese and ducks are killed to make *foie gras* and *confit*, no part of the bird is wasted. The skeletons of these birds, which have been fed gargantuan meals for several weeks before their apotheosis, make the basis of a wonderful soup, especially if bits and pieces of the flesh are left clinging to them. When this soup is ready to serve it gives off an aroma quite unlike any other. The flavour is slightly gamey and smoky, more so if you cook it over an open fire; it is a sad truth that you won't be able to achieve the same result with the carcass of an unfattened bird.

Now that birds are fattened at most times of the year, except in high summer, it is often possible to buy a carcass for a euro or two at market – in the country or in the street markets of large towns like Toulouse and Brive.

LA SOUPE À LA CARCASSE DE CANARD OU D'OIE GRAS

Soup from the carcass of a fattened duck or goose

Serves 6

For the soup:
1 carcass of a fattened duck or
  goose
2 large onions
350 g (12 oz) carrots
3 leeks
1 small cabbage heart
250 g (8 oz) potatoes
2 sticks celery with their leaves
1 bouquet garni
8 peppercorns
salt
slices of country bread

for the *fricassée*:
2 tablespoons goose or duck fat
1 ladleful of root vegetables from
  the soup
3 cloves garlic, finely chopped
3 tablespoons chopped parsley
2 tablespoons flour

First wash the carcass. Then put it into a large soup pot, broken up if need be, and cover with water. Bring slowly to the boil, skim and allow to simmer for 1 hour. Meanwhile chop all the peeled or washed vegetables and add to the soup with the bouquet and seasonings. Simmer all together for another hour and a half. At the end of this time discard the carcass, taking care to add back to the pot any pieces of meat still clinging to it. Also remove the bouquet garni.

In a small saucepan prepare the *fricassée* as described on page 18. Gradually add stock from the soup and when the mixture is thin enough, return it to the stock pot. Mix well together and simmer for a further 20 minutes.

Tremper the soup in bowls by pouring it over coarsely cut pieces of country bread.

———— • ————

After such richness, it is no bad thing to get back to basics, and what could be more basic than *le tourin* – or *torril*, *tourri* or *ouliat*, as it is variously called in patois. This is a soup which every region in the South-West claims to have invented, and is found all over the area in various forms. If you need something to offer to guests who won't go, or who arrive unexpectedly, it is easy and fairly quick to make.

The most important point to note is that the onions and garlic must not be allowed to take on colour – they must retain their sweetness and on no account become bitter.

LE TOURIN
A thin onion soup

Serves 4

2 large sweet Spanish onions, about
   350 g (12 oz) each
2 tablespoons goose or duck fat
2 tablespoons flour

1.5 litres (2½ pt) water
salt, pepper
3 eggs
4 slices bread

Slice the onions very thinly but do not chop them into a purée – the pieces can be quite large as long as they are very thin. Melt the fat in a large, heavy sauté pan or casserole, put in the onion, cover and allow it to sweat as gently as possible for up to half an hour. When the onion is well softened, stir in the flour and allow to cook for a few moments, raising the heat if necessary. Add a little of the water and amalgamate well, then add the remainder little by little until the soup is smooth. Season with salt and plenty of pepper, cover the pan and simmer gently for 45 minutes.

While it is cooking, separate the egg yolks from the whites. Put the whites into a greased bowl and put the bowl into a saucepan containing an inch or so of water which should be brought gradually to the boil but should never be allowed to bubble fiercely. As the whites solidify, stir them so that the transparent uncooked parts get their turn to cook. When they are done, remove them from the bowl, chop them up and add the pieces to the soup.

When the soup is ready, lightly beat the yolks of eggs, then add three tablespoonfuls of water to them. Remove the soup from the heat and when it is well off the boil, add the egg mixture and stir it in. Put slices of bread into the soup bowls and spoon the soup over.

———— • ————

There is a curious custom in the region which is often told to incredulous tourists. After a country wedding, the young couple disappear half-way through the wedding party to hide in a friend's house, where they spend their wedding night. The party continues without them but, when everyone has had enough to eat and drink, they all set off to *chercher les mariés*, taking with them a large bowl, or even a chamber pot, filled with *le tourin*. This, however, is no ordinary *tourin* because it is so excessively seasoned with pepper as to be virtually undrinkable. The bride, blushing at having been surprised *in flagrante delicto*, gets some of it down somehow, her throat on fire, coughing and sneezing. Meanwhile the bridegroom consumes it as nonchalantly as possible as if to demonstrate that for a man of his strength the *bouillon* is as gentle as milk.

We once lent our house to some eccentric English friends who received a late night call from merrymakers looking for a missing newly-wed couple. The visitors refused to believe our friends' innocence and were dispersed only by firing off a round of shot from some antiquated firearm. The moral is that if you are ever invited to join such a search party, make sure you choose the right house.

You can give more body to *le tourin* by using the water in which dried pulses have been cooked or by cooking some vermicelli in it. The onions can be replaced partly or wholly by leeks. You can add some Gruyère cheese or even a poached egg in order to make a more substantial dish. A *tourin* can also be enriched by adding a piece of *confit* (page 36) and this would make it a *tourin bourru*.

The following more sophisticated version containing tomatoes and an egg-liaison makes a beautifully light and creamy soup. The few aniseed grains add a delicious subtlety to the flavour, but do not overdo them.

Le Tourin à la Tomate Toulousain
Onion soup with tomato and aniseed

Serves 4

3–4 medium-sized onions, sliced	salt, pepper, sugar
2 tablespoons goose fat	bouquet garni
1 or 2 cloves garlic	½ teaspoon aniseed grains
500 g (1 lb) tomatoes, peeled,	2 eggs
or 1 small tin	4 slices country bread

Soften the onions in the fat. Add the chopped garlic and deseeded tomatoes and leave to cook for another few minutes, then add 1 litre (1¾ pints) of water and the seasonings including the aniseed grains. Bring to the boil, cover and allow to simmer for half an hour. Remove the pan from the heat and leave it to stand for five minutes. Beat up the eggs and then stir into them a ladleful of the soup. Tip this mixture back into the soup and stir it thoroughly. The soup must be cool enough not to allow the eggs to curdle.

Put the slices of bread into each soup bowl and ladle the soup over.

Soup is a mainstay in the South-West all the year round; during the hot summer days, the fire is lit in the hearth only in the evening for just long enough to cook whatever has to be put in front of the family that evening. The problem of the midday soup is solved in some areas by warming up a *tourin*, often one enriched with some salted meat or bones from the *saloir* (the crock in which pieces of meat are preserved in dry salt or brine), in the ashes at breakfast time. The soup pot is then buried in the warm bedclothes of the farmer and his wife. This *soupe à l'édredon* is said to retain its warmth until midday when the family comes in from the fields; an old-fashioned custom still practised in some of the more remote areas of Quercy and Périgord, where it is also known as *soupe mitonnée*.

It is not surprising that in the mountains the peasants like a more solid soup than those living in the plains. Our neighbours find the traditional *tourin* a bit thin for their taste, and they have borrowed from the Auvergnats their famous hard-pressed cheeses and their fondness for cabbage in order to make a wonderful synthesis, the Aveyron's *soupe au fromage*.

La Soupe au Fromage
Vegetable soup with cheese

The bread should of course be country-style French bread and the cheese Cantal or Laguiole. Gruyère or Emmenthal will not do and Parmesan will be too strong. Cheese wrapped in plastic is often too soft to grate. Cheddar would be the nearest English equivalent.

This soup will be more attractive if served in deep, individual ovenproof soup bowls as the top layer rises slightly and browns rather like a soufflé.

Serves 6

1 small stale loaf, cut into slices 1 cm (½-inch) thick	1 medium-sized onion, thinly sliced
1 green cabbage, the size of a Charentais melon	1 tablespoon goose fat
350 g (12 oz) grated Cantal cheese	1.5 litres (2½ pt) well-seasoned chicken stock
	black pepper

Place a layer of bread in each bowl. Take the cabbage apart, leaf by leaf, discarding the outer ones according to taste, also the inner core.

Blanch the chosen leaves in boiling salted water for 5 minutes and drain thoroughly. Cover the bread in each bowl with a layer of the cabbage and a sprinkling of the grated cheese. Continue with more bread, cabbage and finally cheese until your bowls are not quite full, reserving a little cheese.

Make a *tourin* by gently frying the onion in the fat without allowing it to brown. Add this mixture to the stock and divide it between the bowls until the liquid covers the solids. Season with a little freshly ground black pepper and add a final layer of cheese. Put the bowls on a tray or into a roasting tin (to catch any overflow) in your oven, pre-heated to 150°C, 300°F, Gas Mark 2, and allow to brown for about 40 minutes. At the end of the cooking time some of the liquid will have evaporated, so if there is not enough broth add further stock.

———— ● ————

The *oule*, the traditional earthenware cooking pot from the Languedoc, has given its name to a style of soup enjoyed all over that region. Once a staple diet in the Cévennes, it uses dried, white haricot beans. For preference try to buy the kind called Soissons, otherwise choose Lingots. Butter beans will not do because they disintegrate. The beans and the potatoes, all of them well cooked, blend with the goose fat to thicken the liquid and to give it an almost creamy consistency. This is a soup without meat for a change; made with good fresh vegetables, it tastes far better than the ingredients might suggest.

L'OULADE
White haricot bean soup

Serves 4

250 g (½ lb) dried white haricot
   beans, soaked overnight
salt, pepper
350 g(¾ lb) leeks

1 small heart of a cabbage
500 g (1 lb) potatoes
2 tablespoons goose fat

Put the beans into 1 litre (1¾ pt) of water and bring to a boil in your soup pot. Cook them over a medium heat for an hour, perhaps more if your beans are old, adding salt and pepper after the first half hour.

Clean and cut the leeks, cabbage and potatoes into small pieces and add them to the pot with the fat. Cook for another half-hour and serve hot. If you *tremper* this in the traditional way you will not need much else for your meal.

Another soup featuring white beans and co-starring garlic, comes from the Périgord. We stopped once for the night at the Hotel des Voyageurs at La Coquille between Limoges and Périgueux without knowing that Madame Saussot-Fontaneau was dedicated to her regional cooking. Here is one of her favourite soups. It illustrates the local penchant for adding extra oil at the end of the cooking, this time the lovely walnut oil of the region.

LA SOUPE À L'AIL
Garlic broth

Serves 4

350 g (12 oz) shelled or dried haricot beans (500 g (1 lb) in the pod)
1 large onion, chopped
1 tablespoon pork or goose fat
60 g (2 oz) garlic

1 litre (1¾ pt) beef or chicken stock
salt, pepper
4 slices of bread
2 tablespoons walnut oil

Soak the beans overnight if you have not bought them as *demi-sec*, still in the pod.

Soften the onion in the fat. Add the beans and turn them in the fat to coat them before adding the cloves of garlic, whole or, if they are large ones, cut in half. Pour in the stock, bring to the boil and leave to simmer gently until the beans are cooked – anything from half an hour to an hour according to their age. Add seasoning to taste.

Put the slices of bread in each soup bowl; just before serving the soup stir in the walnut oil.

———— ● ————

The midday break for lunch in France, however humble, is a feature of life in the countryside and in country towns. Everything shuts at *midi* (noon). Sirens blow, the towns empty and everyone goes home to lunch. There are certain seasons, however, when work has to go on regardless, and the break for nourishment takes place out in the fields. In the Auvergne omelettes are taken out to the haymakers. At the time of the vintage in the Gironde, it is a kind of *pot-au-feu* taken to the vineyards. Eaten among the vines after a morning's satisfying work, this soup and the meat cooked in it (served afterwards with the vegetables, gherkins and mustard) is 'better than all the menus to be found in the most fancy of restaurants'. The vigneron's wife would have to be up quite early in the morning, however, to have it ready for *midi*. Even though mechanical grape pickers are being more and more used in the Bordeaux vineyards, many traditional winemakers insist on hand-picking, and sometimes the same pickers come back to the same properties each year. Perhaps this recipe will survive despite the machines.

LA SOUPE DES VENDANGES
Winemaker's soup

Serves 8

For the pot:
1½ kg (3 lb) boiling beef, eg
   shoulder
4 cloves garlic
500 g (1 lb) carrots
1 large onion
500 g (1 lb) turnips
heart of a small cabbage
salt, pepper, bouquet garni

for the *fricassée*:
1 leek
1 small turnip
1 carrot
1 stick celery
2 tablespoons goose fat
2 tablespoons flour

500 g (1 lb) tomatoes
1 tablespoon oil

Spike the beef with the garlic cloves and put it in your *marmite* (soup pot) with enough water just to cover. Bring it very slowly to the boil, skimming off all the scum which rises to the top. Add the vegetables to the pot with the seasoning and herbs and cook very slowly for 2 hours at least. (If at the end of the cooking time there is too much fat on the top for your liking, scoop some of it off.)

Prepare a *fricassée* (page 18). Cook it for a few minutes and return all to the pot.

Peel and deseed the tomatoes, chop them and simmer in a saucepan with a little oil, stirring frequently. When they have cooked to a purée, add them to the soup and allow it to simmer for a further hour and a half, very gently. Remove the bouquet garni.

Tremper the slightly thickened *bouillon* in the usual way, and serve the meat and vegetables separately afterwards.

———— ● ————

The same method is employed when cooking chicken, as we shall see when we come to *poule au pot* and *poule farcie*. Sometimes, however, chicken *bouillon* is not prepared with bread as in the recipe for *mourtairol*, nor is it *trempé* over slices in the bowl. Instead thin vermicelli is cooked in it; the soup is then much lighter and makes a less filling first course. The *bouillon*, full of the flavour and goodness of a free-range chicken, is something now rarely found in Britain but is taken for granted in the simplest country home or restaurant in France. The stock is not skimmed of its fat: the country people expect their soup to contain a good deal of it. According to one old peasant woman:

> Soup is no longer any good these days. My daughter-in-law doesn't like fat, she doesn't put the right things in her soup. When I cook, I do what a woman from Montpellier once told me: half butter, half oil and half lard and I feel very well on it.

The pasta seems to mop up the fat and the flavour is better and fuller if some of it is allowed to remain. The use of pasta, incidentally, in country cooking in the South-West is by no means modern, as we shall see when we come to some of the traditional everyday dishes. This is the soup described at the beginning of this chapter and which we always call 'Maz soup', though Louis Mazières does remove most of the fat before serving it, no doubt because that is what his customers expect.

Le Bouillon Gras au Vermicelle
Bouillon from a plump fowl, with vermicelli

Serves 4

1 litre (1¾ pt) strong chicken stock (see recipe for *poule au pot* on page 51)	100 g (3½ oz) very fine vermicelli salt, pepper

See that the stock is as clear as possible and if necessary, reduce it until it has a concentrated flavour. Add salt and while it is on the boil, drop in the vermicelli. Allow to simmer gently for about 10 minutes until the pasta is cooked. Check the seasoning, adding a little freshly-ground black pepper.

———— • ————

Finally, one of the most unctuous soups of all, kept until last because it is the exception which proves the rule; it is a *soupe* though it is not *trempée*. Who can deny, however, the true rustic character of this perfect marriage of local ingredients? A word of warning first – only the ripest continental tomatoes will be suitable. They must be sweet but must be fleshy too, so use the local varieties like Marmande or St Pierre. Most of the English home-grown varieties where the emphasis is on juice rather than firm flesh will not do. It would be hard to imagine a more evocative souvenir of summer days in the Dordogne, from where this recipe comes.

LA SOUPE AUX TOMATES ET AUX HARICOTS
Tomato soup with green and white haricot beans

Serves 4

500 g (1 lb) ripe tomatoes
1 tablespoon goose or duck fat
1 medium-sized onion, sliced
salt, pepper, sugar lump
1 litre (1¾ pt) chicken or veal stock
350 g (12 oz) fresh white haricot beans (Cocos or Lingots) or 250 g (8 oz) dried beans, pre-soaked overnight

125 g (4 oz) *haricots verts*, cut into 2.5 cm (1-inch) lengths
bouquet garni
hachis (see page 18–19)
tomato purée or concentrate (optional)

Peel the tomatoes. Cut them into quarters and deseed them in a strainer over a small bowl to keep the juice.

Melt the fat in a saucepan, add the tomato pieces and juice, and the onion. Cook gently until you have a smooth purée. Meanwhile bring the stock to a boil in your *marmite*. When the tomato mixture is ready, season with salt, pepper and sugar and tip it into the stock, followed by both kinds of beans and the bouquet garni. Cover the pot and allow it to simmer gently for 40 minutes (an hour if you are using dried white beans). Stir occasionally to prevent the beans sticking to the pan.

During the cooking time prepare the *hachis* and use it to thicken the soup. It should be added to the soup at least 15 minutes before the end of the cooking. Check the seasoning. If you feel you need a stronger tomato taste, add some tomato purée or concentrate, but if you have started off with the right kind of tomato this should not be necessary.

— ● —

Here is one more way of adding weight or character to thin soups. While the soup cooks in the big *marmite* suspended over the fire, the other main cooking utensil – *la poêle* or frying pan – can be brought into play to prepare a savoury kind of pancake with which to *tremper* the soup, in addition to the usual bread. Add it about twenty minutes before serving the soup so that it can flavour the whole pot. It can be eaten cold as well. Note the use of mint, seldom found in the South-West as a flavouring.

LA ROUZOLE
Savoury pancake

Serves 4

175 g (6 oz) fat belly of pork	1 sprig mint
175 g (6 oz) *jambon de campagne*	125 g (4 oz) fresh breadcrumbs
4 cloves garlic, peeled and chopped	3 eggs, beaten
salt, pepper	60 g (2 oz) flour
1 tablespoon chopped parsley	2 tablespoons goose fat

Chop the pork and ham finely and mix in the garlic, seasonings and herbs and stir well together. Add the breadcrumbs and egg. Leave the mixture to rest for an hour if possible. Then roll it out into a thickish pancake and flour it on both sides.

Melt the fat in a frying pan and cook the *rouzole* on both sides until it is a good russet colour – hence its name. Chop it in small cubes and add to soups or stews twenty minutes before serving. It goes particularly well with broad bean soups (eg. pages 163, 164) and any of the *soupes aux choux* in this chapter.

———— ● ————

La rouzole is found in the Languedoc. Up in the Périgord they have another way of adding a certain something in a traditional fashion. When the geese or ducks are cut up to make into *confit*, *foie gras* or other delicacies, there is nearly always some skin left over. There is also usually some spare fat surrounding some of the intestines which must not be wasted. These spare pieces of skin and fat are called respectively:

LES PÉTASSOUS ET LES GRAÏS
Pieces of goose or duck skin and fat

Cut them into small pieces of 2–3 cm (1 in) square. Put a layer of salt in the bottom of a preserving jar, then a layer of these pieces, more salt, more skin and/or fat in layers until your jar is full. Seal it as well as you can and keep it for several weeks in a cool place. At the end of this time you can start using the pieces, which will have gone slightly rancid – that is why they are treasured. Simply add them to your soup during the cooking.

— ● —

Another useful addition to soup is a round of a *confit de couennes* which are strips of pork rind, rolled up and tied before being cooked in pork fat and then stored in it (see page 70). The Périgord also boasts *la mique levée*, a kind of large savoury dumpling which can be poached in the soup. But, as this is more frequently used as an accompaniment for salt pork and other dishes of meat and game, it is fully described on page 144.

There are recipes for other *soupes* and a range of *potages*, including some of the loveliest of the region, in the chapters covering the produce which specially feature in the South-West: the vegetables, the mushrooms and the chestnuts. The references are:

LES OIES ET LES CANARDS

U NTIL WE SPENT our first Christmas in the South-West we had no idea of making such things as *confit* of goose and duck ourselves, nor did we realise that when we bought our bird for Christmas Day we would have to bring it home from market alive and vigorously complaining!

We were lucky to have the help of a dear friend Charlette, who with her husband Marcel had lived many years in French Equatorial Africa. Charlette said that out there if you weren't prepared to kill and pluck your own chicken you never got any meat to eat. So that solved the problem of our roast goose on Christmas Day. Incidentally, for many French people all the excitement happens on Christmas Eve when the great feast is held on the family's return from Mass. Christmas Day is very quiet, so quiet that one year the local electricity board took advantage of the fact that no one gets up till lunchtime to cut off the supply while they carried out repairs. This hardly helps when you are trying to prepare a formal Christmas lunch.

Where Charlette was so really kind and instructive – she had been a schoolteacher for many years – was in introducing us to the mysteries of *conserves*. We went to market together. It was bitterly cold and all the farmers offering their fattened birds for sale were muffled up with thick scarves and several layers of woollies. There were whole birds, and fattened livers on their own, and some birds for sale without livers, these being called *paletots* or *manteaux*. All of course had been force-fed. We ended up with a whole bird, complete with liver, and for good measure we bought some extra goose fat in a tin, though it turned out this was far from necessary. Charlette would not let us negotiate for a truffle or two. They were *mauvaises* she said.

So we arrived home with a live goose in the boot of the car, and a plucked, fattened one on the back seat. Charlette promptly did for the former, and we all set out to deal with the latter. The results and methods form the basis of much of this chapter. In retrospect one's memory is of a kitchen awash with bubbling goose fat, and feathers floating round the courtyard. When we had finished we wanted never to see a goose again. That mood passed and we have since undergone the whole performance again with much amusement and pleasure.

It is the Toulouse goose, particularly the male, which, from the age of five months when it is not yet sexually mature, is force-fed. This feeding – *le gavage* – has to be done three times a day for a period of four to five weeks. In the old days the farmer's wife had forcibly to funnel the *maïs* down the bird's gullet. Nowadays where there are larger flocks a machine-driven feeder is used, although each bird has still to be held during the feed. Many experienced farmers maintain that they build up a calming and coaxing relationship with the birds while feeding and this improves the end result.

Today they often fatten ducks rather than geese because these require only two feeds a day from the time they are three months' old until they are just over four months. Several rearings and fattenings can thus be fitted into a year. By cross-breeding, varieties of duck have been produced which grow larger and heavier than normal. There is, for example, the male Barbary duck which, fully grown, can average 4½ kilos (10 lb). This may then be crossed with another variety like the Peking or Rouen, then producing offspring which can grow even heavier, and are particularly valued for the production of *foie gras*. Some argue that the flavour of a fattened duck's liver is deeper than that of a goose, but it does have the disadvantage of reducing more in the cooking. A fresh goose liver can weigh up to 800 g (about 1¾ lb) whereas a duck's would be roughly half that.

On most farms one flock of young birds is raised during the year for family consumption. The fluffy yellow goslings, dozens and dozens packed into large containers, are on sale in the country markets in early autumn. Young birds feed on greenery out-of doors until the final fattening. At this point they are kept indoors, becoming adipose and almost immobile until they reach a weight of nine or ten kilos (20–22 lb) when they are killed. During November and December the goose markets are a great attraction, the wooden trestle tables laden with enormous birds, plucked to show their creamy skin stretched tight over the plump flesh and enlarged liver. Often an incision is made along the breast bone to expose the liver for inspection by the purchaser: it should be pale ivory-pink in hue, firm in texture and have no blemishes.

With the goose and duck the variety of ways of using every bit of the bird shows both thrift and imagination. The feathers are either kept at home to fill the family eiderdown and pillows, with the quills serving as a brush or feather duster, or sold to gipsies for treatment and later resale to manufacturers. From one fattened goose you can put into your larder one tin of *foie gras*, four tins of *le confit d'oie*, a tin of *le confit de cou farci* (the skin of the neck filled with a forcemeat to form a large sausage), a tin of *confit d'abattis* (the giblets and wings) and a small jar or tin of *rillettes d'oie* (a soft *pâté* which is made from the scraps of flesh left on the carcass). Last but not least you will have a good quantity of honey-coloured goose fat.

The word *confit*, which you will find widely used and exclusively in the South-West, either on the labels of canned meats or on restaurant menus, translates as 'preserved'. The preserving is done with goose or duck fat in which the goose or duck meat is submerged and very gently cooked – preferably over a wood fire so that the wood smoke can play its part in adding savour. It is then stored in the fat – *sous la graisse* – the two processes giving it a particular unctuousness and a flavour which can only be described as slightly gamey. You will by now be starting to understand the fundamental role of goose and duck fat in the cooking of the region. It is a vitally important by-product of the *gavage*. Bring a few tins home with you from France if you can; it makes potatoes most wonderfully golden and crisp to go with your Sunday roast.

LE CONFIT D'OIE
Preserved goose

1 specially fattened Toulouse goose, already plucked
gros sel (coarse salt) 30 g (1 oz) per ½ kg (1 lb) of meat
black pepper

quatre-épices (a ground mixture of pepper, cloves, nutmeg, ginger or cinnamon, sold ready made)
thyme, bay leaf

With a really sharp knife, cut off the bird's head and feet and break off the last joint of the wings. Crack the second wing joints, sever them and put them to one side. Cut round the neck near the base and pull the skin off the neck bone without tearing it, rather like peeling off a glove. This will later be used to make *le cou d'oie farci* (page 42).

With the breast uppermost, make a deep incision on both sides along the length of the breast-bone from neck to tail. When you get to where the liver is, be careful only just to break the skin. Keeping the blade of the knife facing towards the bone, start easing off the flesh from the carcass, working carefully downwards towards the backbone and along the length of the body until the two sides fall away. Cut through the joints of the wings and legs so as to leave them attached to the meat and skin (*le manteau*).

You will find a membrane covers the liver: lift this, taking care not to break the surface of the liver. Peel it off as you did the neck. Then, preferably with poultry secateurs, cut away the carcass from the backbone so that you can ease away the liver and intestines which rather resemble a football. The larger lobe of the liver contains the gall which must be removed extremely carefully. Part the lobes gently with your fingers and cut away the gall. Put the liver to one side.

Separate the unusable intestines from their fat. All the fat can be melted down for the preserving. (A little jar of it kept in the fridge makes excellent hand cream.) Find the crop and separate the gizzard from it. Detach the neck from the carcass and put both of these with the heart, wings, and neck skin into a separate dish. Rub them with seasoned salt and leave to macerate for 24 hours.

Cut the boned bird into four, each consisting of a leg bone or a wing bone and its surrounding meat, some fat and skin. Trim off any excess fat and skin to make a tidy joint, especially any coarse bits around the edges. Put these aside for using to make *rillettes* (page 43) or to put away under salt as *pétassous* (page 32). Mix together the salt with some freshly ground black pepper, powdered thyme and crushed bay leaf, and rub it into the flesh sides of the joints, then leave them in a cool place for 24 hours.

The following day take a large, heavy-bottomed pan and put into it any goose fat you have already rendered. Wipe off any excess salt from the goose quarters and place them, skin side downwards, in the pan. Start heating the fat slowly; a lot of fat will melt out of the pieces and you should get enough to cover them. If not, add additional goose or pork fat. Bring the fat barely to simmering point and then keep the pan very gently simmering for 2–2½ hours. The quarters are ready when the flesh is soft and no more pink juices run out. If there is room in the pan you can add the carcass and the giblets. Remove the giblets after a ½ hour but leave the carcass to continue cooking very slowly for another hour after the quarters are done.

Allow to cool slightly while you sterilize a large glazed stoneware jar – traditionally this is the *toupine*. Transfer the goose pieces to this, if necessary cutting off any protruding bones from the wing and leg ends and dividing the leg pieces into three. Boil up the fat until bubbles appear on the surface and a scum is formed. Skim the fat and when it looks golden and clear, allow to cool slightly before straining it over the meat, covering it completely with at least a 2.5 cm (1 inch) layer of fat on top. When this has set, place a layer of greaseproof paper or foil on top and then the lid. Store the jar in a really cool, dark and dry place.

The confit will keep for from six to twelve months and improves with age as it lies immersed in its own fat. Before the days of sterilization it was thought best to consume it during the winter and early spring – '*Qui veut manger de bon confit salé, doit l'avoir achevé à Pâques*'. If it is kept longer it will be necessary to reboil the contents in its fat for a few minutes to prevent the fat turning rancid in the higher summer temperatures.

You can also conserve the quarters of goose in the special large glass jars called *les bocaux*, of the type with a rubber sealing ring and a clip-on glass lid (size 1000). In this case the goose is only half cooked in its fat – for about half an hour – then packed tightly into the jar and filled to within 2 cm (¾ inch) of the top with fat. The jars are then sterilized in boiling water at 100°C (212°F) for 2–3 hours. This method is safer if you are doubtful about being able to store the *confit* in the traditional *toupine* for a long period.

When a piece of *confit* is required, stand the pot in a warm place and when the fat has melted, remove the meat, taking care that the remaining pieces are completely covered again by the fat.

———— ● ————

These pieces of confit can be used in various ways. For immediate consumption they are sautéed gently in the fat still clinging to them until they are warmed through; *confit* is never served piping hot. There are several traditional accompaniments, all delicious. *Pommes sarladaises* (page 176) and a purée of sorrel (page 182) are perhaps the best known but there is also *confit à la basquaise* which is with sautéed *cèpes*, garlic and parsley, or *confit caussenarde* which is with a fresh tomato and caper sauce. *Confit* can equally well be eaten cold with a green salad, preferably made with *endive* or *scarole*, and dressed with walnut oil. It is said by some local gourmands to be best this way. Whether hot or cold, it is regarded by all as a special treat, to be used for occasions of family gatherings or feast days. It nearly always appears on the gastronomic menu in those restaurants which specialize in regional dishes, and can also be bought in sterilized jars from some of the local producers. A piece of *confit* is a traditional ingredient in *cassoulet* and *garbures*.

The pieces which we would call the giblets (the neck, heart, gizzard) and the wings are conserved separately in goose fat. Known as the *abattis*, they are cut up into pieces and later used to make a stew known as *alicot*. The recipe for this on page 44 uses fresh giblets as this dish was prepared as a 'treat' on the day of the killing of a bird for the *confit*, but conserved ones can also be used. Nowadays in the markets, particularly in the Périgord, you can buy *les abattis confits* separately. The gizzards have recently found their way into a fashionable *salade de gésiers confits*, slightly warmed and served on a bed of lettuce. The upper wings are known as *confit de manchons* or muffs – they have a circle of flesh round the bone – and, warmed through, make a delicious snack.

The cooked carcass can be broken up, grilled and eaten hot or cold: the pieces are known as *les demoiselles* and make a good starter or light lunch. Alternatively the meat can be picked off the carcass and with the juices from the bottom of the preserving pan, made into what are called *grillons* in the Périgord (or further south in Quercy, *fritons*). Any skin which had been preserved with the *confit* but not eaten with the meat, should not be discarded. This can be used to make a delicious omelette filling (page 97).

LE FOIE GRAS
Liver from the fattened goose

1 fresh goose liver, weighing about (575 g) 1¼ lb	black pepper
fine salt	2 teaspoons armagnac

This recipe is for conserving the *foie gras* in sterilized glass jars and a liver of this weight will be enough for at least six or seven people.

You will see that the liver is made up of one large and one smaller lobe. Carefully remove the thin outer membrane, together with any blood vessels running through it. Remove every scrap of white fat and gristle from the smaller lobe, if necessary cutting grooves into the liver. Do the same with the larger lobe, also cutting away any discoloration caused by the gall bladder. At the thick end where the liver was attached to the carcass you will have to make a long incision in order to remove the cord and the bits connected to it. Then press the lobes together again as tightly as possible. Season them with salt and freshly ground black pepper and leave for 24 hours in a cool place.

Next day take either one large (750 size) or two small (350) French glass preserving jars. Sterilize the jar and rubber by plunging into boiling water, remove with clean wooden tongs and place upside down to dry on a clean tea towel. Try to handle the jar as little as possible. When completely dry, start packing the liver into it, pressing it down firmly and carefully, ensuring that there are no air pockets between any pieces. Take great care at the same time not to touch the lip of the jar with greasy hands as this prevents a proper seal. Sprinkle the brandy over.

Fill the jar only as far up as the line indicated on it, wipe the top thoroughly, then slip the rubber ring on to the lid, with the 'ear' to one side of the hinge so that it is in a handy position when it comes to opening the jar. Close the lid and clip it down.

Fill a large sterilizing pan with sufficient water to cover all the jars if you are preparing more than one. Lower in the jar(s) and bring the water to the boil, then keep it simmering actively for one hour. Allow the jar(s) to cool in the water.

Keep the jar in a cool, dark place for at least a month before use, preferably longer. To serve, chill the jar in the refrigerator before opening it – about an hour before eating. Turn it out on to a plate; it will be surrounded with its own fat. Some eat this with the *foie gras* though others may find it too rich. In any case, do not provide butter, just slices of warm toast or brioches.

——— ● ———

A modern variant on the traditional terrine of *foie gras entier* is a half-cooked version called *mi-cuit*, which calls for only 20–30 minutes' cooking. It is more tender and unctuous even than the fully cooked version but even under its own fat it will not keep more than a fortnight. It is, however, possible to buy it vacuum-packed, for consumption within three weeks or, if put in sealed glass jars or in tins, within a year.

Foie gras need not be preserved at all and is delicious fresh, cooked in escalopes and served with apples or grapes, or with a few capers sautéed briefly in the fat. Allow about 100 g (3½ oz) of goose liver or 150 g (5½ oz) of duck liver per person. A duck's liver is fattier and shrinks more in the cooking.

LE FOIE GRAS DE CANARD CHAUD AUX POMMES
Hot duck liver with apples

Serves 4

1 fresh *foie gras* of duck
salt, pepper
150 ml (¼ pt) chicken stock
4–6 dessert apples
30 g (1 oz) butter
1 tablespoon *eau-de-vie*
2 tablespoons double cream

for the mirepoix:
1 medium-sized onion, peeled
2 small carrots, peeled
1 stick celery
1 leek, cleaned
125 g (4 oz) salt belly of pork
bouquet garni
30 g (1 oz) goose or duck fat

Check that the liver is clean and free from veins and gristle. Season it well and put to one side.

Prepare a mirepoix by dicing the peeled vegetables and pork and sweating them in the fat with the bouquet garni in a covered casserole. When they have softened add the stock and cook for 20 minutes.

Preheat the oven to 200°C, 400°F, Gas Mark 6, and put the mirepoix into an ovenproof dish, placing the *foie gras* on top. Allow 10 minutes' cooking time for a liver weighing up to 400 g (14 oz).

Meanwhile peel and thickly slice the apples, then sauter them in butter, adding a little salt and pepper. Do not let them collapse. Take the liver out of the oven and keep it warm while you finish the sauce. Deglaze the dish with the *eau-de-vie*, then press it all through a coarse sieve into a clean pan. Stir in the cream and heat gently until the sauce has thickened slightly.

Quickly slice the *foie gras* on to a hot platter, coat it with the sauce and arrange the apples round it. Serve immediately.

———— • ————

Originally the preservation of *foie gras* was a means of providing the family with a winter's supply of protein and energy. Nowadays you can buy a fresh liver at market in late autumn or winter; indeed many housewives in the country towns prepare their own conserves in this way. But if you happen to be in the region only at other times of year the answer is to buy the finished product. There are three principal areas of production. The Périgord, with its centre at Périgueux and also including Brive-la-Gaillarde just over the border into the Corrèze, is considered the leading producer. This is followed by Les Landes, with its centres of Mont-de-Marsan and Dax, and by the adjacent county of Gers where Mirande has a famous goose market.

But there are some smaller concerns throughout the South-West that preserve their own or local produce on a basis known as *artisanal* to distinguish it from mass-produced. Indeed what was originally a village butcher's sideline has on more than one occasion blossomed into a thriving local business.

Danielle and Jean-Louis, who have a small farm near Brive, have taken the process one stage further. They have converted one of their buildings to provide a few comfortable bedrooms, a good-sized sitting-cum-dining room and a kitchen where up to four couples can spend the weekend learning all about ducks and geese. Across the courtyard is their *laboratoire*; each visitor is provided with a goose (mercifully dead and plucked) and is taught how to deal with it from start to finish. There are now a number of farms in the region which do this and we strongly recommend them as sources of entertainment as well as information.

Buying from a smaller concern will often secure a better product than picking one of the country-wide labels which may be processing imported raw materials; the demand for *foie gras* is now such that the big producers in France are importing from as far afield as Hungary and Israel.

For all producers there are rigorous controls, and laws concerning content, labelling, manufacture and expiry dates as well as standards of hygiene during production. Because of the variety of tinned products which the *foie gras d'oie* or the *foie gras de canard* will yield, the French Government has enacted a strict code of labelling (see Appendix on page 324). We strongly recommend a thorough study to all who read this book before they buy any product containing *foie gras*.

The flesh of the goose and its liver have now been preserved. There remain the neck, the bits of meat clinging to the bones, and the giblets. The skin of the long neck of the goose is put to very good purpose: for making a large sausage which is then also preserved for future use.

LE CONFIT DE COU D'OIE FARCI AU FOIE GRAS
Goose neck stuffed with foie gras and preserved

Serves 4

1 goose (or duck) neck	100–125 g (3½–4 oz) *foie gras*
350 g (¾ lb) pork sausagemeat	salt, pepper, *quatre-épices*

As we shall see later, sausagemeat is usually made with two-thirds lean pork to one third fat. The *foie gras* makes this recipe rather rich so try to find a leaner sausagemeat mix, say three-quarters to one-quarter. A simpler version might omit the *foie gras* in which case the fattier sausagemeat mixture would be better. Either way it should be finely minced or chopped, following the method given on page 66.

The neck of the goose should be cut off level with the body to give as long a length of the skin as possible. Cut off the head if it has not already been removed and then carefully pull the skin off, turning it inside out like peeling off a glove. Salt it all over.

If the goose giblets are not being conserved separately, these can be added to the stuffing. Pick the flesh off the bones of the neck into a bowl. Any bits off the carcass which are left when the quarters have been put into *le confit* can be added. Add the sausage meat and the *foie gras* and mix them all together with some salt, pepper and spices. Leave overnight.

Next day sew up one end of the neck with fine cotton, then stuff the mixture into it – not too tightly as it will swell in cooking. Stitch up the other end. Put this 'sausage' to cook gently in goose fat for 2 hours, as for the recipe for preparing *le confit d'oie* – they can cook together if need be. When cool, store in its own fat in a jar in the same way. If you intend to can or bottle the neck, cook it for only half an hour before the sterilizing process.

———— ● ————

This *cou d'oie farci* can be eaten hot or cold, or put into a *pot-au-feu*. Warm the whole neck in the oven or fry slices and serve these on a bed of sorrel purée (page 182), with lentils or with some *petits pois*. Serve it cold, sliced, as an hors d'oeuvre or with a salad (cut off and discard the ends where the stitches are). Remove as much of its preserving fat from it as possible by heating it slowly: it is very delicious but rich. It is made even richer in the South – *à la façon de Limoux* – where they add truffles, wild mushrooms, wine-soaked currants, pistachio nuts and herbs to the stuffing.

When you prepare *le confit d'oie* you will find at the bottom of the preserving pan of fat in which it has been cooked a marvellous collection of debris – fragments of meat, fat, crisp skin which have fallen from the joints. These are strained from the fat, then served as a special treat, the long cooking in the fat having given them a specially nutty flavour. In the Périgord they call this delicacy the *grillons* or *fritons* referred to earlier. Stored carefully with a covering of fat, they will keep for up to two or three weeks in a cool place. Alternatively *les rillettes d'oie* can be made. They are eaten like a *pâté*, with fresh bread, as an hors d'oeuvre.

LES RILLETTES D'OIE OU DE CANARD
Potted goose or duck meat

Serves 6

1 carcass, plus giblets, wings, pieces of skin and fat
some cubed belly of pork (optional)

salt, pepper, clove
bouquet garni

Break up the carcass and put it together with the other pieces into a heavy-bottomed pan with a cupful of water. Add the seasonings, cover and cook very gently, stirring often, for at least 2 hours.

When all the flesh falls easily from the bones and the liquid has almost evaporated, remove the bones and tear up the meat and fat, mixing it well together but *not* pounding it into a paste. Fill earthenware pots with the mixture and any remaining liquor, leave it to cool and then cover with a layer of goose or duck fat. Or put it into glass jars and sterilize them for half an hour.

•

If the carcass is not being used for this *pâté*, it can be grilled over the fire to make titbits at a festive meal or reserved to make the delicious *soupe à la carcasse d'oie* (page 23).

L'ALICOT OU L'ALICUIT
Poultry giblet stew

At the other end of the spectrum from *foie gras* and *confit* is a rustic stew which we first tasted as prepared by Louis Mazières' old mother one day when their hotel was closed and we were invited to join a family meal. It contains not only the giblets – neck, heart, gizzard – but also the wing tips and even the feet. One recipe includes the head as well but lest anyone be too discouraged, this version comes from the poorest area of the South-West and is not one we have ever tasted.

It is said that the word comes from *aile* (wing) and *cou* (neck) which is consoling. Our recipe is found both in the Périgord and in Languedoc, although the Béarnais like to claim it. The giblets can be of goose, duck, turkey or chicken and can be fresh or *confits*.

Serves 4

giblets of 3 birds (necks, hearts, gizzards)
wing tips of 3 birds
2 tablespoons goose fat
1 large onion, chopped
2 cloves garlic, chopped
500 g (1 lb) carrots, sliced
350 g (¾ lb) salsify, cut into 3 cm (1¼ in) lengths (optional)

2 tablespoons flour
300 ml (½ pt) chicken stock
1–2 tomatoes or 1 tablespoon tomato sauce (page 190)
bouquet garni
salt, pepper, nutmeg

Cut the pieces of bird into portions and brown them in a casserole in the goose fat.

Remove the pieces and set aside. Put in the vegetables to brown. When they have coloured a little, put back the giblets, sprinkle the flour over, then slowly blend in the stock. Add the tomatoes, peeled and chopped or the tomato sauce, plus the herbs and seasonings, adjusted to taste. Cover and simmer very slowly for about 1½ hours, until the meat and vegetables are tender.

Lou Magret
Steak from the breast of fattened duck

How the various parts of a fattened goose or duck are treated is not complete without mention of *lou magret*, the grilled or fried breast of fattened duck which is served like a steak. The name in Gascon dialect derives from the French *maigre* in its sense of meat without any fat, although it seems unlikely it was a common Gascon recipe in previous times. After all, if *le confit* has been made there will be no *magret*.

Monsieur André Daguin, who claims to have revived the fashion in his restaurant in Auch, has said that in his youth it was a family treat – 'fried rapidly, served still *rose*, and considered an original and amusing dish'. Whoever deserves the credit for the popularity of the *magret*, it has rapidly become one of the most characteristic *plats* of the region. The demand is such that tins or jars of *confit* of duck tend more and more to be of leg joints. The *manchons* (upper wings) which have to be detached from the breasts are made into *confit*.

The art of cooking a *magret* is to have a crisp skin on the outside while at the same time liberating all the fat which lies between the skin and the meat. This explains why you cannot achieve the same result with a non-fattened duck: you may product an adequately grilled duck breast but it will not be a *magret* because there is simply not enough fat to lubricate the lean meat below it. Moreover the process of *gavage* lends a very special savour and texture to the meat. *Magrets* will be more tender than rump steak of beef, and should be cooked rare in the same way. Their flavour is slightly gamey, the pink juices providing the only gravy really necessary. If you do not like underdone beef, then *magrets* are probably not for you, because if they are completely cooked through they become tough and even dry. But for those who like their meat or game *saignant*, a properly prepared *magret* is one of the most delicious and succulent dishes in the repertoire of the South-West.

Madame Rosy Gagnard runs a small restaurant in Toulouse called La

Côte de Boeuf where she grills ribs of beef over hot charcoal. She also grills the best *magret* you are ever likely to find. She says there are two secrets to this. Never be frightened of over-salting the fat side of the breast, and allow the fat to run gradually by slowly melting the fat side before beginning the cooking proper.

Serves 4

2 breasts of fattened duck
salt, pepper

thyme, parsley, bay leaf
2 tablespoons armagnac

Leave the skin on the breasts and make four criss-cross cuts in it. Rub a good quantity of coarse salt into the skin side and a very little salt but plenty of freshly-ground black pepper into the other. Sprinkle with the herbs and armagnac and leave to marinate for an hour, turning the pieces from time to time.

The best way to cook the breasts is to grill them over a wood or charcoal fire. Failing that they can be fried like steaks but the grilling process enables a lot of the extra fat under the skin to melt and produces a better result. So place the pieces on the grill, skin side down, over a low fire to start with, and watch until the fat has melted and the skin crispened without burning. Turn the pieces over and move the grill to a hotter part of the fire to seize the meat, leaving the inside pink like an underdone steak.

If you do not have an open fire, you will need a cast-iron griddle or heavy frying pan. The advantage of a griddle is that it sustains a much higher heat and also produces an attractive cross-hatching of the steak.

Heat your griddle or frying-pan over a low flame and on it lay the *magrets* skin side down. Allow as much fat as possible to run without the heat getting through to cook the lean meat (about 10 minutes depending on the thickness of the fat). When the skin is browned and crisp, remove the *magrets* from the stove and raise the heat to the maximum. When the griddle or pan is really hot, brush the lean side of the meat with a little oil and place face down to cook for 6 to 8 minutes for average-sized *magrets*, 350 g (12 oz). The time will also depend on how pink you want the meat to be. If the skin is not as crisp as you would like, give it a minute or two in contact with the hot griddle or pan.

To serve, carve the *magrets* into thinnish slices, cutting them on the slant, and serve either plain, or with sauté potatoes and perhaps a few cèpes or mushrooms, or a few sautéed cubes of apple.

———— • ————

If you are a garlic lover an *aillade toulousaine* – a wonderful walnut and garlic sauce – goes very well with it.

L'AILLADE TOULOUSAINE
Garlic and walnut sauce

Serves 4

75 g (2½ oz) walnuts, if possible
  newly picked, and shelled
50 g (1¾ oz) cloves of garlic, peeled

salt, pepper
150 ml (¼ pt) walnut oil
1 tablespoon chopped parsley

Pound together the walnuts and garlic in a mortar. If you have no mortar, you can short-cut the process a little with the aid of a food mixer. If the garlic and walnuts are fresh and juicy, it will grind them fairly finely and you can finish them off in a bowl with the aid of the thick handle of a wooden spoon. You need to get as finely-ground a mixture as possible.

Stir in one or two tablespoonsful of cold water to help the mixture to amalgamate. Add salt and pepper, then slowly beat in the oil until you have a thick sauce, almost like a mayonnaise. Finally stir in the chopped parsley.

LA BASSE-COUR

THE *BASSE-COUR* is not like either the pigsty or the garden which you can point to as physical parts of the farm. It is more of an activity than a place, denoting the rearing of rabbits and poultry, including the larger birds such as geese and turkeys. This is exclusively the domain of the mistress of the house and explains why on old postcards showing geese being stuffed with corn, it is the women who are doing this very hard work.

The peasant community is to us highly sexist; the roles of men and women are clearly demarcated and the *basse-cour* is allocated to women. On the other hand, they literally 'rule the roost'; within their own sphere their word is law. Our nearest neighbour across the valley was told, when he ventured to comment on the ripe aromas wafting from the duck sheds into the kitchen, 'If you want to have some *confit de canard*, you will have to make some small sacrifices'.

It goes without saying that even today any home-grown poultry is reared entirely naturally. The birds come and go as they please, feeding on whatever they can find in the farmyard or the fields plus a bonus of maize from the mistress when she gathers them in for the night to preserve them from any marauding fox. Sometimes baby chicks are bought at market but even though these may have been hatched under artificial conditions, they then spend their lives in natural surroundings. What a contrast with the battery bird, with its tough muscles, gritty carcass and flesh which at best tastes of nothing and at worst of fish meal! Let those who protest against the force-feeding of ducks and geese consider the appalling conditions of industrial farming and ask whether these can be justified. The results are horrid too.

This said, it has to be frankly admitted that nothing whatever can be said by way of mitigation of *le gavage*: it is a cruel practice which causes the poor suffering birds a great deal of discomfort initially and pain finally. The only explanation of its survival is that the French are not sentimental about their farmyard animals; they are there to be exploited to the maximum. Those who object to *gavage* can, if they like, avoid consuming its consequences, which is why we have given the recipes a chapter of their own. On the other hand, there will be many people who, while they would not dream of perpetrating *gavage* themselves, are not put off the results and see no reason why they should not enjoy them.

In many a *basse-cour* ducks, like hens, are reared for family consumption. They forage for themselves for the most part, lay away and may suddenly reappear with a family – a bonus for the farmer's wife. The killing of even these ducks is not an everyday event but if there were some special occasion, Madame might serve a duck in one of several ways, not simply plainly roasted. In the Limousin where cherries grow abundantly she uses a variety called Griottes to counteract the fattiness of the duck. They are casseroled with the duck to make the sauce. Further south, turnips and onions are favourite accompaniments and make an excellent combination. We were once given this dish as a *plat d'honneur* and we knew we had seen the duck roaming the farm. The sauce and vegetables were beautiful but alas the bird was as tough as old boots – it must have been the doyen of that particular *basse-cour*.

LE CANARD AUX NAVETS ET AUX OIGNONS
Duck with turnips and onions

The young white turnips, either long or round, which appear at the end of the winter combine beautifully with duck. The Muscat de Frontignan or Rivesaltes which flavours the sauce are local sweet fortified wines. Madeira or port would do as a substitute if necessary.

Serves 4

1.5 kg (3¼–3½ lb) duck, dressed
  weight
2 tablespoons duck or goose fat
125 g (4 oz) salt belly of pork, diced
1 carrot, sliced
2 small onions, sliced
1 glass dry white wine
4 tablespoons chicken stock
bouquet garni

salt, pepper
24 button onions, peeled
500 g (1 lb) small white turnips,
  peeled
1 tablespoon goose fat
a little sugar
1 tablespoon flour
1 glass Muscat de Frontignan or
  Rivesaltes

Truss the duck well. You can put a thick slice of country bread well rubbed with garlic (known as a *chapon*) inside. Season the bird well and brown it all over in the goose or duck fat in a large frying pan.

Pour any remaining fat into a large casserole – one big enough to take the bird – and soften the pork, carrot and onion in it. Place the bird on top and pour over the wine and stock. Cover and braise the bird gently for about an hour – or longer if you think it is not very young. Baste with the pan juices from time to time.

Steam or blanch the button onions and turnips briefly. Brown them in some fat in a separate pan and when they start to turn golden, add a little of the juices from the duck. Allow them to continue to cook gently and when the liquid has almost evaporated, add a good pinch of sugar to glaze them.

When the duck is ready, transfer it to a heated dish and keep it warm while you finish the sauce. Strain the contents of the casserole through a sieve into a clean pan, reduce if necessary, removing any excess fat. Mix the flour with the sweet fortified wine and blend this into the sauce. Reheat and cook for a few minutes, checking the seasoning.

Arrange the small onions and turnips round the duck and serve the sauce separately.

—— ● ——

The great stand-by of the *basse-cour* is still the chicken which will range freely. In one rambling and chaotic farm near us we even found a hen perched on the television set in the only sitting room. Free range indeed!

If guests or family arrive unexpectedly, a *poulet sauté* makes a quick and tasty supper, jointed and fried in fat with onions and tomatoes. When you are in France, if you can buy your chicken from a farm be sure to do so. Otherwise most medium-sized towns will have shops specializing in *poulets fermiers*, and in the markets there should be stalls selling organically-reared birds. The better butchers and supermarkets will also sell good quality dressed poultry although the battery bird is as much a commonplace, unfortunately, in France as in England. There is a complicated system of labelling but birds carrying a *label rouge* or described as *poulet fermier* should be good quality. Many will have been raised on yellow maize but, contrary to popular belief, this does not turn the bird's skin yellow. The yellow chickens are a different variety and need never have seen a grain of *maïs*. Conversely, some of the best French chickens such as those reared near Le Mans are the same pinkish-grey which one associates with the lowest battery bird in Britain. Visitors not familiar with French markets should also be warned that if there is no specialized stall, all the chickens for sale will be live and clucking. Tradition apart, the reason for this is that a prudent farmer's wife bringing her hens to market can never be sure how many she might sell.

LA POULE AU POT
Chicken in the pot

This Sunday dish has been attributed to Henri IV of France. When he came to the throne he united France, and proclaimed that all families would be able to *mettre la poule au pot chaque dimanche*, just like those in his native Gascony. This recipe is to be found all over France; here we give it with a sauce associated with the small town of Sorges in the Périgord. Originally the eggs for this sauce would have been cooked in their shells *sous la cendre* (under the ashes). As an alternative sauce a fresh tomato one is quite traditional. In the Languedoc they might add a knuckle of veal to the pot and perhaps some minced veal in the stuffing. The *bouillon* that is served first can have a little vermicelli cooked in it in place of the slices of bread. The recipe is particularly useful for a bird no longer in the first flush of youth.

Serves 6–8

for the stuffing:
1 thick rasher of country ham or slice of belly of pork, about 150 g (5 oz)
the chicken's liver
1 shallot or small onion, peeled
2 cloves garlic, peeled

100 g (3½ oz) fresh breadcrumbs
2 tablespoons chopped parsley
salt, pepper
1 large or 2 small egg yolks

for the bird:
1 boiling fowl, 1.5–2 kg (3–4½ lb)
   dressed weight, with its giblets
4 medium-sized onions, peeled
8 large carrots, sliced
2–4 leeks, according to size
celery leaves, thyme, bay leaf,
   parsley, chervil, chives, tied in
   bouquet

10 peppercorns
salt
1 glass dry white wine
700 g (1½ lb) small potatoes

for the sauce:
3 eggs
salt, pepper
4 tablespoons oil
1½ tablespoons vinegar

1 shallot or small onion, finely
   chopped
parsley and any other *fines herbes* to
   hand

First simmer the giblets of the bird with water just to cover, for half an hour. While this stock is cooking, make the stuffing. Dice the ham very small and chop the liver, shallot or onion and the garlic as finely as possible. Mix these all together with the breadcrumbs, parsley and the seasoning, and bind with the egg yolks. Stuff the fowl with this mixture and truss it with string.

Put the bird in a *marmite* or saucepan with a close-fitting lid to simmer gently. The bird should fit snugly into the pan so that the stock will be concentrated. Add the onions, whole, the carrots, the green parts of the leeks and the bouquet garni and seasonings. Add the stock from the giblets, the glass of wine and enough water very nearly to cover the bird. Bring the pot slowly to the boil, and allow about 1½ hours, depending on the age and quality of the bird, from the time it comes to the simmer. Keep it simmering very gently for the whole cooking time, adding the whites of the leeks, cut in two, with the potatoes, half an hour before serving time.

Meanwhile make the sauce. Put the eggs into boiling water in a pan with a tight-fitting lid. Cover, remove from the fire and leave to stand for 7 minutes. Break open the eggs, separating the yolks from the whites which you leave on one side. Put the yolks together with all the other ingredients for the sauce into a tepid bowl and whisk with a fork quite vigorously. The sauce requires no further cooking. If you like you can decant a little of the *bouillon* into a small saucepan, scoop the whites out of the shells and drop them into the *bouillon* to finish cooking. Then chop them and add them to the sauce.

As a first course, serve the broth from the chicken poured over slices of bread in the soup bowls. Remove the chicken and vegetables from the remaining stock, take the stuffing out of the chicken and serve all together, passing the sauce separately.

●

A recipe for a younger chicken comes from Toulouse and so has Toulouse sausage and olives in the stuffing. Toulouse sausages are made of 100 per cent pork, coarsely minced and well-salted, and they feature in many ways in local cooking. Full details are to be found in the pork chapter on page 66.

LE POULET FARCI TOULOUSAIN
Chicken stuffed with forcemeat and olives

Serves 4

a roasting chicken, 1–1.5 kg
  (2¼–3 lb) dressed weight, with its
  giblets
250 g (½ lb) Toulouse sausage
2 tablespoons goose or duck fat
2 cloves garlic
100 g (3½ oz) stoned green olives
  (approx 20 olives)

salt, pepper
1 medium-sized onion, sliced
bouquet garni
150 ml (¼ pt) dry white wine
3 medium-sized tomatoes, skinned
  and de-seeded

You will need the liver from the chicken to add to the stuffing, and the other giblets can be used to make stock for a soup. Wipe the interior of the bird with a damp cloth.

Prepare the stuffing by first cutting up the sausage into small pieces, then browning these in a tablespoonful of the fat. Add the chopped chicken liver and garlic and continue the frying for a minute or two. Leave this mixture to cool before adding the olives, roughly chopped. Season lightly and mix all together. Fill the chicken with this stuffing and sew up the opening. Truss the bird so that it fits neatly into whatever largeish casserole or pan with close-fitting lid you have. Brown it on all sides in this pan in the remainder of the fat, add the onion, bouquet garni and seasoning and pour over the white wine. Reduce the heat to get a gentle simmer, cover and leave to cook for three-quarters of an hour.

Chop the tomato flesh and add it to the pot for a further 10 minutes' cooking but with the lid off. If the sauce still seems too much at the end of this time, transfer the chicken to a warm place and reduce the liquor by brisk boiling. Check the seasoning. Pass the sauce round separately.

The same kind of stuffing is also used for *lapin farci toulousain*, using a whole rabbit.

———— ● ————

One of the most delicious of chicken dishes is a chicken and salsify pie. Our first acquaintance with it was in the depths of the southern

Périgord at a small old-fashioned country *auberge* at Bouzic. It was run by Madame Sylvestre who offered no menu but did not mind if you pottered round her kitchen watching her preparing this, her best-known speciality. Made with puff pastry in a round shape, her method of serving it was to cut out a complete circle from the lid of the pie and spoon out the contents. The pastry crust was apportioned later and eaten with a green salad.

La Tourtière aux Salsifis
Chicken and salsify pie

The shape of your dish determines how much pastry will be needed: *la tourtière* was the round, cast-iron pot, sometimes with three legs, which stood over the open fire. The lid and inner rim were indented below the top of the pot so that the hot ashes could also be piled on top. This gave an all-round heat – *feu dessous, feu dessus* – approximating more nearly to an oven. A wide and flat-bottomed dish, like the *tourtière*, will probably take 700g (1½ lb) of pastry whereas an oval *pâté* or pie dish may only require 500 g (1 lb). The *tourtière* can also be made with *pâté brisée* and probably was in the old days, then cooked over the fire. Or it was prepared on bread-making day and cooked in the bread oven after the bread was finished. The dish is a speciality of the Quercy but it is also found in the Rouergue as *Croustade aux salsifis*.

This is a lengthy dish to prepare; leave yourself plenty of time for the first stage which can take up to two hours. Allow sufficient time after that for the filling to cool, just as for a steak and kidney pie. Some salsify sold in shops in Britain such as Belgian salsify does not seem to need half such long cooking as the *scorzonera* we have bought at market in France. So keep testing it as it may take longer than the chicken to cook.

Serves 6-7

1 roasting chicken, 1.5 kg (3 lb) dressed weight	5 tablespoons flour
	8 tablespoons cream
1 kg (2¼ lb) salsify	2 crushed cloves garlic
2 tablespoons vinegar	2 tablespoons chopped parsley
2 carrots, finely chopped	salt, pepper, nutmeg
1 onion, finely chopped	2 egg yolks
1 tablespoon goose or duck fat	juice of one lemon
bouquet garni	500-700 g (1-1½ lb) puff pastry
150 ml (¼ pt) dry white wine	1 egg yolk and a little milk
3 tablespoons goose or duck fat	

Skin and joint the chicken into six or seven pieces, reserving the skin and giblets. Scrape the salsify (the rotating type of potato peeler is particularly useful for this) and cut it into lengths of about 3.5 cm (1½ in). Keep them in a bowl of water containing lemon juice to preserve their colour.

Soften the carrots and onion in the goose fat. Add the chicken pieces and simmer together for a few minutes, then add the salsify, bouquet garni, chicken skin and giblets, wine and enough water to cover. Season lightly, bring to the boil and simmer slowly for 30 to 45 minutes. Test the salsify to see if it is done when the chicken is. If not, remove the chicken and finish cooking the salsify on its own. When both are cooked, remove them and strain the liquor which should be about 850 ml (1½ pt). Put it to one side. (Throw away the skin and giblets.)

Make a roux with the melted goose or duck fat and flour, adding enough of the stock to bring it to the consistency of a thick béchamel. Add the cream, garlic, parsley and seasoning, and put back the chicken and salsify. Cook together for 5 minutes, then remove from the heat and stir in the yolks of egg, beaten up with the lemon juice. Allow the mixture to get quite cold so that it thickens; it is important that the consistency is not too thin otherwise the pastry will go soggy.

Choose an appropriate pie dish, grease it and line it with just over half the pastry, leaving an overlap round the edge of the dish. Put in the cold chicken mixture and a support for the pastry lid. Brush the edges with an egg and milk mixture and cover with the remaining pastry. Pinch the edges together and brush the top with egg and milk. Make a hole in it for the steam to escape.

Heat the oven to 230°C, 450°F, Gas Mark 8, and bake the pie for 20 minutes, then lower the heat to 190°C, 375°F, Gas Mark 5, and cook for a further 30 minutes.

To serve, cut out a complete circle of crust and lift out the contents. Divide the crust into six or seven and serve it afterwards with a green salad.

●

As we have already seen many recipes prove to be ways of making meat go a long way. This would have been second nature to a farmer's wife when you consider that on a farm there were usually three generations of a family, apart from any farm workers, to feed three times a day. Family reunions or festive occasions like Christmas or New Year's Eve were opportunities to present special dishes, like this galantine. It includes a large truffle which nowadays would seem pretty academic for most cooks. You *can* buy truffle pieces or small whole ones in tins, highly priced, and it must be said that though they are not a patch on a fresh one, they do add something to this dish. It comes from the region of Brassac in the Lot-et-Garonne. It is a real party dish – pretty to look at and delicious to taste.

LA GALANTINE DE VOLAILLE TRUFFÉE
Galantine of truffled chicken

Serves 10–12

1 chicken, about 2 kg (4½ lb)
  dressed weight
150 g (5 oz) lean stewing veal
150 g (5 oz) lean pork
300 g (10 oz) *jambon de campagne*, in 2
  rashers
175 g (6 oz) *foie gras* or *pâté de foie
  gras*

3 tablespoons *eau-de-vie*, cognac or
  dry white wine
1 large truffle
quatre-épices
2 glasses dry white wine
1 veal marrow bone, cut into pieces
salt, pepper

It is not too difficult to bone a chicken, leaving the skin all in one piece with the flesh attached, but if you 'chicken out', ask your butcher if he will do it for you, telling him you want to stuff and re-shape it. Ask him also to saw the veal marrow bone into three or four pieces.

Remove the breast fillets, season them and leave them to macerate in a tablespoonful of *eau-de-vie* or brandy for a while.

Chop the veal, pork and ham into small dice, put them in a bowl and add the *foie gras*, the finely sliced truffle and 2 tablespoonsful of *eau-de-vie*. Mash well with a fork and add seasoning, but balance the salt against the ham.

With needle and thread, sew up the neck end of the boned chicken, then put half of the stuffing mixture into the cavity of the bird. Lay the fillets on top, then add the remainder of the stuffing on top of them. Sew up along the back and the tail opening – when you have finished you should have a tight, compact, sausage-shaped 'bird'. Wrap it in a muslin and tie with string as if it were a joint of meat, though not too tightly; this way the sausage shape will be retained throughout the cooking and the muslin will keep the string from marking the skin of the bird.

Choose a pan into which the chicken and the pieces of marrow bone fit as snugly as possible – you want the minimum of cooking liquid so as to make a stiff and strongly flavoured jelly. Pour in the wine and enough water to cover. Put the saucepan, with its lid on, over a low heat and bring it gradually to the boil. Simmer gently for 2 hours and then leave it to cool in its liquor.

Remove the bird from the pan and untie and discard the muslin. Pour the pan juices into a bowl and allow to cool for several hours, then remove the fat risen to the surface. Decant the juice underneath, leaving the sediment behind in the bottom of the bowl. You can, if you like, clarify the stock further (as for consommé) but more simply, chill it as it is, adding any truffle juices, and when it starts to set, spoon some over the bird to glaze it.

To serve, slice the galantine vertically; the various meats and the chicken fillets give the slices a marbled effect, set off by the studs of black truffle. Spoon some of the extra jelly, chopped up, over the slices.

———— ● ————

The same method can be used for a turkey, duck or guinea fowl. The *farce* can be made with pure pork sausage meat (as for the *saucisses fraîches* on page 66) with the gizzard and liver added, or for a very special occasion, a piece of *foie gras* can be placed in the centre of the pork stuffing.

LA TERRINE DE FOIE DE VOLAILLE ROSTASSAC
Chicken liver terrine

So many chicken liver *pâtés* are too strong for our taste. We asked the lady who runs the auberge at Rostassac in the hills above Cahors why hers is gentler than most, and she explained that she softened the pungent liver flavour with other meats.

Serves 8

250 g (8 oz) stewing veal	1 clove garlic
250 g (8 oz) fairly lean pork belly or shoulder	salt, pepper, nutmeg
	1 tablespoon brandy
250 g (8 oz) chicken livers	1 beaten egg
2 shallots	1 bay leaf

Mince the veal and pork finely. Chop the livers, shallots and garlic and add them to the mixture together with the seasoning, brandy and beaten egg.

Pack the mixture into a small earthenware terrine or pie dish and lay the bay leaf on top. Cover with the lid or a piece of silver foil and bake in a *bain-marie* (dish of boiling water) in the oven at 180°C, 350°F, Gas Mark 4, for 1½ hours, removing the lid after the first hour.

Leave to cool before chilling in the refrigerator for at least 24 hours. The *pâté* is a better consistency if it is kept for a day or two before serving.

———— ● ————

Next to the hen, the rabbit provides the other staple from the *basse-cour*. It grows more quickly than other domestic animals and will weigh, when skinned, 1.5–2 kilos (3¼ – 4½ lb). The female can produce 30 offspring a year – in French a young rabbit is a *lapereau*, a term often found on restaurant menus. Although there are now special feeds on the market, the peasant farmer's wife feeds her rabbits largely on home-grown products or wild ones – grass, hay, turnips, carrots, corn, and part of her regular chores is to gather the fresh grasses and clovers from the fields and hedgerows.

The ways of cooking these well-fed rabbits range from simple to more sophisticated. Again any surplus rabbits are brought live to market for sale but can also be bought, skinned and gutted, at market or in poultry shops. The two following recipes are for more special occasions, while for a simple meal it is not difficult to prepare *Lapin Dame Jeanne*, using a jointed rabbit which is casseroled with lots of fresh herbs, onions and tomatoes, the sauce finished at the end with fresh cream.

LE LAPIN EN CABESSAL
Stuffed rabbit in the shape of a headband

Some families in our village, even if they have no other livestock, keep a few rabbits in a hutch. Apart from their value for the table they amuse the children and grandchildren. This local recipe, and its curious name, goes back to when the women, who had to carry the pails of water from the well on their heads, rolled a towel or piece of cloth into a crown which they wore to support the weight – the *cabessal*. This dish takes the name because the rabbit's fore and hind feet are tied together to form a circle like the old *cabessal*.

Serves 6

for the stuffing:
175 g (6 oz) *jambon de campagne*, diced
125 g (4 oz) lean pork, chopped
100 g (3½ oz) fat pork, chopped
30 g (1 oz) breadcrumbs
175 g (6 oz) button mushrooms, chopped
4 cloves garlic, chopped
60 g (2 oz) shallots, chopped
2 tablespoons armagnac
1 egg
salt, pepper, *quatre-épices*

for the pot:
175 g (6 oz) fresh *couennes* (pork skin)
a 1.5 kg (3¼ lb) rabbit
3 tablespoons goose or duck fat
30 g (1 oz) shallots
1 tablespoon flour
400 ml (¾ pt) stock
300 ml (½ pt) dry white wine
salt, pepper
bouquet garni

Prepare the stuffing by mixing together all the ingredients listed, then leave it to marinate for an hour. Cut the pork skin into 3 cm (1¼ in) squares.

Remove the head from the rabbit if it has not already been done – in France you usually buy the whole skinned animal including the head. At market you might have to buy the animal live and have to kill, skin and gut it yourself.

Fill the interior with the stuffing and sew it up. Then tie its legs so as to form it into a circle, pushing the forelegs between the hind ones. In a large, round flameproof casserole, heat 2 tablespoonsful of the fat, put in the rabbit, the diced *couennes* and shallots and sauter them, turning the rabbit carefully to brown it on both sides.

During this time, prepare a roux with a tablespoonful of fat and of flour, mix in some stock and white wine and season it. Cook this sauce, stirring it continuously, for several minutes before pouring it over the rabbit. Add the bouquet garni, put on the lid and reduce the heat. Leave to simmer *very* gently for about 2 hours.

Fresh noodles or macaroni go well with this dish.

———— ● ————

The famous prunes made in the valleys of the Lot and Garonne go wonderfully well with rabbit and this is a *ragoût* to be found with variations all over the South-West.

LE LAPIN AUX PRUNEAUX D'AGEN
Rabbit with prunes

Serves 6

20–24 prunes (Agen)	2 tablespoons goose or pork fat
575 ml (1 pt) red wine	24 button onions
a 1.5 kg (3¼ lb) rabbit, cut into pieces	1 tablespoon flour
	300 ml (½ pt) stock
1 carrot	1 clove garlic, chopped
1 onion	2 carrots, sliced
2 tablespoons oil	bouquet garni
1 tablespoon vinegar	salt, pepper
125 g (4 oz) fresh belly of pork	

Soak the prunes overnight in half the red wine, and marinate the rabbit pieces in the remainder, with the sliced carrot, onion, vinegar and oil and plenty of freshly ground black pepper.

Next day cut the pork belly into strips and brown it in the fat in a casserole. Take it out of the fat with a slotted spoon and set it aside. Brown the rabbit pieces all over and set them aside. Brown the onions. When they are coloured, sprinkle in the flour, then blend in the wine which you have drained off the prunes and off the rabbit, also the stock. Add the garlic, carrots, bouquet and seasonings.

Put back the rabbit and pork lardons and bring the pot to a simmer. Cover and leave it to continue simmering very gently for an hour before adding the prunes. Continue the cooking for another half hour and then check to see if the rabbit is tender.

Can be served with *millas* (see page 143).

———— ● ————

Finally a word about *pigeonniers*. These fall within the ambit of the *basse-cour* and thus the woman in charge. Visitors to the region cannot help but notice the wide variety of structures specially built for pigeons – not the common-or-garden type of pigeon we are used to but pigeons specially bred and reared for the table. Sometimes these picturesque buildings are free standing in the middle of a field, raised on stone pillars which have protruding rings halfway up to keep out marauding rats or cats. Others are incorporated into the farm buildings and even into the farmhouse itself. Ours represents one whole additional storey with three dormer windows, but it is nowadays more likely to attract barn owls than pigeons.

After the Revolution everyone suddenly had the right to keep pigeons, so a *pigeonnier* became a kind of status symbol, families vying with each other to produce more and more elaborate versions. It was soon found that, beyond the benefits of having delicious table birds, the fertilizer provided by their droppings was priceless, so much so that when a farmer died the pigeon manure was counted into his estate for the purpose of ensuring a fair division of assets among the family.

These semi-domesticated pigeons are killed when young and are either spit-roasted or cooked *en cocotte* with diced salt belly of pork and little onions and garnished with *petits pois* – or *mangetout* peas if Jane's customer had been allowed to give us the details (see page 171).

LE COCHON –
'LOU MOUSSUR'

W E MUST ADMIT straight away
that we have not so far had the
courage to attend the ceremonial
slaughter of the family pig. However, this is still
in some country farms a ritual and a joyous
occasion in which the whole family takes part.
One small child has passed a proverb into the
folklore of the Ariège by answering the school-
master's question of what are the three great
feasts of the year – 'The Ascension, the Assump-
tion, and the Fête du Cochon'.

Great pride is taken in the family pig. It will
have the finest bristles, the pinkest skin, the
curliest tail, the broadest beam – the last
promising short but round hams. It will be the
most sensible, lively and greedy of all pigs. It will
receive the maximum attention and care,
representing as it does months of work and
investment. It is always referred to respectfully
as *lou moussur* – 'Sir'. The time for slaughter is
carefully chosen: the weather should not be
windy or the meat will not salt properly. The
atmosphere should be dry. The new moon is
avoided. All the utensils associated with the
operation will have been prepared and sterilized where necessary: tubs,
cauldrons, pots, preserving jars and the salting jar, of course. On many
farms a part of the attic is set aside to store all these, with enough
draught to prevent the dreaded mould which, for example, can ruin a
precious ham to the point that not even the dogs will touch it.

The moment of sacrifice at hand; this is what happens, according to
M. Joseph Vaylet, quoted at length in *Les Mangeurs de Rouergue*:

> The slaughterer would have brought with him his big, sharp knives: he
> would seek out the pig in his sty, pass a rope through his mouth to pull

him by and to grab him by the snout; then he would get him outside. There would be two people waiting to get hold of him, one by the front feet and the other by the back feet. They laid him flat on a kind of grid, then they put a similar piece of metal on top of him. Then the farmer's wife, whose job it was to catch the blood, would bring up a cauldron and roll up her sleeves. The slaughterer would then bare the skin of the pig, and do for him with his knife, and the blood which flowed into the cauldron the woman would strain through her fingers, turning it over so that it did not coagulate.

Then they had to purify the animal with fire. Strips of wood would be laid on the ground and the pig laid on them on its belly. Straw would be laid all round and set alight. The people would also have small tapers because there were places where the blood and other matter had run, either on to the feet or the ears and it wouldn't burn off. Then they would scrape the pig with a knife and a pumice stone and pour hot water over it to carry away any impurities. When they had burnt it, they brought the pig back into the house.

Where I was brought up, they always opened the animal up inside, never outside the house. In the kitchen they laid down straw and a wooden frame to keep the animal standing up, then the slaughterer cut off its head, opened it and took out the brains. There were little piles of straw and baskets all over the place to receive the various pieces of the pig. It was customary to present the brain to the farmer's wife to cook.

But the first piece to be eaten was from the fillet. Once he had killed the pig, the slaughterer wanted to be on his way – he never hung around to make the sausages – so he was given a glass of something to drink and a piece of the pig to eat. He went off too with the finest bristles . . . an additional perk of the slaughterer.

So the slaughterer, after killing and opening the pig, takes out the tripe and offal which he puts in a special flat wide basket. One of the women will take this and clean it at the spring: she takes with her a wicker basket so as to be able to lay out the skin of the guts. Then the slaughterer asks the woman of the house 'Do you want the leg bones left or taken out? What do you want to make . . . hams? All hams? or what?' So, he cuts accordingly. And he cuts off the feet which he puts aside on some straw. Then there are the *grattons* – *fritons* they are called too – which were melted down, but later. That day was for making the sausage. The men and women sat down at the table . . . one boned the meat, chopping it on a board into small pieces to make the sausage . . . and the *saucisson* too, but that was made separately because it was salted in quite a different way . . .

They made two kinds of fresh sausage. There was the sausage 'for the cousins'; it was made with the heart – it was less good, it wouldn't keep long. The heart was pre-cooked then salted. It was then hung up to dry but it didn't have the lovely pink colour of the other kind which was hung up on hooks from the ceiling with the *saucissons*.

Les Mangeurs de Rouergue, A. Merlin & A.Y. Beaujour (Duculot 1978, pp 91–3)

Quite a performance, you might think, but that is only the beginning. There is the salting to do, in particular the hams to prepare. Here of course we are talking about the country hams to be cured and eaten raw, in the manner of *jambon de Bayonne*. All too often one finds, even in otherwise reputable *charcuteries*, the so-called *jambon de campagne* is made from pigs raised on industrialized farms, granule fed, whose flesh is thus unsuitable for salting and has to be injected with brine. Nevertheless, given properly produced meat, patience and a good chimney, the production of quality ham is neither as difficult as is made out, nor as expensive as the *charcuterie* trade would have you believe.

Apart from the salting of ham, the other choice joints will all be preserved unless required for immediate consumption, as for example, if a pig is killed at Carnival time (Mardi Gras). These meats will either be kept in brine, or perhaps cooked and preserved in pork fat in tins or preserving jars. The parts which are dried or smoked like the *saucissons* and hams will be hung from the beams, out of the reach of mice and rats. As the patois saying goes:

> *Un porc pendjat demorro pla dins un oustal*
> (A pig hanging from the beams is the best ornament
> in the house)

All the fat is rendered down for long-term domestic use, and the intestines form the casings for sausages and *boudins*. Not even the bones are thrown away: they are preserved in brine, often with some small pieces of meat still attached to them, and enrich many a good soup during the winter. The brain, a delicacy, is awarded either to the oldest or youngest member of the family.

Once all the urgent problems had been dealt with, some districts used to have a tradition of taking a *présent* to neighbours like the schoolteacher, the parish priest or even the farm next door. Sometimes this would be a *sanguette*, which is quite simply a sort of pancake made with some of the blood and cooked with diced pork fat and parsley, or perhaps a *boudin* (blood pudding). It is a pity that this idea has all but died out because the *présent* was naturally reciprocated and it enabled a neighbourhood to enjoy over an extended period of time those parts of the pig which not even French ingenuity has yet found a way of preserving.

Nowadays in our Aveyron village the local people will pay someone to rear a pig for them and when it is fully grown, they will summon the slaughterer – *le tueur* – to come and kill the animal. Many country people will have their own pig so that they have a supply of pork products all through the winter. It will probably not be long before even the domestic killing of pigs is forbidden under Common Market rules. The private killing of other animals is already illegal. The old tradition described here may seem cruel and bloody but once the manufacture of sausages, *saucissons*, *pâté* and hams passes exclusively into the hands of big business, what price standards? On the other hand, many country towns have managed to expand agriculture round canning and preserving, creating a long-term and much needed demand for jobs.

'Why all the fuss?' you may ask. 'Why should the killing of a pig be such a big event?' As so often in the South-West, the answer lies in the basic principles of peasant life: insistence on self-sufficiency, which includes the need to produce one's own meat and fat for cooking in. Most farmers do not produce beef in quantity because they do not have the necessary grazing land to spare from the few hectares which make up their farms; sheep are only viable in quantity and do not provide the fat required for general household purposes. The pig is the natural choice. Until fairly recently most country people never went to the butcher's at all except to buy the odd piece of beef or mutton for a special occasion; they paid out good money for meat only on high days and holidays. Today the tendency persists, though more general prosperity has enabled even the poorer upland farmers to vary their diet rather more than their forebears could. Even so, pork constitutes the basic meat intake. The belly in the soup, as we have seen, the fat with the vegetables, sausage or brawn as a snack, the same enriched with liver for Sunday lunch, *confits* as a special treat, and ham on real feast days.

The pigs are specially fattened during the autumn for slaughter either at the onset of winter or before the beginning of the following Lent. A more prosperous farmer will have more than one pig to kill so that he can spread the availability of meat over a longer period.

A St-Thomas [December 21] si tu as un porc, tue le. Qui n'en a pas, aille en voler. St-Thomas le pardonnera.
(On St Thomas's Day, if you have a pig, kill it. Anyone who hasn't got one should go and steal one; St Thomas will pardon it.)
goes an old country saying.

The pigs are encouraged to grow to enormous size, with much more fat than would be acceptable in this country. According to one old-timer:

> If you wanted to fatten a pig, you had to look after it properly. You had to make it eat, you had to stuff it full of food . . . really stuff it. To start with, you gave it as many raw chestnuts (shells and all) as it would eat; when it wouldn't eat any more of those, you gave it peeled chestnuts, and when it was fed up with those, you gave it cooked ones, even roasted ones. You gave it all that to make it really big.
>
> Pigs used to grow to 250 kilos (5 cwt), some even weighed 300 kilos (6 cwt). In those days they made lots of fat, but it's not the same any more.

Les Mangeurs de Rouergue, A. Merlin & A.Y. Beaujour Duculot (1978, p 91)

In the Cévennes where so many chestnuts are grown, pigs are fed on a sort of chestnut soup for the last three months of their lives. In the Périgord, the diet is more varied: a balance of mashes consisting of greenstuff, cabbage leaves and beet, mixed with potatoes and roots together with coarsely ground maize, corn and barley. This could be moistened with whey if there are cattle on the farm, or in past times with the washing-up water – this at a time when soap was too dear and detergents had not been dreamed of. Some farmers also make a point of warming the pig's drinking water – considered beneficial. There are also chestnuts, both cooked and raw. During the last weeks the mash may be thickened with flour and cooked overnight in a great cast-iron cauldron suspended in the hearth to simmer till morning and then be broken up in the trough to grunts of pleasure. The high quality of feed is the best guarantee of both the quality of the meat and the longevity of the cured hams.

Most readers of this book will not be in the habit of slaughtering their own pigs and for this reason alone they will not be able to attempt all of the preparations which the French farmer's wife can. The recipes which follow are included because we have found them all practical in spite of not having raised one's own *moussur*.

One of the most urgent tasks, once the pig has been opened up and bled is to remove the intestines and tripe. Most importantly, the intestines will yield the casings for the blood puddings which are closely related to our own in content and method, and for the fresh sausages, whether those generally known as *saucisses de Toulouse* or those simply called *saucisses fraîches*. In either case, if you buy them from the butcher or *charcutier*, they will be coiled up like serpents, ready to be purchased by the length.

If you have a sausage-making attachment in your *batterie de cuisine* you will have no difficulty in making either style of sausage and they really are some of the best all-purpose sausages in the world. They contain no cereals or artificial matter whatsoever. Even if you don't make your own sausages, the recipe for the basic sausage meat is fundamental to many dishes of this region as well as being far superior to anything you are likely to find at your own butcher in Britain.

LA SAUCISSE FRAÎCHE
Fresh pork sausage

2 parts lean neck or shoulder of
    pork to 1 part of fat pork, eg.
    neck, back, belly
salt, pepper
a pinch of sugar

a pinch of saltpetre
white wine – 4 tablespoons per 1 kg
    (2¼ lb) meat (optional)
pork sausage skins (3 cm (1¼ in)
    diameter when filled)

The lean and fat meat should be fairly finely chopped or minced. Try using a *hachoir*, one of those crescent-shaped metal choppers, first heated in hot water. Put the chopped meat into a bowl which you can cover easily, add the seasoning and the wine (an extra ingredient favoured in the Périgord). Cover and leave overnight. Fill your skins the following day. This sausage will keep for a few days in a cool, dry place but if you want to put it by for later use, it should be prepared *en confit* as described on page 70.

To cook it, simply prick the skins as you would for any sausage and either fry in a frying pan or bake in a greased dish in a medium oven. Either way it will need about half an hour's cooking; a few rounds of onion added half-way through are an improvement. Serve with lentils, mashed or sauté potatoes and a green salad.

LA SAUCISSE DE TOULOUSE
Fresh Toulouse sausage

This differs in being somewhat leaner; 3 parts of lean to one part of fat. The lean meat should come from choicer parts of the animal such as loin or shoulder and the fat should be all hard back fat. The leaner and coarser mix of the Toulouse sausage makes for an altogether more substantial sausage – good eaten cold and an admirable contribution to picnics. Otherwise the preparation is precisely the same as for *saucisse fraîche*.

An amusingly different way of using Toulouse sausage comes from the Gaillac area where the Co-operative at Técou makes a good pink wine. One has to admit, though, that any good *rosé* would do.

La Saucisse au Vin Rosé

Sausage in a rosé wine sauce

Serves 4

2 red peppers	1 dessertspoon tomato purée
500 g (1 lb) Toulouse sausage	2 wine glasses dry *vin rosé*
6 cloves garlic, chopped	1 tablespoon capers
1 large onion, chopped	salt, pepper
2 teaspoons flour	

Blanch the peppers in boiling water for 10 minutes, drain and de-seed them.

In a thick frying pan, cook the sausage gently in little or no fat but take care to prick it well all over to allow it to give out all its own fat. Allow 20-30 minutes according to the thickness of the sausage. Remove the sausage to a warm place.

Add the garlic and onion to the pan juices and let them take on a little colour. Sprinkle with the flour, stir in the tomato puree, and pour in the wine, stirring until the sauce is smooth. Then stir in the diced peppers and the capers. Check for seasoning, put the sausage back into the sauce and simmer all together gently for 5-10 minutes.

•

Madame Delmur, the wife of our local baker, makes a dish of sausages with green lentils but she first immerses her sausage in oil for three weeks, alternating it with layers of onions, carrot and bay leaves to mature the sausage and add flavour.

Fresh from your triumphs in making Toulouse sausage, you could venture forth into another kind of sausage called *le melsat*. This is said to have been invented in the village of Aiguefonde, a mile or two to the south-west of Mazamet in the Tarn. The casings are stuffed with a mixture of sausage meat, eggs and bread to which pork *couennes* or fat may be added. It is well-seasoned. The *melsat* can be eaten grilled like any other sausage, poached in the soup or cold like a *saucisson*. In the Cévennes it is sliced and fried in a little duck fat and the pan is deglazed with a glass of Muscat de Frontignan. The sausage is then served on a bed of slightly sweetened chestnut purée and the pan juices poured over.

The kind of sausage called *saucisson sec*, which is rather like salami in texture and taste, is quite expensive to buy in France and not at all easy to find in England. Practice is required to bring it to a professional standard and few people have access to a source of supply of the coarse skin needed to encase the sausage. We therefore do not give a recipe but recommend buying it from a local *charcutier*, most of whom make their own. Standards are high though quality can vary. Our favourite local *charcutier* has just won a gold medal at an international exhibition for *la saucisse sèche de campagne*. Note, incidentally, that French butchers (*bouchers*) – unless they are also *charcutiers* – do not sell fresh pork and pork products.

Pig's liver has so many uses in *pâtés* that it tends to be ignored in other kinds of dishes. It is also rather strong in flavour. The following recipe, however, seems to tone down the strength and as long as the liver is not cooked for too long most people would take it for calf's liver. This is not a dish that can be kept waiting.

Le Foie De Porc en Escabèche
Pig's liver with piquant sauce

Serves 4

500 g (1 lb) pig's liver, in slices 2cm (¾ in) thick and 5-7.5 cm (2-3 in) long
flour, oil
12 cloves garlic, chopped
1 large onion, or 1 smaller onion and 2 shallots, chopped
1 glass dry white wine
125 ml (4 fl oz) chicken or veal stock

2 tablespoons wine vinegar
4 medium-sized tomatoes, peeled and de-seeded
powdered thyme and bay leaf
6 chopped gherkins
chives
salt, pepper

Heat some oil in a thick frying pan until it starts to smoke. Dip the pieces of liver in seasoned flour and fry them for about half a minute on each side. Remove the pieces to a warm place and lower the heat. Add the garlic, the onion (and shallots if you have them) and sauter them all gently. Sprinkle with a dessertspoonful of flour and moisten with the wine, stock and vinegar. Add the tomatoes to the pan with a little of the powdered herbs. Cook the mixture gently for 15 minutes and check for seasoning. Put the liver back into the pan, add the chopped gherkins and cook all together so that it scarcely boils, for another 5 minutes. Sprinkle with chives, season and serve. The liver should be quite pink and the sauce fairly short.

——— • ———

A classic method of conserving the pig for later use is the same as we have seen used for poultry, namely *le confit*. The pig gives so much fat of its own that the farmer's wife finds no trouble in putting aside enough to preserve all sorts of pieces. Here are three suggestions, all perfectly feasible in your own kitchen with very little trouble.

LE CONFIT DE PORC
Preserved pork

The best *confit* is made from the loin or fillet, boned and trimmed, but you can also use cuts from the shoulder and leg. The meat should be cut into parcels of about 300 g (10 oz) and well tied with thread so that it keeps it shape during the cooking. Bear in mind that the meat is destined to be stored in glass preserving jars or stone pots and will shrink in the cooking, so the exact size of each piece of meat will depend on the shape and size of your preserving container and whether you want one or more pieces in each pot.

The basic method is much the same as for preparing *confit d'oie*.

1 kg (2¼ lb) fillet or other lean joint of pork
3 cloves garlic
45 g (1½ oz) salt

1 teaspoon saltpetre (optional)
1 kg (2¼ lb) lard, or more according to need

Spike the meat with tiny slivers of the garlic, rub the pieces with the salt and saltpetre and leave them to stand for 48 hours. Turn them often in the salt so as to impregnate the meat as much as possible. After the two days, wipe off the salt, melt the lard in your cooking pot and plunge the meat into the fat, which must cover the pieces entirely. Bring the fat to a gentle simmer, then reduce the heat and leave to cook slowly for 2–2½ hours. The meat will be ready when you can pierce it through with a skewer.

Meanwhile you will have sterilized your preserving jars and kept them hot.

Put in your pieces of meat and cover with the lard, which should be strained to catch any debris. The meat must be covered with at least 2.5 cm (1 inch) of fat since the level will sink as the meat and fat cool. Top up the next day with fat if necessary.

Confit de porc is best eaten cold. Remove what you want from your jar and put it in a frying pan over a low heat to melt off the surplus fat. Top up the jar with this melted fat to ensure that the remaining pieces are completely covered. If necessary add new lard.

Warm the *confit* through then drain off any fat and allow it to cool. Slice it thinly and serve it with a really fresh green salad.

LE CONFIT DE SAUCISSE DE TOULOUSE
Preserved Toulouse sausage

1.25 kg (2½ lb) Toulouse sausage	bay leaf
1 kg (2¼ lb) lard	1 cup water

Prick the sausage and cut it into manageable pieces. Heat the lard in a good-sized pan into which the lengths of sausage will fit without curling them up too much. Add the bay leaf and water – the water is to keep the temperature of the fat down so that the sausages do not fry. Put them in when the fat is gently bubbling and bring them up to a very gentle simmer. Leave to cook at this rate for 1½ hours. Allow to cool slightly, skimming off the top fat as necessary.

Sterilize a glass preserving jar or earthenware pot, dry it and keep it hot. Put in the sausages, packing them vertically or horizontally. Pour over the lard in which they have cooked, passing it through a fine muslin to strain off any bits.

Fill the jar sufficiently to cover the sausage and to allow 2.5 cm (1 in) of fat above. Leave to set and cover. Keep in a *cool* place.

A *confit* of Toulouse sausage is best fried as if it were fresh, and well browned in some of its own fat – with a little onion. Like all *confits*, it will have acquired a nutty maturity which no other method of preserving food can achieve. It can also be used to enrich a *cassoulet* or any similar bean stew, or indeed in any way in which a fresh sausage would be used.

LES COUENNES CONFITES
Preserved pork rind

A fundamental difference between the French and English treatment of pork shows up in the ways we respectively treat the rind. We love to make crackling of it when it surrounds a roasting joint, but the rest of the time we throw it away, or don't know what otherwise to do with it.

The French, on the other hand, don't know about crackling, which is a shame because it is very much in the mainstream of their taste for crispy pieces of fat. On the other hand, they don't waste an inch of a pig's rind. They call it *couenne* (pronounced Quan). They use it to enrich stews, soups, *cassoulets* or dishes of pulses. They also know how to preserve the rind for future use – by making *confits* of it. We shall see that the preparation involves rolling the skin on itself so as to make a kind of Swiss roll. One slice of this does wonders for a dish of white haricots, for an otherwise rather plain soup or for green lentils.

a piece of skin, from loin or belly of pork	coarse salt (*gros sel*) pork fat

This is really not worth doing unless you have a large piece of pork skin, at least 15 cm (6 in) square – perhaps left over after preparing the *enchaud de porc périgourdin* on page 76.

Lay the skin on a board with the fatty side uppermost and pare off as much of the fat as possible, until you are left with the thin rind. Rub this piece all over on both sides with coarse salt and leave it in a dish overnight.

Next day, render down the fat you have cut off and, if necessary, melt some additional pork fat. Wipe the salt off the pork skin and cut it into strips about 7.5 cm (3 in) wide. Roll these tightly up round each other into a Swiss roll, about 5–6 cm (2–2½ in) in diameter. Tie the roll firmly round at 1 cm (½ in) intervals with thin string and place in a small, thick-bottomed pan. Cover completely with melted fat, bring to simmer over the lowest possible heat, cover the pan and keep barely simmering for about 4 hours. It is finally cooked when you can pierce it easily with a skewer or needle: French cookery books say 'when it can easily be pierced with a piece of straw' – not many English kitchens nowadays have easy access to one.

Transfer the *couennes* to a sterilized glass or stoneware jar and pour the cooled fat over until it is completely covered. It may be necessary to do this in stages, only partly covering the rind at first and letting the fat set; otherwise the roll tends to float to the top of the melted fat. Put an airtight cover on the jar and keep in a cool place for at least a month before using it – cut up in soups or when cooking lentils (see page 175), *haricots* or *cassoulet* (page 93).

———— • ————

Other parts of the pig lend themselves to the *confit* process. Local *charcutiers* market a *confit* made from the ears, muzzle, spare ribs, and many other unidentifiable pieces of pig, all described as *fritons*. These cheaper cuts are best crisped up in the frying pan and served with lentils or beans.

But there remain some parts which do not preserve well by this method, so these are eaten fresh. In any case, having devised so many ways of looking after future needs, the farmer is entitled to the treat of some fresh pork – especially at the beginning of Lent – and what better when the weather is still cold than a comforting stew of pig's trotters with *flageolets*.

Pig's feet are eaten all over France. Breadcrumbed and deep-fried, they are called *Ste-Ménéhould* up in the North-East. Otherwise they are good on a bed of mashed potato with a vinaigrette, or stuffed with a savoury meat mixture. Cooks in the South-West remain faithful to the following dish. Two days are needed for it in English kitchens because fresh *flageolets* are unobtainable in England. If you can get fresh ones in France and are cooking this dish there, you can telescope operations into one day.

LES PIEDS DE PORC AUX FLAGEOLETS
Pig's trotters with flageolet beans

Serves 2

2 pig's trotters, cleaned and scraped	bay leaf
2 onions	125 ml (4 fl oz) dry white wine
2 carrots	125 ml (4 fl oz) red wine vinegar
1 stick celery	salt, pepper
3 large cloves garlic	125 g (4 oz) dried *flageolets*

1st day: put the trotters in a casserole with a close-fitting lid. Add one of the onions, a carrot, the celery, one garlic clove, all chopped, plus the bay leaf, wine and half the vinegar. Season. Add water to cover, bring it slowly to the boil and barely simmer for 4 hours. Remove the trotters and keep in a cool place overnight, together with the strained stock in which they were cooked. Put the *flageolets* to soak.

2nd day: Sweat the other onion, carrot and 2 cloves of garlic, all chopped, in the fat which has congealed on top of the stock. Put in the trotters, the beans and the rest of the vinegar. Add seasoning and cover with the stock. Bring to the boil and simmer, covered, for about 1 hour by which time the beans should have absorbed most of the liquor and thickened it, though it may be necessary to top up with a little more if it is all absorbed before the beans are cooked.

Another way of presenting pig's trotters in a thoroughly country style comes from the upper valley of the Lot where they add some lean beef to a stew which might otherwise have been just too rich. The flaming of the trotters helps to reduce the fattiness too.

LA POUTEILLE
Stew of pig's trotters with beef

Serves 6

4 pig's trotters, split down the middle
1 tablespoon goose or pork fat
8 shallots or 1 large onion, thinly sliced
700 g (1½ lb) lean stewing beef, cut into 5 cm (2-inch) cubes

1 small glass *eau-de-vie* or brandy
salt and pepper to taste
60 g (2 oz) flour
1 bottle red wine
bouquet garni
700 g (1½ lb) potatoes, peeled and cubed

Ask your butcher to split the trotters for you. Clean and dry them. Melt the fat in a heavy frying pan and gently brown the trotters all over without letting the fat get too hot. Meanwhile warm a flameproof casserole and preheat your oven to 150°C, 300°F, Gas Mark 2.

Transfer the trotters to the warmed casserole and keep them hot. In the remaining fat in the frying pan, sweat the shallots or onion, then add the beef pieces to seal them. Then transfer the onion and beef to the casserole and put this over a medium heat on the top of the stove while you *flamber* the contents. Warm the *eau-de-vie* in a soup ladle, set it alight and pour quickly over the meat in the casserole. When the flames have died down, season well and sprinkle in the flour. Add the wine gradually, mixing it with the flour, and bring the sauce back to the boil. Add the bouquet garni, cover the pot and transfer it back to the oven, leaving it to cook for 2 hours. Check from time to time that it is not simmering too fast.

After this time, add the potatoes. See that the pot comes back to the simmer, if necessary heating it on the top of the stove. Continue to cook for another half hour or so, until the potatoes are ready. Check the seasoning and serve on to hot plates.

———— ● ————

Moving up off the ground a little, one arrives at the *jambonneau*, literally 'baby ham' which is a polite title for the shin or hock. The hind ones are more tender and contain less bone. After a light salting, they are often cooked and then rolled in breadcrumbs to form the pear-shaped cones, their bone sticking from the top like a stalk, such as grace the counters of most *charcutiers* as *jambonneaux panés*. They are also salted, cooked and boned before being canned rather like a *pâté*. (Plenty of black pepper is used for this so be prepared for dark colourings on opening a tin of *jambonneau*.) In the old days they were steeped in a saline solution with the hams and then used to flavour soups and stews. Here is one that is the basis of a more substantial country stew in which turnips nicely balance the sweet-and-sour style of the other ingredients.

LE JAMBONNEAU AUX NAVETS ET AU CIDRE
Pork hock with turnips and cider

Serves 4

1 *jambonneau*, lightly salted
2 onions, sliced
1 kg (2¼ lb) small turnips, peeled
4 slices of *jambon de campagne*
2 cloves of garlic

1 tablespoon sugar
2 pinches cinnamon
1 pinch nutmeg
250 ml (8 fl oz) dry cider
salt, pepper

Ideally the *jambonneau* should be taken from your *saloir*, or it can be bought from the *charcutier*. Either way it must be soaked in fresh water overnight to get rid of any excessive saltiness.

Next day, line the bottom of your casserole with the onions and add half of the turnips. Put the baby ham on top. Add the four slices of ham and the rest of the turnips, together with the seasoning and the cider. Be careful about the salt as the ham is also salty. Cover the pot and put it in a low oven, 150°C, 300°F, Gas Mark 2. Gradually raise the temperature to 190°C, 375°F, Gas Mark 5, and cook for a total of an hour and a half.

———— ● ————

Moving gradually towards the higher grade cuts of the pig, we come to the pork chop. This is a particularly difficult joint: often it is tasteless, more often it is tough and sometimes both. Safety suggests cooking it *en papillote* with chopped onion, fresh sage and a little white wine or cider: the method tends to keep the chop moist and the flavourings give it some zest. But you might like to try this very attractive recipe from the far South-West.

LES CÔTES DE PORC À LA GASCONNE
Pork chops with olives and garlic

Serves 4

4 thick pork chops	24 green or black olives
	24 cloves garlic
for the marinade:	goose fat
1 clove garlic	1 glass dry white wine
thyme, bay leaf	a little beef or chicken stock
salt and pepper	chopped parsley
oil, lemon juice	

Marinate the chops (spiked with slivers of garlic) in the herbs, seasonings, oil and lemon juice for a couple of hours.

Stone the olives and peel the garlic. Blanch these separately in boiling water for 2 minutes, then drain them. Roughly chop the garlic.

Fry the chops quickly on both sides in some fat for 3 minutes a side. Add the chopped garlic, coat it with the fat, then cover the pan and reduce the heat. Allow to cook really slowly for 30–45 minutes, turning the chops half way through, until they are cooked.

Transfer the chops to a warmed dish in the oven and arrange the olives round them. Deglaze the cooking pan with the wine and add some stock, then allow the liquid to reduce until you have a nice sauce. Pour this, garlic and all, over the chops and sprinkle with some chopped parsley.

———— ● ————

A recipe which is good fun requires not only an open fire – though perhaps a barbecue might do at a pinch – but also the *capucin* or *flambadou* described on page 15. We first came across it at a wonderfully old-fashioned village *auberge* on the Causse de Gramat in the Lot, where the main dishes were roasted over the open fire in the bar. We then searched for some time before finding one to buy for ourselves. Although we felt the need to add it to our *batterie de cuisine* for authenticity's sake we were not at first sure of its merit. But it gives a splendid nuttiness and succulence to a joint or bird. If you cannot procure one, simply baste your chops with fat in the ordinary way.

La Carbonnade au Flambadou
Pork grilled at the fireside

Serves 4

4 pork chops	175 g (6 oz) pork fat or fatty bacon,
olive oil	in a piece
pepper	salt
700 g (1½ lb) potatoes	
dried herbs – thyme, rosemary,	
lavender, marjoram, as available	

Paint the chops with olive oil and season them with pepper but not salt at this stage. Slice the potatoes lengthways in slices 2 cm (¾ in) thick; this will minimize the possibility of their falling through the bars of your grill. Coat them also with olive oil and sprinkle with pepper.

When your fire has settled to a good *braise* – not too hot or the food will char – throw on the herbs and put the chops and potatoes to cook on the grill. Heat the *flambadou* till it is red-hot, put half the piece of fat pork into it and when the fat is flaming, baste the chops and potatoes thoroughly on one side. If the falling fat causes flames to reach the food, take it temporarily off the fire until the heat has once again subsided. After a quarter of an hour, turn the chops and potatoes and repeat the process with the *flambadou*. They should be ready in another 15 minutes but the cooking time will depend on the thickness of the chops and the heat of the fire. Salt just before serving.

●

The finer cuts of pork, such as the loin, are often simply roasted, stripped of their rind but well barded and spiked with plenty of garlic. A loin of pork can, however, be transformed into a dish of great beauty by cooking it like this – *en cocotte* – especially if you have a truffle to spare . . . The recipe goes back to a time when truffles were two a penny whereas nowadays their price is largely prohibitive. But anyway this dish is almost as good without them.

L'Enchaud de Porc Périgourdin
Loin of pork with wine and truffles

Serves 6

1.5 kg (3 lb) boned loin of pork,	1 large clove garlic
with the fillet	salt, pepper
1 large truffle, fresh or tinned	150 ml (¼ pt) dry white wine
(optional)	

Ask your butcher to bone the loin and to give you the bones. If the rind is still on the joint, don't let him score it which some British butchers do automatically. With a sharp, pointed knife, pare off the skin in one piece as thinly as possible. This can then be used to make *couennes confites* – the preserved pork rind described on page 70.

Then carefully cut off another layer from the underlying fat, again in one piece, leaving a thin covering of fat on the joint. Put this piece of fat on one side. Trim off as much of the excess fat as possible from inside the joint, particularly round the fillet. Season the meat all over. Peel the truffle if it is a fresh one, and keep the peelings for later. Slice it and arrange the slices in the grooves along the length of the joint, along the sides of the fillet and also where the bone was. Put slivers of garlic inside as well. Roll the meat up and place the extra layer of fat you cut off round the lean side so that you have a large sausage enveloped in fat. Tie it round with string at 1 cm (½ in) intervals and leave the joint to rest for a few hours.

Preheat the oven to 190°C, 375°F, Gas Mark 5, and put the joint into a casserole together with the bones. Put it to cook, uncovered, for half an hour so as to brown the fat a little, then add the wine and 150 ml (¼ pt) water – and if you are using a tinned truffle, the truffle juices. Cover the pot, reduce the oven to 160°C, 325°F, Gas Mark 3, and leave it to cook for a further 1½ hours. Turn the oven off but leave the joint to rest a little before transferring it to a warmed serving dish. Decorate it along the top with the peelings from the fresh truffle, very finely chopped, and serve the juices separately after you have reduced them slightly.

This joint is just as delicious served cold, when the juices set to make a delicate jelly.

———— • ————

Another recipe for a pork roast, *porc en cocotte aux châtaignes* can be found on page 275 in the section on chestnuts.

There are still recipes which are peculiar to quite small communities and will not have been heard of outside them. In the hilltop fortress village of Najac, perched 150 metres above the gorges of the river Aveyron, the roasting spit is called by its Languedoc name of *aste* and they have evolved a pungent way of roasting pork which is unknown even one station up or down the railway line. The one butcher now left in the village will prepare and season this joint for you but he will need a couple of days' notice. He will wrap it in a caul, the stomach lining which in French is known as *la crépine*. This is a sheet of thin membrane interspersed with small pieces of fat, giving a pretty openwork lace effect. You will need an oblong about 30 cm x 22.5 cm (12 in x 9 in). Soak this in some tepid water (to which you have added a tablespoonful of vinegar) to make it pliable; otherwise the membrane tends to tear. Drain well, then roll it round the joint before tying it up. Caul is quite difficult to obtain in Britain so here is a version that uses the fat of the joint itself as a protective covering – the finished effect is, unfortunately, nothing like so attractive.

L'ASTET DE NAJAC
Pork on the spit with garlic and parsley

Serves 6

1.5 kg (3 lb) boned middle loin of pork with the fillet
3–6 cloves garlic, according to size, chopped

2 tablespoons chopped parsley
salt and pepper

Trim as much fat as possible off the inside of the meat. If the fillet is still on it, there will be fat covering it. With a really sharp knife, very carefully carve a thin slice off the outside layer of fat and put this to one side. (If the rind is still on the joint, carve this off thinly first.)

Spread a thick covering of garlic, parsley, salt and pepper inside the joint between the fillet and the rest of the meat. Roll the meat together and put the spare slice of fat over the lean side. Start to tie up the joint into a roll, tying it with string at 1 cm (½ in) intervals. Roll it in more seasoning and parsley and leave at least 24 hours in a cool place.

Spit roast the joint for 1½ hours, basting it from time to time, reducing the heat after the first hour if it is cooking too fast.

This joint is equally delicious eaten cold, when it is often served with an *aïoli*.

———— ● ————

We shall see in another chapter the diversity of mushrooms to be found all over the South-West of France. Pride of place, if one ignores rarities, must go to the *cèpe* (*boletus edulis*). This and other kinds of mushroom make a savoury garnish for all roast meats, including pork, as this next recipe shows. It comes from a district called the Sidobre which is a strange outcrop of the Cévennes in the Tarn. The landscape is littered with huge granite boulders as if there had been a battle between armies of giants. There are plenty of chestnut woods too, where *cèpes* grow particularly well.

LE RÔTI DE PORC DU SIDOBRE
Roast pork with ceps

Serves 4

1 kg (2¼ lb) roast from the loin of pork, on the bone	250 g (½ lb) fresh *cèpes*, or 45 g (1½ oz) dried ones
salt, pepper	1 large clove garlic
2 tablespoons lard	2 tablespoons chopped parsley
1 medium-sized onion, sliced	

If you are using dried *cèpes*, put them to soak in warm water. Remove the rind from the pork and keep it for future use – to make *couennes confites* (page 70) or to enrich a stew. Bone the meat, season it well inside, roll and tie it securely round. Put a tablespoonful of lard in the roasting tin, together with the joint and the bones, and roast the meat in a hot oven, 220°C, 425°F, Gas Mark 7, for one hour, basting it from time to time with the pan juices.

Remove the roast to a serving dish and allow it to stand in the oven, turned to its lowest heat, for half an hour. In this way the meat will be more juicy and tender than if you had roasted it at full heat for a longer period.

While the pork is resting, cook the onion slowly in a thick frying pan in a tablespoon of lard. Do not allow it to brown but when it is soft, remove it from the pan and keep warm. Replace with the *cèpes*, cut into quarters or other suitable chunky pieces, season them well and cook over a moderate heat for twenty minutes. Towards the end of the cooking time, add a *hachis* made by combining the chopped garlic, parsley and the cooked onion. Simmer all together for a minute or two and then serve it round the roast.

——— ● ———

One of the great delights of country eating all over the South-West is raw ham. It reaches its apotheosis in the *jambon de Bayonne*, a misnomer, since most of it is made in Orthez (just as most of the *pruneaux d'Agen* are made in Villeneuve-sur-Lot and not in Agen). It is a ham which, like its peers from Parma and Westphalia, is intended to be eaten in paper-thin slices. It is, however, extremely expensive as well as impossible to emulate in an English kitchen. Real *jambon de Bayonne* has to be made from pigs reared in the extreme South-West and to have been salted with a specially produced local salt made from the spring waters at Salies-de-Béarn. Nowadays the production of Bayonne ham is largely an *artisanal* industry, organized into a syndicate of local producers whose business it is to preserve what is essentially an *appellation contrôlée*.

Bayonne is far from being the only ham worth imitating. All over the region ham is salted and often smoked for consumption over a long period of spring and early summer. It is described as *jambon de campagne* and, as its name implies, is a country version, less delicate and refined than Bayonne or Parma hams. It is highly salted, and plenty of coarsely-ground black pepper is also used in the preserving, its dark flecks clearly visible on each slice. The tenants who last occupied our farmhouse built elaborate pigsties in the outbuildings and must have salted hams in a big way because the floor of one large room was entirely impregnated with salt. The village of Najac, which is not far from us, used to be famous for its ham and the village street still boasts an octagonal structure rather like a bandstand in a park, from which the hams used to be auctioned. Today the hams of Lacaune in the Tarn are particularly well-known.

This raw ham is usually eaten as an hors d'oeuvre either with the juicy Charentais melons or otherwise, strangely enough, with a little butter, the only time this fat appears on the table.

You can produce a perfectly acceptable *jambon de campagne* at home without either boning it or smoking it, provided that you are assured of enough mouths to eat it all within a period of perhaps four or five weeks from the time you first cut into it. Essentially the method is the same all over the South-West, the Bayonne version differing from the rest principally in the sophistication of its manufacture.

LE JAMBON DE CAMPAGNE
Country ham

Do not attempt to cure a ham unless you have suitable facilities for storing it. You will need somewhere, preferably dark, where the temperature does not rise much above 16°C (60°F) and which is at the same time quite dry. Damp will send ham rancid more quickly even than heat. In the country, the cellar of the farmhouse, dark but always airy, makes an ideal spot. Some farms even allocate an upstairs room for the purpose. If you are lucky enough to have an old-fashioned larder or a cool but dry cellar, the exercise is well worthwhile and is very satisfying too.

The first thing to decide is whether you are going to smoke the ham or not. Most people will not have access to an open farmhouse chimney and even if they do, the chimney can be used for no other purpose while the smoking is in progress because of the low heat at which the fire has to be kept. Let us assume that you will not be smoking your ham but dry-curing it. For this you will need:

1 leg of pork	optional:
1 kg (2¼ lb) coarse sea salt	45 g (1½ oz) *quatre-épices*
100 g (3½ oz) sugar	1 tablespoon cloves
60 g (2 oz) black peppercorns	1 tablespoon juniper berries
100 g (3½ oz) saltpetre	up to 20 bay leaves
	up to 20 sprigs of thyme

Saltpetre or potassium nitrate is added to meat when salting to turn it a more attractive pink colour. It is combined with sugar which aids the chemical process and counteracts the bitterness. Saltpetre is used only in small quantities as it tends to toughen the meat. It is sold by chemists but, as it is also a constituent of gunpowder, may have to be specially ordered. Buy as small a quantity as possible as it easily goes hard.

Remove the thigh bone from the ham; you will find it easier to hang the meat up if you leave the knuckle bone in. Beat the joint all over with a piece of wood to extract as much of the blood and juices as possible. Hang the ham up in a dark, cool place for three days to complete this process.

At the end of this time, wipe the ham dry and clean with a cloth, then rub it all over with ground black pepper. Prepare the salt by mixing in the saltpetre and as many of the herbs and spices as you fancy. (Refined kitchen salt – which contains chemical additives – will not do.) Rub the ham with the mixture and put a generous quantity where the thigh bone was, and put some more pepper there too.

Take a large piece of linen or muslin, about 2½ times the size of the ham. Spread a good layer of the salt on one half of the cloth and lay the ham on it, skin side uppermost. Cover the rind with the rest of the salt, fold the cloth over the ham gently so as not to disturb the salt more than necessary. The cloth must envelop the joint like a tight-fitting glove. Tie it securely.

Find, or make, a wooden box into which the ham will fit fairly snugly and which has a lid or cover. It must be scrupulously clean (a wooden wine crate is one possibility). Put a good layer of wood ash in the bottom, deep enough so that its weight will not force the ham into contact with the wood. Lay the ham on the ash and then cover it with more ash until it is completely submerged. Cover with the lid and leave in a dry, cool place for one month. At the end of this time, take the ham out, remove its covering and brush off all the salt before rubbing it all over with cooking brandy or other spirit. Then tie it up in a clean muslin and hang in a cool, dry and airy larder or outhouse where, if conditions are right, it will keep for up to three months.

You can use the ham any time you like during that period but if you want to keep it longer, you will need to smoke it. In any case it is always wise to test a ham before broaching it: push a larding needle right through to the bone and it should come out clean and sweet, without any suspicion of rancidness.

The smoking process
The ham is suspended from a bar stretched across the chimney about seven feet from ground level. There must be plenty of smoke but the meat must not be allowed to get any hotter than 29°C (85°F) or the fat will start to melt. Green wood makes more smoke than dry, and pine, sage, bay and heather all make for a particularly aromatic smoke.

You will need about 35–40 hours' smoking in all and you may find it easier to do in stages. You may find it easier still to get the local bacon curer to do the whole job for you – provided there are any in your district.

When a ham is smoked it loses about a quarter of its weight and the rind takes on the familiar lovely golden brown colour. After smoking, it can be stored in a dry cool place for months. Avoid the temptation of hanging it in the kitchen which will almost certainly be too warm. Be careful too of cellars which are usually damp and of attics which can get hot in summer. Wrap the ham loosely in muslin to keep the flies off.

———— • ————

As well as being eaten raw, country ham features in various local dishes, for example in the *omelette brayaude* from the Auvergne (page 98); as a garnish and stuffing for *cèpes* (page 112); in the *gratin* of potatoes from the Landes (page 149); with *mange-tout* peas (page 172); or calf's liver *au vin de rancio* (page 221).

Here is one way of showing it up very well on its own, the sweetened pan juices offsetting the saltiness of the ham.

Le Jambon à la Poêle
Sweet and sour ham slices

for each person:

1 dessertspoon goose or pork fat	1 thinly cut slice *jambon de campagne*
1 lump sugar	2 tablespoons red wine

Melt the fat and dissolve the sugar in it slowly over a very low heat. Cook the ham very gently on each side until it turns colour but not too long in case the juice becomes too salty.

Remove the ham slice to a hot dish or direct to a heated dinner plate. Add the wine to the pan juices, allow it to reduce until it is slightly syrupy in consistency and then pour it over the ham.

———— • ————

Country ham can also be cooked whole if it has not been smoked, and made into an attractive and quite sensational *plat de résistance*. The ham is cleaned and desalted in frequent changes of water over a 24-hour period. Those parts blackened by the salting process are trimmed and the joint boiled with vegetables in the usual way. The rind is removed and the ham cooled in the broth, which should turn to jelly. It is served in the Dordogne with decorative salads dressed with walnut oil. Smaller joints can be cooked in the same way but will not look as attractive as a whole ham.

Ham is the most de luxe product of the salting process but many other joints are preserved by salting; sometimes dry, sometimes in brine. Whichever method is used requires sea salt, or at a pinch rock salt, but never refined salt, which contains chemical additives. The salted belly of pork which goes into so many soups, stews and composite dishes is usually dry cured. You will need 100 g (3½ oz) of salt to 500 g (1 lb) of meat and in addition small quantities of saltpetre, granulated sugar and juniper berries (15 g (½ oz) of each to every 500 g (1 lb) of salt), peppercorns, bay leaves, crushed thyme and cloves. All these ingredients are mixed with the salt which is then rubbed into the skin of the piece of belly, which is then buried as far as possible in the salt. A weight is placed on top and the meat left for at least a week.

A brine crock is very handy for odd pieces of meat for which there is no immediate use, as well as for keeping joints of belly, spare ribs and so forth. A typical brine (quantities depending on the size of crock) can be made with 1.75 litres (3 pt) of water (the purer the better), 250 g (½ lb) sea salt, 100 g (3½ oz) sugar and 30 g (1 oz) saltpetre. These are brought to the boil in a pan and a muslin bag added containing the same herbs as listed above for a dry cure. A piece of nutmeg is optional. Any scum is skimmed from the pan before the brine is poured into the brine crock, which must be scrupulously clean. The meat to be pickled is then added and the contents allowed to cool. A weighted board may be needed to stop the meat rising above the surface.

LES PÂTÉS ET LES TERRINES

All *pâtés* rely on at least the fat and often also the lean of the pig. Pork gives a *pâté* smoothness and the fat enables other meats to cook regularly and slowly. We have seen in the chapter on the *basse-cour* how pork enters even into *foie gras* preparations as well as duck and chicken *pâtés* and galantines. To round off this chapter on the pig are three *pâté* recipes from different parts of the South-West in which pork is the dominant meat. What is fascinating about *pâtés*, and incidentally, no distinction is to be drawn these days between *pâtés* and *terrines*, is the endless variety and combination of possible ingredients.

Certain basic points, however, are worth noting. Be careful in the use of smoked ham or bacon. It is best avoided unless you particularly want to include that flavour. Many cooks make their *pâtés* too lean; as a general rule a *pâté* should contain equal quantities of fat and lean meat. An egg helps to bind a *pâté* if its general character is of coarsely chopped ingredients. If a *pâté* is not for immediate consumption it should be sealed, when cold, with an inch-thick layer of lard and then covered with greaseproof paper and the lid of its terrine.

LE PÂTÉ DE FOIE DE PORC
Pork liver pâté

Serves 10

1 pig's liver, approx. 750 g (1½ lb)
equal weight of fresh belly of pork
2 cloves garlic, chopped
3 shallots, chopped
quatre-épices
salt and pepper
3 tablespoons armagnac or *eau-de-vie*
1 wineglass dry white wine

couennes (pork rind) or slices of
    unsmoked streaky or fatty bacon
1 pig's trotter, split into two
bouquet garni

Remove any skin from the liver, chop it until it has the texture of a purée and put it into a mixing bowl. Finely chop the belly of pork, keeping any rind in a piece for lining the terrine, and add this to the liver in the bowl with the garlic and shallots, a good pinch of *quatre-épices* and plenty of seasoning. Add the brandy and wine and mix well.

Line your terrine with the pork rind or bacon, then fill it with the liver mixture and lay the pig's trotter and bouquet garni on top. Cover with its lid.

Stand the terrine in a baking tin containing hot water and cook in a cool oven, 130°C, 275°F, Gas Mark 1, for 2½–3 hours. The pâté is done when it appears to be floating in its own juice and when a needle will go through it and come out clean. Do not overcook it. Remove the trotter. Leave to cool when you will find there is a lovely jelly surrounding it, made by the trotter. The *pâté* will be all the better for being kept a day or two in a cool, dry place.

LE PÂTÉ MONTALBANAIS
Pork and veal pâté

In this pork-based *pâté* the appearance and the texture is set off by the strips of veal running through it.

Serves 6

500 g (1 lb) escalopes of veal, cut thin but not beaten
150 ml (¼ pt) armagnac
150 g (5¼ oz) pig's liver
250 g (8 oz) pork neck or upper hand
250 g (8 oz) Toulouse sausagemeat (see page 66)

salt, pepper
quatre-épices
175 g (6 oz) *couennes* (pork rind) or unsmoked streaky bacon
2 onions
2 bay leaves

Cut the escalopes into strips, the length of your terrine and about 2.5 cm (1 in) wide, and put them to marinate in 125 ml (4 fl oz) of the armagnac for 6 hours.

Chop and mix together all the pork meats, season them and spice them with the *quatre-épices* and the rest of the armagnac. Line the terrine with *couennes* or bacon and lay on the bottom one of the onions, cut into rings, and one of the bay leaves. Add a layer of the pork mixture, then a layer of the veal strips, another of the pork and so on until the meat is used up and ending with a layer of pork. Put the other onion, cut into rings, and a bay leaf on the top and cover with more *couennes* or bacon.

Cover and seal on the lid with a flour and water paste. Put the terrine into a baking tin containing hot water and cook in a moderate oven, 180°C, 350°F, Gas Mark 4, for 1½ hours.

LA TERRINE D'ALBAS
Pork and rabbit terrine

This uses a variety of meat but pork is predominant. If you are unable to buy hard back fat, substitute 500 g (1 lb) pork belly and omit the pork neck.

Serves 10

a half rabbit, about 1 kg (2 lb)
  weighed on the bone
250 g (½ lb) leg of veal
250 g (½ lb) pork neck
250 g (½ lb) chicken livers
250 g (½ lb) back fat (*gras dur*) of
  pork

3 egg yolks
30 g (1 oz) salt
pepper, thyme, bay leaf
3 tablespoons armagnac

Chop the boned rabbit and all the other meats into very small dice. In a mixing bowl combine these with the beaten eggs and the other ingredients, crumbling the bay leaf in your fingers.

Put the mixture into a terrine and leave it to stand in a cool place for a day. Then cook it in the usual way in a cool oven, 130°C, 275°F, Gas Mark 1, for 3 hours.

L'AIL

S HOULD WE HAVE dealt earlier with garlic in this study of the country cooking? Seventy-five per cent of our recipes include at least one clove of garlic, while *la gasconnade* calls for half a kilo of it. The quantities could seem excessive but not so to the people of the Haut Languedoc, the Quercy and the Périgord. They are great lovers of this flavouring, not caring for bland food. If challenged, they will mention the medicinal properties of garlic, recommending it as an aid to digestion and a cure for colds, apart from its ability to improve the memory and the gift of the gab. So they put a clove or two into most *soupes*, *pâtés* and meat dishes, while the garlic soup of Languedoc, *l'aigo boulido*, contains little else.

South-Western cuisine is diffused with *l'ail* and you soon recognize the garlic-scented whiffs of cooking which tantalize your nostrils as you pass opened kitchen windows towards midday. It is in fact a distinctive but different aroma from the pungent one which clings to the fingers when you chop a raw garlic clove. Once it is introduced into cooking, the heat changes the fierceness of the oils in the clove into a more subtle seasoner which seems to blend into the foods it is married to. It is said that mixing parsley with garlic will counteract any lasting odour and this is no doubt why these two are chopped together to make a *persillade* or *un hachis*, so beloved of the Périgourdins in their soups. The only time garlic is used raw is to flavour a salad or a croûton of bread and then only by rubbing a cut clove round the salad bowl or over the bread to give just a hint of the flavour, no more.

Shopping for garlic at market in the South-West in October involves searching for the supplies of the variety known as *l'ail rose* which will last through the winter almost until the next season's young bulbs are lifted in mid-summer. These bulbs or *têtes* are left on their stalks for three months to dry in the warm air out of direct sunlight so it is no uncommon sight to see rows of the huge bunches hanging to dry under the eaves of a barn or on a covered balcony. They are then brought to market in October. By careful purchase or clever planting, everyone has a store of garlic throughout the year. Garlic likes to grow in a moist but sandy soil with plenty of sun to plump out the cloves.

In the Garonne valley around Toulouse there are huge areas of garlic production. Grenade-sur-Garonne claims to produce the best garlic in the South-West but it is also grown extensively over towards Albi in the Tarn. A rival area, around Saint Clar towards the Gers, specializes in *l'ail blond de Lomagne*. This, together with another white-headed variety (it is the colour of the outer skins of the cloves which earn them their names) called *l'ail rond de Limousin*, appears first, to be followed by *le violet* with its large, purple-veined heads which keep quite well. But these are out-classed by *l'ail rose de Lautrec*. This is the most expensive variety as it is the long-keeper and so is always in great demand. There are special garlic fairs from July onwards but at local markets the garlic stalls also appear, laden with neatly-bound bunches. Garlic is sold by weight and the tresses usually weigh half a kilo or one kilo. How many heads make up one kilo depends on the variety and their freshness. There are on average eight *gousses* (cloves) per *tête* (head), though there are variations in size of the cloves, with the *violets* and *blancs* slightly larger than the *rose*. Recipes in this book refer to a clove of these local varieties – which are roughly the size of a butter bean. All of them are larger than those imported from the New World and which appear out of season in English and French shops and are much stronger.

The green 'germ' which may start to sprout inside a clove in winter can be indigestible and for that reason, some cooks remove it before chopping. By the way, we have never seen a garlic crusher in a peasant kitchen: chopping or gently crushing with the blade of a knife are the methods recommended locally.

LE CASSOULET

S EVEN GREEK CITIES claimed to be the birthplace of Homer. As many towns in the South-West of France claim the distinction of having invented the *cassoulet*. Definitive proof would be a prize dearly to be won, for the *cassoulet* is to many the emblem of the region, like roast beef to the British or *sauerkraut* to the Germans. Essentially, it is a bean stew, perfumed with garlic and goose or pork fat and enriched by a variety of fresh or preserved meats which vary according to district. But some magic chemistry manages to fuse the aromas and textures to produce a creamy amalgam of flavours, topped with a crispy crust which sets off to perfection the gently bubbling richness beneath. It is a gloriously original and distinctive dish: no other cuisine has produced anything quite like it. It is so different from any other *plat* that it is difficult to know which section to put it in – hence this one all to itself.

Connoisseurs of the *cassoulet* are justified in claiming that the beans are just as important as the meats. Anyone, they say, can prepare a *confit* of duck or goose, or make sausages in the Toulouse style or provide from his own farm or buy at the local butcher any other meat that is required. But the beans are something quite different. As many towns and villages claim to produce the finest beans as to have invented the dish itself. Tarbes, Lavelanet, Luchon, Pamiers, Cazères; the list is endless and each has its supporters. The bean is elevated almost to poetic status with fancy claims to the derivation of its patois name *mounjetto* – *'un petit moine'* perhaps. More likely that the word is derived from the more modern French *mange-tout*, used simply to describe a vegetable of which every part is eaten.

It is by no means certain that the white haricot bean, now universally assumed to be the basis of the authentic *cassoulet*, is anything of the kind. It is known that broad beans, or something like them, were a common and well-liked staple food in the foothills of the Pyrenees as far back as the Middle Ages, while the haricot bean probably did not make its appearance until much later. Robert Courtine claims that the original *cassoulet* was probably made with broad beans and André Daguin used to serve a modern version with them at his restaurant in Auch. The white bean, which is simply the bean that grows inside the green haricot, has nowadays taken over, perhaps because it dries better and also because *cassoulet* is a dish best enjoyed in winter, when broad beans are out of season.

It is also quite likely that early versions of the *cassoulet* contained little or no meat. Peasants in the far South-West still enjoy an *estoufét de moungétos* which uses potatoes and carrots instead of meat. You would need to be very cold or hungry to be able to get that down so it is perhaps not surprising that such a dish does not appear on restaurant menus. It is easy to imagine a half-way house which used *couennes* and pieces of belly of pork, for example, or other cheap cuts, and perhaps the exotica such as butcher's meats and *confits* came later.

However we are jumping ahead and must get back to the beans – where the *cassoulet* began. The beans you buy in the shops can come from a huge variety of different kinds of haricot. The haricot arrived from the New World in the fifteenth century but was called by the same name as the indigenous broad bean – *fève*. Haricot was already a word in the French language meaning something which is cut up, eg mutton. Indeed the French still make a *haricot* of mutton, traditionally served with white beans, so the name seems at some stage to have transferred itself to the white beans to distinguish them from the broad beans. Nowadays green haricot beans are grown for two purposes: first, to be eaten young and whole during the summer and early autumn; and secondly for the white beans which expand inside the pod as the bean ages on the plant. Modern growers have developed quite distinct varieties for each purpose, as well as countless other varieties of edible bean. Here we are only concerned with the white haricot.

It must be stressed that what we call 'butter beans' simply will not do for a *cassoulet*; they will fall to pieces in the long cooking, and anyway, they have the wrong texture and flavour. Having said that, any plain white haricot of good quality will do, whatever the purists may say, but some discretion must be used in the light of the age and size of the bean. The large white haricots called kidney beans will do well.

Beans straight from the pod, which have shrivelled on the plant, will need less cooking time than fully dried beans. They are already partly dried, and are likely to be those found at the markets in the South-West in the autumn. If they were to be cooked for eating straightaway they would need about 45 minutes. Once the beans have been allowed to dry out fully, they need rehydrating before cooking and will also take longer in the cooking.

If you buy beans from a supermarket, watch for the 'best before' date – beans older than one season may never come round at all and should not be used. If you are in the South-West your first choice of beans should be the expensive Tarbais, or perhaps the Pamiers. Generally the white beans called Lingots (those called Soissons are larger) will do very well. In any French market you can buy in October what are called Coco beans, which are round rather than elongated and they do very well in *cassoulet* too. Incidentally, it is as well to remember that salt will harden the beans and so should not be added till later in their cooking. The essence of a good *cassoulet* is that the beans, while not falling apart, should be tender and should have absorbed the aromas and savours of the other ingredients. The quality of the raw materials cannot therefore be stressed too much.

Cassoulet is called in patois *cassolet* and is named after the special kind of pot called *cassole or cassou* which was designed for the purpose and used to be made in the village of Issel, just eight kilometres north of Castelnaudary. The *cassole* was made from the red clay of the region and highly glazed. Nevertheless it remained slightly porous and improved with use and age like a tobacco pipe. It is quite a deep bowl with sloping sides, its open top being specifically proportioned for the finishing of the dish, as we shall see. The *cassole* will not go on a naked flame, and it was originally intended to go into the bread oven. It is perfectly suited to the modern gas or electric oven. You can make a *cassoulet* without a *cassole* but in selecting your cooking pot, bear in mind the specifications of the original and keep as close to these as possible.

You may think that we have resolved all the controversies about *cassoulet* and can get on with the recipe. No such luck because the quarrels about what goes into it are only just beginning. The Castelnaudary version, which probably starts a firm favourite in the authenticity stakes, is made exclusively from pork – shin, loin, spareribs, *saucisson* and fresh *couennes*. In Toulouse the pork is accompanied by lamb (boned) and pieces of *confit* of goose or duck. Carcassonne also keeps to the same pork base as Castelnaudary but adds a leg of lamb and, if in season, partridge.

The Périgord makes no claim to having invented the *cassoulet* but that has not inhibited them from devising their own version, where meats are lamb, Toulouse sausage and *cou farci* of goose or duck (see page 42). In the Ariège there are many versions current. One prescribes individual terrines and the principal ingredients are duck giblets and sausage; another contains just about all the meats used in the Castelnaudary, Toulouse and Carcassonne versions combined, but is interesting principally for the inclusion of carrots and potatoes, as in the *estoufét de moungétos* referred to earlier as a primitive meatless version. *La mounjétado* is clearly a close relative: while opting for individual terrines, it eschews both potatoes and the gratin process. Some hold that the breadcrumb fetish – you are supposed to plunge the crispy top back into the dish seven times if you live in Castelnaudary – is unnecessary and detracts from the creaminess of the finished dish.

It would be tiresome to give detailed recipes for all the variations on the theme of *cassoulet*. What follows is a compromise which adopts a consensus approach. Not being confined to the purism of Castelnaudary, it is a good mainstream version which translates quite well to an Anglo-Saxon kitchen. A few preliminary tips may be useful:

1 The *confit* of duck or goose can be replaced by partly roasted fresh joints from the same birds. They will provide the same fat that gives so much towards the unctuous quality of the finished dish. Shoulder of lamb, part roasted, would be another possibility.

2 It is important to try to find 100 per cent pork sausages. Any containing bread will really not do.

3 This is a filling dish, best avoided late in the evening. No starter is needed except perhaps a few *crudités*. Accompany with a crisp green salad and follow with fresh fruit.

4 It is very difficult to know how much *cassoulet* to make for any given number of people. If you make it really properly, few of your guests will have tasted anything like it, even if they claim to know what a *cassoulet* is. Newcomers may either want a second helping or treat the dish warily, because it is exceedingly rich. The quantities given here should make ten average portions.

5 A fruity young red wine, Corbières or Minervois, will go quite well. Do not splash out on anything too good, because it will probably not be able to cope with the strong flavours.

6 If you come across tins of *cassoulet* in French shops, be careful; you are

liable to be sadly disappointed. If you have never had the real thing you may wonder what all the fuss is about. Study the tin's label carefully because many brands contain all too little meat. It is recommended that meat should constitute 30 per cent of the total net weight. The beans in many tinned versions tend to be soggy and the mixture ill blended. There are good brands but you would do well to take advice locally.

LE CASSOULET
White bean stew with sausages, tomatoes, garlic and meats

There are three distinct processes. The beans and meats are partly cooked separately to start with. Both are then cooked together in the cassole. If you are using *confit* or partly cooked meats, they are added only for the final stage.

Serves 8–10

for preparing the beans:
1 kg (2¼ lb) dried white haricot beans, preferably Lingots or Cocos
350 g (¾ lb) salt belly of pork with its rind, previously soaked if very salty

carrot
onion stuck with 2 cloves
bouquet garni
ham or pork bone (optional)
2 cloves garlic (more if you like)
salt
peppercorns

the meat:
2 tablespoons goose fat
350 g (¾ lb) lean pork shoulder
2 medium-sized onions
carrot
700 g (1½ lb) Toulouse or pure pork sausage
250 g (½ lb) Marmande or beef tomatoes (or small tin tomatoes)

1¼ litres (2 pints) stock or water
2 large cloves garlic (more if you like)
bouquet garni
salt, pepper

for the *cassoulet*:
2 quarters *confit d'oie* or 3 pieces *confit de canard*

fresh white breadcrumbs
goose fat

To prepare the beans:
Soak the beans overnight in plenty of water. Drain and rinse them and put them into a large enamelled pan. Cover with cold water and bring slowly to the boil. Boil hard for 10 minutes then skim before adding the belly of pork, onion stuck with cloves, sliced carrot, bouquet garni, ham or pork bone, garlic and peppercorns. Allow to simmer very slowly, covered, until the beans are just tender, adding salt half way through this cooking time if there is not enough in the ham/salt pork. The time will depend on the age and quality of the beans but a further half an hour should be enough because of the cooking they will have later. Be sure they do not become overcooked. While they are cooking, prepare the meat.

To cook the meat:
If you do not already have any goose fat to hand, open your jar or tin of confit and put it in a warm place. You will then have all the fat you need. In a casserole heat the fat and in it seal the shoulder of pork, cut into 2.5 cm (1 inch cubes). When they are well sealed add the chopped onions and carrot and colour them. Prick the sausages and fry them separately until their skin turns golden and they have given off some of their fat. Drain them and cut into bite-sized pieces, then add these to the sautéed pork and onions. Stir in the skinned and de-seeded tomatoes and pour over enough meat stock to cover. Add the chopped garlic and seasonings and leave to simmer quite gently for 50 minutes.

To assemble the cassoulet:
During this time prepare the confit, i.e. open its jar or tin and set it in a gentle oven to heat through and to melt the fat. Remove the skin from the *confit* (pop it back into the jar of goose fat to use later for an omelette filling, as on page 97). Break up the goose meat into bite-sized pieces, discarding the bones.

When the beans are just tender, drain them but keep their cooking liquor. Cut off the rind from the cooked salt belly of pork and cut up the meat. Discard the onion and carrot. Take your large earthenware casserole or *cassole* and lay the pork rind in the bottom, fat side down. Put in half of the beans and then a layer of all the meat. Cover this with the rest of the beans. Pour over the sauce from cooking the meat and top up with the stock plus, if necessary, some of the bean liquor so that the beans are nearly covered.

Sprinkle a good layer of fresh breadcrumbs over and put into a cool oven (150°C, 300°F, Gas mark 2) for one hour. You should top up the level of the liquid with the bean stock so that the contents of the casserole are again nearly covered. This preparation can be done the day before. When you resume, stir in the breadcrumbs gently and put another good layer of crumbs on top. Sprinkle this all over with melted goose fat and return the dish to the oven for another 2 hours, or until the crust on top has become an appetising golden colour.

LES OEUFS

ANGLO-SAXONS BELIEVE that all French cooks can make wonderful omelettes. This is almost true but certainly the best omelettes we have ever had anywhere are at our local *auberge*, run until recently by Louis Mazières and his wife. Louis, in fact, played a catalytic part in the purchase of our farmhouse because he provided the base and much of the practical help from which the negotiating and buying was carried out. We have been firm friends with his family for over twenty-five years. Their younger son Jacques, whom we helped to read at the age of five, has now taken over the kitchens of the hotel.

Louis' mother, alas no longer with us, was a wonderful old lady. After Louis took over on his father's death, Grand'maman continued, in spite of the most awful rheumatism, to look after the kitchen garden which was terraced out of the hillside slopes behind the hotel. She kept numerous rabbits – '*mes petits lapins*' – as well as chickens, and grew every kind of vegetable needed for the hotel in prodigious quantities. Once picked, the *haricots verts* and *petits pois* were sorted into various *qualités*; we never quite knew why – unless the best ones were kept for *à la carte* customers and the not-so-good ones for the *pensionnaires*. She was a very kind old lady, and taught us a great deal about local produce and local history in her clear French, which she spoke more slowly even than General de Gaulle, but with a wonderful Midi accent. We once confessed to her that we had been so disloyal as to have eaten at the rival local establishment. She crossed herself and replied '*Je vous donne absolution*'.

Old Easter traditions in the far South were that after the plain fare during Lent, everyone celebrated on Easter Monday with *l'omelette pascale*. This could be an omelette with a filling of *fines herbes*, perhaps accompanied by rounds of sausage or bacon. *If* the weather permitted, it would be the first outdoor meal of the year. But one of the first local proverbs we learned was:

> *Noël au balcon*
> *Pâques aux tisons*
> *(Christmas on the balcony, Easter by the fireside)*

On Easter Saturday mothers took hard-boiled eggs to church to be blessed, then painted them gay colours and hid them outside for their children to hunt for next morning. Another custom was a sort of carol-singing group who toured the farms, singing religious and secular songs in the hopes of receiving eggs as a reward – eggs being required for the Monday's omelette. If eggs were plentiful at other times of the year it was a bonus and meant they could be combined with those wonders which nature provided free – the truffle and the *cèpe* being the most prized.

Omelettes were the answer, cooked quickly in the *poêle* over the fire. As we have said, Louis' were marvellous and he has often shown us how to do them, but obviously he has a *tour de main* which cannot be taught. Here is an old country recipe which he cooked for his *pensionnaires*.

L'OMELETTE AUX CROÛTONS
Omelette with diced fried bread

per person:

1 thick round of bread	2 large eggs
1-2 tablespoons pork or goose fat	salt, pepper

Cut the crusts off the slice of bread, then cut it into cubes. Brown these on all sides in some of the fat until they are crisp. Season the eggs, beat them very lightly.

Heat a frying pan well until you can feel the heat on the palm of your hand held a few inches above it. Put in the rest of the fat and see that it is well spread before tipping in the eggs, covering all the area of the pan.

Scoop the edges towards the middle with the side of the fork and let the uncooked egg flow into its place. While it is still half set, sprinkle the croûtons over the top and roll it up.

●

In spring there is almost sure to be some home-cured *saucisson* still in the kitchen, some Cantal cheese and in the *potager* some fresh herbs – for an *omelette de la Rouzille*.

L'OMELETTE DE LA ROUZILLE
Omelette with country sausage slices

per person:

2 eggs	1 tablespoon goose fat
salt, pepper, nutmeg	1 tablespoon grated Cantal cheese
1 tablespoon fresh chopped herbs, including parsley, chives, tarragon, chervil	3 or 4 slices of *saucisson sec* or *andouille* (black-skinned tripe sausage)

Beat the eggs lightly, season and add the chopped herbs. Pour them into a very hot, lightly greased omelette pan. Make the omelette in the usual way, then sprinkle the cheese along the top and arrange the slices of sausage round.

———— • ————

After a piece of *confit* of goose or duck has been taken from its preserving jar, the fatty skin attached is often too much and too rich to eat with the meat. This is not thrown away as it makes a most delicious omelette filling, quick and easy to prepare; you could well believe you were eating a bacon omelette. It is now many years since we were first taught this recipe by Monsieur Coscuella, who has since made of his restaurant, La Ripa Alta, one of the most famous gastronomic shrines of Gascony.

L'OMELETTE AU PEAU DE CANARD OU D'OIE
Omelette with crispy duck or goose skin

a piece of skin from preserved duck or goose	2 eggs per person salt, pepper

Cut the skin up into small cubes and heat these fairly gently in a small frying pan until some of the fat has run out and the cubes have browned a little. Make an omelette in the usual way and spread the drained, crisp cubes of skin inside before rolling it up.

———— • ————

A slightly more substantial omelette comes from the mountainous Auvergne where everything needs to be that bit more nourishing.

L'OMELETTE BRAYAUDE
Omelette with ham, potato and cheese

This is named after a gastronomic club formed by local farmers at Riom in the Auvergne. Their unusual breeches were called *braies*, hence the title:

Serves 2 or 4

175 g (6 oz) *jambon de campagne* cut in one slice (or gammon steak with as much fat on it as possible)
250 g (½ lb) waxy potatoes
1 tablespoon pork or goose fat
4 eggs

100 g (3½ oz) Cantal cheese, cut into strips
60 g (2 oz) Cantal cheese, grated (or Lancashire or Cheddar cheese)
pepper, salt

Have the ham cut in one slice about ½ cm (¼ in) thick. Cut it into dice and melt these in a frying pan over a low heat so as to extract the fat. Remove the pieces when they start to brown.

Dice the potatoes and cook them slowly in the fat for 12–15 minutes. Stir them regularly to stop them from sticking and if there is not enough fat in the pan, add a tablespoonful of fat. When the potatoes are cooked, mix them with the ham and season with pepper.

Heat your omelette pan, beat the eggs, add the ham and potatoes, the strips of cheese and, depending on the saltiness of the ham and the cheese, a little further salt. Cook your omelette, and when it is done, sprinkle the grated cheese all over, fold and serve immediately.

These quantities are for a starter for four people. As a main dish they serve two; all that is required by way of accompaniment is a crisp green salad with the usual dressing – walnut oil if you are to be regionally authentic.

——— ● ———

Other fillings for omelettes can be gathered free in spring and early summer from the hedgerows and fields, the young dandelion leaves being a favourite or the shoots of *le tamier*, in patois *reponchous* or *respounjos* (see page 186.)

Later in the year, at harvest time, the farmer's wife would have to prepare snacks to be taken out to the fields. This onion and garlic omelette is therefore a fairly solid affair because the haymakers need to be able to eat it in their fingers. It appears under various names in different areas. We give it our local patois title. In the Périgord it is *la gourgousse* and in the Midi-Pyrenées *matafam aux oignons*.

LOU MEISSOUNENCO
Thick onion omelette

per person:
½ tablespoon pork fat   2 eggs
1 onion the size of a billiard ball   1 clove garlic

Choose a frying pan in which the eggs will be about 1 cm (½ in) deep. Melt the fat and fry the sliced onion gently in it, allowing it to take on only a little colour. While it is cooking, break the eggs into a bowl, season and add to them the garlic, very finely chopped. Beat the mixture lightly and make your omelette when the onion is cooked.

As this was traditionally intended to be carried out to the hayfields, it was well cooked. At home it can be less well done and served, folded, on to a hot serving dish or straight on to the plate in the usual way.

●

It is impossible to say which combination with eggs makes the most delicious omelette: the marvel is that the arrival of sorrel, *cèpes* and truffles is spread over the year, so as each appears it is a new joy. But in among these first three there has also to be the tomato omelette, made with the large fleshy varieties like Marmande or St Pierre which grow so well all over the region.

L'OMELETTE AUX TOMATES FRAÎCHES
Tomato omelette

Serves 2

for the filling: 4–6 eggs, according to size
350 g (¾ lb) tomatoes   salt, pepper
1 small onion   1 tablespoon goose fat
1 clove garlic
1 tablespoon chopped parsley
2 tablespoons oil
salt, pepper

First make a fresh tomato sauce for the filling by peeling and chopping the tomatoes and slicing the onion finely. Chop the garlic and parsley. Heat the oil in a small pan and cook the tomato, onion and herbs in it over a medium heat for 15–20 minutes until the sauce has formed – by then most of the liquid should have evaporated. Season.

Beat the eggs lightly with some salt, pepper and a tablespoonful of water. Heat the fat in a large omelette pan and when it starts to smoke pour in the eggs and make an omelette in the usual way. While it is still *baveuse* – that is, creamy on top – spread the tomato over one half, fold the other half over and slide it on to a hot plate.

This quantity will serve four as a starter or two as a lunch dish, served with a green salad to follow. The sauce must be made with *fresh* tomatoes – tinned ones will not do at all.

●

Those who falter at making an omelette can use this same fresh tomato sauce to bake the eggs *à la sarladaise*. On to garlic-flavoured rounds of toast you slip an egg which you have baked whole in tomato sauce (made as above). Even more simply, you can break some eggs into a small ovenproof dish, season them and sprinkle them with a mixture of fresh parsley and chopped garlic before baking them in a moderate oven for 5–8 minutes.

It is not surprising to find that eggs and bacon is not an English invention – pork in whatever form combines well with eggs. *Lard maigre de poitrine salé* is the French equivalent of bacon. In the valley of the river Tarn the country people call these crisp fried slices *rabanels* and they have a recipe for serving them with fried eggs – *oeufs aux rabanels*. More surprising is to find them described as *Salade campagnarde* when served on a lightly-dressed bed of lettuce. The egg and bacon juices mix beautifully with the vinaigrette, all ready to be mopped up with some fresh crusty bread.

Hard-boiled eggs feature frequently in the *hors d'oeuvre* dish, as an accompaniment to sorrel (page 183) and stuffed with *rillettes*.

LES OEUFS FARCIS AUX RILLETTES
Eggs stuffed with potted duck

Serves 4

4 hard-boiled eggs	salt, pepper
2 tablespoons goose or duck *rillettes* (see page 43)	1 white of egg
	fat for frying
chopped chives, tarragon, parsley or chervil	fresh tomato sauce (see page 190)

Cut the hard-boiled eggs into two lengthwise, take out the yolks and mix them with the *rillettes*, the herbs and a little seasoning. Refill the whites with this mixture.

Whisk a white of egg, dip each stuffed half of egg into it and then fry them in hot fat or oil, turning them over until they are golden.

Serve on a hot dish surrounded by the hot tomato sauce.

———————— ● ————————

Soft-boiled eggs which had been cooked in the hot ashes of the fire were considered excellent nourishment for the very young, the old or any invalid. A book of old recipes from the Rouergue describes the method, saying that since it is advisable to let the air out of the egg before putting it into the ashes, the custom was to crack one end. The patois recommendation is that you must 'give it a crack on its bottom to prevent its breaking wind'.

Only those who have cooked on nothing but a wood fire, and so have got to a fine art how to judge its heat, would be recommended to cook eggs in this way. You are just as likely to end up with a perfectly raw egg as one which is as hard as a bullet.

More recipes based on eggs are in other sections of the book:

LES CHAMPIGNONS
ET LES TRUFFES

SOME SPECIES OF mushroom are admittedly deadly poisonous and others will make you feel more or less ill; on the other hand, some of the most highly prized varieties are impossible to confuse with the dangerous ones, and this happens to be particularly true of those which grow quite commonly in South-West France. If you go to the market in any country town you will usually find some of the farmers' wives with a basket of whatever mushroom happens to be seasonal, and you will soon learn to identify the varieties quite easily. Because the seasons of the different species seldom overlap, you will find that any variety is referred to simply as *champignon*, confusing, as the word does not refer only to what we understand by a field mushroom. The French use the word rather as they do *gibier*, which means anything wild that moves on however many legs, so long as it can be eaten.

What we call mushrooms are generally on sale at every French greengrocery but the other varieties are usually to be found, if the weather is propitious, only in the markets or in the countryside – usually in deciduous woods of oak, beech and chestnut. Mushroom hunting is a favourite pastime throughout France, not only because the prize is free but also because it is so highly esteemed as a delicacy. It is one of the most important functions of the village chemist to give free advice on the edibility of any mushroom presented to him, including the most unlikely looking fungus, and this is one pressing reason why their shops are open on Sunday mornings.

It is very hard to extract from the locals the secret of where mushrooms may be found; even our best friends will give only the vaguest general directions; there are certain spots where they tend to grow season after season. The places are so reliable that you look there first and if there is nothing, you know it is not worth looking anywhere else. It is almost impossible to deter the poacher: certainly he will take no notice of a faded warning nailed to a tree saying *champignons interdits*, a phrase which suggests, incidentally, the opposite of what was meant.

The peasant resents bitterly the invasion of his woods by town dwellers who seem to spend whole weekends with their families searching for *cèpes*. You often see cars parked by the roadside, their owners pretending to have stopped to stretch their legs but the tell-tale basket on the back seat of the car is an instant giveaway.

One of the most prized mushrooms is the *morille* (morel in English), to be found in May in open woodland, especially where brushwood has been burned away. It also grows in orchards. *La morille* is instantly recognisable by its conical shape and its pitted, sponge-like cap; it is small and its colour varies from yellowish brown to dark grey. Its flavour is perhaps more suggestive of the woods and damp leaves than that of the other main edible species. In many parts of France this mushroom is most frequently cooked in cream, which lends a marvellous contrast both in colour and texture (*morilles* tend to remain fairly firm even when cooked). In the South-West, however, cream is little used and *morilles* tend to be used interchangeably in any dish where mushrooms are called for; in fact the recipes we give for mushrooms – except that for *cèpes à la bordelaise* – can be used for any species. *Morilles must not, it should be noted, be eaten raw: they contain a poison that is neutralized only by cooking.*

In June and July, if the weather is wet, come *chanterelles* or *girolles* as they are more often called in the region. *Girolles* can be found again in the autumn. They are quite small, horn-shaped, with a hollow in the top of the cap. The tapering stem is short and stout but the most striking feature is these mushrooms' orange-yellow colour, like an apricot and, indeed, when fresh they give off a smell of that fruit. They are one of the most delicate and delicious of all mushrooms and have a particular affinity with eggs. They grow in the oak and chestnut woods as long as the undergrowth has been kept under control, and often in little clearings where the warm sun can conjure them out of the cool, damp woodland floor.

The French call fairy-ring mushrooms *mousserons* from which word ours is said to be derived. Throughout the year, when the weather is particularly wet, *mousserons* are common on open grassland. So too are they in England but nobody bothers to pick them because they are regarded as 'toadstools' and so assumed to be poisonous. As their English name implies they grow in wide rings and usually turn the pasture or grass into a circle of dark green. When young they have a rounded cap but this soon gives way to a boss-shape. The *mousseron* is small and so is most suitable for use in soups and stews. Raw it tastes nutty, and cooked it has a beef-like flavour. It also goes well in an omelette. The stalks on the whole are rather tough and are best discarded. It dries well – for this reason it is locally called a *sécadou* although in the Toulousain it is known as *le bouton de guêtre* (gaiter button). If you can gather enough at one time, this is a useful and delicious species.

Another unmistakable variety is the parasol mushroom, *la coulemelle*. This is to be found by the side of deciduous trees and sometimes in open fields in the late summer and autumn and, as its English name implies, it is shaped like a sunshade. It is a large species, the cap being between 10 and 20 cm (4 and 8 in) across, covered with shaggy scales. The stem can be up to 30 cm (1 foot) high. This is a popular variety with quite a strong porky flavour but must be picked young; otherwise it tends to be leathery. Again the stems are rather dull.

There is no doubt whatever that the variety of mushroom most closely associated with the South-West is the *cèpe*. It is quite different from any of the other commonly found edible mushrooms: it has no gills on the under surface of the cap but a mass of spongey spores. The cap itself is a reddy brown, up to 15 cm (6 in) or more across and the stem is bulbous, thickening towards the foot, and almost as good to eat as the cap. The smaller ones are if anything better than the larger, which can grow to a prodigious size, weighing a kilo or more. By that time, unfortunately, they are more than likely to be past their best and overtaken by worms.

The *cèpe* is most commonly found in the areas where sweet chestnuts grow best, with plenty of hot sun in the summer but also rain in September. *Cèpes* from the Cévennes and the Corrèze are particularly highly prized in the markets, although they grow in wooded land all over the South-West when conditions are right. They favour half-shaded conditions. The sunlight must get through the leaf cover to heat the earth in July and August. It is said that they need five days after heavy rain to appear, and a waning moon is the best time. As a subject of conversation we find they rank second only to the weather; word spreads like wildfire round our village if *cèpes* are known to be about. If you go after them yourself you will need a pair of wellingtons and a stout stick: the mushrooms are hard to distinguish from dead leaves on the floor of the wood. They are one of the best examples of natural camouflage.

It is a rare privilege to be invited along with a local peasant on a mushroom hunt. Not only must the spoils be shared but you will inevitably find out the best places to look in the future. It was nearly twenty years before we had such an invitation, and then it was to go searching in our own woods! And our guide didn't even particularly like *cèpes* – the fun was all in the hunt.

The spongy underside will identify the *cèpe* immediately. There is only one poisonous variety and that is bright red, so is instantly recognizable. It is also rare. Some other varieties are not so good as the *cèpe (boletus edulis)*or the even finer *tête de nègre* which has, as its name implies, a darker cap. *Cèpes* are characterized by their bulbous feet. The spores should be pale: when young they are a creamy colour, turning yellow-green as they age. If the spores are too dark or soggy the mushroom will be too old. The cap can be any shade of brown and should be free of holes bored by insects. It is best to avoid the relatively common variety that has a cracked cap and is a really vivid yellow underneath. It is not dangerous but is of little culinary value.

Cèpes should be cooked or processed as soon as possible. They should never be kept for any length of time in any plastic or other bag, and need air to circulate round them if they are to remain fresh. They quickly deteriorate and develop worms which, though harmless, are hardly appetizing. These can be evicted by putting the mushrooms in a very low oven for ten minutes.

Some of our villagers pickle baby *cèpes* raw, in vinegar, as a de luxe accompaniment to a cold *confit*. In quantity, however, they need thorough cooking to be digested easily and so lend themselves well to stews and other slow-cooked dishes. They should be tender but not soggy in texture; and the flesh has an almost meaty flavour.

Just as the autumn days start to get a little cooler and the *cèpes* are nearly finished, nature produces a marvellous rabbit from her hat. The brilliantly coloured *oronge* does indeed have an aura of magic about it. It grows, like the *cèpe*, in the woods just as the chestnuts start to fall from the trees. Its cap is a flame-like orange on top and its gills a bright lemony-yellow. It does not have spores like a *cèpe* so cannot be confused with the one dangerous variety of *cèpe*. The *oronge* may grow to 15 cm (6 in) across and its long stem has a double ring, and what is called a *volve* at the base. This is in fact the bud from which the mushroom has sprung and which has burst open but does not disintegrate. *L'oronge* is not only quite obviously distinguishable from other mushrooms but also one of the most delicious. It can be fried like *cèpes* or grilled with a little oil, or stuffed. Garlic and parsley are, needless to say, obligatory seasonings.

Sweetbreads go particularly well with mushrooms, so the following recipe will be useful all the year round, depending on what mushrooms are to hand. Ordinary field mushrooms are lovely with this dish so do not wait for something more exotic to turn up in the woods.

LE RIS DE VEAU AUX CHAMPIGNONS
Sweetbreads with mushrooms

Serves 4

500 g (1 lb) calf's sweetbreads
60 g (2 oz) butter
4 shallots
1 tablespoon flour
575 ml (1 pt) chicken stock
salt, pepper
250 g (½ lb) field mushrooms, or
   mousserons, morilles or *girolles*

lemon juice
seasoned flour
125 g (4 oz) butter
2 egg yolks
2 tablespoons double cream

Put the sweetbreads into running water for 30 minutes to clean them.

Meanwhile prepare a velouté sauce: melt 60g (2 oz) butter and soften the chopped shallots in it, then stir in the flour and after a minute or two, add the stock. When the sauce has come to the boil and thickened a little, reduce the heat to a minimum and leave it barely simmering for 20 minutes. Slice the mushrooms.

When the sweetbreads are clean, prepare a pan of boiling salted water with a good squeeze of lemon juice in it. Plunge in the sweetbreads and blanch them for a couple of minutes, drain them and cool them in running water. Drain them again and remove any membrane covering them. Cut into bite-sized pieces and roll them in seasoned flour.

Heat another 60 g (2 oz) of butter in a frying pan and when it is barely smoking, put in the sweetbreads. Fry them on all sides, not too briskly, for 5 minutes or so, then transfer them to a heated casserole and keep them hot while you fry the mushrooms in the same pan, adding the remaining butter as required. When these are soft, add them to the sweetbreads.

Mix together the egg yolks and cream and stir them into the sauce. Add plenty of lemon juice and seasoning to taste, then pour the sauce over the sweetbreads and mushrooms. Mix well together and simmer very gently for 5 minutes to amalgamate the flavours before serving.

Boiled potatoes or *fleurons* of flaky pastry go well with this dish.

Soups can be made with all manner of mushrooms but the following recipe is particularly good with *mousserons*. If you can pick these yourself, fresh and clean, do not wash them – it is basically wrong to wash any mushrooms if you can avoid doing so. Discard the stalks; they are tough and have no flavour. This soup can also be made from rehydrated dried *mousserons*, in which case 125 g (¼ lb) of the dried mushrooms will be enough.

LE POTAGE AUX MOUSSERONS
Soup from fairy-ring mushrooms

Serves 4

500 g (1 lb) *mousserons* or other fresh wild mushrooms
2 tablespoons goose fat
2 shallots
2 tablespoons parsley, finely chopped

2 cloves garlic
1 litre (1¾ pt) veal or chicken stock
salt, pepper and nutmeg
2 egg yolks
juice of half a lemon
bread croûtons, fried (optional)

Wipe the mushrooms clean and dry, discarding the stalks, and put them in your soup pan with the goose fat. Add the chopped shallots, parsley and garlic and allow all to stew together for a few minutes. Add the stock, season and cook gently for 30 minutes. Check again for seasoning and add a little freshly grated nutmeg to taste.

Prepare your croûtons. When you are ready to serve the soup, beat the egg yolks gently in a bowl and dilute with a ladleful of soup. Add the lemon juice and return all to the soup. Mix well and serve over the croûtons in the soup bowls.

———— ● ————

Up in the high pasture country of the Aubrac, the border country between the Auvergne and the Rouergue, it rains quite a bit, even in summer. *Mousserons* are commonly found and the locals have devised this attractive kind of mushroom quiche, to which *mousserons* give a very special added perfume. The recipe also uses the local Cantal cheese. Cantal is used a great deal all over the South-West and approximates roughly to our farmhouse Cheddar, although it is nuttier and when fully mature, tough and strong. If you are in France and want some to cook with, ask for it *doux* (mild) or *entre-deux* (half way between mild and strong).

LA RECOULETTE
Fairy-ring mushroom flan

Serves 4

350 g (12 oz) shortcrust pastry
(page 258)
150 g (5¼ oz) fresh, or 30 g (1oz)
dried *mousserons* (fairy-ring
mushrooms)
30 g (1oz) butter

salt, pepper, nutmeg
3 eggs
3 tablespoons double cream
100 g (3½ oz) Cantal (or Cheddar)
cheese

The dried mushrooms should be soaked in cold water for half an hour.

Line a 20 cm (8 in) buttered flan case with the pastry and leave it to rest in a cool place for 20 minutes. Prick the base, cover it with foil or buttered paper weighted down with dried peas or beans, and bake it 'blind' in a moderately hot oven, 200°C, 400°F, Gas Mark 6, for 20 minutes.

Sauter the mushrooms in butter for 5-10 minutes or so and season them; if they are fresh quite a lot of liquid will come out of them and they should be well drained before transferring them to the bottom of the pre-baked pastry case. Beat the eggs together with the cream and more seasoning, including a pinch of freshly grated nutmeg. Cut the cheese into thin slices and spread them over the top so that the egg mixture is completely covered.

Bake in the moderately hot oven for a further 25-30 minutes until the top is golden and has risen slightly.

— ● —

Mushrooms are particularly good in omelettes but in Britain it is rare to find them made with anything other than button mushrooms which are not really suitable at all. *Girolles or chanterelles* – the names are interchangeable – make a particularly lovely dish, especially when really fresh, in late spring and wet summers. The flavour is very delicate with a touch of pepperiness. They are a bright marmalade colour, their tops slightly resembling umbrellas blown inside out rather than the normal, rounded mushroom cap. They are particularly full of moisture and so should not be washed unless they are very dirty. In order to seal in their liquid they should be plunged into hot fat and cooked over a high heat with parsley and garlic before being laid across the finished omelette.

While the technique of omelette making is the same whatever the garnish or filling, each variety of mushroom requires slightly different preparation. *Morilles* must be well cooked (*remember they are poisonous when raw*). The stalks have no flavour and should be removed while the heads may need very careful washing to get rid of the sand and earth in them. This is because their pitted texture prevents your being able to clean them in the usual way by wiping with a damp cloth. Their texture is firmer than other mushrooms of their size so it is a good idea to blanch the heads by plunging them for a few minutes into boiling water with a tablespoonful of vinegar or lemon juice. Then cook your *morilles* in goose fat or oil, season them and add some chopped parsley. Add half a tablespoonful (per person) of *verjus* (the juice of unripe, fresh grapes, see page 132). Simmer for 15 minutes before adding them to your raw omelette mixture. Cook the omelette in the usual way.

Cèpes are more commonly to be found than *morilles*, and an *omelette aux cèpes* features frequently on restaurant menus all over the South-West, usually with a *supplément* of a few euros. Even in season, *cèpes* in restaurants will usually be canned or bottled, nowadays sometimes frozen or perhaps dried. They need be none the worse for that if they have been correctly processed (see p. 116). If you have some fresh *cèpes*, clean them and slice them, seal them in hot oil then reduce the heat, cover the pan and simmer for 15 minutes, adding the parsley and seasoning halfway through. Make your omelette in the usual way and lay the *cèpe* mixture across it as the omelette starts to set.

There is no reason why you cannot use dried *cèpes* to make an omelette, or indeed in most of the recipes which call for fresh ones. You will need only about a quarter of the weight compared with the fresh *cèpes* and they will need soaking for up to three hours. Drain them and dry well before using. Dried *cèpes* are much more frequently to be found in Britain than bottled or canned ones, especially in shops specializing in German and Austrian food imported from Central Europe.

Dried *mousserons* are very successful too and should be rehydrated in the same way. They are particularly good with eggs and complete our quartet of mushroom omelettes. They need only a little prior cooking in oil with a sprinkling of chopped shallot before you add them to your egg mixture. This omelette has a particularly subtle and flowery perfume.

Any kind of mushroom goes well with a dish of braised rabbit. The *basse-cour* will nearly always include plump rabbits in its population and most French butchers sell really good, unfrozen, indigenous rabbit, but at prices somewhat higher than we are used to. However the quality is quite different, the animals have much more flesh and the texture and tenderness are reminiscent of a slightly gamey chicken. The mushrooms in this recipe enhance the illusion of *la chasse*.

LE LAPIN EN COCOTTE AUX CHAMPIGNONS
Rabbit braised with mushrooms

Serves 4–6

strips of pork rind or slices of
   unsmoked streaky bacon
1 rabbit
125 g (4 oz) salt belly of pork
12 small white onions

½ bottle dry white wine
4 tablespoons *eau-de-vie*
bouquet garni
salt, pepper
30 g (1 oz) dried *cèpes* or 175 g
   (6 oz) fresh mushrooms

Line the bottom and sides of a thick cocotte, which must have a close-fitting lid, with the strips of pork rind (skin side down). Joint the rabbit into six or eight pieces and lay them on the pork. Add the rabbit's giblets, if you have them, and the salt pork, diced, and the onions, peeled but whole. Set over a moderate flame and pour over the wine and the *eau-de-vie*. Add the bouquet garni and seasoning. Allow to bubble fiercely for a minute or two, then transfer, covered, to a moderate oven (160°C, 325°F, Gas Mark 3).

If you are using dried *cèpes*, these should have been put to soak for an hour or more beforehand in tepid water. In any case, add the mushrooms – fresh or rehydrated – to the rabbit after 45 minutes and then cook the dish for a further 45 minutes.

This recipe is particularly useful if you are not too confident of the age, tenderness or provenance of your rabbit.

———— ● ————

The bigger mushrooms, like horse mushrooms, parasols or *cèpes*, can make a very good filling for a kind of savoury tart called *une tourte* in the South-West. This dish makes an excellent light meal with perhaps a salad, or, in half quantities, an unusual *entrée*.

LA TOURTE LANDAISE AUX CHAMPIGNONS
Mushroom and ham pie

Serves 4

350 g (¾ lb) *cèpes* or other
   mushrooms
3 tablespoons oil
1 small onion, finely chopped
3 cloves garlic, finely chopped

250 g (8 oz) raw *jambon de campagne*,
   diced
60 g (2 oz) fresh breadcrumbs
2 egg yolks
1 tablespoon armagnac
pepper, salt
350 g (¾ lb) *pâte brisée* (see page 258)

Preheat the oven to 220°C, 425°F, Gas Mark 7. Clean then chop the mushrooms into dice and fry them gently in the oil. Add the onion and garlic without allowing them to colour but let the mushrooms first give off their liquid and then allow it to evaporate. When there is only a little moisture left in the pan, remove it from the heat, stir in the ham and breadcrumbs, mix well and bind with one of the egg yolks. Add the brandy and seasoning, but go easy on the salt because the ham may already have enough.

Roll out half the pastry and line a greased 20 cm (8 in) flan case with it. Fill this with the mushroom mixture. Roll out the rest of the pastry and cover the *tourte* with it. Press the sides together, trimming off any excess, and brush the top with the other beaten egg yolk. Make two or three ventilation cuts in the top and then put it to bake on a baking sheet in the oven for 40 minutes.

—— • ——

In the Sarlat district of the Périgord there is a saying that if you have *cèpes* to cook, there is no need to go to the butchers. Even so *cèpes* are often found as a garnish for roast and grilled meats; these are rarely served with sauce in the South-West – '*La faim est la meilleure des sauces*'. Roasts are well suited by the moist texture of these mushrooms. *Cèpes* are fairly filling and give the impression of richness. If you cook them a long time, as the older regional recipe books instruct you, they become soggy and lose their taste and texture. Before giving the classic recipes for the different ways of preparing *cèpes* in different districts, here is the best basic method which preserves flavour as well as texture. It is the way Monsieur Cardaillac told us that he cooked them when he had his restaurant by the river Tarn in the middle of the Gaillac vineyards.

LES CÈPES À L'ETUVÉE
Ceps cooked in oil

Cèpes should be trimmed and wiped dry, never washed or peeled. They are cooked in oil, not fat. The stalks are nearly as good as the caps; slice the former into rounds and the latter into thick slices.

Serves 4

500 g (1 lb) *cèpes*
4 tablespoons oil
3 tablespoons chopped parsley

4 cloves garlic, finely chopped
salt and pepper

Heat the oil in a frying pan which has a close-fitting lid. Use a non-stick pan if you can. When the oil begins to smoke, throw in the *cèpes*, parsley and garlic, stir well to mix and immediately reduce the heat to low. Cover the pan and simmer undisturbed for 10 minutes. Season and serve. One school of thought objects to peppering *cèpes* but surely a little brings out the flavour rather well?

——— ● ———

The frying of *cèpes* in oil and with parsley and garlic is common to nearly all of the regional variations of which brief notes are given as follows:

LES CÈPES À LA BORDELAISE
Ceps as in Bordeaux

as for basic recipe, plus
1 shallot (chopped) which you cook with the *cèpes*. Optional extras are a little *verjus* (page 132) and/or a few fresh breadcrumbs to give a change of texture.

LES CÈPES À LA GASCONNE
Ceps from Gascony

as for basic recipe, plus
125 g (4 oz) lean *jambon de campagne*   1 tablespoon flour
125 ml (4 fl oz) dry white wine

Fry the mushroom heads gently in oil for half an hour or so. Take from the pan and keep on one side while the stalks, thinly chopped and the ham, cut into small cubes, the garlic and parsley are all fried like a *hachis* in the pan juices. After cooking a little, sprinkle the *hachis* with the flour, stir well, gradually add the wine, then season. Put the *cèpes* back in this mixture and simmer together for 10 minutes.

——— ● ———

Further South, in the foothills of the Central Pyrenees, the *cèpes* are grilled over a wood fire.

LES CÈPES À LA BIGOURDANE
Ceps from the Pyrenees

as for basic recipe, plus
125 g (4 oz) fresh belly of pork

Cut off the stalks half an inch or so from the caps and put the stalks aside for another use (in a stew or in a pan of *sauté* potatoes). Grill the caps over an open fire in the chimney so that they give out their liquid.

While they are cooking, cut the pork into small spikes and insert them into the flesh of the mushrooms. After about 15 minutes, by which time the mushrooms will be about half cooked, finish them in a frying pan with the oil. Sprinkle with the garlic and parsley before serving.

LES CÈPES À LA BÉARNAISE
Ceps from the Basque country

In the Basque country they like their *cèpes* grilled too. Spike with garlic and sprinkle with oil. If you wish, add an *hachis* made with the chopped stalks, breadcrumbs, garlic and parsley.

———— ● ————

If you are lucky and find *cèpes* in the woods or at the market, you can make a real feast by opening some *confit* of goose or duck to go with them. The farmer's wife would kill a chicken, joint it and sauter the pieces with the *cèpes*, the bird taking on the flavours from the pan juices, the parsley and the garlic.

In the Bordelais they start off a *poulet aux cèpes* in two separate pans.

LE POULET SAUTÉ AUX CÈPES À LA BORDELAISE
Fried chicken and ceps

Serves 4

1.25 kg (2¾ lb) chicken, jointed into 8 pieces	4 small or 2 medium-sized cloves garlic
oil or goose fat for frying	2 tablespoons chopped parsley
2 large or 4 medium-sized *cèpes*	4 tablespoons dry white wine or
salt, pepper	verjuice (see page 132)

Heat the oil or fat in a large frying pan, and when it is just smoking, put in the chicken pieces and fry them over the high heat on all sides for 5–7 minutes. Then reduce the heat and leave them to cook for a further 10 minutes, turning them from time to time.

In another pan with a fitting lid, put a covering of oil and bring to a high heat. When the oil is smoking, throw in the *cèpes* – the caps sliced into pieces and the stalks into rounds. Turn them in the oil and, after a few minutes, reduce the heat to a minimum, sprinkle over some salt and cover the pan. Leave to cook gently for 10 minutes.

At the end of this time, transfer the *cèpes* to the chicken in the frying pan and add the chopped garlic and parsley plus further seasoning. Mix all together, stir in the white wine or verjuice and leave to cook gently for a final 10 minutes.

——— • ———

If you are lucky enough to find some big *cèpes*, a lovely Périgord dish can be made by stuffing the caps with a mixture of country ham, breadcrumbs, parsley and garlic, all well-seasoned and bound with an egg. In the Cévennes they stuff *cèpes* rather like tomatoes. Incidentally, unmarried daughters in the Cévennes are allowed to pick, dry and sell mushrooms and to put the proceeds towards their bottom drawer.

A different way of combining the same flavours is to braise the *cèpes* in a cocotte, sandwiched between two layers of an *hachis* (see page 18). In this case the long cooking time required is not only essential but beneficial to the finished texture of the dish.

The idea of *cèpes* as a meat substitute is perhaps the rationale behind cooking them *en salmis* as if they were game birds. The cooking time is long but only the gentlest of heat is needed.

LE SALMIS DE CÈPES À LA GIRONDINE
A rich stew of ceps from the Gironde

Serves 4

125 g (4 oz) *couennes* (pork rind)	salt, pepper
4 tablespoons cooking oil	bouquet garni
500 g (1 lb) *cèpes*	1 teaspoon sugar
100 g (3½ oz) belly of pork, diced	150 ml (¼ pt) red wine
6 shallots	2 tablespoons armagnac

The caps of the *cèpes* should be kept whole and the stalks cut into thin rounds. In a frying pan start the caps to cook in the oil with the diced belly of pork and the chopped shallots.

Preheat your oven to 180°C, 350°F, Gas Mark 4, and take a casserole with a tight-fitting lid. Line it with the pork rind cut to cover the whole of the base and sides of the pot. When the mushroom mixture in the frying pan has absorbed the juice given out by the *cèpes*, put it into your cocotte. Add seasonings. Heat the wine in a small pan and add it to the mushrooms. When the dish is bubbling well, cover and transfer to the oven where the heat must be reduced to an absolute minimum and the *cèpes* allowed barely to simmer for 3 hours.

Just before serving dribble the armagnac over the mushrooms. The *couennes* are not, of course, eaten but will have given much richness to your *salmis*.

———— ● ————

Lovers of *oeufs bonne femme* – eggs on fried bread baked together with mushrooms – will not be surprised to learn that the Périgourdins have their own thoroughly characteristic version, based on *cèpes* although, as with nearly all *cèpes* dishes, other large well-textured mushrooms can be substituted.

Cèpes go extraordinarily well with potatoes, which seem to take on the flavour of the mushrooms just as eggs do with truffles. This, however, is a more economical miracle; indeed you can adapt the following recipe to use just a few tinned or bottled *cèpes*, or any left over from another dish.

LES POMMES DE TERRE AUX CÈPES
Potatoes and ceps

Serves 4

500 g (1 lb) waxy potatoes	1 clove garlic
2–3 fresh *cèpes*	chopped parsley
1–2 tablespoons goose or duck fat	salt, pepper

Peel the potatoes and cut them into thinnish rounds. Cut off the stalks of the *cèpes* and set them aside. Wipe the heads with a damp cloth, then cut them into slices. Clean the stalks and chop them finely with the garlic and some parsley.

Heat the fat in a large, thick-bottomed frying pan and when it starts to smoke, toss in the potatoes and *cèpes*. Keep the heat high at this point and turn the pieces in the pan continuously until they start to colour. Watch them carefully as they tend to stick.

When they are nicely sealed, add the *hachis* of stalks, garlic and parsley, with plenty of salt and pepper. Lower the heat and cover the pan with a tight-fitting lid or with foil. They should then be left to cook for half an hour or so but you will need to turn them every 10 minutes to crisp all sides and to ensure they are not catching on the bottom of the pan.

You will find the mushroom flavour penetrates the whole dish. It is excellent with a pork roast or a steak, although in the countryside it might be eaten as a dish on its own with a green salad.

——— ● ———

Dried *cèpes* are easily and quickly reconstituted and you can adapt the above recipe to produce almost as good a result. Keep the liquid in which you soak the mushrooms. Parboil the potatoes and fry them sliced with diced pork or bacon, a *persillade* (see glossary) and the mushrooms which should be first patted dry in a clean cloth. After a few minutes add the mushroom water, season, cover the dish and simmer slowly for about 40 minutes. There should be a little sauce left when you serve the mushrooms.

TO DRY CEPS AND OTHER MUSHROOMS

The best varieties for drying, other than *cèpes*, are *mousserons*, field and horse mushrooms and *morilles*. *Girolles* do not dry very well. The mushrooms should be young and free from worms or other inhabitants. Sever the feet from the caps and depending on their size, either dry the two halves as they are or cut them into smaller pieces, remembering that a dried mushroom is only a fraction of the size it was when fresh. Spread the pieces out on a wattle surface so that the air can get at them from all sides. Depending on the temperature, you can lay them in the sun if it is not too hot, bringing them into the warmth of the house at night. Alternatively they can be dried entirely indoors. The process will take four to six days, at the end of which they should be left in a faintly warm oven overnight. The whole process can in fact be done in the oven but the experts rather frown on the idea. Perhaps it is too simple? Store the dried mushrooms in airtight containers.

To reconsitute dried mushrooms, simply soak them in water but they may need up to three hours if you have kept them for any time. You need only weigh out about one fifth of the weight you would need for fresh mushrooms. Don't throw away the water you have used for soaking them; it may come in handy for flavouring purposes. Dried mushrooms are particularly useful in sauces and as garnishes.

To Bottle Mushrooms

For dishes in which mushrooms are the star turn, bottling is the best method of preservation. *Cèpes* and *morilles* are both very well suited to bottling. You will need some of the glass preserving jars with clip-down lids and rubber sealing rings which the French call *bocaux*. The jars can be re-used as many times as you like, using fresh rubber rings and as long as the metal closure device is functioning properly. *Bocaux* must be sterilized before use by boiling them in water.

As far as you can, bottle mushrooms whole or in the largest possible pieces. The stalks of *cèpes* may be detached and cut into 2.5 cm (1 inch) thick rounds. Although scrupulous cleanliness must be observed, never wash mushrooms unless absolutely necessary. Wipe them clean with a damp cloth. Reject the bottom ends of any feet which remain obstinately dirty.

If *cèpes* are not so young as they might be, for example if the spores are tending to disintegrate or are getting mushy in texture, you can scrape the spongey part away, keeping the cap itself (as long as its flesh is firm and pale).

Never blanch mushrooms before bottling them or they will acquire the texture of slugs. This is what is wrong with so many tinned *cèpes* and however much you try and wash away the canning juices and dry the flesh of the mushrooms, they will always be soggy and slimy.

Now you have your beautifully clean mushrooms on the one hand and sterilized jars on the other. The rest is simple. Find a saucepan big enough to take the mushrooms in comfort and as wide and shallow as possible. Put into the bottom as much oil (a mixture of olive oil and sunflower oil is ideal) as you would need if you were cooking the mushrooms. Heat the oil to smoking point, put in the *cèpes*, stir all about and cook briefly and briskly over a good heat for 10 minutes, seasoning with salt but no pepper.

At the end of this time put the *cèpes* and their juices into the jars, never filling a jar more than three-quarters full. Seal the jar. Stand the jar(s) in a deep preserving pan, cover them completely with water and bring the water to the boil. You may have to weight the jars down with a piece of wood and a stone or some such weight. Boil the jars for two hours. Allow to cool, remove the jar(s) from the water and store in a cool place.

LES TRUFFES

There is one fungus, if that is the right name for it, which is not only the most sought-after speciality of the South-West but cannot be rivalled for quality anywhere else. Truffles are becoming increasingly important in Provence and Italy; a poor relation grows in Spain and is increasingly imported into France to supply an impossible demand; there is, however, no real substitute for *la truffe noire* of the Périgord and Quercy. Aptly christened 'black diamonds', they sell in the local markets for £15 to £30 a half kilo; almost double in the smart *épiceries* of Paris. Perhaps our Puritan instincts suggest that no foodstuff can be worth that price? In any case those of us who have eaten them have more probably tasted them in their tinned form, when no amount of care or expertise can prevent their losing a large part of their flavour. A fresh truffle is a true marvel of the soil, incredibly pungent – *l'odeur est déjà une fête* – and only needing very small quantities to flavour a large dish. It is no myth that one truffle put overnight in a sealed box of eggs will flavour the eggs through their shells. We once brought three truffles home to England in a paper bag in the boot of the car. When we stopped for the night at Chartres the hotel porter lifted the tailgate of our car to extract our luggage and cried '*Mon Dieu! Vous êtes venus du Périgord!*'

'*Qui dit truffe prononce un grand mot,*' said Brillat-Savarin. 'Black as the souls of the damned,' as the peasant saying goes. More charming is the Périgord legend that a truffle is a potato turned into treasure by a good fairy. But what are truffles? They are a subterranean fungus growing in winter 7–40 cm (3–15 in) below the level of the soil and are parasitical on the root-ends of certain trees, particularly oaks. They only grow where the soil is very chalky and scarcely capable of sustaining any vegetation other than scrubby trees, juniper bushes and wild herbs and grasses. A tree claimed by truffles as their home can be recognized instantly by the burnt appearance of the soil around it. This area is called *la brulée*, the mycelium of the truffle having poisoned the soil against other forms of vegetation. Even when growing conditions are right, no one ever knows whether there will be truffles in any given place or not. Truffles are capricious – '*capricieuse comme une fille*'.

In theory the best conditions exist on the plateaux of the Périgord and Quercy and occasionally elsewhere in the South-West where a thriving industry flourished a hundred years ago, sending truffles to Paris to become an essential feature of the *haute cuisine*. When phylloxera devastated the vineyards of the South-West, there was a mass emigration to cities; the truffle trade, too, went into a decline. The loss of so many further lives in the First World War accelerated widespread depression and poverty in these already under-privileged areas, almost wiping out the harvesting of truffles for commerce.

Today attempts are being made on a serious scale to revive it, by clearing the old plantations of undergrowth and generally by encouraging the conditions in which truffles will thrive. The truffle mycelium will live for a hundred years, so it is not too late to revive areas where truffles are known to have grown in former times. Secondly, scientific experimentation is starting into the artificial inducement of truffle growing in areas where conditions are thought to be propitious. Jean-Louis, whom we met in an earlier chapter rearing fattened ducks on his farm near Brive, is fanatical about the revival of the truffle. He is systematically planting young oak trees, though these will take 15 years to develop the fungus. He is also part of a group of enthusiasts concerned with the development of new breeds of tree which will, it is thought, be particularly successful in producing the required conditions. Meanwhile the poaching of truffles is considered a serious offence and more severely punished than many other forms of larceny.

The hunting of truffles is the subject of legend and folklore, which seems to grow in direct proportion to the mounting price of the marketed product. It is generally accepted that specially trained sows, with a highly developed sense for scenting the truffle, are the best 'mine detectors'. Fed on miniscule portions of truffle peelings, they acquire the capacity to sniff out a truffle even 50 cm (nearly 2 feet) below ground level. Pigs are also easier to control than dogs when the treasure is brought to the surface. Dogs nevertheless are also used to hunt and presumably have to be well trained not to eat the truffle. They can cover more ground than a pig, are more agile and easier to get into the Deux Chevaux. A third technique involves the human hunter lying on the ground and watching the movement of flies. A cluster of insects above a well-known truffle-ground is said to pinpoint the position of a truffle. The method has its devotees, perhaps because it cuts out the middle man, but the failure rate must be high.

Truffles are not everyday fare and in a sense are peripheral to the peasant cookery of the South-West. Because they are particular to the region, and because they have contributed so much to the *haute cuisine* of days gone by, they cannot be ignored in a book that includes the Périgord in its territory. The truffle is probably at its best served simply, either on its own or in an omelette, or with the pork and poultry for which the region is famous. Its scented, earthy flavour also goes well with sweetbreads.

Although tinned truffles are a pale shadow of the real thing, they are still not to be despised. It is important to buy only the best quality whole truffles. If you happen to be in the South-West over Christmas and New Year and want to bring some truffles home you would be better off preserving them under goose fat, and we give the method for this (page 121). You will find it surprisingly difficult, however, to find any truffles for sale. Any peasant who brings a few to market does not expose them publicly for sale: he will keep them in a paper bag and, when he sees a likely customer, will offer them furtively for inspection as if they were dirty postcards. As with all expensive goods, the buyer must take great care if he is not to be disappointed. A good truffle should not be offered with too much earth attached to it – defects are easily concealed in this way.

The size of the truffle is not important but it should be quite firm to the touch and give off its powerful aroma instantly upon acquaintance. It should be round in shape, not irregular, and can vary from the size of a large grape to that of a large plum. It should be very dark brown, almost black; a pale truffle will be insipid and useless for cooking. They come into season in the early part of December but are really not at their best until well into the New Year. They are not found after the beginning of March. Because of the risks involved in the purchase, and in view of the large cash outlay to buy even one or two, a non-expert is probably best advised to seek out a dealer, by enquiring in local cafés. He may have to pay a little more this way but at least is less likely to be disappointed. If you buy casually at market, the seller is more than likely to pass on inferior specimens which he has acquired cheap from a dealer.

The beginning of the truffle season coincides with the festivities for Christmas and the New Year, more accurately Christmas Eve and New Year's Eve. The markets just before Christmas are full of poultry, and even quite humble people have saved enough at least to make a gesture with truffles, because the tradition is to flavour your turkey with as much or as little as you can afford. At that time of year, if at no other, you may well find the occasional furtive peasant with his little bag of black gold, tempting the bourgeois housewives of the country towns into a mad spending spree.

As we have seen, geese and ducks are fattened and cultivated for their liver. The French therefore concentrate on turkey for their table poultry, just as we do. Capons which have been surgically castrated are no longer available: nowadays they are a creation of the chemist and are to be avoided. Poorer households may have to make do with a chicken but whatever the bird, the truffle makes it something special.

Christmas Eve in France has always been one of the great days in the calendar for good eating and drinking. After midnight mass, families would return home to enjoy their best *conserves*, whether it were *foie gras* in more fortunate households or perhaps a simple *jambonneau* on poorer farms. There would always be the bird, roasted over the fire and, with luck, perfumed with the divine flavour of truffle. Truffles would be mixed in with the stuffing, the kind of *farci* we have already seen used as a basic way of preparing *poule au pot*. Alternatively a chestnut and pork stuffing, or slivers of truffle would be slipped between the skin and the flesh of the bird (as early as eight days before cooking) allowing the flavour to permeate the meat, to be released again under the subtle influence of the juices released by the roasting. This method gave rise to the phrase *demi-deuil* to describe the impression of half-mourning created by the slices of black truffle against the nearly white flesh of the turkey or chicken.

Before canning techniques were invented, the farmers' wives developed a method of preserving truffles beneath goose or duck fat, and this is still the best way of keeping them. The method is simplicity itself.

LES TRUFFES CONSERVÉES SOUS LA GRAISSE
Truffles preserved in fat

2 or 3 medium-sized truffles, weighing together approx 175 g (6 oz)	250 g (8 oz) goose or duck fat

Brush the truffles well to remove all particles of grit. Put the fat into a small saucepan; when it is just at boiling point add the truffles. Allow to poach in the scarcely boiling fat for 15 minutes.

Have ready a small sterilized preserving jar. Carefully remove the truffles from the saucepan and place in the jar. Cover with the fat, seal the jar and store in a cool, shady place away from abrupt temperature changes; an old-fashioned larder would be best.

———— • ————

If you are travelling in the South-West, your most likely introduction to truffles will probably be in an omelette. The French prepare such delicious omelettes: they seem to have been born with the technique developed to such perfection that it is difficult to choose between the huge variety in their repertoire. An omelette with truffles has to be near the top of anyone's list, not necessarily for its rarity value but because the combination of flavours is quite sensational. Alas, many restaurants are mean with the truffle. The more truffle you can afford the better, but the following proportions will at least give you some idea of the Lucullan possibilities of doubling or trebling up on the quantities.

L'OMELETTE AUX TRUFFES
Truffle omelette

Serves 2

1 medium-sized truffle of about
   50–60 g (2 oz)
4 eggs

1 scant tablespoon fresh cream
1 tablespoon goose or duck fat
salt, pepper

If your truffle is fresh, place it with the four eggs in their shells, in a bowl with a close-fitting lid. Leave until next day. If possible, a few hours before making the omelette, slice the truffle into thin rounds and poach these for 10 minutes, uncovered, in a small pan with a glass of water. These preparations will have already flavoured the eggs and the cooking water to perfection. Reduce the water to a tablespoonful.

When the time comes to make your omelette, beat the eggs in the usual way, add the cream, truffle, seasoning and the liquid you have poached it in. If you are using preserved truffle, you need not poach it. Simply slice and add it to the beaten eggs a few hours before making the omelette, together with any juices in the tin. Heat the fat in your omelette pan, and make the omelette in the usual way, taking care to leave the top *baveuse*, not quite set. Fold and serve without delay.

———— • ————

This is quite one of the best ways of enjoying the flavour of truffles. It is difficult to know whether to prefer it to the following recipe, which ennobles scrambled eggs to the status of *cuisine de luxe*.

LES OEUFS BROUILLÉS AUX TRUFFES
Scrambled eggs with truffles

Serves 2

The ingredients are exactly as for *l'omelette aux truffes*.

Put your truffle with the eggs as for an omelette, then poach it as indicated. When you are ready, slice the truffle and add it to the eggs and scramble them in the usual way.

Serve with slices of toast or country bread. These are two egg dishes which call, unusually, for a rather special red wine.

—— ● ——

A fairly small amount of truffle will elevate an already lovely dish into a memorable experience. One example is the recipe for *enchaud de porc périgourdin* on page 76; without the truffle it is quite one of the best ways of cooking a joint of pork but the addition of a truffle turns it into something really festive. A small truffle also works wonders for calf's sweetbreads.

LE RIS DE VEAU À LA SAUCE AUX TRUFFES
Sweetbreads with truffle sauce

Serves 4

700 g (1½ lb) calf's sweetbreads
1 large onion, finely chopped
2 tablespoons goose or pork fat
2 tablespoons flour
300 ml (½ pt) chicken stock

2 tablespoons brandy
125 ml (4 fl oz) dry white wine
salt, pepper
1 small truffle

Soak the sweetbreads whole for several hours, changing the water as often as possible. Blanch them in boiling water for 5 minutes, then lift out and take off the membrane encasing them as well as any fat or other waste.

Sweat the onion very slowly in a tablespoonful of the fat for about 30 minutes. Use a wire gauze mat if you cannot get the heat low enough (because the onion must not colour and should cook almost to a purée). Add the flour, cook for a few minutes, stirring constantly, then add the stock. Amalgamate well so that the sauce is completely smooth.

In a small casserole melt the remaining fat and sear the sweetbreads in it over a high heat so that they take on a little colour all over. Flamber with the brandy and add the wine. Allow to bubble fiercely for a minute or so, then add the onion sauce and seasoning to taste. Reduce the heat, add the finely sliced truffle, cover the pan and simmer for a quarter of an hour over the lowest heat.

———— • ————

In country households food went straight from the cooking pan to table and the cooking method itself provided all the seasoning and extra flavours required. The emphasis was on the raw material and the processes it underwent. The peasant therefore finds not only mint sauce and horseradish sauce difficult to understand but also finds no use for the elaborate classic French sauces based on long reductions of stock, such as the *espagnole* or the butter-based sauces in the *hollandaise – béarnaise – beurre blanc* tradition.

There are exceptions, and they serve to prove the rule. There is the kind of wine-and-butter based sauce which the Bordelais serve with an entrecôte steak (page 217). But meat of that quality rarely came the way of a farmer's wife in the *haut-pays* and the Bordelais style was developed within the bourgeois ambiance of the town. Of the same kind is the sauce called *sauce périgueux* which was probably christened by some Parisian chef as epitomizing in his view just what Périgord cookery was all about – the use of the black truffle as the ultimate condiment. Historians seem to agree that *sauce périgueux* is no more than a hundred years old, and for a relatively new creation there is such a wide variety of different versions (some including *foie gras*, others ham, and with such diverse liquids as dry white wine, brandy, Monbazillac and even Madeira) that the sauce has almost certainly little or no regional authenticity.

Some regional cooks have adopted it as their own. The best have stripped away the *haute cuisine* trappings and have got back to something which has the true feeling of the Périgord. It goes well with any roast of beef or veal, or any steak.

LA SAUCE PÉRIGUEUX
Périgueux truffle sauce

Serves 4

2 tablespoons goose or duck fat
3 good-sized shallots, finely
    chopped
1 large glass white wine
4 tablespoons armagnac

1 medium-sized onion, thinly sliced
1 tablespoon flour
300 ml (½ pt) strong veal or beef
    stock
truffles, according to your purse

Even the smallest tin of truffles (25 g) will be enough but with 50 g you will be in for a *régal*, as they say.

For this sauce you will need two pans. In one melt a tablespoonful of the fat and soften the shallots over a very low heat until they are pliant and quite translucent. Turn up the heat, pour in the wine and the armagnac and flamber. When the flames have gone, reduce the heat and allow the shallots barely to simmer over a very low heat.

In another pan fry the onion in the second tablespoonful of fat as gently as you softened the shallots. When the onion is starting to colour, add the flour, mix it well with the onion and cook together for 3 or 4 minutes to avoid any risk of a 'raw flour' taste to the sauce. Add the stock little by little and cook together until perfectly smooth.

Now mix together the contents of your two pans and simmer as gently as possible, preferably with the pan over a wire gauze, or stand the pan on the very edge of the heat, and cook for 2 hours, covered, stirring from time to time to ensure the smoothness of the sauce. If you are using truffles from a tin, add the juices to the sauce.

Just before you are ready to serve your meat, strain the sauce and cook the truffle peelings in it for a few minutes before adding the truffles themselves, very thinly sliced. Gently simmer all together but without boiling, for 5 minutes, then serve.

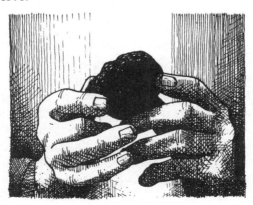

LES POISSONS

La pêche, c'est en sorte la chasse domestiquée

RAYMOND VIALELLES HAS the farm across a small valley from us. Very early on in our French days we allowed him to send his small herd of cattle to graze in our small field, usually accompanied by one of his old parents.

Our properties are divided by a stream which runs in quite a steep gorge, and one hot summer day Monsieur Vialelles invited us to go *écrevisse* hunting with him – at night. Now *écrevisse* hunting is illegal except during a very short season which we were not in, and the fines can be fairly steep. We really had no choice: to refuse his invitation would have made us a laughing-stock in the village café. Armed with strong torches we fumbled around in the cool clear water, turning over the stones which protect these rather sinister creatures from predators. Our catch was small but that was hardly the point. We were enjoying the excitement of *la chasse*, and we were not caught.

We must be quite clear what an *écrevisse* is. It is a freshwater fish. It translates as crayfish, thus becoming confused with its salt-water relation the *langouste* which we call crawfish. *Écrevisses* are much smaller, usually about 7–10 cm (3–4 in) long, a dark and rather evil-looking muddy brown in nature. They live in rivers and streams where they are to be found lurking under stones. They can be caught by simply paddling and turning the stones over or, in deeper or less transparent water, by bait such as rotten meat (mutton is traditional). The well-tried method in France in which all members of the family, wives as well as children, participated was *à la balance*. This consisted of a circular net stretched across a hoop on which bait was fixed before it was lowered into the stream. After a suitable wait, sitting on the river bank, the family would haul up the nets which might yield sixty or eighty *écrevisses* during the course of an afternoon.

The country people will be quick to tell you that an *écrevisse* is not worth having unless it was fished from a local stream. They could be right, because commercially marketed crayfish are often of an inferior variety. You must hope that the fish you secure is of the breed called *pattes rouges*. On the other hand, if you ask for advice on where and how to find these, you will be met with the same kind of glassy look and mumbled response which greets similar questions about mushrooms.

So *écrevisses* are miniature freshwater *langoustes*. They too go bright red when cooked, a wonderful dark brick colour even more spectacular than that of a lobster. Their size does, however, make them difficult and messy to handle. First, it is essential that you get them home alive. A French fishmonger will not boil them for you and would be amazed if you asked him to because they need very little cooking time and once cooked, there is little you can do with them. All French recipes call for just the single cooking, whatever the sauce or garnish.

There *is* the problem of killing the crayfish. English sensitivity is probably best assuaged by raising the water temperature very gently. They appear to go to sleep and not to feel the end at all. The French have no qualms about these matters and if a recipe calls for the poor creatures to be thrown into boiling water or oil, *tant pis*. It is important first to remove the intestinal tract which runs down the centre and which otherwise gives a bitter taste to the fish when cooked. This is done by applying a knife to the end of the tract below the tail and pulling it out.

As far as eating is concerned, the tail is the only part really worth bothering about. The claws are so small that the amount of flesh they contain is miniscule. And diners should be warned that *écrevisses* are difficult to enjoy in polite society. The sauce is liable to run up to your elbows and it is common in French restaurants for bibs to be provided.

Écrevisses are, nevertheless, well worth experimenting with, particularly if your home rivers or streams are inhabited by them. Despite their rarity they are highly traditional to the whole of the South-West, threaded as it is with such a wonderful variety of mountain rivers and streams. Furthermore, *écrevisses* used always to be free.

LES ÉCREVISSES À LA FAÇON DE RODEZ
Crayfish in a spicy sauce

Serves 4

32 crayfish
100 ml (3 fl oz) olive oil
salt and pepper
100 g (3½ oz) finely chopped onion
2 shallots, chopped
2 cloves garlic, chopped
½ wine glass armagnac

2 glasses dry white wine
1 wine glass water
60 g (2 oz) butter
2 tablespoons fresh breadcrumbs
a little cayenne pepper
3 tablespoons finely chopped parsley

Check that the live *écrevisses* have had their intestinal tract removed. If not, detach it with the point of a knife from under the end of the tail.

Put the oil in a large pan, add the crayfish and season with some salt and pepper. Start the heat very low and cover the pan with its lid, shaking it from time to time. As the *écrevisses* turn from dark brown to bright red, remove the lid and raise the heat, cooking them for 3 or more minutes. Add the onion, shallot and garlic and stir the pan thoroughly. Flamber with the armagnac and when the flames have died down, add the wine and water.

Heat a serving dish in a low oven. When the crayfish have cooked for a further 5 minutes (not more or they will lose their texture) transfer them to the serving dish. Strain the sauce and while you reduce it by about a third over a good fire, mix the butter and breadcrumbs together with a fork and thicken the sauce by adding a little of this at a time, off the heat, and whisking it in thoroughly.

Add cayenne pepper to taste, the sauce should be quite spicy, and check for salt and pepper. Reheat the sauce and as soon as it comes back to the boil, pour it over the *écrevisses*. Sprinkle the dish with chopped parsley and serve hot.

———— ● ————

This is the Aveyronnais version of a recipe which crops up all over the South-West with local variations. In the Périgord the brandy is used but not lit, nor is the sauce thickened but it is cooked longer so as to extract the maximum flavour from the vegetables which, incidentally, include carrots and celery. In the lower Dordogne tarragon is sometimes used instead of parsley and the sauce is thickened with egg yolks, reflecting perhaps a more comfortable style of living. In Bordeaux tomatoes also go into the sauce but their colour detracts from the startling red of the fish which is surely much better set off simply by the herbs. So it is really up to the flair of the cook and what she has to hand but the basic indispensable ingredients to all versions of this sauce are the three members of the onion family, the alcohol and the herbs.

LES ÉCREVISSES À LA NAGE OU À LA PAYSANNE
Crayfish in the peasant style

This is the simplest and most basic method of preparing *écrevisses*, perhaps also the best if their quality can be relied on.

Serves 4

32 *écrevisses*
400 ml (¾ pt) dry white wine
1.5 litres (2½ pt) water
3 carrots
3 onions

3 shallots
bouquet garni, including celery
    leaves and leek tops
salt, pepper

Put the *écrevisses* in a deep saucepan, cover with the wine and place over a gentle heat. They will in due course turn red. Turn off the heat while you make a *court-bouillon*: put the chopped vegetables, bouquet garni and seasonings into another pan and cover with the water. Cook for 45 minutes.

At the end of this time, reheat your *écrevisses* and as the wine comes to the boil, add to them the strained *court-bouillon*. Cover the pan, cook for 7 minutes over a lively heat. Check the seasoning and serve the fish in soup plates with as much or as little of the broth as wished.

In the Auvergne they thicken some of the *court-bouillon* with a *roux*, season it well and enrich with egg yolks and cream – but then the Auvergne is cattle country.

———— ● ————

Our crayfish stream rises just a kilometre or two up the road so is not polluted in any way. The same cannot, however, be said for so many other rivers, small and large, in the South-West, where the effects of damming rivers for electrification and the pollution caused by towns and factories have emptied the water of fish altogether. A century ago salmon was so plentiful (and available free) that farm workers engaged for harvesting made it a term of their employment that they were not to be fed salmon more than three times a week. Today salmon survives only in the river Adour and some of the Pyrenean streams.

Trout is probably the most commonly fished of the fresh water species and for centuries has provided an attractive alternative to meat. Although it used to be found in most clear-running streams, early summer being the best time, demand has now outstripped supply and trout farms have developed to cater in quantity for shops and restaurants. Sometimes a trout farm has been established where once there was a water-mill, by diverting the mill stream to fill fresh water tanks in which the fish are bred. There used to be a trout farm near us in an idyllic valley setting. It provided useful pin money for a 'retired' farmer who had passed on his property to his son. Unfortunately, a long summer drought deprived him of his running water. He lost all his fish and any enthusiasm to start again.

If you should see a trout farm sign-posted in the countryside – *pisciculture* – it is well worth buying your fish there, freshly netted before your eyes. Also unless you find a local fishmonger you may have no alternative, since trading in river trout is now forbidden, to stop further drain on the natural supplies.

Fishermen claim that a trout is best eaten straightaway, grilled over a wood fire on the bank of the river from which it has been landed. If, however, the fish are brought home, they should be soaked in slowly running water for a couple of hours to avoid any chance of their tasting muddy. This also allows time for the nerves and sinews of the dead fish to relax; a trout which has stiffened for an hour or so after death curls up in the frying pan.

LES TRUITES AUX LARDONS
Trout with diced salt pork

This is a recipe which comes from Naucelle in the Rouergue. The late Monsieur Fraysse ran the Hostellerie des Voyageurs in this pretty market town above the banks of the river Viaur, and gave us his recipe, simple but delicious. The idea of salt belly of pork with fish may seem unusual but Jane Grigson in her *Fish Cookery* gives a recipe called *Brithyll a cig Moch* from Wales which uses the combination of trout and bacon. This seems to be another fascinating example of the parallels in dishes to be found in the same kind of countryside in France and in Great Britain, in this case hilly with mountain streams. Or perhaps it is simply a common Celtic background.

Serves 4

4 trout
125 g (4 oz) salt belly of pork
flour
pepper

2 cloves garlic, finely chopped
   (optional)
1 lemon

Clean the fish, removing any blood along the spine. Before cooking them, allow plenty of time to extract sufficient fat from the pork. Cut it into small dice and sauter these as gently as possible. The cubes should eventually become crispy and quite golden. They should then be taken out and kept warm or pushed to the side of the pan if there is sufficient room.

Season the flour with freshly ground pepper (no salt unless the pork has been cured very mildly). Coat the fish lightly with it and put them into the pan over a gentle heat together with the chopped garlic if this is being used. Five to six minutes' cooking on each side should be enough.

To serve, simply pour the pan juices over the fish and garnish with the lardons and the lemon, cut into quarters, not slices which are quite unsqueezable and useless except for decoration.

———— ● ————

Grilling or frying trout is considered by many as the finest way to preserve its delicate flavour but poaching the fish, then serving it with a buttery sauce is an alternative which is found all over France.

It was in Sarliac-sur-l'Isle in the Dordogne twenty years ago that we learned a delicious but simple way of preparing buttered trout. Our gourmet dentist friend from Périgueux invited us out to lunch, to a small country restaurant – Chez Basile. Here is his recipe:

La Truite Féterne
Trout with wine and butter

Serves 4

4 trout	3 tablespoons salt
court-bouillon: onion, carrot, celery,	125 g (4 oz) unsalted butter
parsley, 125 ml (4 fl oz) dry	1 glass red wine
white wine	1 tablespoon wine vinegar

Clean the trout, removing any blood along the spine. Make a *court-bouillon* by simmering the vegetables, herbs, wine and salt with sufficient water to cover the fish, for 30 minutes. Slide in the trout and barely simmer for 5-10 minutes according to their size. They should be just right when the pupils of their eyes pop out like pearls.

Transfer the fish to a heated serving dish and keep warm while you prepare the sauce. Heat the butter and at the moment when it is starting to turn nutty-coloured, pour it over the fish. In the same pan bubble up the wine and vinegar until reduced by half then pour over the fish.

Until the arrival of the lemon as a means of accentuating flavours as well as off-setting the sweetness of fish or fowl, cooks had turned to other acidic seasonings. Wine vinegar is an obvious one although it is often too strong for the more delicately flavoured proteins. But as far back as the sixteenth century the French and the English made great use of *verjus* or verjuice. As its name implies, this is the juice of green or unripe fruit, usually made with grapes although in England more often with crab apples. Wherever a vine would grow in the South-West of France it was not difficult to make your own *verjus*; in fact it was more tricky to store than to make. You had, however, to plant the right variety of vine to make the true *verjus*, not a wine-making plant but a type on which the grapes never fully ripened and so was reserved for making jam. A passable substitute can be prepared with unripe winemaking grapes, but not the dessert varieties. Although this practice almost died out last century, happily it is being revived by some local restaurateurs.

LE VERJUS
Verjuice

Around the middle of July when the grapes are formed and beginning to lose their strong green colour although not their acidity, pick sufficient for your needs. Blanch them briefly and spread them out to dry before crushing them, pushing the liquor through a sieve. Leave the juice to settle then pour it through a paper filter into sterilized bottles. To prevent any fermentation, some cooks recommend filling the top inch of the bottle with a layer of oil to exclude the air before inserting tight-fitting corks. Always store the bottles in a cool place.

———— ● ————

This was the original way of conserving verjuice, but there is less risk of fermentation in bottle if the verjuice is first heated to 80°C/172°F, allowed to cool and strained again before bottling. Its flavour is not as sharp as lemon or vinegar and for this reason it goes especially well with fish, as the next two recipes show.

LA TRUITE AU VERJUS
Trout with verjuice

per person:

1 trout	2 tablespoons verjuice
1 handful of sorrel, de-stalked	½ clove garlic, chopped
a little seasoned flour	a little chopped parsley
1 tablespoon lard or cooking oil	salt, pepper

Clean the trout, removing any blood along the spine and dry in a cloth or with kitchen paper. Season the insides and fill the slit with a handful of sorrel before rolling the trout in seasoned flour.

Heat the fat in a frying pan and put in the trout to cook over a moderate heat. Baste with the fat while they are cooking – watch they do not stick to the pan – giving them 4 or 5 minutes on each side, no more.

Transfer the trout to a hot serving dish, salt and pepper them and keep warm. Deglaze the fat in the frying pan with the verjuice, scraping the cooked flour off the bottom but do not allow the juice to boil. Tip this over the trout and sprinkle with garlic and parsley. The combination of the lemony sorrel, the garlic and the sweet-sour *verjus* with the trout is quite delicious.

LES TRUITES FARCIES
Stuffed trout

Serves 4

4 medium-sized trout	salt, pepper
3 tablespoons oil	parsley and any other herbs
1 large *cèpe*, or 30 g (1 oz) dried	available
cèpes (rehydrated)	2 tablespoons flour
one 100 g (3½ oz) slice of *jambon de*	1 egg
campagne (or gammon)	verjuice
3 shallots	3 tablespoons *persillade* (chopped
	parsley and garlic)

Check that the trout are thoroughly clean, removing any blood along the spine, then dry them with a clean cloth or kitchen paper.

Oil the centre section of four pieces of aluminium foil, large enough to wrap each fish in, and lay each trout on one. Chop the *cèpes*, dice the ham and chop the shallots and some parsley. Heat a little oil in a frying pan and fry the mushroom lightly for a few minutes before adding the ham and shallots and cooking all a little longer before stirring in the parsley and seasoning. Transfer this mixture to a bowl and when it has cooled a little blend in the flour and then the beaten egg. Put two spoonfuls of this stuffing into the cavity of each fish, sprinkle a little salt and pepper on top. Wrap each one up, not too tightly, in the foil, taking care to make a good seal on top and at each end and without tearing or puncturing the foil.

Cook in a preheated oven, 190°C, 375°F, Gas Mark 5, for 30 minutes.

When ready to serve, you can unwrap the trout and arrange on a hot serving dish, sprinkling over them a little verjuice and *persillade*. But better still, a packet can be given as it is to each diner who then opens it, savouring the wonderful mushroomy aroma which arises. The verjuice and *persillade* can be handed separately for sprinkling over the trout after it has been slit open and the backbone and head removed.

—— ● ——

Not all green vegetables blend well with fish but sorrel and spinach are both excellent partners largely because of their acidity.

LES TRUITES AUX ÉPINARDS À LA LIMOUSINE
Trout on a bed of spinach

Serves 4

1 kg (2¼ lb) spinach
125 g (4 oz) butter
salt, pepper, grated nutmeg
cooking oil
4 medium-sized trout, cleaned and
   all blood removed

flour
2 tablespoons chopped parsley
2 cloves garlic, chopped
4 tablespoons dried breadcrumbs

Wash and de-stalk the spinach and blanch it in plenty of boiling salted water for 5 minutes. Drain thoroughly, then reheat in half the butter together with seasonings and a dash of nutmeg. Spread the spinach over the bottom of a heated gratin dish and keep warm in the oven while you cook the trout.

Heat some clarified butter or oil in a large frying pan and cook the floured trout in it, allowing about 5 minutes a side. Transfer them to the dish of spinach, sprinkle the *persillade* of parsley and garlic over, followed by the breadcrumbs, and dot with the rest of the butter. Brown quickly under the grill and serve immediately.

—— ● ——

Apart from trout there are many other fish to be found in the rivers of the South-West. Larger varieties include pike (*brochet*) and carp but the irregularity of the supply hardly justifies including any recipes for them here. Smaller river fish such as *goujon* are frequently caught, sometimes netted in large quantities, but are best fried simply in a little oil or in batter and served with lemon slices.

There has always been a steady demand for fish on Fridays and during Lent in South-West France, which is predominantly and sometimes very strictly Catholic. Farmers' wives, however, never expected to rely on the family's skill at fishing: they might come back with nothing. Even on fast-days one had to eat something. Furthermore, the rest of the household had their work to do, and to go fishing was a treat which brought occasional bonuses to the table, but that was what they were.

Until the late nineteenth century refrigeration was unknown, so there was little prospect of remote farms being able to buy sea fish that might have to be brought 200 miles overland. The solution lay in salted and dried fish. Even today, when there is a marvellous system of fish distribution all over France, the country farmers hardly ever buy it. The traditional ways of preparing salted and dried cod, on the other hand, survive intact.

The salting and drying of fish to preserve it for long periods goes back to ancient times. French fishermen have sailed to arctic waters off Newfoundland and Iceland since the Middle Ages in search of cod, herring and mackerel, all of which feature in the cuisines of their largely Catholic population.

The men sailing to northern waters for cod had their work cut out. Having caught the cod, it was cleaned, filleted and then salted on board (*la morue*). The French fleets brought crystallized sea salt with them from the salt marshes of Poitou. Not all the fish was preserved in salt; some after gutting were taken ashore in Newfoundland or Norway and, strung up by their tails, were hung out to dry for up to twelve months before being brought back to Europe (*le stockfisch*).

There is a long tradition all over the South-West, and along the Mediterranean, of eating salted or dried cod, and not only as a penance. It gave a taste of the sea to those living their entire lives in their inland village. They were accustomed to salty pork and the salted fish made a welcome but familiar alternative. In the Périgord, the Dordogne and the Rouergue they soaked the *morue* for some days before cooking it, then blended it into a smooth, light purée with local ingredients – potatoes, walnut oil and eggs. Others cooked it with tomatoes but this was less traditional.

Le stockfisch, being air-dried until it became shrunken and stiff as a board, could be kept for long periods in the coolest part of the scullery, which suited those peasants living far inland. Its name probably derives from old Dutch meaning a piece of wood or stick, and when it reached the Rouergue the peasants' version in patois was *éstofi*. During the last century when river barges were the chief means of transport, it is said that the bargees would bring the *stockfisch* on their upstream trip – both for their own consumption and also to trade inland – and that they trailed the dried fish on lines behind their boats for the week-long journey so that it would be reconstituted and ready for sale when they reached their destination. Since it takes that long to re-hydrate it – and the purists say it should be in a running stream – it is not surprising that people nowadays mainly take the trouble to prepare and serve it only on feast days or in large quantities for the grape pickers at harvest time.

It is only in the region around Decazeville and Villefranche-de-Rouergue that *éstofinado* has become a local speciality and is still prepared for feast days in the winter. However, in view of the high cost nowadays of *stockfisch*, *éstofinado* is probably also made with *morue*.

L'ÉSTOFINADO ROUERGAT
Stockfish as in the Rouergue

Serves 6–8

1 dried *stockfisch*, approx 700–750 g (1½ lb)
500 g (1 lb) potatoes
50 ml (3 fl oz) milk
a *persillade* of 2 tablespoons chopped parsley and 4 chopped cloves of garlic

6 eggs, 3 of which hard-boiled
300 ml (½ pt) walnut oil
salt, pepper

Soak the fish for seven days, changing the water twice a day.

Put it into an enamelled pan and cover with plenty of cold water. Bring very slowly to just below boiling point so that this process takes up to 15 to 20 minutes. Turn off the heat and leave to stand for 20 minutes.

Remove the fish from the water and in its place boil the potatoes in their skins. When they are cooked, peel and mash them. Skin and fillet the fish and flake it back into the enamelled pan, pounding it with a fork or wooden spoon until it is reduced to a fine pulp. This is quite hard work but has to be done.

Mix in the mashed potato over a very low flame, then the milk. Make a hole in the centre of this mixture and tip in the *persillade* and the three raw eggs, well beaten beforehand. Mix all together thoroughly, still over a very low heat, then add the heated walnut oil and continue to beat until you have a light purée. Add seasoning and the sliced hard-boiled eggs. Serve immediately.

This dish is just as delicious made with salt cod which has only to be soaked for 24–36 hours, still changing the water frequently.

———— • ————

If you visit the open-air weekly market at Villefranche-de-Rouergue in autumn you can see the long, stiff, shrunken forms of the fish, their skins slightly golden, hanging up on the fish stalls. There will also be the giant flat filleted slabs of *morue*, white and glistening with their coating of salt crystals. This is also used to make the same dish as *l'estofinado*. On Good Friday the flaked, cooked fish is served in a potato salad. A dish which is nearly as lovely as *estofinado* is this one for which the creamed fish is baked with potato and eggs until it has risen into a golden cake.

Le Gâteau de Morue
Salt cod loaf

Serves 4

500 g (1 lb) salt cod	500 g (1 lb) potatoes
4 tablespoons walnut or other oil	3 eggs, separated
2 cloves garlic, chopped	salt, pepper, nutmeg

Soak the fish in an earthenware or enamelled dish for at least 24 hours, changing the water at least twice. Then poach it in fresh water.

Flake the fish, removing the skin, and pound it to a cream with the oil and garlic. Cook the potatoes and mash them to a purée, then beat them into the fish together with the three egg yolks and the seasonings. Mix very well. Whisk the egg whites and fold them into the mixture.

Butter an ovenproof soufflé or gratin dish and fill it with the mixture. Bake in a preheated oven, 190°C, 375°, Gas Mark 5, for 40 minutes or until risen and golden.

———— • ————

The salt fish even found its way into the High Auvergne where, cooked with haricot beans, it was a dish served after a funeral. In the hills of the Cantal they make a rustic kind of fish omelette. The walnut oil gives it a wonderful nutty flavour.

LA MORUE À LA CANTALIENNE
Salt cod with eggs

Serves 4

250–285 g (8–10 oz) salt cod
3 tablespoons walnut oil
3 eggs
3 tablespoons double cream

persillade: 1 tablespoon chopped
parsley and 2 cloves garlic,
chopped
freshly ground black pepper

Soak the fish in an earthenware or porcelain dish for 36 hours, changing the water frequently. Drain it and pat it dry with kitchen paper. Skin and fillet the fish and slice it very thinly.

Heat the walnut oil in a frying pan and when it starts to smoke, tip in the fish. Reduce the heat slightly and stir briskly, turning the fish over and over. It will break up and soften and as you continue to stir, it will become a pulp.

After 15 minutes turn up the heat slightly and pour over the beaten eggs followed by the cream and the *persillade.* Just as the eggs start to set, remove the pan from the heat, sprinkle with pepper and serve while hot.

———— ● ————

The Atlantic coast forms the western boundary of South-West France but, as we have seen, problems of freshness and transportation prevented its produce from reaching most country areas. Bordeaux had none of these difficulties and was able to profit to the maximum from the oysters of Arcachon, the mussels which are farmed all along the west coast from the mouth of the Loire southwards, and the lamprey which thrived in its own river estuary of the Gironde. The culinary repertoire of Bordeaux is largely bourgeois, not peasant in character, so we do not deal with it in this book. But there are recipes that are peasant in origin and derive obviously from the inland styles of the Dordogne and Gascony.

LES MOULES BORDELAISES
Mussels as in Bordeaux

Serves 4

2 kg (4½ lb) small mussels
1 onion, roughly chopped
2 tomatoes, peeled and de-seeded
1 glass dry white wine (Graves)
bouquet garni

salt, pepper
2 or 3 shallots, chopped
1 tablespoon chopped parsley
2 tablespoons fresh breadcrumbs
60 g (2 oz) butter

Scrub and de-beard the mussels, discarding any that are slightly open.

In a large pan sweat the onion and tomato in the wine, together with the bouquet garni and seasonings. Then add the mussels and heat them over a brisk heat for 5 minutes or so. As soon as the shells start to open, move the pan off the heat and start to remove the upper shell of each one. Place the mussels in their half-shell in a large frying pan or casserole and strain over them the wine and liquid left in the first pan.

Add the shallot, parsley, breadcrumbs and butter and stir all together over a brisk flame to cook them a little and brown the crumbs. Serve while very hot.

———— • ————

As with other fish a little acidity accentuates the fleshy, fishy flavour of mussels. And, as we have seen, the combination of pork and trout works well. In the following dish, the salt belly seasons the shellfish and an accompaniment of sorrel purée also brings out the flavour.

LES MOULES À L'OSEILLE
Mussels with sorrel

Serves 4

2 kg (4½ lb) small mussels	1 tablespoon oil
1 glass dry white wine	1 tablespoon chopped parsley
30 g (1 oz) salt belly of pork, diced	sorrel purée (see page 182)
1 clove garlic, chopped	fried bread triangles

Scrub and de-beard the mussels and put them into a large, wide-bottomed pan with the glass of wine. Cover and heat briskly for 5 minutes. As soon as the shells start to open, take out the mussels.

Fry the salt pork and garlic in the oil for 5 minutes and then add the mussels and parsley. Mix all together until heated through but not too long or the mussels will be overcooked.

Have ready the heated sorrel purée and some triangles of fried bread. Serve the mussel mixture on one or two spoonfuls of the sorrel purée, surrounded by the fried bread.

———— • ————

Coquilles St Jacques (scallops) when cooked *à la bordelaise* are prepared in much the same way as the mussels.

LES COQUILLES ST JACQUES À LA BORDELAISE
Scallops as in Bordeaux

Serves 4

12 large scallops
60 g (2 oz) butter
2 shallots, chopped
3 tablespoons armagnac
1 medium-sized tomato, skinned,
   de-seeded and chopped

2 cloves garlic, chopped
salt, pepper
6 tablespoons dry white wine

Clean the scallops if the fishmonger has not done so, cutting off any ligament and black part, and peeling off any skin round the whites. Separate the corals and slice the whites into two rounds. If the corals are large, cut them in half.

Melt the butter in a frying pan large enough to take all the scallops in a single layer and soften the shallots without letting them colour.

Raise the heat under the frying pan and when it starts to sizzle, slide in the white rounds of scallop and let them cook over a moderate heat for a couple of minutes before turning them over. At this point add the corals and continue cooking for another 2 minutes – the secret with scallops is not to overcook them (when they become rubbery).

Heat the brandy, pour over the scallops and set fire to it. When the flames have died down, tip in the chopped tomato and garlic, salt and pepper. Pour over the white wine and bubble all together for 2 or 3 minutes.

With a perforated spoon lift out the scallops and divide them between four heated scallop shells or cocotte dishes and keep warm. Reduce the liquid in the pan, strain over the fish and serve immediately.

———— ● ————

Rougets (red mullet) and fresh sardines, two small salt-water fish landed at Atlantic fishing ports, are prepared similarly. Red mullet, bony, firm-fleshed with a distinctive flavour, is simply fried and coated with a spicy sauce. The Provençal word *escabèche* has come to denote such a sauce.

LES ROUGETS OU SARDINES FRAÎCHES EN ESCABÈCHE

Red mullet or sardines in a spicy sauce

Serves 4

4 red mullet, weighing approx
   150 g (5¼ oz) each or 8 small
   fresh sardines
flour
salt, pepper
3 tablespoons cooking oil
1 onion, sliced

2 cloves garlic, chopped
1 small red pepper deseeded and
   cubed
a pinch of thyme
4 leaves of fresh mint
2 tablespoons vinegar

Clean and scale the red mullet, leaving any roe inside. Roll in seasoned flour and fry in a little cooking oil for 5 minutes or so on each side. Transfer to a heated serving dish and keep warm.

Add a little more oil to the pan and tip in the onion and garlic, red pepper and the herbs. Allow to fry gently until the onion begins to colour, then pour in the vinegar and reduce the sauce a little before pouring over the fish. Serve hot or cold.

———— • ————

Les royans is the Bordelais name for the tiny sardines found in the Atlantic because one of the principal sardine fishing ports is at Royan at the mouth of the Gironde. This small variety is considered the finest, and is at its best simply grilled or fried. A recipe for *tomates farcies aux royans* can be found on page 158.

LES PLATS DE TOUS LES JOURS

THE ACCOUNTS OF country life in the poorer areas of the South-West during the eighteenth and nineteenth centuries reveal that diets were very simple, quantities meagre and, when grain harvests failed from time to time, the peasants were reduced to starvation point, even leaving the countryside for ever.

Everyday cooking showed extreme resourcefulness; meat had to go a long way and could not possibly feature at every meal. Since the farm work was so arduous, particularly at harvest times, the men needed plenty of sustenance. After a bowl of soup in the early morning, there could be a snack at ten, followed by the main meal at noon. In the middle of the afternoon another snack would appear, then in the evening a light supper finished the day. With the narrow range of resources, it was difficult for a cook to ring the changes.

Some areas could not grow wheat for bread-making; the foothills of the Pyrenees, now the Ariège, were too wet, infertile or just too mountainous; the West of the Rouergue, now the Aveyron, then known locally as the *Ségala*, earned its name because only *seigle* (rye) could cope with the acidity of the soil. If millet, buckwheat or maize could be cultivated, they were the peasants' chief source of flour. Even where some wheat was grown this was sold, since it fetched a good price. Bread made from wheat was food only for the *bourgeoisie*, though even for them it was considered a luxury and often kept under lock and key. The poor had somehow to survive largely on a sort of porridge known as *la bouillie*, made from maize flour boiled up with milk.

Throughout the Languedoc they also made *le millas*, a kind of bun made with maize flour and eaten in place of bread. The flour and the liquid – milk, stock or just plain water – were blended together with a 'trident' made from a branch of willow – *un toudeillo*. After cooking, *le millas* was left to cool, then used in numerous ways. Cubed, it was added to soups; sliced, it was toasted with cheese or battered and fried, or plainly fried and eaten with jam or sprinkled with sugar. This was *le millas maigre*. In winter when there would be a nice supply of fat in the cauldron after the killing of a pig or some poultry, it became *le millas gras* and would be sliced and toasted for serving with a *daube* (page 206) or a *civet* (page 248). A further luxury might be some added ham fat, chopped onion and garlic. *Le millas* is now making a come-back on the menus of some of the restaurants that specialize in regional dishes.

LE MILLAS GRAS
Maize dough

Serves 4

60 g (2 oz) lard or goose fat	salt, pepper
575 ml (1 pt) water or milk	125 g (4 oz) maize flour

Bring the fat, water and seasonings to the boil. Sprinkle in the maize flour, stirring briskly to prevent lumps from forming. Reduce the heat and continue stirring while it cooks for 10–15 minutes until the mixture leaves the sides of the pan. It should be quite firm at this stage.

Spread it out on a greased tray or leave as a ball; allow to cool before slicing. Although *le millas* feels rather leaden when cold it becomes much lighter after reheating in the frying pan or the soup. Served as an alternative to potatoes with a stew or as croûtons in a soup it is delicious.

———— • ————

Further north in Quercy and the Périgord an alternative to bread is a dumpling the size of a loaf but lightened with eggs and yeast. It is called *la mique levée*. After it has risen, the large golden ball of dough is poached in a *court-bouillon* and is eaten hot, either with the pork and vegetables from the *court-bouillon*, or as an accompaniment to *daubes* and *civets*. It should be as light as a sponge cake, belying its English title.

LA MIQUE LEVÉE
Dumpling

Serves 8

for the *mique*:
500 g (1 lb) flour
3 eggs
1 heaped tablespoon goose fat or
   lard
1 teaspoon salt
15 g (½ oz) fresh yeast or 7.5 g (¼
   oz) dried yeast
½ teaspoon sugar
150 ml (¼ pt) warm water

for the *court-bouillon*:
1 kg (2 lb) salt pork, belly, hock or
   spare rib
4–5 carrots
4–6 potatoes
3–4 white turnips
4 leeks

Sift the flour into a bowl and break the eggs into a well in the centre. Add the melted fat or lard, and the salt. Dissolve the yeast with the sugar in a little warm water and stir it in, then knead the dough for up to 15 minutes. The mixture will be quite sticky to start with but continue with the kneading until you have a smooth dough. If it becomes too stiff, add a little water – it should be the consistency of a soft bread dough. Roll it into a ball, flour it and leave in a bowl, covered with a cloth, in a warm place for 3–4 hours. It is ready for cooking when it has doubled in size.

Meanwhile cook the salt pork (not pre-soaked) in plenty of water in a *marmite* large enough to hold the *mique*, for 2 hours or more before adding the vegetables. Half an hour later, slip in the dumpling and let it simmer for an hour. Some cooks turn it halfway through, others say it does not matter.

Serve the *mique* hot, divided into portions with two forks – it is not correct local fashion to slice it with a knife.

———— ● ————

Bread made from wheat gradually replaced the other starches as principal foodstuff even more than did potatoes when they arrived on the scene. And it is a tradition which still remains although, as Madame Guinandeau-Franc says in her evocative book *Les Secrets des Fermes en Périgord Noir*

> *Il est loin le temps ou l'on mangeait du pain avec un petit bout de quelque chose: aujourd'hui on mange quelque chose avec un petit bout de pain.*
> (It is a long time since people ate bread together with a little piece of something; nowadays they eat something accompanied by a little piece of bread.)

So it is clear why so much bread still continues to be eaten with meals even when other carbohydrates are included; it is inborn.

Until the Second World War many farms and larger houses had their own bread ovens, often constructed as part of the house or the outbuildings. You can still sometimes spot these stone and tiled ovens, shaped like a bun loaf cut in half and stuck on to the end of a farmhouse or barn. Once a fortnight or so a batch of loaves was baked on the stone floor of the oven which had been heated to a very high temperature by a wood fire previously lit on the same floor. The kneading of huge quantities of dough, sometimes up to 30 kilos or more, was a man's job. Natural leaven was used – a piece of dough being kept from one baking to start the next, or handed on from one farm to another. Most villages had their communal oven where you could take your loaves to be baked, paying a small amount in cash or grain. Other dishes could also be cooked there after breadmaking, while there was still some heat in the oven.

Our farmhouse has its own bread oven and, though still in excellent condition, sadly it is no longer used. We have been told by our neighbours that during the Occupation in the war our oven was quietly put back into use in order to supplement the meagre bread supplies, and that sacks of grain were taken secretly on horseback during the night to the local flour mill to be ground. Only recently we learned that that same mill was still working and the same miller, also a baker and now well into his eighties, was still baking twice a week the most wonderful country bread in the traditional way. Thanks to an introduction via our friend Alain, one day we paid a visit to watch, even help, the miller and his wife prepare and bake a batch of fifty loaves.

The mill sits tucked in a fold of a valley by a small stream, which even at the end of a dry summer had enough water in it to drive the machinery which first ground the wheat into flour and then kneaded 80 kilos of flour into bread dough. After that it was all hard manual work, starting at 4.30 am, later kneading and shaping loaves of various weights, putting them to rise in wicker baskets while the oven was heated to white-hot heat by burning in it brushwood and planks of conifer wood. Raking out the ashes from a fifteen foot square blazing hot oven and then loading in the loaves by means of a long wooden shovel was clearly a hot and exhausting occupation. After less than an hour golden crusty loaves emerged, and the one we brought home, almost too hot to hold, looked so good we cut into it straightaway, although we knew it would keep well for up to a week. (In peasant families, they would resist the temptation to eat the fresh loaf, knowing that too much would disappear quickly, leaving none for the end of the week.)

High bread consumption remains a feature of country life. What has changed is the style of bread. The sturdy, thick-crusted *pain de campagne*, made with leavening, which keeps well, such as our miller was making, can still be found at some *boulangeries*. But there is a fashion now for a lighter-textured dough, the result of modern steam-baking ovens and more refined flours. Loaves made in this style are the long *flûtes* or *baguettes*. At best they can be wonderfully crisp and light when fresh from the oven, but can very quickly dry out and harden.

Over to the east in the Cévennes and north into the Rouergue and the Périgord the hilly country makes grain-growing difficult but sweet chestnut trees grow well; so from October to spring chestnuts were at one time the staple diet. Since medieval times another source of carbohydrate has been the various kinds of haricot bean. Vegetables as we know them, apart from these beans, were not grown until the end of the last century. It was towards the end of the eighteenth century that the potato made its appearance, revolutionizing the meals of those who could not afford white bread. Potatoes appeared on the table at least once a day, boiled, braised, mashed or whatever, and in those years when grain harvests failed were an invaluable substitute. In an account of life in the Rouergue, *Les Mangeurs de Rouergue*, a local reminisces about what his parents had told him of the hard conditions they remembered in the 1860s and 1870s:

> Ah yes, there was much misery at that time. My mother often told me the story of how the people near her gave away one of their fields in exchange for a loaf of bread. . . . You know that they used to eat more bread than vegetables, or one but not the other because at that time people grew very few vegetables. One grew a few in the garden and some beans in the field but the principal food one had was potato, a little pasta – macaroni or whatever, perhaps some rice, and that was our chief sustenance in the way of vegetables.
>
> *Les Mangeurs de Rouergue*, A. Merlin & A.Y. Beaujour (Duculot, 1978, p. 114)

If you grew corn or rye, and kept cows and chickens to provide the milk and eggs, then you could make various kinds of *galettes*, solid pancakes, which could easily be carried to the fields as snacks. The fillings would depend on what was in the larder or the vegetable garden. Fillings wrapped in pastry were an alternative, slightly more ambitious and obviously needing more time to prepare.

Some of the dishes which follow have now become well-known specialities of their area. Originally they would have been the only dish of the meal. When times became more prosperous or when a special occasion warranted *un grand repas*, they were served as an additional course before the meat. And now, happily, one or two have found their way into restaurants, appearing on the *goût du terroir* menus.

The next recipe shows how potato cakes can be elaborated into a more sustaining dish. It uses local cheese made in the Cantal in the Auvergne. Its nearest equivalent in Britain is Cheddar and, like Cheddar, it is made in varying strengths.

LES CRIQUES DE GRAMAT
Potato cakes with ham and cheese

Gramat is a sprawling market town built in the pale local limestone on the top of the Causse de Gramat in the Lot. Use floury old potatoes – waxy ones have too much moisture and alter the texture of the cakes which then tend to stick to the pan.

Serves 2

350 g (12 oz) floury potatoes
100 g (3½ oz) *jambon de campagne*,
   finely diced
60 g (2 oz) grated cheese, Cantal,
   Gruyère or other strong-
   flavoured kind

1 clove garlic, chopped
salt, pepper
1 large egg
flour
goose or pork fat for frying

Grate the peeled, raw potatoes on a medium grater over a clean tea towel. Pat them dry and transfer to a mixing bowl. Add the diced ham, cheese, garlic and seasonings. Lightly beat the egg and stir into the mixture until you have a softish ball. Divide this into four balls, then flatten them to a thickness of just under 2.5 cm (1 in) having first floured your hands. Dip the cakes into more flour then fry on both sides in shallow fat until they are golden brown and crisp on the outside – about 8 minutes each side – but soft and light inside.

These quantities make a good main lunch dish for two, with a salad.

——— • ———

Cantal or Laguiole cheese (for more details of these see the chapter on cheeses) is called *la tomme fraîche* when it is at its unfermented stage. The town of Murat in the Auvergne is the centre of production for the *tomme fraîche de Cantal* while the *tomme fraîche de Laguiole* comes from the Aubrac further south. Before it has fermented the cheese is white and sponge-like in appearance with a slightly sour cream taste, and it melts easily when heated. It is made during the summer months and cheese shops sell it from then on into winter. The nearest English substitute would be Lancashire.

La tomme is an essential part of three dishes from the upland prairies of the Auvergne; these are *l'aligot, la truffade and la patranque.*

The most famous is *l'aligot*, perhaps rightly so. This wonderful creamy potato and cheese purée is often served at village fêtes, marriages and other festivities as a course on its own. As it is hard work to beat the mixture, this is traditionally the job of the man of the house, sometimes even assisted by another strong man. There are numerous stories concerning its correct preparation just as there are for making mayonnaise, one of which is that the mixture should always be stirred in the same direction.

L'ALIGOT
Potato, cheese and garlic purée

Serves 4

700 g (1½ lb) floury potatoes	2-3 cloves garlic, chopped
60 g (2 oz) butter	salt, pepper
4 tablespoons double cream	250 g (½lb) *la tomme fraîche de Cantal*,
4 tablespoons milk	cut into thin slices

Boil or steam the potatoes in their skins then peel them. Mash them in the pan in which you will continue the preparation of the dish as finely as possible to a smooth purée.

Over a low heat beat in first the butter, then the cream and milk and keep beating until the mixture is really light. Do not be put off by the time and effort required. Stir in the garlic and seasoning, still over a low heat and when the purée seems heated through, drop in the slices of cheese all at once. Continue beating and lifting the mixture as if you were adding egg whites to a soufflé. The cheese has to melt – you will notice that at a certain point the purée becomes a little tacky and shiny and comes away from the sides of the pan in an almost pouring consistency. It is ready and should be eaten immediately.

If there is any of the purée left over it makes delicious fried potato cakes. It is sometimes served with a grilled Toulouse sausage, an *andouillette* (sausage made with offal) or even a pig's foot.

Although it is not authentic, a non-stick pan is quite an asset in the preparation of *l'aligot*.

LA TRUFFADE
Potato cake with pork and cheese

La truffade is a large potato cake bound together with melted cheese. When bread is used instead of potato it is known as *la patranque*.

Serves 4

6 medium-sized potatoes
2 tablespoons pork fat
125 g (4 oz) fat belly of pork or
   green streaky bacon

175–200 g (6–7 oz) *la tomme fraîche de Cantal* or, as best substitute,
   Lancashire cheese
salt, pepper

Peel and slice the potatoes thinly and dry them well. Melt the pork fat in a large frying pan and soften the pork or bacon, cut into small strips or cubes. Then arrange the potatoes in circles on top, seasoning each layer. Cover with a large lid and allow to cook gently in their own steam for 20 minutes.

Meanwhile cut up the cheese into strips and when the potatoes are cooked, crush them with a fork. Add the cheese, mixing it together with the potatoes and continue stirring until it is blended into the purée. If there is too much fat in the pan, remove any excess and then leave, uncovered, for a few minutes without stirring so that the underneath colours and crispens.

To serve, tip out upside down on to a plate – you should have a huge golden cake.

LE GRATIN LANDAIS
Potato cake with ham

Serves 4

This is made with Bayonne ham, hence its name, but any *jambon de campagne* can equally well be used. Since they are each highly salted, no further salt is used in the recipe.

60 g (2 oz) butter
700 g (1½ lb) potatoes
4 slices raw ham
125 g (4 oz) Cantal cheese (or
   Cheddar)

300 ml (½ pt) milk
1 egg
pepper

Coat a large gratin dish with butter.

Peel the potatoes and slice them into thin rounds. Remove the rind from the ham and cut it into pieces which will make whole layers in the dish. Grate the cheese. Beat the egg into the milk in a bowl.

Preheat your oven to 180°C, 350°F, Gas Mark 4.

Line the dish with a layer of the potato, cover with a layer of ham, then a coating of about one-third of the cheese. Season with pepper. Continue with another layer of each of the ingredients. Finish with a layer of potato, then pour over the egg and milk mixture. Finally sprinkle over the remaining cheese, season with more pepper and dot with pieces of butter. Place in oven and bake for 1–1¼ hours.

●

There is nothing new about the use of pasta in French cuisine since it was brought to France from Italy at the time of the Italian Renaissance. But it was largely regarded as a luxury item, except that, as the old peasant in *Les Mangeurs de Rouergue* recounted, it had to replace flour and potatoes during bad times.

The farmer's wife would add flavour to it with home-produced garlic and eggs, while the more prosperous would dress it up with the juices from a roast, or, for special occasions, with the added richness of the fat which surrounds a conserved *foie gras*. Our neighbour, Madame Miquel, explained to us this traditional dish.

LES PÂTES À L'ANCIENNE
Pasta with garlic and eggs

Serves 2

250 g (8 oz) macaroni	3 eggs
oil	1–2 tablespoon chopped parsley
garlic	salt and freshly ground pepper

Cook the macaroni in salted water with a dash of oil in it. At the same time hard-boil the eggs. Shell them and separate the whites from the yolks. Chop up the whites with some garlic and fry them gently in oil in a large frying pan with the parsley.

Mash the yolks with a fork and dilute them with a little water to make a cream. When the macaroni is cooked, drain it well, put it into the frying pan and mix it with the egg white, garlic and parsley. Tip in the creamed yolks, turn it all together, season well – especially with pepper – and serve immediately.

Macaroni cheese is found in every beginner's cookery book in England, and it is also a way of preparing the pasta here in France, at any rate for those with access to an oven. In the Périgord and in Les Landes they make a richer gratin of it by adding ham, eggs and tomato.

LE MACARONI AU GRATIN
Macaroni cheese

Serves 4

250 g (8 oz) macaroni
1 litre (1¾ pt) stock
250 g (8 oz) Cantal cheese, grated
250 g (8 oz) slice of *jambon de campagne*, diced

2 egg yolks
4 tablespoons fresh tomato sauce (see page 190)
salt, pepper

Cook the macaroni in the boiling, seasoned stock. Put a gratin dish in the oven to warm. Drain the macaroni, then mix into it three-quarters of the grated cheese and all the ham, moistening it with a little of the stock. Check the seasoning. Whisk the egg yolks together, and stir into the pasta with 4 tablespoonfuls of fresh tomato sauce. Sprinkle the rest of the cheese on top and put under the grill for 5 minutes to heat through and to brown.

Serve very hot and hand round a black pepper grinder for each to pepper his own.

———— • ————

In those parts of the region – the old Rouergue, Quercy and towards the Cantal – where corn would grow, the availability of flour meant that omelettes could be expanded into pancakes. They were more substantial and thus appropriate for the often harder climate. They did not need as many eggs as an omelette and would feed more. So these solid pancakes became 'the poor man's omelette'. One of the local sayings is that a mean woman is one who makes a *pascade* for the whole family with one egg. This plain pancake was served instead of bread for a mid-afternoon summer snack with a piece of cheese, or it was sweetened with sugar to make a dessert. In the Rouergue it is known as *la pascade*, in the Auvergne as *la farinette* and in the south of the Aveyron where buckwheat and rye grew, it is called *la pescajoun* or *la galette de blé noir*. The addition of the flour bound the egg into a 'cake' as the English name implies so that it could be turned in the pan to brown the other side. The skill and pride in tossing the pancake was such that a mother only relinquished the role to her daughter when she was no longer strong enough to wield the frying pan.

LE POUNTI
Pork, spinach and prunes in batter

Pounti is a filling country dish from the Auvergne which is baked in the oven, and would originally have been made on bread-making day. Its ingredients depend on what comes to hand, particularly in the way of meat, e.g. cold minced pork, provided it is a mixture of lean and fat, or pure pork sausagemeat. Meat might not always have been added in the poorer homes, being replaced by prunes. However, the pork and prune combination, a well-tried and successful one, is definitely the making of this dish.

    Pounti is served nowadays in Auvergnat restaurants as an entrée – how we first tasted it at Les Remparts in Salers in the Cantal. In the past *pounti* would, with a bowl of soup, have constituted a meal in itself in many homes.

Serves 4

for the filling:
125 g (4 oz) prunes
125 g (4 oz) *jambon de campagne*
125 g (4 oz) fatty fresh (or salt)
   belly of pork or streaky bacon
125 g (4 oz) chard or spinach
60 g (2 oz) onion
1 clove garlic
2 tablespoons chopped parsley
salt, pepper

for the batter:
100 g (3½ oz) flour
3 eggs
300 ml (½ pt) milk
salt, pepper

Soak the prunes in some *tisane* or hot tea for an hour.

    Make the batter by blending the eggs and milk into the flour. Add seasoning and leave to stand for an hour.

    Put the meat, greens, onion and garlic through the fine blade of your mincer or chop it all very finely by hand. Add the herbs and seasoning and mix all together. Drain the prunes, stone them and roughly chop the flesh.

Butter an oblong (or even round) tin or pie dish – a small bread tin is ideal. Do not use one too large as the *pounti* has to fill its mould to a height of 5 cm (2 in). Cut and fit a piece of buttered aluminium foil into the base of the container to make it easier to turn the *pounti* out after cooking.

Now mix together the batter and filling and tip half of it into the tin. Spread the prunes in a layer on top of this, and cover with the rest of the mixture.

Cook in a preheated oven (200°C, 400°F, Gas Mark 6) for 15 minutes, then reduce the heat to 180°C, 350°F, Gas Mark 4 and leave to cook for another 45 minutes. It is cooked when the top starts to colour and it shrinks a little from the sides of the tin. Turn it out and serve in slices.

Pounti can be eaten hot, cold or reheated – fry the slices in butter.

———— • ————

Another very rustic dish which was sometimes prepared for bread-making day is *tripoux*. It was, perhaps, not an everyday dish since you would make it only if you were killing a sheep. And while it makes use of the stomach, and so in theory is perhaps not to everyone's taste, it is a particular speciality in the Auvergne, the Cévennes and the Rouergue – where you might also find it under the name of *les trenels*. Tripe lovers will become addicted. The stomach lining itself is cut up into 10 cm x 15 cm (4 in x 6 in) rectangles, which are filled with a stuffing of diced meat consisting of the rest of the tripe, the sheep's trotters, some ham or belly of pork, and of course garlic and parsley. The little *paquets* are rolled up and tied and then braised very slowly with the usual ingredients which make up a savoury sauce – pork rind, pig's foot, wine, onion, carrot and tomato – for up to seven or eight hours. *Les tripoux* were made in large quantity, and cooked overnight in the bread oven as it cooled. Nowadays you can buy them already prepared in tins or sealed jars from some of the *charcutiers*; they are excellent and merely need to be heated through. Some restaurants in the Rouergue serve them as an entrée. There are recipes which include veal tripe as well, but traditionally *tripoux* was made from the sheep's stomach.

The special cooking pot for pies and cakes – *la tourtière* – has already been described in the chapter on farmyard fowls (page 54). It held *les tourtes* which were usually chicken or meat pies, the fillings depending on the season or the larder. The simpler ones were *la tourte au pauvre* where the meat was sausagemeat, wrapped in a tomato, olive and mushroom sauce (it sounds as if the poor man did quite well), or *la tourtière aux noix* which was for meatless days and was filled with walnuts and breadcrumbs. There is also this relative of the Cornish pasty:

L'ÉTOUFFE CHRÉTIEN
Sausagemeat and potato pasty

Serves 4

350 g (¾ lb) *pâte brisée* (*see page 258*)
350 g (¾ lb) potatoes
salt, pepper
1 clove garlic, chopped

1 tablespoon chopped parsley
350 g (¾ lb) pure pork sausagemeat
1 egg, beaten

Line a greased 20 cm (8 in) pie dish with half the pastry and fill the bottom with the peeled potatoes, cut into rounds. Season them and sprinkle over the garlic and parsley. Cover with a layer of sausagemeat and season again.

Roll out a lid from the rest of the pastry and after brushing the edges of the lower pastry case with egg, cover the pie with the pastry to make a lid, trimming round the rim and sealing the edges together. Cut vents in the lid before painting the top with beaten egg.

Cook in a preheated oven, 220°C, 425°F, Gas Mark 7, for 45 minutes.

●

In the Périgord there is the delicious *tourtière aux salsifis*, given on page 54, and down south in the pig country you find an equally unusual but less extravagant pie –

LA TOURTE LANGUEDOCIENNE
Pork and apple pie

This is a fairly near relative of the Leicestershire pork and apple pie, though the addition of fresh thyme and bay leaf does make an important and delicious difference. The bay leaf chops easily with an *hachoir* – the two-handled crescent-shaped rocking chopper.

Serves 4

350 g (¾ lb) *pâte brisée* (*see page 258*)
350 g (¾ lb) pork fillet
350 g (¾ lb) semi-sweet apples,
   Reinettes (or Cox's)

½ teaspoon fresh thyme
1 large fresh bay leaf
2 eggs and a little milk
salt, pepper, sugar

Roll out half of the pastry and line a greased 20 cm (8 in) pie plate. Preheat your oven to 220°C, 425°F, Gas Mark 7. Dice the pork fillet as finely as you can – do not mince it as this alters the finished texture of the pie. Peel and quarter the apples and slice them finely.

Put a first layer of half the apples into the pastry case, cover with the diced pork, season and add chopped thyme and bay leaf. Cover with the rest of the apples, sprinkle with a little sugar. Beat up one whole egg with the white of the second one plus a little milk, salt and pepper, and pour this over the filling.

Roll out the remainder of the pastry. Brush the rim of the pastry case with a little of the remaining yolk of egg mixed with a little water, and place the rolled-out pastry on top. Cut off any excess and press the edges together. Cut two or three ventilation holes in the top and brush over with the egg yolk. Cook in the preheated oven on a baking tray for 40–45 minutes.

Double quantities will fill a 30 cm (12 in) flan case. A tomato sauce (page 190) goes well with this tart which can also be made in a grander version using puff pastry. On the other hand, it tastes equally good if cold pork, left over from a roast, is used instead of fresh pork fillet.

It can also be made with a piece of *confit d'oie* – becoming *la tourtière d'oie gasconne*.

LE CHOU FARCI
Stuffed cabbage

This is a traditional dish of the more hilly areas of the South-West towards the Auvergne. In England we consider the cabbage as one of the more mundane vegetables – redolent of school dinners. In France *le chou farci* is something of a treat, combining meat and vegetables. It used to be specially prepared on Saturday night and cooked slowly on the corner of the fire next morning while the family went to Mass.

Serves 4

1 firm green cabbage, weighing about 575 g (1¼ lb)

for the stuffing:
250 g (½ lb) pure pork sausagemeat
250 g (½ lb) minced veal
50 g (2 oz) pork fat
1 clove garlic
2 shallots
30 g (1 oz) breadcrumbs, soaked in
   milk and squeezed dry
2 tablespoons chopped parsley
½ tablespoon chopped chives
salt, pepper, *quatre-épices*
1 large egg

for braising the cabbage:
1 piece *couenne* (fresh pork skin)
1 carrot
1 onion
bouquet garni
125 ml (4 fl oz) dry white wine
125 ml (4 fl oz) stock or water
salt, pepper

Cut off any very coarse or damaged outer leaves of the cabbage, and cut away any thick parts of the centre stalk and white stems of the outer leaves but take care not to allow the leaves to fall off. Plunge the cabbage into a bowl or pan of acidulated water for 15 minutes to kill off any insects that may be inside.

Bring a large pan of water to the boil, immerse the cabbage in it, then leave it, barely simmering, for 8–10 minutes, or steam it for this length of time. This is to soften the leaves so they are easier to manipulate. Drain the cabbage and leave upside down to cool while you prepare the stuffing.

Put all the ingredients except the egg into a bowl and mix well. Beat the egg and stir it in until you have a well-blended stuffing. You will then need a large piece of muslin or cheese cloth to wrap round the stuffed cabbage. Fill the cabbage with the stuffing – a simple but fascinating operation. Place the cabbage, stalk end down, on a board and starting with the very outer leaf begin to fold each one back so that they lie virtually flat on the board. Slowly the cabbage will take on the appearance of an overblown green rose.

Starting with the centre, push teaspoonfuls of the stuffing inside each leaf and press the leaf round it to reshape the cabbage into a ball. Work your way round, holding the filled leaves in place with one hand. When all the leaves have been filled and you have a larger round cabbage again, slip it into the middle of the muslin cloth, pull it up and tie firmly so that the cloth gives support to the cabbage.

Line the bottom of a tall braising pan with the piece of pork skin, fat side down, and cover this with the chopped onion and carrot. Fry these for five minutes or so on a gentle heat so that the pork fat melts a little, then place the cabbage on top with the bouquet garni. Pour over the wine and water and bring gently to simmering point. Cover and cook very gently for 3 hours. There should not be a lot of liquid left at the end.

Variations of this dish include chestnuts or prunes in the stuffing.

LE CHOU À L'AUVERGNATE
Cabbage with ham, cream and cheese

Here the cabbage is taken apart and the leaves layered with ham, cheese and cream. It has a breadcrumb topping and is baked until it is golden.

Serves 6

1 large cabbage
250 g (½ lb) grated cheese, Cantal
   or Cheddar
400 ml (¾ pt) single cream
250 g (½ lb) *jambon de campagne* or
   lean salt belly of pork

salt, pepper, nutmeg
fresh breadcrumbs
60 g (2 oz) butter

Cut out the centre stalk of the cabbage and separate the leaves. Blanch, then drain them well.

Grease an ovenproof gratin dish and fill it with layers of the cabbage leaves, grated cheese, cream, cubes of ham or pork, all seasoned with not too much salt, plenty of pepper and a little grated nutmeg. Finish with a layer of cream and sprinkle the breadcrumbs over the top. Dot with butter and put into a preheated oven (180°C, 350°F, Gas Mark 4) for half an hour, then raise the heat to 200°C, 400° F, Gas Mark 6, for the final 15 minutes or so until the top is golden.

———— • ————

Continuing the idea of the all-in-one dish, here are two more recipes for stuffed vegetables, this time tomatoes. The large Marmande and St Pierre tomatoes that are grown throughout the region are essential, just as they are to make a tomato salad or a tomato sauce. Both varieties have plenty of flesh, hardly any white core, and not too much liquid. The flavour is very sweet and fruity; a fresh tomato sauce made with these, plus a little onion, parsley and garlic, has to be tasted to be believed (page 190). A keen gardener can grow his or her own Marmandes from seed – these are available from some seed merchants, or can be brought back from a trip to France.

LES TOMATES FARCIES À L'ALBIGEOISE
Stuffed tomatoes

Serves 4

4 large tomatoes
350 g (¾lb) sausage meat
2 thick slices bread, crustless
1 small onion, chopped
2 cloves garlic, chopped
2 tablespoons chopped parsley

1 slice *jambon de campagne* or 2
   rashers unsmoked bacon
1 egg yolk
salt, pepper
pork or goose fat

Cut the tomatoes in half, score the flesh in several directions with a sharp knife and sprinkle them with salt. Leave the salt to dissolve slightly then invert the halves to allow them to drain.

Prepare a stuffing with the sausage meat: soak the bread in water then squeeze it dry before adding it to the meat together with the onion, garlic and parsley, diced ham or bacon, seasonings and the beaten egg yolk. Mix very well.

Scoop out as much of the seeds and liquor as possible from the halved tomatoes and fill the cavities with the stuffing. Place them on an oiled baking dish, and dot with a piece of bacon or ham fat, or failing that some lard or goose fat. Cook in the oven, pre-heated to 190°C, 375°F, Gas Mark 5, for 45 minutes.

These make an excellent light lunch or supper dish by themselves or a good accompaniment for a roast chicken or leg of lamb.

LES TOMATES FARCIES AUX ROYANS
Tomatoes stuffed with sardines

Another way of stuffing tomatoes is with the tiny, fresh sardines called *royans*, found in the Bay of Biscay.

Serves 4

4 large tomatoes	4 tablespoons chopped parsley
4 medium-sized fresh sardines	60 g (2 oz) butter
2 shallots	salt, pepper

To make replaceable 'hats', cut a thick slice crossways from the top of each tomato. Empty the juice and pips and inside each tomato crush to a pulp with a fork the remainder of the flesh. Season them with salt and pepper, replace the 'hats' and cook in a buttered dish in a moderate oven (180°C, 350°F, Gas Mark 4) for 20 minutes.

While they are cooking, clean the sardines and dry them. Grill them until they are cooked, fillet them and mash the fillets. Chop the shallots and parsley finely, add them to the sardines and cream the mixture with the butter. Season it.

Remove the tomatoes from the oven, fill them with the fish stuffing, replace the tops and return to the oven for a further 10 minutes to heat the stuffing through and glaze the tomatoes.

LES CROQUETTES DE POULET
Chicken croquettes

We first tasted these in Millau, the glove-making town on the river Tarn, and we have since found a version made with veal down in Les Landes. The meat has to be pre-cooked, so it is a way of using any left-overs.

Serves 4

350 g (¾ lb) chicken meat
1 medium-sized onion
salt, pepper
bouquet garni
400 ml (¾ pt) very thick béchamel
  sauce

1 egg
dried breadcrumbs
60 g (2 oz) butter
1 tablespoon cooking oil

Cook the chicken with the onion, seasonings and bouquet garni. Then mince it together with the onion.

Blend the minced chicken into the béchamel. Set it aside to cool, then form this mixture into small cylindrical-shaped croquettes. Dip them into the beaten egg and roll in the crumbs.

Heat the butter and oil in a frying pan and fry the croquettes, rolling them over, until they are crisp and golden.

Serve with a fresh tomato sauce (page 190).

LES LÉGUMES

N O VISIT TO South-West France ever fails to re-create the initial enchantment of shopping for vegetables at the market, feasting the eyes on neatly arranged bunches, bulging boxes or just a few bundles of produce, all displayed with loving care by the smallholders who have grown them with skill and affection, picking only the best to sell. Monsieur and Madame Testas, for example, an old couple who live in the valley below us, go to market each week with, say, a basket of walnuts, three or four fresh vegetables, some heads of garlic or a few dozen eggs, delighted to chat to two English people because a niece of theirs once went to stay in Littlehampton. Further along the same trestle table in the market place a furious woman chastises a rabbit in a basket for stealing a stick of celery from the stallholder next door while her own chicken is demolishing a lettuce displayed too near it. Market day shows the local populatation at its most gregarious and noisy.

In spring there are small, fat pods of peas, bunches of tiny carrots or white turnips, piles of sorrel or spinach. In summer there are glistening heaps of fresh green salad, bouquets of radishes and herbs, bright red tomatoes and tiny *haricots verts* no thicker than shoelaces. These are followed in autumn, alongside nuts and mushrooms, by the green-topped celery and *blettes* (chard), enormous snowy cauliflowers, plump white beans in their pods and massive orange pumpkins. When you have no *potager* of your own, the attraction of a market proves irresistible: all local shopping has to be planned round the market days so that fresh provisions can be stored away in larder or cellar, and there is no better way to be plunged into local life than by touring these stalls, studying which vegetables, salad or fruit are *en primeur* and which *en pleine saison* before buying.

When country towns developed, they spread round a central square; sometimes arcaded to give protection from sun or rain; sometimes featuring a covered area, a handsome pillared and roofed *halle* (market hall). Some of these *halles* still standing in the South-West date from the thirteenth century. Where there is no covered hall, markets still take place in the open, in the middle of *la place*. After the Revolution, as these towns developed, the townspeople's living standards rose. They created demand for fresh farm produce: poultry, eggs and cheese. So the peasant women started coming to the towns weekly – as opposed to the previous tradition of selling their produce at the occasional fairs which took place during the year on feast days.

These market places provided a shopping centre; the poor bought and sold in small quantities on a weekly basis. And markets came to serve a dual function by catering also to a social need as the exchange of news became as interesting as the sale of goods. Rural people would otherwise see few neighbours or relatives throughout the year except at the fairs. These larger fairs were periodic and offered a wider choice than only food – cattle, clothing, tools and household utensils – and as cattle-rearing increased, so did their importance.

Over the years the markets and fairs have lost their distinctive roles, and *le marché* and *la foire* now differ in size and frequency rather than purpose. More recently, the stricter control of meat slaughtering and marketing as well as the guaranteed markets provided by the EC has reduced the importance of cattle sales, but the fresh vegetable, fruit and dairy products are more than ever sold at markets throughout the region. Toulouse, for example, has its daily vegetable and fruit market, which extends a good half-mile along the pavement of the Boulevard de Strasbourg, right in the middle of town. Brive-la-Gaillarde has boldly converted a park in its centre to provide a huge market place – la Place du 14 juillet – with a covered area for stall-holders and ample car parking beneath. Many of the larger towns have some kind of covered market, open daily, and these are most sensibly marked on the town maps in the red Michelin Guide. (Would that this Guide still listed the principal market days as it used to do!)

On market day the country people arrive early in the morning, by car, bus or even on foot pushing a handcart, bringing everything they have produced which is surplus to their own needs, whether it be cattle, poultry, eggs, cheese, vegetables or fruit. The farmers congregate around the livestock whilst their wives set up stall in the central market place with their produce of *basse-cour* or *potager*. The care and enthusiasm with which they part with their produce demonstrate their attitude to life as they know it; their unassuming pride in cultivating to a high standard.

You may not pay much less than in the greengrocer's or the supermarket and the standards of hygiene may be a little primitive but more often than not you are buying *les produits de la ferme*, produce of a certain individuality and quality . And you may find items that never appear in the shops – rare and delicate mushrooms like *coulemelles* or *trompettes de la mort*, large, fat *cèpes* or the new season's fresh white haricot beans already podded and chestnuts already *blanchies*. There are many local specialities which can only be sold in small quantities – to buy some of these you must get to market really early before they are snapped up. The list is mouth-watering: wild strawberries or medlars, local honey or goats' cheese, fresh herbs, dried leaves to makes *tisanes*, home-made *gâteaux*, country-baked bread, fresh walnuts and chestnuts, garlic, home-reared rabbits, chickens and ducks, sometimes dressed but more often still alive. And in season, lovely free-range eggs with real feathers and dirt still clinging to them.

During the last hundred years standards of living have substantially improved, with a higher protein diet matched by a demand for more vegetables. But at the same time, in the agriculturally poorer *terrains*, right up to the Second World War, there remained a distinction between the carnivorous townspeople and the vegetarian peasants. The latter still relied on potatoes and onions, with carrots and beans as Sunday treats. Local patois nicknames for the occupants of various villages on the *causses* of the eastern Rouergue at the beginning of this century translate as 'the bean eaters' or 'the onion eaters'. And even nowadays, an old farmer living across the valley from us, eating out with us one market day recently, chose after *le potage*, *le pot-au-feu* followed by *le bifsteck* followed by *le fromage*; for him it was still a real treat to indulge in such a non-stop parade of protein.

By the end of World War I, in the alluvial river valleys where irrigation was easy, the range of vegetables widened. The beans, potatoes and cabbages which were winter staples were augmented by salsify, celery and cauliflowers, while in spring there came fresh peas and sorrel and in summer, green beans, salads and tomatoes, artichokes and pumpkins. But local tradition dies hard here and potatoes still play a principal part as an accompanying vegetable, as do the true *légumes* – the botanical family of the bean and the pea.

LES FÈVES

One of the oldest vegetables known to the region was the broad bean, its position only diminishing with the arrival of the haricot bean and the potato. In spite of this, broad beans are still widely grown and particularly esteemed in the Dordogne and the Périgord, where you will find a row or more in most *potagers* and where they are made into wonderful spring soups, *râgouts* and purées.

Ideally, broad beans should be picked when they are so young that the pod is little thicker than your middle finger. At this size or smaller they are eaten pod and all, cooked round a joint after a preliminary blanching. Or the tiny beans are eaten raw as an hors d'oeuvre *à la croque-sel*, out of their pod but just as they are, each one dipped into the salt cellar for a little seasoning. At this size they taste as sweet as peas. Left to grow larger, you may have to peel away the outer skin of the bean itself, which becomes coarse even after cooking although it does have a more concentrated flavour. If you peel off the outer skin after blanching for a minute or two, it is a simple operation. It is this skin which turns the liquid in which it is cooked a dark colour so some prefer to peel it off for this reason too. Several leaves of sorrel cooked with the beans will prevent this blackness. The French put a sprig of fresh *sarriette* (savory) in with broad beans to bring out the flavour while the English, not knowing this herb so well, use parsley. *Sarriette* is often found growing in among broad beans, looking like a tougher kind of tarragon. It is a pungent herb and should be used with caution.

This recipe was collected many years ago from the small restaurant run by the late Mme Délibié-Veyret in the tiny village of Marquay in the Dordogne. So parochial are the food repertoires of different areas that when we offered this soup to dear friends and neighbours of ours it was described as '*pas mal du tout, cette soupe anglaise*'. And the author of this comment had three helpings.

LE POTAGE AUX FÈVES
Broad bean soup

Serves 6

2 large onions, finely chopped
3 carrots, finely chopped
2½ tablespoons goose fat
1.75 l (3 pt) chicken or veal stock
6 slices *saucisson sec* or 3 rashers lean
    unsmoked bacon, chopped

2 cloves garlic, chopped
2 tablespoons flour
salt, pepper
1 kg (2¼ lb) broad beans, in the pod
3 tablespoons chopped parsley

Soften the onions and carrots over a low flame in a tablespoonful of the fat for 5 minutes before adding the stock. Cover and simmer gently for half an hour. Meanwhile sauter the sausage or bacon gently in a separate pan in the rest of the fat. Add the garlic and stir in the flour so that you have a thick paste. Stir in some of the soup liquid little by little until it is thin enough to pour back into the soup. Bring back to the boil, add the peeled beans (see above) and chopped parsley and simmer gently for as long as it takes to cook the beans. Don't allow them to overcook and go to pieces.

———— • ————

La soupe aux fèves à l'ancienne – a more substantial affair – was prepared at haymaking when it was made at breakfast time and kept hot until midday, tucked under the eiderdown – the fire was not kept in while everyone was out working.

LA SOUPE AUX FÈVES À L'ANCIENNE
Broad bean soup with preserved pork

Serves 6

1 medium-sized onion, chopped
1 leek, chopped
1 tablespoon goose fat
1 kg (2¼ lb) broad beans, in the pod
250 g (½ lb) potatoes
500 g (1 lb) *confit de porc* (page 69)
small piece of *saucisson sec*
sarriette

125 g (4 oz) salt belly of pork, finely chopped
3 cloves garlic, chopped
2 tablespoons parsley, chopped
2 more tablespoons goose fat
1½ tablespoons flour
6 thick slices bread
salt, pepper

Before you start it is important to choose the right pans. Unless they are enamelled or otherwise highly glazed, the soup will discolour and even then it is advisable to add a few sorrel leaves to help preserve the fresh green colour. You may also like to remove the outer skins from the beans after podding.

In the first pan, melt a tablespoonful of goose fat and soften the onion and leek in it for 10 minutes or so without allowing them to colour. Add 850 ml (1½ pt) of water and while this is coming to the boil, pod the beans and chop the potatoes into dice, then add them to the boiling water. Put in the *confit* and *saucisson*, some salt and pepper and a little fresh *sarriette*, reduce the heat and simmer very gently for an hour and a half.

Towards the end of the cooking time, take your second pan, which should for preference be an earthenware *marmite* in which the soup is to be served.

Warm it on a protective mat over a moderate heat. Melt in it the other two tablespoonfuls of goose fat and sauter the salt pork, the garlic and parsley. When they have taken on some colour, add the flour and cook for a few minutes. Now start to transfer the contents of the first pan to the *marmite*, spooning in the liquid a little at a time to avoid lumps, then tip in the solids. Stir well together, check for seasoning and allow to simmer for 10 minutes.

To serve, either *tremper* the entire contents over the slices of bread in the serving bowls, or the meats may be taken out and served as a second course with a salad or other vegetable.

———— ● ————

Another haymaking recipe is:

LE RAGOÛT DE FÈVES
Casserole of broad beans

Serves 4

1.5 kg (3 lb) broad beans, in the pod	pinch of sugar
1 tablespoon goose fat	1 tablespoon flour
60 g (2 oz) salt pork, diced	300 ml (½ pt) water
8 small white onions, weighing not	salt, pepper
more than 30 g (1 oz) each	pinch of *sarriette*

Pod the beans. If they are old or large, it is well worth the trouble of removing the inner skins.

Melt the fat in a pan which has a good fitting lid and cook the diced salt pork in it gently for 5 minutes or so. Add the beans, then the whole onions and a pinch of sugar and cook all together over a moderate flame for another 5 minutes. Stir in the flour and amalgamate well, add the water little by little until you have a smooth sauce. Stir in some seasoning and the *sarriette*. Cover the pan and cook as gently as possible for half an hour or so.

LES HARICOTS

When the English think of French beans they usually picture *les haricots verts*, the tender, slim green pods less than 15 cm (6 in) long. But *le haricot vert* has been bred to be like this and is just one of the larger family of French beans – *phaseolus vulgaris* – which gives a range of beans not only through the summer months but throughout the year. The season begins with *les haricots verts*. By nature their pods can become hard and stringy quite quickly so they have to be picked really young, though modern horticulture has bred stringless versions (*sans fil*). There are in addition *les haricots mangetout* which come with both green (*vert*) or yellow (known as *beurre*) pods which do not grow leathery or stringy as they develop. Their pods are flatter in form, and although they lack the strength of flavour of *haricots verts*, they can better survive heat and drought. Then there is a variety grown for its white bean inside the pod, usually dried for winter use – known correctly as *les haricots blancs* but more often just referred to as *les haricots*.

When the tiny *haricots verts* first appear, they fetch the highest prices; *en primeur* as the first of the season are described, coming from around Villeneuve in the *département* of the Lot. Even later in the season these finer, smaller beans are carefully sorted and sold separately at a higher figure. Whatever their size, they make the ideal accompaniment to a slice of roast leg of lamb or an *enchaud* of pork. The simplest preparation is the best for the most delicate specimens, simmered in salted water or, better still, steamed until they are *al dente*, and then finished in butter or oil and sprinkled with a *persillade*. However in the Quercy and further south, when they are served as a vegetable it is customary to finish the beans with a liaison of egg yolk and vinegar, which makes a slightly tart but creamy sauce. This same sauce is used for *les pois mangetout de Chez Jane* on page 171. In the Rouergue they also make a soup with *les haricots verts*.

La Soupe aux Haricots Verts
Green bean soup

Serves 4

1 l (1¾ pt) chicken stock
300 g (10 oz) *haricots verts*
350 g (¾ lb) potatoes, diced
125 g (4 oz) salt belly of pork,
    finely chopped

salt, pepper
slices of French bread
1 tablespoon goose or duck fat

Bring the stock to the boil. Top and tail the beans and chop them into lengths suitable for eating with a soup spoon. Put all the ingredients into the boiling liquid, season lightly, cover the pan and cook over a moderate heat for 25 minutes.

Line four soup bowls with the slices of bread. Add the additional fat to the soup and ladle spoonfuls over the bread.

You will recognize *les haricots beurre* by their bright yellow pods, though these turn a pale green when cooked, so do not jump to the conclusion when buying that they are faded and old. Not only does their colour suggest butter but they taste of it too. And as a *mangetout* variety, the complete pod is eaten.

LES HARICOTS BEURRE
Yellow haricot beans

Serves 4

500 g (1 lb) *haricots beurre*	salt and freshly ground black
60 g (2 oz) butter	pepper
2 cloves garlic, chopped	lemon juice
2 tablespoons parsley, chopped	

Top and tail the beans and peel off any strings, then cut any long pods in half. Cook them by steaming or boiling in salted water for 10 minutes or so until the pods are soft. They take a little longer than *haricots verts* but retain their crisp texture when cooked. (If you steam them, you may hear them popping as they cook.)

Heat the butter in a frying pan. When the butter is hot, turn the beans in it for a few minutes without letting them fry, then mix in the garlic, parsley and seasoning. Sprinkle plenty of lemon juice over and stir well before serving.

———— • ————

The French cultivate varieties of the bean family just as much for their beans as their pods; in fact, this was their primary use in olden days when they ousted the broad bean in the diet. Some varieties such as Michelets and Cocos are sold fresh, either still in their pods or if you are lucky, ready podded, and these must be used straightaway. Michelets come in a creamy-coloured pod which quickly turns blackish, discolouring the grains if they are not extracted. The bean maintains its shape well during cooking, which takes 15–20 minutes. Cocos, rounder and less kidney-shaped, are also sold fresh in early autumn, still in their pod, but the bean does tend to shed its outer skin on cooking. Lingots, which are more lozenge-shaped, are a local variety of white bean sold commercially already dried, and available for use during the long winter months. What a blessing it must have been to discover that the bean would dry well and so keep over a long period! Both of these white *haricots* are the ones that feature in the *cassoulet* and the thick bean soups; they are grown all over the upper valley of the Garonne and they play an important part also in the hearty diet of the Gascons.

The following recipe is based on the use of fresh beans but if you are using dried ones, they must be soaked overnight. The subsequent cooking time can vary and always depends on their age. The *beurre de gascogne* in which they are finished is typical of the southern half of the region. In the north on the Limousin-Poitou borders they like a variety of bean called Mojette and the local style is to replace the '*beurre*' with thick fresh cream.

LES HARICOTS À LA GASCONNE
White beans with 'Gascony butter'

Serves 4

700 g (1½lb) fresh *haricots* in the pod	for the *beurre de gascogne*:
– Cocos for preference	6 cloves garlic
575 ml (1 pt) stock or water	2 tablespoons pork or goose fat
salt, pepper	1 tablespoon parsley, chopped

Cook the beans and unpeeled garlic cloves in unseasoned stock or water for 15 minutes. Remove the garlic and continue cooking the beans until they are tender, adding salt only towards the end. Fresh beans will take about 30 minutes and can be started in boiling water; dried ones take up to an hour or more and should be started in cold water. After cooking, drain them.

For the *beurre de Gascogne* six cloves are specified but this depends on their size and age, and also on one's taste for garlic – although their ferocity is reduced by the preliminary cooking. At the end you should have about one generous tablespoonful of pounded garlic.

Simmer the garlic cloves for 10-15 minutes until quite soft, then transfer to a mortar or small bowl. Pound them to a cream and then blend in the pork or goose fat. When the mixture is smooth add a tablespoonful of chopped parsley and stir this 'butter' into the beans.

———— ● ————

La sobronade is a rustic winter dish from the Périgord where haricot beans are also cultivated. The climate and soil are ideal for their success – they like to have 'their feet in the water and their heads in the sun'.

LA SOBRONADE
Stew of white beans, pork and vegetables

Serves 4

250 g (½ lb) white haricot beans,
    pre-soaked
500 g (1 lb) salt belly of pork
1 winter turnip or several spring
    turnips
3 carrots
1 stick celery
onion stuck with 2 cloves

bouquet garni
6 peppercorns
2 medium-sized potatoes, sliced
1 large clove garlic, chopped
3 large sprigs parsley
salt, pepper
4 slices of bread

Drain the soaked beans and put them into a large, earthenware pot or a flameproof casserole. Trim off as much of the layer of fat from the pork as possible and cut the lean meat into 3 cm (1¼ in) cubes. Add these to the beans and cover with water to about 2.5 cm (1 in) above the meat. Bring slowly to the boil and skim off any scum.

While the pot is coming to the boil, dice the fat from the pork and put it into a frying pan on a low flame to soften and give off its fat. Peel and slice the turnip into rounds and fry gently with the fat until golden on both sides and the pork fat crispy. When the beans and pork are on the boil, add the turnips and fat, also the carrots, cut into rounds and the celery in 3 cm (1¼ in) lengths. Put in the onion, bouquet garni and peppercorns. Bring back to the boil, cover and allow to simmer for one hour before adding the potatoes, garlic and parsley. Continue cooking until the beans are tender and the potatoes cooked. (If during this time the water reduces too much, top it up with *boiling* water; cold water would harden the meat and vegetables.)

Just before serving, check for seasoning, put the slices of bread into a soup tureen and spoon the stew over them. The bread should absorb the broth so that you could stand a spoon up in the dish.

LES PETITS POIS

Peas in France are always true to their name and never bigger than a small pearl. They are picked at this size whether they are for eating straightaway or for canning. In fact the French skill in canning has developed a large market for tinned *petits pois* which somehow manage to keep their shape during this process. They are cultivated on a large scale in the Lot but in a smaller way in most domestic *potagers*. This is the 'household' way of serving them.

LES PETITS POIS À LA MÉNAGÈRE
Peas as cooked on the farm

Serves 4

700 g (1½ lb) young fresh peas in the pod
1 tablespoon goose fat
60 g (2 oz) salt belly of pork
30 g (1 oz) *jambon de campagne*

4 or 8 small white onions, according to size
½ tablespoon flour
1 lettuce heart
salt, pepper, sugar

Shell the peas and sauter very gently in the fat with the pork and ham diced small, and the little onions, for about 10 minutes. Sprinkle with the flour and add cold water little by little until you have a smooth, slightly thickened sauce. You will need just to cover the peas. Add the shredded lettuce heart and a lump of sugar and check for seasoning – watch the salt because of the pork and ham.

Simmer gently for 15 minutes or until the peas are tender – this will obviously depend on their size and age. You can, if you like, serve them sprinkled with small pieces of onion, fried quickly to a deep brown but not burnt.

———— ● ————

Peas are one of the earliest of the summer's green vegetables and arrive at the time of the new seasons's sorrel, so they can be blended together into a wonderfully fresh bitter-sweet soup. Sorrel can be found growing wild in the fields but nowadays a superior, cultivated variety is grown in the *potager*. It closely resembles spinach to look at but the leaves are more delicate, with pointed ends where they join the stalk, which is itself sometimes tinged with red. Sorrel is a much valued herb and vegetable and other recipes for it appear later in this chapter.

LA SOUPE AUX PETITS POIS ET À L'OSEILLE
Sorrel and pea soup

Serves 4

125 g (4 oz) salt belly of pork
1 tablespoon goose fat or butter
500 g (1 lb) peas
2 tablespoons flour
1 litre (1¾ pt) hot water
salt, pepper

1 clove garlic
6–8 spring onions
1 tablespoon goose fat
1 handful sorrel leaves
1 egg yolk

Chop up the pork and fry it gently for a few minutes in a tablespoonful of fat in your soup pan. Then add the peas and turn them in the fat so that they keep their bright green colour. Sprinkle them with the flour and stir in the hot water. Season and add the garlic and onions, chopped, and leave to simmer for up to an hour. Wash the sorrel if it is gritty, drain and remove the stalks before chopping it up.

Just before serving, fry the chopped sorrel in a little fat until it melts, then add it to the soup and remove the pan for 5 minutes or so from the heat. When it has cooled slightly, beat up the egg yolk, stir a ladleful of the soup into it (if it is too hot it will curdle so watch this) and then pour it all back into the soup.

To serve, pour ladlefuls over slices of bread in individual bowls.

—— ● ——

As mentioned at the beginning of this book, *mangetout* peas were a discovery in the markets of the South-West twenty years ago. But they already had *haricots mangetout* so when the peas arrived, they were treated in the same way. This is the recipe we were given then by Jane. Since then it has gradually become clear that this way of finishing vegetables is traditional all over the South-West, even as far away as Les Landes.

LES POIS MANGETOUT DE CHEZ JANE
Jane's way with mangetout peas

Serves 4

500 g (1 lb) mangetout peas	salt, pepper
60 g (2 oz) salt belly of pork (or unsmoked bacon), chopped	1 egg yolk
30 g (1 oz) butter or fat	1 teaspoon vinegar

Top and tail the peas and de-string if necessary but leave them whole. Soften the pork or bacon in the fat until all the fat runs out of it. If there is too much, drain some off at the end; the finished dish should not be too fatty.

Toss the vegetables in this fat until they are coated all over, then add about one cupful of water and leave them to stew very gently *au coin du feu* – on a very low heat – for about 20 minutes. There should not be much liquid left by this time. Season them, then, just before serving, and off the heat, stir in the egg yolk which has been beaten up with a little vinegar so that it thickens the cooking liquid into a short sauce. The dash of vinegar should just balance the sweetness of the peas. Watch that the peas are not too hot when adding the egg or it will curdle.

———— • ————

Another neighbour later passed on her method:

LES POIS MANGETOUT DE MADAME MADER
Madame Mader's way with peas

per person:
1 handful mangetout peas
a little goose or pork fat
1 slice salt belly of pork or *jambon de campagne*

1 medium-sized potato, diced
salt, pepper

Remove the stalk end and any strings from the peas. Heat the fat and start to soften the chopped pork or ham in it. When it has given off some fat and is hot, add the potatoes and continue cooking, turning them from time to time until they are soft and beginning to crispen. Add the peas and turn them frequently in the hot fat to keep their green colour. Continue cooking for 7 to 10 minutes. Season and serve while still hot.

You can add to this mixture any spare bits of sausage or other meats, cooked or uncooked, to give the dish more body. It then makes a complete light lunch or supper dish of its own.

———— • ————

I am very discourteous in referring to Madame Mader as 'another neighbour'. We count the Mader family among our best French friends. During the latter part of the Second World War when the German Occupation was extended to southern France, Paul Mader was conscripted to serve in the army in Normandy, i.e. to fight the Allies. This he refused to do, fleeing his home and living rough with the Maquis in the chestnut woods round Carmaux for two years.

After the war he decided to concentrate on his smallholding, a typical venture in polyculture. A few cows, a pig or two and, when he duly married Olga, the usual quota of ducks, chickens, guinea-fowl and rabbits, and of course the *potager* in which they both took a keen interest. It was just outside their front door and was watched eagerly for any influence, good or bad, from the weather, slugs, birds, moles or insects. They were not frightened to pick their vegetables really young, so that their peas, *haricots verts* and spring carrots would be enjoyed *en primeur* – for example in a *ragoût printanier*. This dish goes well with the *confits* which Madame Mader put by in winter from her poultry.

LE RAGOÛT PRINTANIER
Casserole of spring vegetables

Serves 4

350 g (¾ lb) tiny new potatoes	60 g (2 oz) goose fat or butter
350 g (¾ lb) small broad beans	1 tablespoon flour
175 g (6 oz) peas	300 ml (10 fl oz) chicken stock
175 g (6 oz) *haricots verts*	salt, pepper, *sarriette*
125 g (4 oz) young carrots	1 egg yolk (optional)
1 medium-sized, or 8 button onions	

Scrub the potatoes, pod the beans (removing the inner skin as it really does make all the difference) and pod the peas. Top and tail the *haricots verts*. Scrape the carrots.

Sweat the onion and carrot slowly in the fat in a saucepan or casserole with a well-fitting lid. If your onions or carrots are too big, slice them first. When these are beginning to soften, add the potatoes, peas and broad beans. Leave to sauter gently, then sprinkle the flour over and slowly mix in the stock. Season and finally add the *haricots verts*. Cover and leave to cook very gently for 30 minutes. If at the end of this time the sauce is too thin, thicken it with an egg yolk.

LES LENTILLES

Lentils belong mainly to the Auvergne – they certainly seem to grow well there, these climbing vetch-like plants with their short, broad pods filled with tiny seeds. The French *lentille* is very small, like the red 'Egyptian' one, not bigger than the head of a nail. The most common variety, known as *les lentilles d'Auvergne* are a dark greeny-grey colour. However, Le Puy, the capital of Velay in the High Auvergne, has its own variety, the seeds being really tiny and bright, marbled pale and bluey-green. The Ponots, the inhabitants of Le Puy (also the name of this variety), claim theirs are superior to the *'turques'* of the Auvergne, charging more for them and insisting that their finer flavour comes from growing them in the volcanic soil in the *bassin* which surrounds this spectacular hill town. Both kinds differ from red lentils by retaining their shape after cooking, not disintegrating into a purée as the Egyptian ones do, and by their distinctive earthy flavour, which is not at all the same. They turn a dull colour while cooking, losing their original green hue. All lentils must be washed carefully before use and any grit or other foreign bodies rejected. Dried lentils do not need soaking before use.

The first lentil soup which follows is almost a meal while the second, vegetarian, one has the excellent combination of the acidic sorrel which counteracts the earthy sweetness of the lentils.

Le Potage aux Lentilles
Lentil soup

Serves 4

125 g (4 oz) green lentils	salt, pepper
125 g (4 oz) fresh lean belly of pork	1 litre (1¾ pt) water
1 onion spiked with a clove	1 tablespoon *crème fraîche*
bouquet garni	

Put the lentils into a covered pan with the pork, onion and bouquet garni. Add seasoning and 1 litre (1¾ pints) of water. Bring to the boil and simmer gently for up to 2 hours. Extract the pork and cut it into cubes, putting it to one side. Discard the bouquet garni and clove. Purée the lentils and onion in a liquidizer or food mill, then return them to their liquor together with the cubed pork.

Stir in a good tablespoonful of *crème fraîche* and reheat gently without allowing the soup to boil.

Le Potage de Lentilles à l'Oseille
Lentil and sorrel soup

Serves 4

100 g (3½ oz) green lentils	350 g (¾ lb) sorrel
1 litre (1¾ pt) water	60 g (2 oz) butter
salt, pepper	4 slices bread

Put the lentils and water into a large soup pan and cook gently for an hour and a half, or until they are quite tender. Towards the end of this cooking time, add a good teaspoonful of salt. De-stalk the sorrel, wash and drain it. Heat 30 g (1 oz) of the butter in a pan and melt the sorrel in it slowly. It will reduce considerably. Allow it to simmer for 5 minutes, then tip the purée into the lentils. Liquidize the lot and return it to the pan. Add the remaining butter and check the seasoning.

Serve the soup over slices of bread placed in each soup bowl.

This soup is a good way of using up left-over lentils prepared as a vegetable, provided they have been covered with stock or water while they were still hot; otherwise they tend to dry out like concrete. Do not, however, keep cooked lentils for long as they tend to ferment.

———— ● ————

South-Western cooking is unique in its use of the skin off a pork joint which is not cooked with the roast to make crackling but is cut off and preserved separately in its own fat – *couennes confites* – to enrich soups or vegetable dishes (see page 70). Perhaps the most delicious way these are then used is in combination with green lentils, which need some kind of fat to enrich them and their sauce. *Les lentilles aux couennes* is a truly winter dish and you can imagine its helping to keep out the cold during the severe months in the Auvergne mountains. It would be eaten on its own or as an accompaniment to some *petit salé* or the local sausage.

LES LENTILLES AUX COUENNES
Lentils with preserved pork rind

Serves 4

250 g (½ lb) green lentils
1 tablespoon goose fat
1 medium-sized onion, chopped
2 cloves garlic, chopped

stock
1 roll of *couenne confite*
salt, pepper

In a flameproof pot that is also suitable for serving the lentils in, melt a good tablespoonful of goose fat. Sauter the onion and garlic in it gently for 10 minutes. Add the lentils and stir well so as to coat them in the fat. Add salt and pepper and just cover the lentils with stock. Bring to the boil, cover and simmer gently for an hour, then add the diced *couenne* and simmer for another hour.

During the whole of the cooking period it is necessary to watch the level of liquid in the pot. When the lentils are cooked they stop absorbing the stock and give off their own thickening to the sauce. They should therefore never be more than *just* covered with liquid, although the level may have to be topped up with new stock kept hot in readiness.

During the last half hour, stir the lentils from time to time and stop adding the stock so that by the end the sauce has a chance to achieve the right consistency. Although it sounds simple, it takes some care to achieve this and unless you do so, the dish will not be correct.

———— • ————

Les couennes confites are also used to enrich white haricots in the same way. The Périgourdins are extremely fond of these beans and will add *un hachis* or sprinkle a little walnut oil over them just before serving.

Madame Zette Guinandeau-Franc in her wonderful book of peasant cookery, *Les Secrets des Fermes en Périgord Noir*, explains a dish we have not come across elsewhere but which sounds excellent. It goes by the name of *le torchis*. A dandelion or *chicorée-frisée* (endive) salad, well-seasoned with walnut oil, vinegar and rounds of onion, is served with the *haricots aux couennes* and each person finely shreds his own helping of salad before mixing it on his plate with the beans. The title comes from the ensuing resemblance to *le torchis* which is mortar made of clay mixed with straw.

LES POMMES DE TERRE

The arrival of the potato in the eighteenth century as an alternative starch to replace the ubiquitous chestnut gave this new vegetable an important place in the family meals, not only as part of *la soupe* but being combined with eggs and cheese (see pages 147–150) or eaten as a vegetable. In any event there is plenty of evidence that potatoes prepared in one way or another were eaten at least once a day.

As a vegetable they were for the most part plainly boiled, or baked in their jackets under *la braise* of the wood fire. But someone soon found that to sauter them in goose or duck fat made a wonderful combination. You do not find in the region quite the roast potatoes prepared in the English manner – although goose fat *does* make the best English roast potatoes of all – but instead delicious variants, the best known being

LES POMMES DE TERRE SARLADAISES
Potatoes with garlic and parsley

It is claimed that the truffle is a traditional ingredient – Sarlat holds important truffle markets in winter – although some locals vehemently deny this. It would seem that for everyday cooking the seasoning has always been just a mixture of garlic and parsley and what seems most likely is that when truffles were more plentiful than now, they were added to the ordinary *pommes de terre confites*, which were awarded the more specific title of *pommes sarladaises*.

Serves 4

750 g (1½ lb) waxy potatoes
3 tablespoons goose fat
1 tablespoon chopped parsley

2 cloves garlic or a small truffle or
    some peelings
salt, pepper

There are two methods of cooking these potatoes. Either they are made in an open pan on the fire, or they are started this way, then covered and finished in the oven.

Peel and slice the potatoes fairly thinly and dry them in a clean tea towel. Heat the goose fat in a heavy frying pan with a good-fitting lid, and when it starts to smoke, put in the potatoes to colour over a high heat. Keep turning them so that they do not stick and when they start to colour, cover the pan and moderate the heat. Allow them to cook on the flame (or in a moderately hot oven – 190°C, 375°F, Gas Mark 5) for 30 minutes, turning them over every 10 minutes to brown in the fat. Towards the end of the half hour, stir in the chopped parsley and garlic. At this stage some cooks break up the potatoes slightly with a fork so as to crisp some of the bits, and add a little more fat if necessary. The finished dish should present a good contrast of crusty, golden outsides and creamy centres.

When the rounds of potato are not disturbed during the cooking but kept together in a mound, then turned out upside down as a golden potato cake, this is known as *un gâteau de pommes de terre à la sarladaise*.

⸺ ● ⸺

The comparative abundance of potatoes in the diet means they are used to 'bulk out' produce in shorter supply and home cooks will often sauter carrots and potatoes together, or if only one or two *cepès* or a few *girolles* have been found, these seem to double or quadruple in the frying pan when mixed with potato, which easily takes on their perfume. In spring a few dandelion leaves or the young shoots known locally as *responchous* (see page 186) may be added to the pan.

In England we are familiar with the idea, if not the practice, that roast beef should be allowed to drip on to the Yorkshire pudding below. In the country districts, and particularly in the Périgord, where roasting used always to be done on a spit in front of an open wood fire, they have a way of doing the same thing with potatoes. The method is easily adapted to a modern rotisserie and is particularly good with boned and rolled joints of pork or with a tarragon-flavoured chicken. The dish which catches the juices dripping from the roast is known as *une lèche-frite* and sometimes the name is given to this way of cooking the potatoes.

LES POMMES DE TERRE AU JUS
Potatoes with meat juices

Serves 4

750 g (1½ lb) potatoes
1 tablespoon chopped parsley

1 large finely-chopped shallot
salt, pepper

Steam or boil the potatoes in their skins for 15 minutes or until cooked. Peel them and crush them coarsely with a fork without making the purée too fine. Mix in the parsley and shallot.

Choose a gratin dish as near to the size as possible of the roast you are cooking. Spread the mashed potatoes in this and season them well with salt and freshly-ground black pepper.

About 45 minutes before your roast is cooked, pour over the surface of the potatoes all the juices that have run into the drip tray under the meat and replace it with the gratin dish. Stir the potatoes from time to time so that the juices still dripping are evenly distributed.

When the roast is cooked, put the potatoes under a gentle grill and the surface will turn a beautiful golden colour, while underneath the potato will be moist and quite rich.

If you are cooking in the oven, do not use a roasting pan but put the meat directly on to the shelf and let it drip on to the potatoes on the shelf below. This is not, however, possible where a roast needs basting so the method is only practical in the oven if you are cooking a larded joint.

If a goose is being spit roasted at Christmas or New Year it is customary to add hard-boiled eggs to the potatoes in the *lèchefrite*.

LES POMMES À L'ÉCHIRLÈTE
Potatoes finished in goose fat

Another traditional recipe from the valley of the Dordogne.

Serves 4

750 g (1½ lb) small new potatoes
575 ml (1 pt) chicken or veal stock
   or water

1–2 cloves garlic, roughly chopped
2–3 tablespoons goose or duck fat
salt

Scrape or peel the potatoes which should be no bigger than a walnut. Parboil them, preferably in seasoned stock, together with the pieces of garlic. Drain them.

Heat the fat in a large frying pan, tip in the potatoes and garlic and let them sauter gently, turning them over from time to time until they have turned a golden colour all over. Don't have the heat too high or they may burn – allow about half an hour for this browning. They should be fairly crisp outside and soft and floury inside. Salt them before serving.

LES PATATES À L'AIL
Garlic potatoes

This is a simple recipe for 'stewed' potatoes from the foothills of the Pyrenees where they are sometimes called *patates* – a frequent dialect word for them. This recipe is for garlic lovers. Put in as many cloves as you like; the aroma fills the kitchen and the potatoes absorb the flavour wonderfully.

Serves 4

750 g (1½ lb) potatoes, preferably
   Bintjes or other waxy variety
6 cloves garlic

2 tablespoons goose fat
salt, pepper

Peel and slice the potatoes thinly. Dry them well. Peel and crush the garlic and heat it in the fat in a heavy-bottomed casserole (or non-stick pan) with a good-fitting lid. When the aroma of garlic becomes really enticing (but don't let it burn), add the potatoes. Turn them in the fat to distribute the garlic. Cover and cook slowly for 20–30 minutes, checking from time to time to be sure they are not sticking – you may need to add a little more fat. The potatoes should not brown but gently stew. Season them at the end and serve hot. They are delicious with *confit* as an alternative to *pommes sarladaises*.

LA BLANQUETTE DE POMMES DE TERRE
Potatoes in a white sauce

We came across this dish at the Hotel d'Europe in Villeneuve-de-Marsan during a marvellous trip we made around the region, exploring the armagnac distilleries. As the potatoes are in a sauce they go very well with a *confit de porc*, a grilled *magret* of duck or any other grilled meat.

Use a variety of potato that does not 'fall' during cooking – any waxy kind or even some King Edwards provided they are new. The pieces must stay whole in the sauce.

Serves 4

6–8 medium-sized potatoes
1 dessertspoon goose or pork fat
1 medium-sized onion
1 dessertspoon flour
400 ml (¾ pt) stock

salt, pepper
bouquet garni
1 egg yolk
1 tablespoon white wine vinegar

Peel the potatoes and quarter them, then brown them lightly in the hot fat. Chop the onion and sprinkle it in, stirring to prevent sticking. Add the flour, mixing it in and then slowly add enough stock to cover. Season and put in the bouquet garni. Cover and leave to cook slowly for about 20 minutes, when the potatoes should be cooked. Just before serving, thicken the sauce with an egg yolk beaten up with a spoonful of wine vinegar.

●

The next recipe for *les crêpes de grand'maman* was given to us in 1972, grandmother being the mother of Monsieur Vanel, the famous chef who at that time had his restaurant at Lacapelle-Marival in his native Lot. It was never clear whether *grand'maman* was actually still making the inexhaustible supplies of these delicious potato cakes served to every customer for Sunday lunch, but young Madame Vanel was only too happy to pass on her *belle-mère*'s recipe. We treasure the card on which it is written, especially since Monsieur Vanel has since gone on to merit two stars in the Guide Michelin for his Toulouse restaurant where he is still serving these *crêpes*.

LES CRÊPES DE GRAND'MAMAN
Grandma's pancakes

Serves 4

250 g (½ lb) floury potatoes
¾ tablespoon flour
1 egg

60 ml (2 fl oz) hot milk
60 ml (2 fl oz) double cream
salt

Steam the potatoes or cook them in their skins, then peel them. Sieve or mash carefully before beating in the flour, followed by the egg whisked up with the hot milk, cream and salt to produce a batter the consistency of thickish cream.

Heat an iron frying pan. Oil it slightly and keep it at a *moderate* heat. Drop tablespoonfuls of the batter on to the pan and wait until the mixture spreads and becomes covered in bubbles and 'sets' before turning over. They should puff up a little. Keep the cooked ones hot while continuing to make further pancakes with the rest of the batter. They should be thicker than pancakes and the size of a scone.

The *crêpes* go very well with roast lamb or veal and are served to soak up the meat juices. You can add chopped *fines herbes* to the batter if you like.

L'Oseille

Sorrel grows wild in the British Isles just as it does in France but since the time of Henry VIII we seem to have lost the taste for it. The French, on the other hand, use it a great deal both as a potherb and as a vegetable. When salt used to be scarce and costly, wild sorrel was even sometimes used in its place and one kind was known as salt grass. They have now cultivated a fleshier leaved variety and you will find a clump of it in most country gardens. In spring and early summer when there is still plenty of moisture about, you may even find it on sale at market. Although it weighs little, buy a reasonable quantity – say 500 g (1 lb) if you are able. This is necessary since the way the arrow-shaped leaves dissolve to nothing when heated is quite magical. However the resulting purée is quite strong and sharply acidic so that it needs to be softened with a béchamel sauce.

The name derives from the old French word for sour – *surelle* – and its oxalic acid content means it is not recommended for the rheumaticky ones among us, nor indeed, in a large quantity, for anyone. For the same reason, care must also be taken to use stainless steel or enamel utensils when cooking sorrel. But none of this should be allowed to deter anyone since the deliciously fresh, lemony taste is a wonderful contrast to the rich, fatty dishes that compose a large portion of the peasant cuisine.

Sorrel with a *confit* of goose or duck is quite the best accompaniment, and if you have never tried this wonderful purée, do not hesitate to buy some sorrel – or to grow some plants if circumstances allow. It is a natural companion to eggs, the sharpness of one being offset by the gentle blandness of the other, and it is also delicious with mussels, as described on page 139.

First, here is a quickly-made soup, using potatoes, sorrel and eggs, which makes a complete light meal.

LE TOURIN BLANCHI À L'OSEILLE
Sorrel and potato soup

Serves 4

500 g (1 lb) potatoes
850 ml (1½ pt) water
250 g (8 oz) sorrel
1 tablespoon goose fat
2 large cloves garlic, chopped
1 tablespoon chopped parsley

1 tablespoon chopped chervil
1 tablespoon flour
2 eggs
salt, pepper, nutmeg
slices of bread

Peel and chop the potatoes and boil in seasoned water for 20 minutes until soft.
While they are cooking, wash and drain the sorrel, removing the stalks, and melt in the fat over a low heat with the garlic and herbs. By the time the potatoes are ready, the sorrel mixture will have reduced to a smooth purée. Stir in the flour.
Liquidize or sieve the potatoes with their water and stir in the sorrel. Bring this to simmering point but do not allow it to boil – the potatoes may separate if overheated. Separate the eggs and put the yolks to one side. Stir in the whites vigorously until they have coagulated. Allow the soup to cool a little, then add the beaten egg yolks, check the seasoning and grate in a little nutmeg.
Pour over the bread with which you have lined the soup bowls.

LA PURÉE D'OSEILLE
Purée of sorrel

Serves 4

500 g (1 lb) sorrel
30 g (1 oz) goose fat or butter
30 g (1 oz) flour

300 ml (½ pt) milk or stock
1 egg yolk or 1 tablespoon cream
(optional)
salt, pepper, nutmeg

Pull off the stalks from the sorrel and wash the leaves. Shake off the water, not too thoroughly as some moisture on the leaves helps the 'melting' process.
Melt the butter in an enamelled pan, add the drained sorrel and cook very gently for some minutes, stirring frequently until you have a smooth purée. Then add the flour, mix it well in and blend in the warmed milk or stock. Continue cooking it very gently for 5 to 10 minutes. Just before using, you can

if you like bind the purée with an egg yolk, beaten with a little water, or substitute a little cream. Check the seasoning.

This purée freezes well so extra supplies can be put in reserve.

L'Omelette à la Purée d'Oseille
Omelette with purée of sorrel

This is, after a truffled omelette, probably the next most delicious omelette of all. If you have a few roots of sorrel in your herb garden, you will always have a quick and delicious lunch or supper dish. Another version of sorrel omelette is to melt the leaves in a little butter, then mix them into the beaten eggs before cooking the omelette. There is the danger that this method, though quicker, can cause the eggs to stick to the pan. And, although simpler, the finished result is not quite so satisfactory.

per person:
2 large eggs
salt, pepper
a little butter

about 2 tablespoons warm sorrel purée (above)

Beat the eggs very lightly and pour into a very hot, lightly buttered omelette pan. Make the omelette in the usual way and when it is not quite set on top and is still *baveuse*, put a line of sorrel purée across the centre. Do not have the purée too hot or it will continue to cook the eggs. Roll up the omelette and slide on to a heated plate. Serve immediately.

———— • ————

As an alternative to a purée of sorrel, *oeufs durs à l'oseille* is a traditional accompaniment for a joint of *confit* or grilled sausage.

Les Oeufs Durs à l'Oseille
Hard-boiled eggs with sorrel

Serves 4

1 thick slice of salt belly of pork or unsmoked streaky bacon (optional)
8 small thick rounds of white bread without crusts

1 clove garlic
a little chopped parsley and chervil
purée of sorrel (above)
4 hard-boiled eggs

In a frying pan heat up very slowly the fatty part of the pork or bacon, cut into cubes, until it has given off all its fat and turned crispy and golden. In this fat, fry the lean bits of pork or bacon, also cubed, until crisp. If the pork is omitted, add some fat to the pan, then brown the croûtons of bread on both sides. At the last minute stir in the garlic but do not allow it to burn. Stir the herbs into the hot sorrel purée. Shell the eggs.

To serve, spoon a bed of the purée on to each heated plate, place two fried croutons on top and on each of them put half an egg. Sprinkle the bacon mixture around and serve immediately.

In our own district of the Rouergue and in the Languedoc where it was an especial favourite of the nineteenth-century weavers, a most delicious version of that recipe crops up by the name of *Tripade* or *Tripada*. The sorrel and eggs are added to potatoes sautéed in goose fat and seasoned liberally with a *persillade*.

———— • ————

In Britain you may not be able to find calf's sweetbreads; the French are fonder of them than we are, and they are considered quite a luxury. If your butcher is able to supply them, this combination with sorrel strikes the right balance.

LE RIS DE VEAU À L'OSEILLE
Sweetbreads with sorrel

Serves 4

500 g (1 lb) calf's sweetbreads	bouquet garni
2 carrots, finely chopped	salt, pepper
8 very small onions	500 g (1 lb) sorrel
2 tablespoons goose fat	1 tablespoon goose fat
4 medium-sized tomatoes, peeled	1 dessertspoon flour
120 ml (4 fl oz) dry white wine	milk or cream
120 ml (4 fl oz) stock	

Soak the sweetbreads in running water or several changes of water for 2 or 3 hours. Do not cut them up but blanch them whole in fresh boiling water for 5 minutes. Drain and refresh them in cold water then cut away all waste and peel off their outer transparent skin.

Colour the carrot with the whole onions in the goose fat in a heavy pan with a tight-fitting lid. Add the sweetbreads, the tomatoes, wine and stock, bouquet and seasoning. Cook the sweetbreads gently on one side for 10 minutes, then turn them before covering the pan and leaving it to simmer slowly for 45 minutes.

While they are cooking, wash and strip the sorrel. Put it in a pan with the tablespoonful of goose fat and let it melt down. Stir in the flour and add enough milk or cream to make a smooth sauce. Season and leave to simmer very gently for 10 minutes (a non-stick pan is ideal for this purpose).

To serve, put the sweetbreads in the centre of the serving platter and surround with the little onions. Sieve the sauce in which they were cooked and pour it over the sweetbreads, then surround them with the sorrel purée.

———— • ————

The chief vegetables to be found on the table, accompanying any meat or presented on their own, are the légumes (peas and beans) or potatoes, with sometimes sorrel as a welcome addition in spring. And in spring thrifty housekeepers in the country turn to other plants growing in the wild – in spite of an inborn unease about eating anything that has not been cultivated by themselves. For instance, when the young nettles first shoot and are too young even to sting, they are collected and the leaves used like spinach. They are first soaked in salt water or else blanched before being finished *au jus* or *à la crème*. Alternatively they are added to soup or to *haricots blancs* in the same way as sorrel. They were welcomed after a meagre winter diet because of their chemical properties which help to purify the system – provided they were not taken in excess.

LE POTAGE AUX ORTIES
Nettle and potato soup

Serves 4

2 handfuls of young nettle tops	350 g (¾ lb) potatoes
a bunch of watercress	salt, pepper

Chop together the nettle leaves and watercress, peel and dice the potatoes. Put these vegetables into the soup pot, cover with 1 litre (1¾ pt) of water and season with salt and pepper. Bring to the boil and cook over medium heat for half an hour. Thicken the soup by crushing some of the potatoes in it with a fork, and serve just as it is, *trempé* over slices of bread or not, as you wish.

———— • ————

Going for a spring walk we often find the locals searching in the hedgerows amongst the brambles for what for them is a delicacy offered by nature. Hard to find unless your eye is trained, this is a climbing plant whose young shoots when first sprouting resemble a sort of wild asparagus. The French call it *le tamier* but it is known locally as *reponchous* or *respounjos*. The 15 cm (6 inch) long shoots are used in rather the same way as asparagus to make into an omelette or for a mixed sauté with potatoes and eggs. They are an acquired taste, not sweet like asparagus but quite bitter and so they need blanching before cooking. They are quite a strong laxative so should only be taken in small quantities. One of our first invitations in France was to stay to lunch with the carpenter who was making new windows for our house. His wife gave us this omelette and we still have the memories of it.

Another almost free vegetable to be seen in spring – and sometimes on sale at market – is a flowering shoot which sprouts from around the stalk after a winter cabbage has been cut. These *pointes de choux* or *choux broccolis* look rather like bolting broccoli; long thin stems with buds of yellow hue rather than violet. They must be picked while still in bud and are either served as a hot vegetable as in this recipe, or cold rather like asparagus vinaigrette – or so the lady told us who was selling them in little bunches at market one Easter in April.

LES POINTES DE CHOUX AUX LARDONS
Cabbage tops with diced pork

Serves 4

2 bunches of *pointes de choux*	salt, pepper
60 g (2 oz) salt belly of pork, diced	30 g (1 oz) butter
1 hard-boiled egg	

Tie the cabbage tops in firm bundles. Bring some salted water to the boil in a tall pot, high enough to cook them with the stalks in the water and the tips in the steam, as you would for cooking asparagus. Simmer them, covered, for 10–12 minutes.

Fry the belly of pork *lardons* in some fat for 10 minutes until they are brown and crisp. When the stalks of the cabbage shoots are just *à point*, drain them thoroughly and pour a little melted butter or fat over them. Chop the hard-boiled egg and sprinkle it and the *lardons* over the top.

LES ASPERGES

Near Narbonne asparagus is grown between the rows of vines. This is not surprising since formerly asparagus grew wild in the Languedoc – another of the free foods.

Nowadays farmers and small holders in other parts of the South-West are planting their rows of cultivated asparagus roots and with modern developments in horticulture these yield much more quickly than used to be the case. Southerners seem to prefer the thinner, purple and green asparagus for its stronger flavour and it is usually this variety that is served in local restaurants – *à la vinaigrette* or in an omelette. If you should have broken or bent stalks, these can be made into a dish which uses only the tips.

LE GRATIN D'ASPERGES
Asparagus baked in a cheese sauce

Serves 4

750 g (1½ lb) asparagus tips
60 g (2 oz) butter
175 g (6 oz) salt belly of pork or 1
    slice of *jambon de campagne*, cubed

salt, pepper, nutmeg
575 ml (1 pt) béchamel sauce
60 g (2 oz) grated cheese

Wash and scrape the asparagus, keeping only the tender tips (use the stalks to flavour a soup) and cut these into 3 cm (1¼ in) lengths.

Heat half the butter in a frying pan and colour the asparagus and pork in it. Add a very little salt, some pepper and nutmeg. Cover, reduce the heat and leave to cook until the asparagus is soft, stirring the pan from time to time to prevent any sticking.

Make a béchamel sauce and season well, then fold in the asparagus and pork mixture. Tip this into a buttered gratin dish, cover the top with the grated cheese and dot it with the remaining butter. Bake the gratin in a hot oven (200°C, 400°F, Gas Mark 6) until the top is crisp and golden.

The same recipe can be used with the white stalks of *blettes* or *bette* (chard) – a vegetable rather popular with the French but whose flavour is so delicate as to be almost insipid and seems to call for a savoury sauce such as this one.

LES NAVETS

These are the nearly pure white variety of turnips which can be found in neat bunches in the market at spring time – either small round ones the size of a tangerine or the carrot-shaped variety. They both have a good crisp texture and a tangy flavour.

LES NAVETS GLACÉS
Glazed turnips

Serves 4

500 g (1 lb) white turnips
a little salt
30 g (1 oz) butter

stock or water
1 teaspoon sugar

Peel the turnips and blanch in salted water for 5 minutes or a little longer if they are not very young. Drain and refresh them in cold water and drain again. If necessary cut them into half or quarters or into rounds, and fry in melted butter, turning them over, for a few minutes. Pour in a little stock and stir in the sugar and cook gently, uncovered, until the stock has evaporated and the turnips are shiny and glazed. Don't use too much stock or they will be overcooked before it has reduced.

LES NAVETS À LA BORDELAISE
Turnips as in Bordeaux

Serves 4

500 g (1 lb) small white turnips
salt
2 tablespoons goose fat

2 tablespoons breadcrumbs
1 tablespoon chopped parsley
1 chopped shallot

Blanch the peeled turnips in salted water for 5–10 minutes. Drain. Cut into smaller pieces if necessary.

Heat the fat in a frying pan and toss the turnips in it. Cook over a gentle heat, covered, turning the pieces from time to time, for about 15 minutes. At the end when they are translucent and golden, stir in the crumbs mixed with the parsley and shallot and let these crisp. Serve immediately while the crumbs are still crunchy.

LES TOMATES

On through the summer comes a bounty of green vegetables, the tiny peas and various beans which are the mainstay of the vegetable garden, the fresh lettuce and other salads and the big, fleshy tomatoes. We are not here talking about the kind of tomato which seems to have taken over the market in Britain, the perfectly round fruit the size of a golf ball, full of rather acid juice and pips but with no flesh. It would be better if tomatoes for cooking had no juice or pips at all: indeed it is a counsel of perfection in France to remove as much of both as possible before starting to cook tomatoes.

French tomatoes of the kind grown in South-West France contain a maximum of flesh and the minimum of juice and pips. One famous variety called Marmande is named after the town of that name on the river Garonne, and large quantities are grown and harvested in the area. Marmande tomatoes are early rather than late and are usually large and quite heavily wrinkled. Sometimes they can assume bizarre shapes and frequently weigh up to half a kilo. Later in the season their place is taken by a variety called locally St Pierre, which tend to be slightly smaller and more orthodox in appearance. Both kinds are noteworthy for the abundance of tender flesh which they contain and which makes them so valuable for raw salads as well as cooking. A tomato salad made from these with a little chopped shallot, a mild *vinaigrette* dressing and a few drops of *eau-de-vie* sprinkled over, is an altogether different experience from the kind we mostly have to endure. If you do not grow or cannot find these tomatoes in Britain, the so-called 'beef' tomatoes are a kind of substitute but they are not usually allowed to ripen sufficiently before sale to allow their flesh to soften, so must be allowed to ripen for a few days in your kitchen. Marmande tomatoes *will* grow in Britain and some nurserymen sell young plants in May. Get them going as soon as possible and allow them as sunny a spot in the garden as you can. Plant African marigolds with them to keep away insect pests.

We have seen in this book how tomatoes can be made into lovely and typically South-Western *potages*; how they can be stuffed, also used as a filling for omelettes. Often they are eaten simply fried or grilled, sometimes topped with a few breadcrumbs and herbs. Inferior specimens are used to make an all-purpose tomato sauce which is a wonderful standby to have, either in preserving jars or in the freezer. With macaroni, or as a way of livening a plain and perhaps otherwise dull pork chop, or with a dish of *haricot blancs* or *topinambours*, this sauce has an endless variety of applications.

LA SAUCE AUX TOMATES
Tomato sauce

for 1.5 kg (3 lb) tomatoes:

1 tablespoon goose fat or lard	1 shallot, finely chopped
1 tablespoon flavourless oil	1 clove garlic, finely chopped
1 large onion, thinly sliced	bouquet garni
1 tablespoon goose fat	salt, pepper, cayenne pepper
1 tablespoon flour	2 tablespoons chopped parsley or
150 ml (¼ pt) chicken stock	chervil

First peel the tomatoes. This is best done either by toasting them on a fork over a gas flame until the skin loosens, or immersing them in nearly boiling water. Either way you must not let the tomatoes cook.

Cut the peeled tomatoes into quarters and extract the pips. Gently squeeze the remaining fruit to get rid of as much of the acid juices as you can.

Melt the fat and oil in a large *sauteuse* (frying pan with fitted lid) and add the tomato pieces and sliced onion. Start to cook the mixture over a good heat for 3 or 4 minutes, then reduce the heat, cover the pan and simmer slowly for a quarter of an hour. Sieve everything through a strainer.

In another pan melt the other tablespoonful of fat and stir in the flour. Cook together then add the chicken stock slowly until the mixture is smooth. Add the tomato and onion mixture, the chopped shallot, garlic, seasonings and bouquet garni and simmer as gently as possible for half an hour. Add more stock if the sauce gets too thick. If it is not thick enough continue cooking until the right consistency is achieved.

If you must use canned tomatoes, choose the Italian, plum-shaped kind but drain the juices away carefully before you start preparing the sauce.

———— ● ————

In years when there is a glut of tomatoes the price falls to a give-away level in the markets. It is then a good opportunity to bottle for later use a concentrated purée of tomatoes. The process is very simple.

La Conserve de Purée de Tomates
Bottled tomato purée

Serves 4

for every kilo (2¼ lb) of tomatoes:
1 large onion, sliced
60 g (2 oz) sugar

thyme, parsley, celery leaves
salt, pepper

Crush the tomatoes as they are, skin, pips and all. Put them into a preserving pan and add the other ingredients. Stirring regularly, boil the mixture until it has reduced by at least half. Strain it through the finest blade of a *mouli-légumes*, or other strainer. Sterilize some preserving jars in the usual way, fill them with the mixture, seal then sterilize in boiling water for half an hour.

———— ● ————

By the end of September the harvest really arrives: there are the root artichokes, the pumpkins, celery and cauliflowers, and on through the winter the salsify and *endives*. This is apart from the soup vegetables – the onions, carrots, leeks and cabbages – which occupy the main part of the *potager*.

Les Topinambours

For the most part the Jerusalem artichoke is grown as animal feed. Its tall stalks topped with their yellow, daisy-like flowers can be seen growing in many fields all over the region. Some peasants regard this root vegetable as fit only for cattle, and certainly Paul Mader treated the idea of bringing it to the table as a hilarious eccentricity. (Perhaps the kind given to cattle are a coarse variety, just as the maize grown in such vast quantities is a somewhat poor relation of the sweet corn so popular across the Atlantic.) In the Dordogne, however, as in Britain, they have known for years what a lovely *potage* can be made from these tubers.

Le Potage aux Topinambours
Jerusalem artichoke soup

Serves 4

1 large onion, chopped
30 g (1 oz) butter
500 g (1 lb) Jerusalem artichokes,
peeled and sliced

850 ml (1½ pt) chicken stock
150 ml (5 fl oz) double cream
1 tablespoon chopped parsley
salt, pepper

Melt the onion in a little butter until it is soft and transparent, then add the artichokes. Turn them in the onion and butter for a few minutes, then add the stock and seasoning. Bring slowly to the boil and allow to simmer for 30 minutes.

Liquidize or sieve and return the soup to the pan. Reheat it, adding a little more stock or milk if necessary to achieve the right consistency. Just before serving, add the cream and parsley and check the seasoning.

———— • ————

Artichokes also appear as an hors d'oeuvre tossed in mayonnaise but even more popular is to make them into *beignets*, those delicious deep-fried morsels which are especially French.

LES BEIGNETS DE TOPINAMBOURS
Artichoke fritters

Serves 4

350 g (¾ lb) Jerusalem artichokes

for the frying batter:
125 g (4 oz) flour   salt
3 tablespoons oil   1 egg white
about 150 ml (¼ pt) warm water   oil for frying

Peel the artichokes, and put them to cook in salted, boiling water for just long enough to soften – watch them as they easily overcook. Drain and leave them to cool before slicing them into rounds.

Make the frying batter by sieving the flour before mixing into it the oil and salt and just enough warm water to have a smooth cream a little thicker than pancake batter. Leave this to rest for an hour or more.

Just before using the batter, whip the egg white stiffly and fold it into the mixture. Heat a good quantity of frying oil in a pan and when it is really hot, (190°C, 375°F) dip a number of slices of artichoke into the batter before sliding them into the hot fat. When they have nicely puffed and turned golden, in 2–3 minutes, not more, drain them and keep them hot while cooking the other slices.

You can use exactly the same method for pre-cooked pieces of salsify or celeriac.

LE POTIRON

Bright orange pumpkins are as much a feature of the autumn landscape in the South-West as they are of the country markets in September and October. As the dense summer vegetation dies in the *potagers* and fields, these unlikely fruits, bigger than footballs, swell and deepen in colour as they mature. The huge orange and gold globes look absolutely splendid, lying on the earth in a state of torpor or sunning themselves on the dry-stone wall of a farm or cottage. Called either *le potiron* or *la citrouille* according to colour, the pumpkin came from the New World and, as it likes the sun, it responds particularly well to the long, hot summers of the region. Pumpkins are a great favourite with the peasants, perhaps because they grow to such an enormous size and so will feed large households. Their other added attraction is their good keeping quality; after drying they are stored in dry cellars or attics until needed during the winter.

In the South they are used to make soup as well as purées and gratins, bread, jam, cakes and tarts. Paul Mader remembered his childhood winters when the soup served three times a day was one composed of pumpkin, potato and dried beans. Pumpkins look rather better than they taste but with a little encouragement from other local produce they do yield unusual dishes like these:

LE POTAGE AU POTIRON
Pumpkin soup

This soup has an attractive flavour with its combination of earthy beans and sweetish pumpkin. The *hachis* gives it an additional savour; this can be replaced by tomatoes, emphasising the sweet element. Potatoes and even a knuckle of ham can be added, making it more of a *soupe* than a *potage*.

Serves 4

175 g (6 oz) dried haricot beans, soaked overnight
salt
1 tablespoon goose fat
1 large onion, finely chopped

2 teaspoons sugar
500 g (1 lb) slice of pumpkin, peeled and cubed
hachis of shallot, parsley, garlic and flour

Put the haricot beans to cook while you prepare the rest of the soup. Add some salt only half-way through their cooking.

Colour the onion in the fat in a large casserole or pan. When the onion is golden, stir in the sugar, then add the pumpkin and reduce the heat so that the flesh will soften without burning. Cover the pan but stir the contents from time to time. When quite soft and almost a purée and when the beans are cooked, ladle some of the bean water into it and blend together. Slowly amalgamate the rest of the water plus the beans and leave to simmer for 5 minutes or so while preparing an *hachis*. Soften the shallot, parsley and garlic in a little fat, thickening it with some flour, then blending a little of the soup liquid into it. Let this mixture cook a little before tipping it back into the soup. Simmer all together for a final 10 minutes and check the seasoning, adding pepper and perhaps a little more salt (but remember the beans are already salted).

LE POTIRON AU SAFRAN
Pumpkin with saffron

Serves 4

350 g (¾lb) peeled, de-seeded
  pumpkin
1 tablespoon goose fat
1 tablespoon maize flour

a good pinch of saffron
60 ml (2 fl oz) milk
salt, pepper

Roughly chop the pumpkin. Heat the fat in a thick-based casserole or pan and let the pumpkin sweat in it until it turns translucent and soft. This may take up to half an hour depending on the age of the pumpkin. Do not let the vegetable fry and if necessary put a lid on the pan. When it is soft enough to pulp, crush it in the pan with a wooden spoon until you have a purée, then stir in the maize flour. Blend in the saffron infused in the milk, season and let simmer gently for 5 minutes or so, stirring from time to time.

You will find you have a beautiful, gold-coloured light purée with a delicate flavour so don't serve it with a meat dish which might overpower it. It does go well, however, with pork chops.

LE GRATIN DE POTIRON AUVERGNAT
Glazed pumpkin purée

This is an enriched purée and would have been a dish on its own. The flavour is rather like a creamed carrot purée and so if served as a vegetable it is best with a slightly piquant dish in order to get the sweet and sour contrast.

Serves 6

1 kg (2¼ lb) pumpkin, peeled de-
seeded and cubed
2 teaspoons sugar
125 g (4 oz) grated Cantal cheese
(or Cheddar)

4 tablespoons flour
2 eggs
salt, pepper
30 g (1 oz) butter

Put the pumpkin into a pan with the sugar and 1 cm (½ inch) of water, cover and simmer for about half an hour with the lid on, until it is quite soft, dry and almost a purée. Stir until smooth and then blend in the grated cheese, flour and beaten eggs. Season.

Butter a gratin dish and spoon the purée into it. Dot the top with butter and put into a moderate oven (180°C, 350°F, Gas Mark 4) for 20 minutes. Flash the dish under the grill to *gratiner* the top before serving.

LE CHOU-FLEUR

The cauliflower is regarded as a winter vegetable but already by October the most enormous white heads are to be seen in vegetable crates on market day, imported from further north. They make a good start, together with the equally large heads of celery and the football-sized cabbages, to the winter cuisine.

LE CHOU-FLEUR FROMAGÉ
Cauliflower coated with cheese

Serves 4

1 cauliflower
salt
125 g (4 oz) Cantal or Laguiole
cheese (or Lancashire)
3 tablespoons double cream or
fromage frais

1 egg yolk
60 g (2 oz) fresh breadcrumbs
60 g (2 oz) butter (for *beurre noisette*)

Cook the whole cauliflower in boiling salted water (or better still, steam it) until it is *al dente* – between 5 and 10 minutes. Be most careful not to overcook it at this stage as it will continue cooking while being *gratiné*.

Drain and cool it and then place it in an oven-proof dish. Cut the cheese into long thinnish slices and with the help of a sharp knife, cut incisions in the cauliflower and poke the cheese down into them. Do this all over the flowering top. Season with salt and pepper. Mix the cream with an egg yolk and pour this over the top. Sprinkle with the breadcrumbs and brown the top under a hot grill.

Then transfer the dish to a cool oven (150°C, 300°F, Gas Mark 2) to melt the cheese. While it is softening prepare the *beurre noisette* by heating the butter until it starts to turn a golden colour. Sprinkle this over the cauliflower and serve straight away.

For a less rich version, substitute *fromage frais* for the double cream and omit the *beurre noisette*.

LE CÉLERI-RAVE

These knobbly roots, the size of a large grapefruit, are a versatile vegetable with a flavour near to celery but of more subtlety. Boiled or steamed as an accompanying vegetable, or even better, made into a purée with butter, cream or *fromage frais*, celeriac goes wonderfully well with pork or game. It is also a useful spring salad vegetable: cut into *julienne* and dressed with a mustardy mayonnaise when it is known as *céleri-remoulade*, it may be found in many a local *hors d'oeuvre*.

LES SALSIFIS et LES SCORSONÈRES

In season in late autumn and in winter, there are two root vegetables that are both often called salsify. True salsify is also known in Britain as the vegetable oyster because, it is said, of its slightly fishy flavour but this seems hard to credit. Its skin is light brown and it is shaped like an over-long carrot. In contrast *la scorsonère* (or *scorzonera*, from an old Catalan word meaning viper because the roots of one kind were used in the treatment of snake bites) is dark, almost black and tapers much less than salsify. They both belong to the daisy family and have a delicate flavour, the *scorzonera* being perhaps the finer of the two. When peeled, their white flesh discolours on being exposed to the air, so it is advisable to cook them in what the French call *un blanc*.

To cook 500 g (1 lb) salsify you will need for *le blanc*:

1 tablespoon flour	1 teaspoon salt
2 tablespoons wine vinegar	1 litre (1¾ pt) water

In a large pan whisk together the flour, vinegar, salt and water and bring to boiling point, stirring occasionally.

Peel the salsify and cut off the leaf end. If necessary, to fit into the pan, cut them in half but the less they are cut up at this stage the better. Simmer them very gently in the *blanc* until they are just tender; the time may vary but should be about ½–¾ hour. When they are cooked, peel and cut them into 3.5 cm (1½ in) lengths.

LES SALSIFIS EN SAUCE
Salsify in sauce

Serves 4

500 g (1lb) cooked *salsifis* (as above)

for the sauce:

1 or 2 small onions, chopped	about 150 ml (¼ pt) stock or water
1 tablespoon butter	salt, pepper
1 tablespoon flour	parsley
1 teaspoon tomato purée	

Make the sauce by softening the onions in the butter. Stir in the flour and tomato purée and blend in the stock or water slowly in order to avoid lumps. Season. Bring the sauce to the boil and leave it to simmer very gently for about 20 minutes.

Add the precooked salsify to the sauce and allow to sit in it for 5 minutes or so but do not continue cooking too long as the salsify should remain firm rather than soft. Sprinkle with chopped parsley before serving.

LES SALSIFIS SAUTÉS AU BEURRE
Salsify in butter

Serves 4

500 g (1 lb) cooked *salsifis* (as above)	chopped parsley
60 g (2 oz) clarified butter	chopped garlic (optional)
salt, pepper	

Heat the butter in a sauté pan until it is quite hot then throw in the salsify. Season with salt and freshly ground black pepper and let the pieces take on colour like sauté potatoes. Turn them over from time to time. Serve with chopped parsley sprinkled over and also a little chopped garlic if wished.

●

When *les scorsonères* start to sprout in the spring and young buds appear but have not yet opened these used to be, and maybe still are, picked to flavour an omelette. Recipes for *l'omelette aux boutons de scorsonères* appear in more than one cookery book of the Périgord and the Rouergue and were evidently regarded as quite a delicacy. We have not had the chance of tasting this.

LES ENDIVES

Les endives or, just to confuse, what the English call chicory, also appear with winter. *Les endives* to the French are the white, tightly packed hearts known also as the Belgian endives, not the related salad chicory which is the *chicorée-frisée* or more often just *la frisée*.

Chicory grows wild all over the South-West and until the end of the seventeenth century was used solely for medicinal purposes. It was developed 'industrially' as a vegetable and as an ingredient for coffee-making from plants in the North of France. Belgium in fact first took the lead in its cultivation but now France claims to head production. You may see at market in the South-West home-grown versions of *endives*, the heads smaller and not so tight or so white. They are none the worse for that but when using them as a vegetable, you should obviously allow several heads per person. All the chicory family are protected from the light as they grow in order to reduce their bitterness and keep their pale colour. Even so, when cooking the white endive hearts these are always best blanched first. If they are then slowly braised, they have a sweet-sour, buttery taste and are a perfect combination for a rich meat dish like *l'enchaud de porc périgourdin* (page 76).

One lunchtime around New Year quite some years ago, Monsieur Fraysse who then owned the Hostellerie des Voyageurs at Naucelle in the Aveyron, served us chicory cooked in this delicious way. Sadly, he is no longer with us but his memory is preserved with his recipe, which we now always use. (It was also the late M. Fraysse who gave us his *truite aux lardons* recipe on page 130.)

LES ENDIVES BRAISÉES
Braised chicory

Serves 4

4 large (and 4 small) chicory	salt, pepper
30 g (1 oz) butter	lemon

Allow at least one large chicory for each person and perhaps a small one as well if it is to be the only vegetable of the meal.

Trim the bottom neatly with a stainless steel knife and wipe each one clean with a damp cloth. Plunge them into a pan of boiling, salted water containing a slice of lemon, reduce the heat and allow to simmer gently for 8-10 minutes. Be careful not to overcook them; they should be only semi-soft at this stage. Test with the point of a knife near the bottom end. Thinner ones may only need 8 minutes and should be lifted out.

Pre-heat the oven to 180°C, 350°F, Gas Mark 4. While it is warming, drain the chicory thoroughly, standing them stalk end upwards. Heat the butter and about one tablespoonful of water in a flameproof casserole large enough for them to fit in one layer. Put in the chicory, baste them with the melted butter, salt lightly, and pepper more generously. Cover, bring the pot to simmering point before transferring it to the oven, which should now be turned down as low as possible. Provided it is hot when the chicory goes in, it does not matter if the pot goes off the boil, indeed it should. Leave the pot to cook very gently like this for at least 2 hours, basting the heads from time to time.

To serve, transfer the vegetables to a clean, warm dish, spoon the buttery juices over and sprinkle in a little lemon juice. Do not worry that the endives will no longer be white but will have turned darker and translucent.

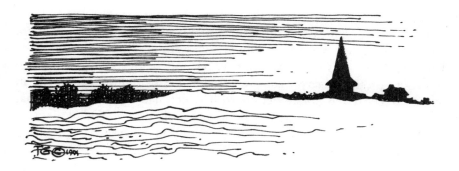

LES SALADES

PHILIP OYLER, WRITING in his second book about country life in the Dordogne after World War II, says 'the peasants here like to have a salad every day of the year and appreciate a gift of lettuce or endive, when they are short of them, more than anything else.' *Sons of the Generous Earth* (Hodder & Stoughton, 1963, p 105).

This is certainly still true; we are often the recipients of one or two crisp lettuces, freshly picked with the roots and earth still attached. When the fine weather arrives, salads swell at an amazing rate and all get ready to bolt at once. Those whose plants are ready, pass them on to family or friends, and later the exchange is opportunely returned.

Until quite recently a tossed green salad used always to be part of the menu in most country restaurants. It was sometimes the only 'green vegetable' of the meal but the lettuce would always be fresh and crisp, picked within hours and probably grown within a stone's throw of the kitchen. Sadly this custom is fast dying out, being replaced in some instances by the *salade composée*, offered at the beginning of a menu in place of the mixed hors d'oeuvre dish which had been the traditional start to a meal. This is due in part to *la nouvelle cuisine*. Today where a chef of the South-West has his roots firmly in *le terroir*, he is devising salads in local style or reviving traditional ones and we all benefit.

In summer the range of salads is wide, though if a long, dry spell sets in, local supplies naturally fall off. If you can grow and water your own, so much the better. Apart from the round cabbage lettuce and the *romaine* (cos), there are the more bitter *chicorée-frisée* and (*chicorée*) *scarole*.

As its name implies, *la frisée* is the curly-leaved, rather flattened salad we call endive, with green outer leaves and a yellowish centre. There is also the less bitter *scarole* or Batavian endive with broader leaves, only slightly curled. This too looks flattened from the blanching it receives as it grows: the plant is covered over to keep it white and reduce its bitterness.

In spring there is *le pissenlit* (dandelion), wild or cultivated, while in late summer and autumn you sometimes find bunches of *la roquette* (rocket) in the market, looking like a cross between dandelion and watercress but of a bluer colour. *La roquette* is quite peppery in flavour so combines well with the sweet-tasting, small fleshy lettuce called *la sucrine* (sold as Little Gem in Britain). This keeps for days, which is more than can be said for the more delicate *mâche*, more popularly known as *la doucette*. We know this as lamb's lettuce or corn salad and it is a tender plant with small spatula-shaped leaves growing from a central root. Another salad to be looked for is *la laitue romaine* whose leaves are prettily tinged with red.

The oil used to dress salads is often olive oil or perhaps the blander *tournesol* (sunflower) or *arachide* (groundnut). But before any of these became widely available in the South-West, salad oil was made from walnuts (see page 282). *L'huile de noix* is very strong in flavour and no doubt the local people were used to it at full strength; for those who are not so accustomed to it, a dilution with a flavourless oil is preferable. Either way, it makes the most delicious dressing and a small tin of walnut oil (best kept in the refrigerator once it has been opened) is an expensive but authentic addition to the larder of anyone cooking in the South-West tradition.

If a flavourless oil is needed, there is sunflower oil. Growing sunflowers for their seed which is then processed to make the oil has become a major crop in areas like the Haute-Garonne, ousting maize as being a more reliable crop in dry years. The large fields of flamboyant sunflowers make a spectacular sight in full summer. You can drive for kilometre after kilometre in the Lauragais south-east of Toulouse and see little else but their golden faces turned to the sun.

Then there is the question of the vinegar. In a region where wine-making has played such a big part for centuries and where many peasant families had, and still have, their own rows of *vignes*, home-made wine vinegar is no problem. All that is needed is some wine, the special container in which it is made, called *un vinaigrier*, and either some ready-made wine vinegar or a piece of *la mère*. *La mère* is the rubbery skin which forms on the surface as bacteria attack any wine that is exposed to the air and to warmth. This will act as a starter for the souring process. Alternatively a mix of two parts wine to one part vinegar will create the right acidic condition, provided always the ambient temperature is high enough (20–25°C). Once the wine has turned into vinegar, it can be drawn off as needed, more wine added and the process will continue under *la mère*. *Un vinaigrier*, made of oak or earthenware, complete with dispensing tap and ventilation holes, can be bought from a good *quincaillerie* (ironmonger) and when this is installed in the corner of a warm kitchen there is a permanent supply of vinegar, not to mention a recipient for any odd ends of bottles of wine.

LA SALADE À L'HUILE DE NOIX
Walnut oil salad

Serves 4

lettuce, *frisée, scarole* or *pissenlit*
1 tablespoon wine vinegar
salt, pepper

1 tablespoon walnut oil
2 tablespoons vegetable oil
8–12 walnuts, roughly chopped

Wash and dry whichever green salad is to be used, or use a mixture of more than one. Dandelion leaves should be young, picked from a plant which has not yet flowered.

Just before serving mix together the vinegar and some salt and pepper, then whisk in the oil. Pour this into the salad bowl, sprinkle the chopped walnuts over and turn the salad.

Autumn salads containing the season's newly-picked walnuts with their tender, juicy white flesh are perhaps the best.

LA SALADE ROUERGATE
Salad with walnuts and cheese

Serves 4

lettuce etc
1 tablespoon wine vinegar
salt, pepper
1 tablespoon walnut oil

2 tablespoons vegetable oil
60 g (2 oz) Roquefort cheese
15–20 walnut halves

Prepare the salad. Mix the ingredients for the *vinaigrette* and cut the cheese into cubes. Toss the salad in the dressing, turn in the pieces of cheese and scatter the walnut halves on top.

LA SALADE AVEYRONNAISE
Salad with Roquefort dressing

Serves 4

1 hearty cabbage lettuce	pepper
1 tablespoon Roquefort cheese	chopped herbs, eg. parsley, chervil,
1 tablespoon single cream	chives
2 tablespoon lemon juice	

Wash and dry the lettuce. Mash the cheese in the salad bowl, then blend in the cream, lemon juice and a good dash of pepper, but no salt because of the salty Roquefort. Add the herbs and taste to check the balance of creamy cheese and lemon flavours.

Toss the salad in this dressing just before serving.

———— ● ————

There are no prizes for guessing where the next salad comes from.

LA SALADE TRUFFÉE
Salad with truffle

Serves 4

1 truffle	salt, pepper
a little white wine	1 tablespoon walnut oil
1 lettuce or *chicorée-frisée*	2 tablespoons vegetable oil
1 tablespoon wine vinegar	a little chopped chervil or parsley

Poach the truffle in a little white wine for 5 minutes. Then slice thinly and mix it with the washed and dried salad. Leave it a little while to impregnate the leaves. Mix the vinegar with the seasonings, blend in the oils and herbs and when you are ready to serve, toss the salad in this dressing.

LA SALADE AU CHAPON
Salad with garlic flavoured bread

Many country households make this simple but delicious salad after the walnut harvest. *Un chapon* or in patois *lou capou* is a garlic and oil-impregnated piece of toasted bread which is not only used to flavour a salad like this, but in poorer homes was eaten with a bunch of sweet grapes in place of dessert.

Serves 4

1 thick slice of bread
1 clove garlic
1 tablespoon walnut oil
2 tablespoons vegetable oil
1 dessertspoon wine vinegar

salt, pepper
lettuce or *frisée*
1 tablespoon chopped walnuts
   (optional)

Toast the slice of bread and while it is hot, rub it all over with the cut clove of garlic. Mix together the two oils and pour a tablespoonful over the toast, then put it in the bottom of your salad bowl.

Make the rest of the oil into a dressing with the vinegar and seasoning. Wash and dry the salad and dress it just before serving, sprinkling in the chopped walnuts, if used. The *chapon* is divided between the guests.

———— ● ————

Our last salad is a spring favourite in the Périgord and the Auvergne; there are charming old picture postcards portraying the women out in the meadows at Easter-time picking the young dandelion leaves before they become too bitter.

LA SALADE DE PISSENLITS AU LARD
Dandelion and bacon salad

Serves 4

125 g (¼ lb) young dandelion leaves
salt, pepper
clove of garlic
1 tablespoon goose or pork fat

125 g (¼ lb) streaky bacon, cut into
   strips
1 tablespoon wine vinegar

Wash and dry the dandelion leaves and put them in a salad bowl. Season them with a little salt, pepper and chopped garlic.

Heat the fat and cook the pieces of bacon in it. When it is crispy and golden and still hot, pour it into the salad. Deglaze the pan with the vinegar quickly and pour this over the salad, tossing it all together. Serve immediately.

A *frisée* salad can be used as an alternative to the dandelion.

LES VIANDES

PORK USED TO be treat enough, especially in the poorer districts, but was enjoyed by almost everyone in the country because it was home-grown, home-killed and home-cured. Cows and oxen were the pride of every peasant farmer, wealth being measured by head of cattle as much as by the area of land you owned. They were therefore used for ploughing and working the land rather than as meat. Nor were they generally raised for dairy purposes, although in the Ariège cows' milk formed a major element in the diet of the poor peasants up to the end of the last century. For milk the peasants often preferred that from ewes or goats. Butter was not a regular commodity and most of the milk produced was used to make cheese, especially where there was good pasture land as in the Cantal and the lower Pyrenees.

As meat, therefore, beef had a rarity value. If you were a successful farmer with a farm large enough to employ, say, a dozen regular workers, you might well have enjoyed a beef Sunday lunch; and the moderately well-off peasant might have enjoyed a good stew on high feasts or holidays. The poorest, however, might hardly ever taste butcher's meat. At the beginning of this century one kilo of beef or veal cost the whole day's pay of a labourer or farm worker. This chapter is therefore concerned with the tables of the relatively fortunate; the owner of twenty or thirty hectares of good land, say, in one of the river valleys; the *petite bourgeoisie* of the villages, rather than those exclusively devoted to cultivation; or even the most humble of peasant families at the time of a wedding when, exceptionally, they would literally kill the fatted calf.

In peasant households the cooking was done, as we have seen, in the big open fireplace. Roasting was on a spit but was restricted to smaller joints; otherwise it would have been necessary to maintain the fire at a much higher temperature. Most chimneys would then smoke uncomfortably; it is true that many chimneys were intended to smoke to enable pork products to be preserved in quantity – not at a high heat, however, because then the fat of the pork would melt. In our house both rooms with large fireplaces have beams blackened with smoke from the days when it was the centre of a prosperous pig farm. We burn logs in the large fireplace of our sitting room, for both heating and cooking, but have had to devise a way of lowering the chimney breast by means of a kind of pelmet in order to make the chimney draw properly, so avoiding a room full of smoke. When a decent amount of ash has collected on the hearth so that a glowing hot heap of embers builds up, it is quite easy to cook a leg of lamb or a chicken in front of the fire, roasting it on a clockwork-driven spit (see the gigot of lamb recipe on page 229). These mechanical spits can still be bought from good ironmongers.

Beef provides few small compact roasting joints so it was more often than not cooked in other ways, notably braised or stewed for long periods. Furthermore, the quality of livestock was probably not in former times good enough to ensure that even the most highly rated parts of the animal would be tender enough for roasting.

Casseroled dishes were cooked either in iron pots called *daubières* in the ashes (with more hot ashes in the hollowed-out lid) or on trivets strategically placed close to or over the fire. The fire itself needed only to be a modest affair, so it was possible to control temperatures fairly easily and the cook could get on with other jobs in or out of the house – feeding the chickens, ducks and geese, nursing the *potager* or foraging for foliage for the rabbits. Alternatively, time-consuming dishes were taken along to the baker's oven and put in when the bread came out. They were left there for hours as the oven gradually cooled down. We have seen that some of the larger farms had their own oven for breadbaking, so could use that for their *daubes* or stews.

LES DAUBES ET LES ESTOUFFATS

Daubes and *estouffats* – the names are interchangeable – were invariably cooked very slowly and for a long time. This poses the first problem for

English cooks: how to keep the heat low enough. We tend to cook our stews at a higher level and the whole operation is over in two or three hours. A *daube* should barely simmer; the very lowest flame in a gas oven, well below Mark ¼ and almost at the point when the gas goes out altogether, will be quite high enough, once the dish has been brought to simmering temperature. Owners of a solid-fuel cooker such as an Aga are in a better position for this type of slow cooking.

There are other differences between our casseroled beef dishes and the French ones. The French farmer's wife will add extra fat meat to the stew – *couennes* (pork rind), pig's trotter, belly of pork or the home-cured country ham. These add body and a slightly gelatinous quality to the dish. Not all of the fat which rises to the surface during the cooking will be removed. Wine, usually red but often white if the dish is to be eaten cold, plays a more prominent part while pre-made stock or water is rarely required. *Eau-de-vie* is often added towards the end, and *haricots blancs* are featured as an accompaniment as well as any mushrooms which may be about – even dried ones rehydrated if there are no fresh.

The cuts of meat vary enormously and may dictate the cooking time. Pieces from the chuck or shoulder are commonly used, but the range goes from sirloin at best to shin at worst. Sometimes the meat is cooked all in one piece, or it may be cut into cubes or steak-like slices, sometimes marinated. There are as many combinations and recipes as there are cooks. The four recipes which follow show a fair range, including one version intended to be eaten cold.

LA DAUBE TARNAISE
Casserole of marinated beef

This recipe is traditional to the plateau above the Tarn valley. The inclusion of pork rind and a pig's foot gives body to the *daube* – flour is not always used except in recipes which call for an initial browning and frying of the meat.

1 kg (2¼ lb) piece of topside of beef, or chuck	3 tablespoons pork fat
	1 tablespoon flour
salt, pepper	2 teaspoons tomato purée or
2 tablespoons *eau-de-vie*	2 tomatoes
60 g (2 oz) fat belly of pork	1 ham knuckle
100 g (3½ oz) lean belly of pork	1 pig's foot
100 g (3½ oz) fresh pork skin	
large piece of ham skin (if available)	

for the marinade:
½ bottle red wine
3 tablespoons wine vinegar
1 large onion
1 sliced carrot

½ head garlic
bouquet garni, including celery and
 leek tops
a few juniper berries,
1 clove

Cut the beef into 85 g (3 oz) cubes, sprinkle them with coarse salt and pepper and the *eau-de-vie* and leave them to marinate for an hour. Mix together all the ingredients for the marinade, pour it over the meat and leave in a cool place overnight.

Next day, cut the belly of pork into largish pieces and drain the meat. Colour them all in the pork fat in a large casserole. Sprinkle in the flour and stir well, still cooking over a moderately high heat, then reduce the heat and pour in the marinade mixed with the tomato purée. Add the ham knuckle, pig's foot and the pork skin (cut into decent sized squares). Cover the top with a large piece of ham skin, if you have one, checking beforehand that all is covered in liquid; if not, add a little stock or water. Cover the top with foil to make a tight fit under the lid, and cook very slowly for at least 6 hours – either on top of the stove or, better still, in a low oven.

At the end of the cooking time, take out the ham skin and transfer the meat to a fresh cooking pot, removing the bones from the knuckle and pig's foot, and cutting up the meat into serving pieces. Strain the liquor, reduce it if rather thin and de-grease it to taste. Pour it back over the meats and reheat for 10–15 minutes.

Serve hot with slices of toasted *millas* (see page 143), a traditional kind of bread substitute.

Saint-André was the brother of St Peter and his feast day falls on 30 November. This coincides with the real beginning of winter and is celebrated with a typically heart-warming *daube* of beef. An unusual approach in this dish is one which crops up all over the South-West from the Périgord to the Landes: the stew is prepared with alternate layers of fairly thinly-sliced meat and a *hachis* made with pork belly, garlic and parsley. Sometimes the meat is lightly crushed with a fork after cooking.

LA DAUBE DE LA SAINT-ANDRÉ
Beef casserole in the style of a terrine

Serves 4–6

1–1.5 kg (2¼–3 lb) piece of top
  rump of beef
salt, pepper
250 g (8 oz) *couennes* (pork skin)
½–¾ bottle red wine, preferably
  Cahors
1 onion stuck with 2 or 3 cloves
bouquet garni
quatre-épices

for the *hachis*:
250 g (8 oz) salt belly of pork
parsley
garlic
shallots

Cut the piece of beef into slices about 2 cm (¾ in) thick. Season them. Using a heavy casserole with a tight fitting lid, line the bottom with the pieces of pork skin, fatty side down. Put in a layer of the beef and cover this with a layer of the chopped belly of pork mixed with some chopped parsley, garlic and shallots. On top of this put another layer of beef followed by more of the *hachis* and a final layer of beef. Pour over the wine and push into the middle the onion stuck with cloves, the bouquet garni and seasonings.

Bring the pot to the boil then cover it tightly, preferably with a layer of foil over the top and under the lid. Leave to cook on the lowest possible heat for 7 hours or so. Before serving, remove as much of the fat from the gravy as you like.

———— • ————

In country districts this dish, the secret of which is the long, slow cooking, would be prepared the evening before and left to cook all night in the embers of the fire.

You will not be surprised to learn that in Gascony generous quantities of armagnac are used in preparing their version of a *daube*. The joint is generally kept whole and not cut into pieces.

In the foothills of the Pyrenees the country people round Foix use white wine for their *daube* and like to add dried mushrooms to give the dish extra savour. Note also that the meat is first floured and sealed in the English manner. *Millas* (page 143) is the traditional accompaniment but croûtons of good country bread, sautéed in goose fat, would be delicious. So would the white haricot beans of nearby Pamiers which the locals boast of as being the best in France.

In the hill country of the eastern Rouergue they have a *daube* of their own, formerly a dish for Christmas and Easter, which goes under the enchanting name of *coufidou*. *Cofir* in the local patois means to simmer. Even in the South-West the French tend not to eat garlic with beef but this is an exception.

LE COUFIDOU OU LA DAUBE AVEYRONNAISE
Beef in a rich wine sauce

Serves 4

700 g (1½ lb) braising or stewing
  steak, cut thick
175 g (6 oz) piece of salt belly of
  pork, with its skin
2 tablespoons beef dripping
1 large onion, chopped
4 cloves garlic, chopped

2 tablespoons flour
3 tablespoons tomato sauce or
  1 tablespoon tomato purée
300 ml (½ pt) Marcillac or other
  red wine
salt, pepper
bouquet garni

Divide the meat into large chunks. Remove the skin from the pork and dice the meat. Cut the skin into strips.

Heat the dripping in a large casserole and seal the meat on both sides. Remove it and put in the pork, the pork skin, onion and garlic. Stir them round for a minute or so then add the flour and tomato sauce, mixing them in. Stir in the wine and bring to the boil, stirring continuously. Add seasoning, lower the heat and put back the pieces of beef. Push the bouquet garni into the centre. Cover with a sheet of aluminium foil under the lid and bring up gently to the boil again – when you can hear a gentle bubbling inside. Cook as indicated above. Remove the bouquet before serving.

Boiled potatoes, jacket potatoes or a purée of chestnuts and potatoes (page 273) would be traditional with this stew.

●

To round off this group, here is a *daube* for eating cold. It is a kind of *boeuf à la mode* only made with wine, not *bouillon*. The presence of the marrow-bones and *couennes* should ensure that you will need no gelatine to set the finished dish. The bigger the *daube* the more spectacular it will look but even for four people and with modest quantities it will still be attractive. All you need to accompany it is a bitter salad, dandelions or *frisée*. Dress it with a vinaigrette that includes some walnut oil. This is an ideal dish for a summer lunch.

La Daube au Vin Blanc
Cold beef in a white wine jelly

Serves 4

1 kg (2¼ lb) sirloin or silverside of beef
2 cloves garlic
2 tablespoons goose fat
350 g (¾ lb) *couennes* (pork rind)
2 marrow bones
3 shallots, chopped
60 g (2 oz) salt belly of pork or *jambon de campagne*, or some of each

575 ml (1 pt) dry white wine
salt, pepper
bay leaf, thyme
500 g (1 lb) carrots, sliced
1 large onion, chopped
3 tablespoons *eau-de-vie* or brandy

The meat is cooked in one piece, spiked with garlic. Brown it in a frying pan in the goose fat until it takes on colour and is well sealed. Line your casserole with the *couennes*, lay the beef on it with the marrow bones, the shallots, the pork and/or ham. Add the wine, seasonings and herbs. Cover the *daube*, bring it just to simmering point and transfer to your lowest possible oven heat for 6–8 hours. During the last 2 hours add the carrots, onions and *eau-de-vie*.

When the *daube* is cooked, check for seasoning, remove as much fat as possible from the surface. Cut the meat into thin and tidy slices – which calls for some care with a piece of beef which has cooked for so long. Now choose a pudding bowl or similar receptacle from which you will be able to turn out your finished dish when it is cold. Put a little of the sauce in this bowl and lay the carrot rings in it, followed by the slices of beef. You can alternate layers of carrot and beef if you like. Strain the rest of the sauce over the mixture, allow it to cool and leave in the refrigerator for 12 hours.

When you are ready to turn it out, place the bowl in a saucepan of hot water for half a minute and it should then turn out cleanly on to your serving dish.

Le Pot-au-Feu
Beef in its broth with vegetables

This dish is eaten all over France and is a great stand-by when there are a lot of mouths to feed. There are once again a great many variations, even from one part of the South-West to another. For example, in the Périgord veal is often the base while in the neighbouring Quercy the principal meat is beef. In the Tarn a piece of pork shin may be added to give substance to the *bouillon* and even a piece of *confit*, while in the

Ariège lean pork meat is used to replace both. If a large party is expected a stuffed chicken may be added to the pot.

Because of all the different kinds of meat which combine to make a good *pot-au-feu*, there need to be six people at least to enjoy it, while to do justice to a more extravagant version, twelve would be a minimum. Two versions are given here which seem to contrast different regional styles, each contributing something essentially *du grand sud-ouest*, and in which various tips from all over the region have been incorporated.

The following 'rules' are basic for all kinds of *pot-au-feu*:-

1 Choose a pan, preferably tall rather than wide, large enough to contain a generous covering of water as well as the solids.

2 The pan (in France a tall cylindrical pot called a *marmite*) must, like the *daubière*, have a really tight-fitting lid.

3 It is difficult to have both the finest broth and the tenderest meat at the same time. The best *bouillon* calls for the meat to be put into cold water and gradually brought to the boil. If you want the tenderest and tastiest meat it should be immersed in water already just boiling. In either case the pot must be skimmed regularly to remove the scum which rises to the surface.

4 Once the *pot-au-feu* approaches the boil, it must barely simmer rather than boil. 'A broth cooked too fast is valueless.'

5 The vegetables – in Gascony called *les sabous* (the savours) – should not be added until the water is hot and most of the scum from the meat has been taken off. So allow the meat to simmer for 20 minutes before adding the vegetables. Alternatively, after 20 minutes of cooking the meat, throw the water away and start again, this time using all the ingredients.

6 Cut the onions into halves or quarters and roast them in a hot oven until the cut sides are nearly black – they will give colour to the broth. Do not chop them up. Tomatoes may be similarly blackened over a flame and put in the pot whole.

7 The broth may be served with some of the vegetables or with vermicelli. The meat will be served afterwards with the vegetables, or what is left of them, and a garnish of gherkins. A tomato sauce (page 190) with capers added, or a selection of mustards, are good accompaniments, and a few potatoes cooked at the last minute in the *bouillon* are all you will need by way of extra vegetables.

LE POT-AU-FEU À L'ALBIGEOISE
Beef in broth, with a variety of meats

Serves 6

575 g (1¼ lb) chuck steak
575 g (1¼ lb) shin of veal, on the
  bone
125 g (4 oz) shin of pork
250 g (½ lb) *saucisson sec*
250 g (½ lb) carrots
175 g (6 oz) leeks
125 g (4 oz) turnips
2 sticks celery
5 cloves garlic, cut into quarters

2 onions, stuck with 2 cloves,
  roasted and halved
salt, pepper
bouquet garni
1 wing of *confit d'oie*, with any fat
  removed
175 g (6 oz) white haricot beans,
  pre-soaked if dried
1 small cabbage, cut vertically into
  6 pieces

The four kinds of meat should each be in one piece, not cut up before cooking. Put all of these except the *confit* into the pot, cover with water and bring gently to the boil, then skim. Roughly chop the vegetables and add them and the seasonings, but not the haricots or the cabbage. Cover and cook very slowly for 3 hours. Then add the *confit*, beans and cabbage and cook all together for another hour. Check for seasoning before serving the broth, followed by the meats.

LE POT-AU-FEU GRANDE FÊTE
Beef in broth, for a special occasion

Serves 10–12

1 kg (2¼ lb) topside of beef
1 marrow bone
575 g (1¼ lb) shin of veal
1 *poule farcie*, prepared as for *poule au
  pot* (page 51)
or
1 stuffed breast of veal prepared as
  for *peau farcie de la Montagne Noire*
  (page 223)

vegetables as above (white haricot
  beans may be omitted)
seasonings as above

The cooking method is the same as already described but the chicken or stuffed veal breast should only be added 2 hours before serving time.

●

Beef enters into many other regional recipes; the cheaper cuts always remained in demand (they still do) and oxtail is no exception. One cannot fail to make a lovely stew with oxtail.

Its meat is fairly glutinous and in the Auvergne they have a way of mopping up its naturally rich juices with chestnuts. This makes a change from white haricot beans.

LE RAGOÛT DE QUEUE DE BOEUF
Ragout of oxtail with chestnuts

Serves 6

There are four cooking processes involving

1) 1 oxtail, cut up
   60 g (2 oz) goose or pork fat
   125 g (4 oz) carrots, finely chopped
   175 g (6 oz) onion, finely chopped
   45 g (1½ oz) flour
   1 litre (1¾ pt) dry white wine
   bouquet garni
   salt, pepper

2) 250 g (½ lb) salt belly of pork, cubed
   250 g (½ lb) Toulouse sausage, cut into 3 cm (1¼ in) slices

3) 500 g (1 lb) peeled chestnuts
   stick of celery

4) croûtons of *pain de seigle* (rye bread)
   60 g (2 oz) goose or pork fat

In a heavy casserole – *une daubière* – put the pieces of oxtail to brown gently in the goose fat. Add the carrots and onions and when fairly browned, sprinkle with the flour, stir well and cook together for a few minutes, allowing the mixture to take on some colour. Add the wine little by little, stirring to amalgamate the gravy, add the bouquet garni and seasonings, and allow the mixture to simmer, covered, over a low heat for 3 hours or so.

Meanwhile fry the pieces of salt pork and sausage very gently in their own fat for 20 minutes. Cook the chestnuts in lightly salted water with the celery for 20 minutes and strain.

When the oxtail pieces are cooked, put them in a serving dish with the chestnuts, the salt pork and sausage. Remove what fat you can from the liquor in which the oxtail has cooked and pour the remaining juice over all. Serve with hot croûtons of rye bread, fried in goose or pork fat.

———— • ————

Another way of cooking oxtail gets away from the idea of stews and gives almost the impression of a quick, barbecued grill. Nevertheless three hours or more of painstaking preparation have gone into what seems like a fast food snack!

LA QUEUE DE BOEUF GRILLÉE PAYSANNE
Grilled oxtail

Serves 4

10–12 pieces of oxtail, 4 large, 6–8 smaller
1–1.5 litres (1¾–2½ pt) beef stock
175 g (6 oz) fresh breadcrumbs

for the marinade:
oil
salt, pepper
parsley and chives, chopped
4 shallots, chopped
4 cloves garlic, chopped

Simmer the pieces of trimmed oxtail in some good beef stock for 2–3 hours until tender though not falling off the bone. Leave to cool in the liquor, then drain them. (Use the stock as a basis for a soup.)

Prepare the marinade and put the meat in it to marinate for an hour, turning it over from time to time.

Roll the pieces in the breadcrumbs, pressing them firmly all round. Heat your grill well then grill quickly, turning them over to brown on all sides. Serve immediately, with a fresh tomato sauce (page 190).

———— • ————

The tripe which in the north of England is eaten with onions, and in Normandy prepared *à la mode de Caen*, is from the ox. In France the tripe of all animals is prepared for the table but nowhere more so than in the country running from Albi north to Aurillac. The cooking of tripe goes back a long way into history, at least to Roman times.

The city of Albi also happened for many centuries to be a centre for the trade in saffron, a spice which was introduced by the Moors into the South-West via Spain. Saffron used to be widely cultivated in the region of the Tarn. Alas, it has all but died out. But it is imported commercially and is easy to buy in even the smallest *épicerie*. Its marriage with tripe is as beautiful as it is unlikely and gives one of the most original as well as savoury dishes of the whole of the South-West.

LES TRIPES AU SAFRAN À L'ALBIGEOISE
Tripe cooked with saffron

Serves 4

for the preliminary cooking:
1 kg (2¼ lb) *gras double* (beef or calf's
   tripe from the stomach)
1 pig's or calf's foot
piece of ham bone (optional)
2 onions, 1 stuck with 3 cloves
2 carrots
bouquet garni
3 cloves garlic
175 ml (6 fl oz) dry white wine
stock to cover, about 1 litre (1¾ pt)
salt, pepper

for the sauce:
2 tablespoons goose fat
125 g (4 oz) salt belly of pork or
   unsmoked streaky bacon
1 onion, finely chopped
2 cloves garlic, finely chopped
2 tablespoons chopped parsley
½ teaspoon powdered saffron
3 tablespoons flour
3 tablespoons capers plus
   1 tablespoon of their vinegar
2 tablespoons armagnac

In this country tripe is usually sold already blanched. If not, you must plunge it in lightly salted boiling water for 5 minutes. This will give off a most disagreeable smell, which you must not allow to put you off the whole dish.

Cut the blanched tripe into 5 cm (2 in) squares and put them in a pan which has a tight-fitting lid, is large enough to hold the other ingredients and is good for slow simmering. Cover with the vegetables and the other meats, packing the whole as tightly as reasonably possible – the more concentrated your *bouillon* in the end the better. Add the wine and stock. Season lightly and bring slowly to the boil. Cover and simmer gently for at least 8 hours, the longer the better – but the heat must be very low.

An hour or so before you intend to serve the dish, take a flameproof *marmite* or similar dish in which you will serve it, and in it melt the fat and the pork, diced small. Add the onion, garlic and parsley and soften all together slowly for 10 minutes. Stir in the flour and cook for 2–3 minutes. Ladle the tripe from the other pan into this roux and gradually moisten with enough of the tripe stock to bring the roux to an attractive consistency – a thinnish cream. Stir in the saffron. Cover the pot and cook all together slowly for 40 minutes. Just before serving, add the capers and their vinegar and armagnac and check the seasoning.

Steamed or boiled potatoes are called for as an accompaniment, with a crisp salad to follow. Whatever you do, do not spurn the stock that you have not used. When it cools it will turn into a marvellous transparent jelly, as deep in flavour as it will be in colour.

●

It would be easy to run away with the idea that the peasants of the South-West disdain the finer cuts of beef. Not at all, but there is the problem of the price differential between the cuts which are used to make *daubes* and which sell very reasonably in every village butcher's, and the finer cuts of steak for grilling. Perhaps that is why the French persist in joints of beef cut into steaks which, as so many people have discovered in restaurants of all classes in France, do not support grilling at all. It is true that the French rate flavour higher than tenderness but that is hardly a recommendation for the many cuts made to do duty as steaks which would be better off in a *daube*.

Not that there is anything the matter with modern French beef. Fillet, *entrecôte* and sirloin can be even more delicious in France than they are from the best Aberdeen herds. The Bordelais have long had a penchant for *entrecôtes*, provided they are cut thick and served underdone. They have a better flavour than fillet and their texture is more reliable than sirloin or rump. This recipe should be in every beef-lover's top five.

L'ENTRECÔTE À LA BORDELAISE
Grilled steak with beef marrow

This dish, which has passed into the national cuisine more completely than many others in this collection, is associated nowadays with a fairly short and strong red wine sauce. Even in the restaurants of Bordeaux the customers would probably look askance at a steak served under this name without a sauce. It seems historically, however, that the original *entrecôte à la bordelaise* was prepared rather in the same way as *entrecôte à la périgourdine* but with the addition of the beef marrow. This latter is the key characteristic of the dish and its omission is as wrong as it is increasingly frequent. The tendency nowadays is to refer indiscriminately to steak '*à la bordelaise*' and steak '*au marchand de vin*' which is a pity if only because they respectively derive from the two great rival areas of fine red wine production in France.

Perhaps the easy way out of the difficulty is to regard the sauce as optional and whether or not you make it might depend on the rest of the menu. A garnish or accompaniment of plain or sauce-less vegetables would cry out for the sauce, whereas if the vegetables or the surrounding dishes were to be complicated or served in their own sauce, the 'dry' version might be preferred. If you make the sauce, it is correct to use white wine (not red, though the latter tends to be more generally used nowadays). It is a good idea to finish the sauce before you cook the steak.

Two points should be noted: first, the steak should be cut about 3.5 cm (1½ in) thick. Thus one entrecôte will weigh about 500 g (1 lb) and will do for two people. Secondly, the beef marrow will be a more attractive pink rather than grey colour if it is soaked overnight.

Serves 4

for the *entrecôtes*:
2 *entrecôte* steaks, 3.5 cm (1½ in)
   thick, each weighing about 500 g
   (1 lb)
1 beef marrow bone cut into 7.5 cm
   (3 in) lengths
oil
salt, pepper
4 shallots, finely chopped
1 tablespoon butter
chopped parsley (optional)

for the sauce (optional):
4 shallots, finely chopped
½ bottle dry white wine
300 ml (½ pt) strong beef stock
125 g (4 oz) butter
salt, pepper

Soak the marrow bones for several hours, changing the water as often as possible. Put them into a pan into which they will just fit to stop them rolling over and the marrow falling out. Cover with cold water, bring to the boil and cook fairly gently for 20 minutes. Remove the bones from the pan, extract the marrow with a teaspoon and allow it to cool until it is quite firm. Chop it into small dice about 0.6 cm (¼ in) thick.

While the marrow is cooking, paint the steaks with oil and season with pepper. (They should not be salted until after cooking.)

Soften the shallots very gently in a tablespoonful of butter – they should not be allowed to brown. Heat a griddle to cook the steaks on. A charcoal or wood fire is even better, especially if the prunings from the vines are burnt on it – *les sarments de vigne* – but the usual grill attached to a domestic cooker is really not fierce enough to seal the meat quickly. As a last resort choose your heaviest frying pan.

Whatever the utensil, grease it and get it really hot. Put the steaks on it and leave for 2 minutes without touching them except to see that they are not sticking to the pan. Turn over and seal the second side also. After 2 minutes remove from the fire, spread the shallots on top and cover with the diced marrow. Return to the heat and cook over high heat until the steaks are done. Flatten the marrow on to the meat from time to time with the flat side of a knife. Halve each steak.

You can, if you like sprinkle on some parsley before serving. If the steaks are to be rare – which they should be – a total of 12 minutes' cooking will probably be about right but much will depend on your pan and your fire. The sauce is served, if at all, separately.

The sauce:
In a small but heavy-bottomed saucepan, put in the shallots and cover with the wine. Bring to the boil and cook fiercely until there is only about one tablespoonful of liquid left. Add the stock and cook this too until it is reduced by about half. Strain the liquid and reheat to boiling point, take it off the fire and add the butter in little pieces one at a time, whisking them in. The sauce should become light and frothy but must not boil after this point. Keep in a warm place until the steaks are ready to be served.

———— ● ————

From beef it is but a short step to veal. It might be thought that if beef is eaten so little in the French countryside because of its price, veal would be scarcely seen at all. In fact, veal is more currently eaten than beef and is the most highly rated butchers' meat of all. There is a regular market in calves, which gives the peasant farmer the francs he needs to buy what he cannot produce himself. Such a market ensures in turn that only some young animals are bought by cattle farmers and the rest are re-sold for the table.

Alas, veal is no longer always produced naturally: milk-fed veal from the farm has given way to modern industrialized methods reminiscent of the battery hen. If you are in France and get a chance to buy veal *élevé à l'ancienne* or *élevé sous la mère*, take it and you will find out what veal really tastes like. Some growers are setting out to produce it in commercial quantities, such as *Les Fermiers du Bas-Rouergue*. An adolescent calf is called *une génisse* and the meat is somewhere in colour, texture and flavour mid-way between veal and beef. In France, much of what is really *génisse* is sold as veal.

Stuffings for meat have to be tasty in the South-West to escape the charge that one's cooking is *fade* – a combination of blandness and tiredness. For example the following way of stuffing a shoulder of veal is particularly successful. The recipe is given for larger numbers than usual – the cut of meat does not lend itself to making small joints, and this is a good way of making expensive meat go a long way. This dish is also good cold.

L'ÉPAULE DE VEAU FARCIE
Stuffed shoulder of veal

Serves 8–10

2 kg (4½ lb) shoulder of veal, in a
  piece

for the stuffing:
250 g (½ lb) pure pork sausagemeat
1 or 2 chicken livers (optional)
3–4 tablespoons breadcrumbs
1–2 shallots, chopped
1 clove garlic, chopped

thin pieces of pork fat
veal or chicken stock

1 tablespoon chopped parsley
½ teaspoon chopped tarragon
salt, pepper, *quatre-épices*
grated rind of a lemon
1 egg yolk

The piece of shoulder should be roughly oblong and cushion-shaped. Either cut or ask the butcher to cut for you a slit along the length of one of the sides – the thicker of the two – to make a pocket to hold the stuffing. The cut should not go right through to the opposite side.

Make the stuffing by mixing together the sausagemeat, chopped liver, breadcrumbs, shallot, garlic, herbs and seasonings. Be generous with salt and pepper unless you know that the sausagemeat has already been well seasoned. Bind it all together with the beaten yolk of egg. Fill the slit in the joint with this stuffing, then prepare to tie it up, having to hand some thin pieces of pork fat to serve as barding on the top and also as a covering for the opening, so preventing the stuffing from falling out during the roasting.

Lay these in place, then tie them down with thin string at 1 cm (½ in) intervals along the length of the joint, followed by one or two loops at right angles so that you have a firmly-tied parcel.

After preheating the oven to 220°C, 425°F, Gas Mark 7, put the joint into a greased roasting tin in the centre of the oven. A 2 kg (4½ lb) piece of veal, allowing 25 minutes per 500 g (1 lb), will take approximately 1¾ hours, followed by quarter of an hour's resting time. After the first half hour reduce the heat to 190°C, 375°F, Gas Mark 5, and baste the meat from time to time with a little stock so that you get the pan juices nicely coloured in the tin. At the end of the cooking time and while the joint is resting in a warm place, scrape up and mix together all the contents of the roasting tin. Dilute with a little more stock if necessary and serve these pan juices separately.

Cut off the strings and remove the slices of fat before carving the joint along its length, serving some meat together with a little of the stuffing.

——— ● ———

Veal lends itself very well to roasting on a spit or over a wood fire. Veal chops with a 'stuffing' of traditional flavourings are transformed into something with *Sud-Ouest* written all over them.

LES CÔTELETTES DE VEAU FARCIES
Veal chops with a savoury garnish

Serves 4

4 trimmed veal chops
salt, pepper
4 slices fresh or salt belly of pork,
   chopped

4-6 shallots, chopped
4 tablespoons chopped parsley
1 large clove garlic, chopped
a little oil or goose fat
1 tablespoon red wine vinegar

Ideally the veal chops should be grilled over an open wood fire or over charcoal to produce the authentic flavour. If this is not possible, sauter them.

Mix together the pork, shallots, parsley and garlic so that you have a fine stuffing or *farce*. Season the chops after painting them with oil or goose fat, then put them to cook. While the first sides are being done, put the *farce* to cook in a separate pan over a low heat. When you have turned the chops, put a spoonful of the stuffing on top of each one. Continue the cooking and just before serving, sprinkle a tablespoonful of vinegar over them.

A *ragoût* of broad beans (page 165) goes well with the dish.

— ● —

In the Tarn they make a glorified version of calf's liver and bacon, using the raw country ham whose saltiness is set off rather well by the sweet sauce, which is based on *vin de rancio*. This is an old sweet fortified wine which has been allowed to maderize, thus Madeira would be an acceptable substitute.

LE FOIE DE VEAU AU RANCIO
Calf's liver in sweet wine sauce

Serves 4

4 thin slices of raw *jambon de
   campagne*
2 tablespoons goose fat
700 g (1½ lb) calf's liver, cut into
   4 pieces, 1 cm (½ in) thick
flour
salt, pepper

250 g (½ lb) mushrooms, *morilles* for
   preference
2 tablespoons chopped parsley
2 cloves garlic, chopped
250 ml (8 fl oz) *vin de rancio*
juice of ½ lemon

Soften the ham in the goose fat in a frying pan and cook slowly until done – for about 10 minutes. If this ham is not available, very thinly-sliced gammon rashers would be the best substitute. When cooked, remove to a serving dish in a low oven to keep hot. While the ham is cooking, roll the liver in seasoned flour and, after removing the ham, turn up the heat and brown the liver briefly on each side to seal it. Reduce the heat and cook gently for not more than 5 minutes on each side – liver should remain pink inside. Remove it and place each slice on top of its own piece of ham.

To the juices in the pan add the mushrooms, chopped parsley and garlic and fry briefly for a minute or two, sprinkle with a tablespoonful of flour, stir it in, then add the wine. Season and cook altogether for 2 or 3 minutes. Add the lemon juice and serve with the liver and ham.

———— • ————

It would be surprising if cooks in the South-West had not come up with regional variations on the theme of *blanquette de veau*. In the Périgord the cuts of meat used are a mixture of shoulder and breast, and the acid flavour in the sauce is provided by *verjus* rather than lemon. In the Rouergue they have a sweet version with chestnuts. But on the southern slopes of the Black Mountain, going down towards Carcassone, they use fat to seal the meat and add *girolles* if they can.

LA BLANQUETTE DE VEAU DU CARCASSÈS
Stew of white veal and mushrooms

Serves 4

800 g (1¾ lb) stewing veal	250 g (½ lb) mushrooms, preferably
1 tablespoon goose fat	*girolles*
150 ml (¼ pt) dry white wine	60 g (2 oz) butter
400 ml (¾ pt) water	45 g (1½ oz) butter plus 2
1 onion stuck with 2 cloves	tablespoons flour (for the roux)
1 carrot	2 egg yolks
1 leek	2 tablespoons double cream
bouquet garni	juice of 1 lemon
salt, pepper, nutmeg	½ tablespoon capers
10–12 little onions or 3 medium-	
sized ones	

Trim the meat and cut it into pieces weighing 60 g (2 oz) each. Blanch it for a few seconds in boiling water, then drain it and plunge straight into cold water, then drain again.

Heat the fat in a casserole and put in the veal, turning to seal it on all sides.

Add the wine and water, onion with cloves, sliced carrot and leek, bouquet garni and salt and pepper. Quarter the onions, or if you are using the small pickling kind, blanch them whole, then add them to the meat. Bring the casserole to the boil slowly and allow to simmer gently until the veal is tender – about an hour.

When the stew is nearly ready, cook the *girolles* or other kind of mushrooms briefly in a little butter. Make a roux in a separate pan and moisten it with the veal stock from the casserole, stirring it all in. Bring this sauce to the boil; leave to simmer gently for 10 minutes. Meanwhile beat up the egg yolks, cream and lemon juice in a bowl. When the sauce is ready, stir a ladleful of it into the yolks and then tip this bowlful back into the sauce. Stir it all together and pour it over the meat. Add the mushrooms and their juice. Check the seasoning and sprinkle the top with chopped capers.

———— • ————

From the same area – which enjoys a wet micro-climate on the northern slopes of the Cévennes, where some cattle are reared – comes a savoury recipe for stuffed veal cooked as if for a *pot-au-feu*. A joint like this is sometimes added to the standard *pot-au-feu* for special occasions or if there are many guests.

La Peau Farcie de la Montagne Noire
Stuffed breast of veal

Serves 6

1 boned breast of veal, weighing about 1 kg (2¼ lb), from the brisket end

for the stuffing:
1 large slice stale country bread
1 cup milk
1 clove garlic, chopped
2 tablespoons chopped parsley
250 g (8 oz) lean veal (leg)
175 g (6 oz) *jambon de campagne*, cut
   0.6 cm (¼ in) thick

125 g (4 oz) fresh fat belly of pork
4–5 large leaves of *blette* (chard)
   without stalks
salt, pepper
2 eggs

for the *pot-au-feu* – see page 211

Ask your butcher to make a suitable pocket in the breast of veal to take your stuffing, which you prepare as follows:

Put the white part of the bread to soak in the milk for an hour. Chop together the garlic, parsley, lean veal, ham and pork, then add the chopped chard. Squeeze the bread out dry and add this, then season – plenty of pepper but only a little salt because of the ham. Beat the eggs and amalgamate all together. Stuff the veal breast with this mixture before sewing up the opening. It is then ready for the pot and requires 2 hours' cooking. If any is left over, it is excellent cold.

———— ● ————

Veal kidneys seem almost impossible to obtain in England – perhaps they are kept for restaurants which have evolved all manner of complex ways of showing off with them. Once again the South-West prefers a simpler approach, avoiding complicated sauces and concentrating on depth of flavour and first-class raw materials. Here is a recipe which makes the best use of Marmande tomatoes and prunes from Agen – produced from opposite banks of the river Garonne.

LES ROGNONS DE VEAU À LA GARONNAISE
Veal kidneys with tomatoes and prunes

Serves 4

12 large prunes
2 veal kidneys
salt, pepper
4 tablespoons cooking oil
2 large tomatoes, skinned and de-seeded
4 shallots, finely chopped

2 tablespoons olive oil
1 tablespoons chopped basil (or parsley)
45 g (1½ oz) butter
1 tablespoon French mustard
6 thin rashers *lard* (unsmoked streaky bacon)

Soak the prunes in some *tisane* or warm tea for six hours.

Leave the kidneys to soak in cold water for 1 hour, drain them and remove any of their outer skin which the butcher may have left on. Cut them in half lengthwise through the core of suet and remove as much of that as you can. Season the four pieces and pour the cooking oil gently over them so as to cover the pieces on both sides. Leave to stand while preparing the tomato mixture.

Chop the tomatoes roughly and put them in a saucepan with the shallots and olive oil. Season and cook over a moderate heat for 15 minutes, by which time the mixture should have reduced to a thickish sauce. Add the chopped basil (or parsley) and keep the mixture warm. While the tomatoes are cooking, heat your grill and cook the kidneys for 8 minutes on each side under a hot flame. Mix the butter and mustard together.

When the kidneys are cooked transfer them to a hot serving dish but keep the grill hot. Cut the bacon rashers in half and roll up a drained prune in each piece, securing them with a stick if necessary and grill them until the bacon is crispy.

To serve, spread the butter and mustard mixture over the kidneys, then fill their hollow sides with the tomato mixture. Surround them with the prunes and pour into the dish the juices which have come out of the kidneys during cooking.

If you think that half a calf's kidney is not enough for one person, you can increase all the ingredients pro rata – except for the prune and bacon garnish. A little mashed potato would be good to mop up the gravy, with a salad to follow.

———— • ————

You could hardly find anything simpler than the next recipe which comes from the Landes and uses the local armagnac to set off the rich taste of the kidneys. Note that, as usual, the sauce is very short and concentrated.

LES ROGNONS DE VEAU À L'ARMAGNAC
Veal kidneys in armagnac

Serves 4

2 veal kidneys	2 tablespoons flour
3 tablespoons goose or duck fat	300 ml (½ pt) dry white wine
salt, pepper	2 lumps sugar
125 ml (4 fl oz) armagnac or other	1 tablespoon tomato purée
brandy	175 g (6 oz) field or other
2 small onions, finely chopped	mushrooms (optional)

Slit the kidneys and remove the white core. Soak them in water for 2 or 3 hours.

Cut them into bite-sized pieces and dry these on kitchen paper. Heat the fat in a frying pan, choosing one with a close-fitting lid. When the fat is really hot, add the kidneys and toss them briefly to seal them. Season generously and flamber them in the brandy.

When the flames have died down, add the onion and cook together over a much lower heat for 2 or 3 minutes. Add the flour and amalgamate it well with the contents of the pan. Pour in the wine slowly, add the sugar and tomato paste and stir all together. (You can, if you like, add to the pan any mushrooms you may have to hand.) Cover the pan and simmer over a low heat for 20 minutes. Check for seasoning, particularly pepper – the effect should be quite spicy.

Serve with rice or steamed potatoes.

It appears that an aristocrat in the Bas-Quercy, the Marquis de Brézolles, employed a talented cook who invented a very savoury dish of veal and named it after his employer. *Brézolles* sounds more like a cut of meat in the local patois than a way of cooking – hence the rather curious title for

LES BRÈZOLLES DE VEAU À LA QUERCYNOISE
Layered veal fillets

Serves 4

700 g (1½ lb) veal (fillet or braising veal)
175 g (6 oz) lean *jambon de campagne*
2 large shallots
2 cloves garlic
2 tablespoons chopped parsley
1 tablespoon chopped chives

salt, pepper, nutmeg
60 g (2 oz) goose fat or 4 tablespoons cooking oil
2 or 3 pieces of fat bacon or fresh pork
125 ml (4 fl oz) dry white wine

Slice the piece or pieces of veal very thinly into escalopes about 10 cm (4 in) long. Their width will depend on the cut of the meat.

Finely chop the ham, shallots and garlic and mix together with the herbs and seasonings. Stir in half the melted goose fat or oil. Put the remaining fat or oil to cover the bottom of a casserole, oval for preference and a little bigger than the escalopes. Then spread a thin layer of the stuffing over the bottom, cover this with slices of veal, followed by another layer of stuffing and so on. Finish by laying the pieces of fat bacon or pork on top, cover and heat slowly over a low flame for 15 minutes.

During this time, heat up the oven to 140°C, 275°F, Gas Mark 1, then place the casserole within. After half an hour, pour over the white wine and continue the cooking. If you are using braising veal, allow 1½ hours cooking time in the oven, or three-quarters of an hour for fillet.

Turn out on to a heated dish, strain the pan juices into another pan and skim off as much fat as possible, then reduce the remaining liquid. Carve this layered meat loaf downwards into slices. Serve the sauce separately.

— ● —

The word *rouelle* means a small wheel in French and cooks use it particularly to describe a perfectly round joint from the leg, usually with its own part of the femur bone left in it.

LA ROUELLE DE VEAU AU VERJUS
Grilled veal with verjuice

Serves 4

1 kg (2¼ lb) *rouelle de veau* or shin of
   veal, in a piece
2 tablespoons cooking oil
salt, pepper

60 g (2 oz) butter
3 tablespoons *verjus* (2 of lemon
   juice as substitute)

In the fireplace prepare a fire with *sarments de vigne*, the thin branches which are pruned off the vines, dried and kept for this purpose. They give grilled meats a flavour like nothing else. Without the *sarments*, an ordinary wood fire will have to do: or this is a dish you could barbecue.

Whatever fire you use, get it to a good temperature. Oil and season the piece of veal on one side and put it face downwards on to the hot grill. Allow it to cook for 15 minutes. Oil and season the top surface before turning the meat to cook the other side for another 10 minutes. When the meat is cooked, sandwich it between two hot plates with the piece of butter and put the plates to cover a saucepan of boiling water for a few minutes. Into the juices which run, pour your *verjus* or lemon juice, transfer to a gravy boat and serve with the meat.

A dish of your favourite mushrooms would be perfect with the *rouelle*, and they will go beautifully with the acidulated sauce.

LAMB

The rearing of sheep in South-West France has undergone remarkable changes since the Revolution. Even from region to region the history of the sheep varies enormously. Until the coming of man-made fibres and cheaper materials, sheep were raised for their wool and huge flocks were sent up to the Aubrac each summer with the cattle to pasture on the high hills which were always lush and green even in the hottest months of the summer. The exodus of the shepherds and the flight of the population towards the towns had a negative influence on lamb production. In those years lamb was little esteemed for its table value. In the Périgord it was regarded as 'black meat' and looked on with something like scorn.

In recent years, however, the huge upsurge in cheese production has given the sheep farmers a real shot in the arm. The ewes of the

Rouergue no longer go up into the mountains. They stay at home to produce milk which is taken to the Roquefort caves for conversion into that wonderful blue cheese. In the Pyrenees the production of ewes' milk cheese has expanded enormously. The consumer does not seem to mind that the small yield from these animals makes their cheese that much more expensive.

Another plus factor for the industry is the establishment of lamb on at least the same gastronomic plane as beef. A leg of lamb is one of the most expensive and popular of all butchers' joints, and even in those areas where lamb meat was traditionally despised, opinion has now swung round. All over the South-West modern *bergeries* are being set up with government subsidies. Lamb producers enjoy the benefit of EC price support although it means they must also face severe competition in price from other Market countries.

Cooks are looking back into their regional history for the traditional ways of preparing lamb and immediately there is conflict between the fans of baby lamb and the mutton supporters. The former are heirs to the traditional view of sheep meat as strong and coarse–flavoured while the latter regard really young lamb as insipid and lacking in taste. However old or young you might like your lamb/mutton, the French butcher will be able to oblige. He is much more expert than English butchers at jointing a lamb. All excess fat will be trimmed from a *gigot* and the knuckle removed. You do not pay for anything you can't eat, except of course the bones down the middle. (It is commonplace in England to find that off a 5 lb leg, up to 1 lb can be thrown away in fat, gristle and bone.) If you ask for a joint to be boned you will not be charged extra for the bones; '*En France on ne mange pas les os*' we were once told rather epigrammatically if cheekily.

Then there is the vexed question of how long you insist on having your lamb cooked. Although the English accept in the main that beef should be at least pink, they are reluctant to eat lamb which is not actually grey right through to the middle. The French cannot understand this: to them lamb should be roasted or grilled rare like beef, although they make an exception of the shoulder which is a fatter joint and for that reason needs more time. *Gigots*, chops and *noisettes* are nevertheless cooked *saignant*. The two points of view are irreconcilable because most of the French recipes for roast and grilled lamb are wasted on meat which is cooked as long as most English people like.

The contrast is nowhere more apparent than in the French style of preparing a roast leg:

LE GIGOT D'AGNEAU RÔTI
Roast leg of lamb

Serves 6–8

1 leg of lamb (with all fat and gristle removed)	pepper
	salt
2–5 cloves garlic	
1½ tablespoons goose fat or cooking oil	

Make incisions all over the lamb with a small, sharp pointed knife and insert spikes of garlic. The amount of garlic must depend on the size of the cloves and personal taste.

Rub the joint all over with the fat or oil, pepper it generously and allow to stand for a few hours. Do not salt it at this stage.

A *gigot* of lamb is one of the best of all joints to spit-roast in front of a fire because it does not need tying up and very largely looks after itself. All the cook has to do is to look after the fire. Place a rectangular receptacle under the joint to catch any juices. The French call this a *lèchefrite*. You can baste from time to time with the contents of the *lèchefrite* but there will not be much because the joint has little fat left on it and the meat will retain most of its natural juices – the whole point of spit-roasting. You can also baste with a little more fat or some *bouillon* or a little of both.

The fire must be already hot and red rather than flaming before you start. Add wood a little at a time to keep the temperature even. You will have to judge the cooking time according to the fire but a rough guide would be 20 minutes to 500 g (1 lb), a little more than if you are cooking in a modern oven.

If you are not using an open fire, preheat your electric spit or oven to 230°C, 450°F, Gas Mark 8, and cook for 20 minutes before reducing the heat to 180°C, 350°F, Gas Mark 4. Allow 15 minutes to 500 g (1 lb) from start to finish.

Whatever method you use, remove the meat when it is cooked and allow it to stand for a quarter of an hour in a warm place, but where it will cook no more. Salt the joint well before this resting time, the object of which is to allow the fibres of the meat to relax and the juices to flow back into them so that the meat is a uniform colour right through when it is carved.

A *gigot* may be carved either across its surface, or – more frequently – in steak-like slices through to and around the bone. For gravy, use whatever has come out of the joint while cooking; more should flow as you carve. The French do not know about mint sauce which they find faintly comic. They take the view that if the meat and its natural juices are good enough, no sauce is needed.

The finest green haricot beans go beautifully with a *gigot* or, in winter, a dish of white *haricots* perfumed with a little goose fat, chopped garlic and parsley.

———— • ————

In England a leg of lamb is roasted and a leg of mutton boiled. That seems to be the extent of our repertoire. All over France there are countless different ways of preparing a roast *gigot*. In Provence the meat is cooked with plenty of fresh herbs, particularly thyme and rosemary. In the Bas-Languedoc they add a little powdered cumin and the zest of a lemon to the herb mixture. Every part of the South-West has its own variations and traditions. In the Cantal and the uplands of the Quercy, where potatoes still are eaten a great deal, a *gigot* is roasted over a dish of potatoes and allowed to drip its juices on to them rather as a joint of English beef drips into the Yorkshire pudding beneath.

On the *causses*, where juniper bushes grow in profusion, the berries are used in the following recipe.

LE GIGOT AU GENIÈVRE
Roast lamb with juniper berries

Serves 6–8

1 leg of lamb	175 ml (6 fl oz) salted water or
4 tablespoons juniper berries	well-seasoned stock
4 large cloves garlic	a chunk of pork fat
2 tablespoons cooking oil	salt
pepper	

You need to start this recipe two days in advance. The *gigot* may be boned or not as you wish; a boned leg of lamb is much easier and more economical to carve and for this recipe more practical since you can put some of the juniper berries into the cavity left by the boning before tying it up.

Bruise the berries with a rolling pin – not too much or you will not be able to spike the joint with them; all that is necessary is to allow their flavour which is sealed inside their outer skin to permeate the meat. If they are not crushed at all they will impart no flavour. Keeping one tablespoonful of the berries aside for the roasting, make small incisions all over your joint and insert the crushed juniper. Similarly cut up the garlic into small lengths and spike the meat with these too. The leg should then be left in a cool larder or meat safe for two days. Failing this, tie it in a muslin and hang it in the coolest place available – it is intended to become a bit gamey. Too warm a temperature would be all too effective but nothing whatever is to be gained by keeping it in a refrigerator for two days.

The *gigot* is then roasted as described on page 229. Towards the end of the cooking time it should be basted with hot pork fat, preferably using your *flambadou* (see page 15).

Serve with white haricot beans.

———— ● ————

In Gascony, where the Atlantic Ocean is never far away, they have discovered an affinity between lamb and anchovies, with garlic as the *agent de mariage*. This is a remarkably subtle and beautiful combination and you must not be put off by the quantities of garlic. When cooked, it will have dissolved into a gentle purée.

LA GASCONNADE
Leg of lamb with anchovies and garlic

Serves 6–8

1 leg of lamb	500 g (1 lb) garlic
12 anchovy fillets	175 ml (6 fl oz) *bouillon*

The *gigot* is spiked not only with the usual few cloves of garlic but with the anchovy fillets as well. You will need to cut them into small pieces in order to slide them into the slits in the meat. If you are roasting the leg in an oven so that it does not revolve on a spit, it is sufficient to lay the fillets across the top of the roast. During the cooking they will melt all over the meat and give it the same effect.

While the joint is cooking (for timing see page 229) peel all the rest of the garlic cloves and blanch them in boiling water until they are almost cooked, then throw them into cold water for 20 seconds and drain them. Heat the *bouillon* in a saucepan, add any pan juices and the garlic and reduce the sauce until it is nearly a purée. Serve as a garnish to the *gigot*.

In the Ariège a little chopped ham is added to this Gascon sauce as well as a *cèpe* or two or some *girolles* if available.

———— ● ————

Older meat may benefit from pot-roasting and larding with fat. The garnish in the next recipe is typical of a more rustic style of cookery. A winter dish if ever there was one.

LE GIGOT À L'AVEYRONNAISE
Pot-roasted leg of lamb

Serves 6–8

1 leg of lamb	2 carrots
8 cloves garlic	bouquet garni
125 g (4 oz) fat pork, cut into thin	salt, pepper
strips for larding	2 strips pork back fat
1 large onion	575 ml (1 pt) meat stock

Ask your butcher to bone the leg for you, if you do not feel up to tackling it yourself. Make sure you get the bones back. Also you or he should make it into a tidy joint, well tied and stripped of all surplus fat and gristle.

Put it into a solid *cocotte* which has a tight-fitting lid, well-spiked with the garlic and the thin strips of pork. Put the vegetables and seasonings with it and arrange the bones around. Cover with the strips of back fat and pour in the stock.

Put your *cocotte* on to a good flame, lowering the heat when it boils. Cover and cook slowly for 2 hours. Then remove the joint to a serving dish, de-grease the juices, reducing them until you have just enough and then serve. Braised cabbage, haricot beans and small onions sautéed in fat and finished with the beans, are suggested accompaniments.

———— ● ————

Shoulders of lamb are nearly as prized in France as *gigots* but the French recognize they need a longer cooking time and are more fatty. They are often boned to enable the fat to be taken off and to make a compact joint for braising. Here is a dish that has a particularly Occitan accent and the alternative title of *Pistache languedocienne* picturesquely describes the garlic cloves in the accompanying sauce.

L'ÉPAULE BRAISÉE (PISTACHE LANGUEDOCIENNE)
Braised shoulder studded with garlic

Serves 6

1 shoulder of lamb or mutton	2 tablespoons pork fat
salt, pepper	2 thick slices of belly of pork
15 cloves garlic or more to taste	2 onions, cut into quarters

2 carrots, cut into quarters
1 bottle *vin rosé* or dry white wine
zest of an orange
a few slices of dried *cèpes*

4 ripe tomatoes
bouquet garni, with celery leaves
1 thick slice of country bread

Bone the shoulder or ask your butcher to do this for you. Salt and pepper it generously inside and range slices of garlic inside. Also make several incisions from the outside and push pieces of garlic into them. Roll up the joint and tie it round at intervals with string to hold it in a neat, sausage shape.

Melt the pork fat in a braising pan large enough to hold meat and bones, then brown the slices of belly of pork, cut crossways into short strips. Put in the shoulder and bones to brown all over, then the onions and carrots. When they have coloured a little, pour in the wine and push down into the liquid the zest of orange, dried *cèpes*, quartered tomatoes and a bouquet garni. Add seasoning. If the vegetables are not fully covered, add a little water; but the joint is to be braised and so should not be drowned in liquid. Bring gently to the boil and then transfer to the oven, preheated to 180°C, 350°F, Gas Mark 4. After an hour or sooner if it sounds to be bubbling too fiercely, reduce the heat and continue for a further 2 hours.

Lift out the shoulder and keep it warm. Strain the liquor through a sieve into a pan and rub the vegetables through. Bubble the liquid strongly to reduce it to about half, then skim off as much fat as possible. Crumble the slice of bread and slowly sprinkle it into the sauce, stirring it until it has thickened slightly. Check the seasoning. Cut off the string from the meat; either slice it on to a hot serving platter and pour the sauce over or carve it at the table and pass the sauce separately.

This dish can be done in just the same way with a half shoulder: reduce the quantity of vegetables and the wine to 300 ml (½ pt) and cook it for 2 hours instead of 3. If you are using a shoulder of mutton and think it is really elderly, a total of 4 hours' cooking time will not harm this dish – it will almost carve with a spoon at the end.

An alternative version which emphasizes its title of *pistache* uses 40 cloves of garlic, blanched first for a couple of minutes and then cooked in the juices for the last hour and not spiked into the meat. This way they are served in the sauce, looking like pistachio nuts. As with the *gigot* recipes, there is no reason to fear the quantity of garlic. Long gentle cooking tames the flavour as it does the sinews of the meat.

———— • ————

A shoulder is a smaller joint than a leg so if eight people are to sit down at table, it is often stuffed. We in England stuff our shoulder of lamb too, but not with as exciting a *farce* as the French. Incidentally, 'a French farce' was originally a comic interlude 'stuffed' between the acts of mystery plays in the Middle Ages.

L'ÉPAULE D'AGNEAU FARCIE
Stuffed shoulder of lamb

Serves 6–8

1 boned shoulder of lamb weighing
   1.5 kg (3½ lb)
24 small onions, peeled
3 tablespoons dry white wine
1 tablespoon *eau-de-vie* or brandy
3 tablespoons meat stock

for the *farce*:
30 g (1 oz) breadcrumbs
125 g (4 oz) minced pork
125 g (4 oz) diced ham
1 shallot, chopped
1 clove garlic, chopped
mushroom stalks (optional)
chopped parsley, chives, sorrel,
   thyme
1 egg
flour to bind
salt, pepper

Spread the shoulder out flat on a firm surface, trim off any excess fat and beat the meat with a meat bat or similar implement to flatten and tenderize it as much as possible.

Mix together the ingredients for the stuffing, binding them with the beaten egg and flour, and place the mixture along the centre of the meat, parallel with its longest side. Pull up the meat round it to form a roll and tie it at 1 cm (½ in) intervals. Season the joint.

At this stage, you can if you like brown the meat in a little fat to give it colour though this is not essential. Then place it in a covered casserole with the small onions, the wine, brandy and stock and cook in a moderate oven, 180°C, 350°F, Gas Mark 4, for 2 hours. Check after 1 hour and reduce the heat if necessary.

To serve, remove the string, surround the joint with the little onions and hand the pan juices separately. This dish is usually accompanied by white haricot beans.

———— • ————

Lamb cutlets and chops can be very unrewarding for their price in France, especially best end of neck, which the French call *carré d'agneau* and which costs as much as *gigot* or even the best escalopes of veal. If it is properly trimmed and comes from a really young lamb, it can still make a lovely dish for two, especially if prepared as it was for Lapérouse. This round-the-world explorer came from Albi and his cook obviously knew a thing or two about preparing a *carré*.

LE CARRÉ D'AGNEAU LAPÉROUSE
Rack of lamb with herbs and wine

Serves 2

1 thick slice salt belly of pork or unsmoked streaky bacon, about 60 g (2 oz)
2 tablespoons goose fat
rack of baby lamb containing 6 chops
2 tablespoons breadcrumbs
1 tablespoon chopped parsley
6 crushed juniper berries
salt, pepper
125 ml (4 fl oz) dry white wine
2 tablespoons armagnac
30 g (1 oz) butter
juice of ½ lemon

Chop the pork or bacon and sweat it gently in the fat in a heavy iron pan. Put in the *carré* of lamb, fat side down, and let it take on a little colour while you pre-heat the oven to 200°C, 400°F, Gas Mark 6. Turn the lamb fat side up and put it in the oven with the pork pieces in a roasting tin to cook for half an hour.

For the final 10 minutes of the cooking, coat the fat side of the *carré* with a mixture of the breadcrumbs, parsley and crushed juniper berries. When the lamb is cooked, season it well with salt and pepper and keep it in a warm place.

Remove the pork pieces and any surplus fat from the roasting tin, deglaze the pan juices with the wine, add the brandy and allow it to bubble fiercely for half a minute. Remove from the fire, add the butter, whisking it in, then finish with the lemon juice.

Serve the lamb with the sauce passed separately.

———— ● ————

A far cry it is from tender baby lamb to old mutton but even the oldest scrag end can be made tasty by this country method. Although obviously intended to be cooked in the fireplace, it adapts very well to a barbecue.

Le Cou De Mouton Grillé, Sauce
À la Moutarde
Scrag end of mutton with mustard sauce

Serves 4

1 scrag end of neck of lamb or
  mutton (*collier* in French and *revers
  de cou* in Languedoc)
cooking oil
125 g (4 oz) fresh breadcrumbs
walnut or olive oil
1 tablespoon French mustard

for the *court-bouillon*:
1 glass dry white wine
carrot
onion stuck with a clove
stick of celery
2 cloves garlic
2 sliced shallots
bouquet garni
salt, pepper

Simmer the neck in a *court-bouillon*, made with the wine and aromatics and enough water to cover, for 2½ hours. Drain and dry the piece of meat and then roll it first in oil and then in the breadcrumbs. Heat the grill very well and then grill the lamb, turning it on all sides to brown nicely.

Serve with a sauce made with walnut or olive oil beaten slowly into a large spoonful of mustard, just as when making a mayonnaise. If this seems too rich, serve a tomato sauce (page 190) instead.

●

That recipe comes from the Périgord. Further south towards the Languedoc they make *collier* into a meat and lentil stew with the green lentils from Le Puy in the Auvergne.

Le Collier de Mouton aux Lentilles
Scrag end with lentils

Serves 4

2 tablespoons goose or pork fat
800 g (1¾ lb) scrag end of neck of
  lamb or mutton, cut into pieces
4 onions, (just under 500 g/1 lb)

250 g (8 oz) young carrots
250 g (8 oz) green lentils
3 cloves garlic
salt, pepper

Melt the fat in a casserole with a tight-fitting lid. When it is hot, add the pieces of lamb, stirring them vigorously round until they are properly sealed – they will otherwise stick quickly to the bottom. Add two of the onions, coarsely chopped. While they take on a little colour, boil some water and add enough to cover the contents of the pot. Cover, reduce the heat and cook gently for 1 hour.

Meanwhile halve each of the remaining onions vertically. Scrape the carrots and if they are too large to use whole, cut them into lengths the size of new young ones. At the end of the hour add these vegetables and the washed lentils, together with the garlic to the pot. Season, cover the pan and cook all together for another hour and a quarter. Check from time to time that there is enough liquid in the pan – the lentils will absorb a lot of it and will thicken the rest towards the end of the cooking time but there should not be too much liquid at the end.

———— ● ————

As with all other animals, no part of the sheep is thrown away. The stomach with its little tripe is made into savoury packets called *tripoux* (see page 153) and served with a spicy tomato sauce. Breast of lamb too is a cheaper cut which they stuff; in the Cévennes the peasants evolved a recipe which makes the most of a fatty joint.

LA FALETTE
Stuffed breast of lamb

Serves 6

1 breast of lamb, boned and
  trimmed
2 tablespoons pork fat
2 carrots, chopped
1 large onion, chopped
250 ml (8 fl oz) dry white wine
575 ml (1 pt) stock
bouquet garni
a few green cabbage leaves
500 g (1 lb) potatoes

for the stuffing:
250 g (8 oz) spinach
1 small onion
1 tablespoon mixed herbs
2 cloves garlic
125 g (4 oz) fresh breadcrumbs
125 g (4 oz) *jambon de campagne*
125 g (4 oz) fresh fatty pork
125 g (4 oz) Toulouse sausage meat
  (page 66)
salt, pepper
2 eggs
125 g (4 oz) lamb's liver

Prepare the stuffing by first blanching, then draining and chopping the spinach, and chopping the other ingredients finely. Mix them all together and bind with the beaten eggs. You will probably have too much but the surplus is for making tiny stuffed 'cabbages' to serve as a garnish.

Open up the pocket at the flap end of the breast of lamb and fill it with the mixture, then sew up the pocket. Roll this stuffed end over and pull the other end over it. Tie firmly with string. Brown the joint in the pork fat in a large casserole. Add the chopped carrots and onion and when these have coloured a little, pour in the wine and stock. The meat should be largely covered so if there is not enough liquid, add more stock. Season and push in the bouquet garni.

Bring gently to simmering point and, while this is happening, fill the cabbage leaves, lightly blanched, with the left over stuffing. Wrap them into parcels and tie them with string. Add these to the pot and bring back to simmering point, lower the heat and simmer very slowly for 2½ hours. Twenty minutes before the end put in the potatoes to boil in the liquor.

When all is cooked, remove the meat and 'cabbages' and discard the cottons or strings. Place the meat on a serving dish, cut into slices, surrounded by the parcels and potatoes, and keep warm. Skim off any fat and reduce the broth in the casserole by boiling fiercely for 10 minutes or so before straining it into a sauce boat.

LA CHASSE

T RADITIONALLY, PEASANT FAR-
MERS regarded themselves as being
permanently at war with nature.
L'oustal could only survive and expand if the
hostile forces outside its boundaries could be
controlled and kept at bay. Nettles and brambles had to be tirelessly cut back. The rooks and
starlings which wrought such havoc on the
crops had to be destroyed, and where there
were no real dangers, superstition created
others in the form of sorcery and fantastic
monsters like the Beast of Gévaudan, the
scourge of the Robert Louis Stevenson country,
which was said to have carried off and consumed countless young children at the end of
the last century.

It was not only those outside forces known to
be destructive that were feared. Every form of
life not actually sustained as part of the
activities of the *oustal* was hostile and needed to
be destroyed. Thus no distinction was made
between jays and songbirds, buzzards and
nightingales. It was enough that they were wild
and no part of the farmers' economy.

Perhaps this explains why so-called sports-
men in the Landes used deliberately to set about
the trapping of hundreds of thousands of
ortolans, thrushes and other harmless, beautiful
birds on migration each year, and why the
woods in France seem much more silent than we are used to, the song
of birds providing a comparatively rare pleasure.

The wild and the unknown are a source of fear, and must therefore
be fought. *La chasse* is one way. *La chasse* in South-West France does not
mean dressing up in fancy clothes, getting on a horse and riding to
hounds, though foxes are as dreaded in France as they are in England.

La chasse means going out, often on a Sunday morning before church, with one's dog, perhaps with a few neighbours and their dogs as well, and trying to bag everything that moves. Rabbits and hares are the most popular targets, and often three or four *chasseurs* will go out in a party to surround an area where one of the dogs picks up the scent of a hare. The runs of the hunted animals are well-known to the countrymen and if a group of them takes up strategic positions, the poor victim has little chance of escape.

The peasant may use the trap – *un collet* – as well as the gun, particularly for hares, rabbits and thrushes. These traps are often of primitive nature and not likely to commend themselves to the squeamish. Thrushes nourished on the wild juniper bushes which grow on the *causses* are regarded as particular delicacies by those who lack any kind of sentimentality for small and beautiful creatures. The restaurants of Millau are the Mecca in August and September for amateurs of *pâté de grives*. No recipes are included for them here because they are, thank goodness, unavailable.

The bag is free to the hunter, an added attraction to the activity of *la chasse*, like mushrooming. The peasant did not, however, rely on hunting for his daily sustenance. It was not a way of life but it could be and often still is a great passion. Before the Revolution, the right to *la chasse* was confined to the aristocracy, which resulted in much resentment and so in the development of poaching as a profession. Even now, on larger estates where shooting rights are reserved – *chasse gardée* – the war between bailiff and poacher continues unabated. Landowners had the good sense to recruit their bailiffs from the ranks of the best poachers, who were highly effective through their knowledge of the tricks of the trade.

In an attempt to stop poaching, hunting permits were introduced in 1844, and much discontent was provoked, even riots in the Gers. The peasants feared a return to the hated *Ancien Régime*. Honest proprietors shooting on their own land frequently clashed with gendarmes trying to enforce an unpopular law. Then the licence fee was lowered and such was the popularity of *la chasse*, by the end of the century nearly 400,000 permits were issued annually in the French countryside.

Unfortunately all kinds of game are getting rarer and rarer. When the official season opens in the early autumn the pent-up passions of the *chasseurs* are unleashed in an orgy of slaughter. For the rest of the season they have to make do with the occasional success. The opening-up of the right to shoot, but above all the increased use of insecticides which kill birds and rabbits as well as pests, has caused the stock of wildlife to shrink dramatically. Birds are nowadays bred to be let loose before guns and they are also farmed for the table, like poultry. These have only a fraction of the flavour of a real, wild species. Partridge seem to have survived better than pheasant, perhaps because of their less flamboyant plumage.

La chasse is an entirely male preserve, the head of the house displaying his shot-gun above the chimney-piece as a prize ornament of the *oustal*. The preparation of game for the table is one of the rare occasions when the man will deign to help with the cooking. Indeed, he may be expected at least to supervise the making of a *saupiquet* to accompany a wild rabbit or a young hare. *Un saupiquet* is a traditional piquant sauce which crops up all over France in a number of different guises. In the South-West, particularly the Languedoc, their version calls for large quantities of garlic and red wine.

LE LAPIN DE GARENNE OU LEVRAUT AU SAUPIQUET
Wild rabbit or hare with piquant sauce

Serves 6

a wild rabbit or young hare
  (including the blood)
1 tablespoon red wine vinegar
2 tablespoons goose fat
salt, pepper
60 g (2 oz) fat pork, cut into
  1 cm (½ in) cubes
flour (optional)

for the *saupiquet*:
2 tablespoons goose fat
500 g (1 lb) garlic
1 medium-sized carrot
2 sprigs of celery leaves
1 medium-sized onion
bouquet garni
¾ bottle good red wine
salt, pepper
pinch of *quatre-épices*
2 tablespoons cognac or armagnac
liver from the rabbit or hare

You will need to set about the sauce before you start thinking about cooking the rabbit, but you must collect the blood of the rabbit in a jug, adding a tablespoonful of red wine vinegar to stop it coagulating.

Melt the goose fat in a heavy cocotte which will go directly on to a flame. Peel and coarsely chop the garlic, carrot, celery leaves and onion and soften all these in the fat without their colouring too much or sticking on the bottom of the pan. After about 15 minutes, raise the heat and add the wine. Bring it to the boil and let it bubble fiercely. Add the seasoning, spices and the brandy, reduce the heat and cover the pan, leaving it to simmer for 2 hours.

Towards the end of this cooking time, you can deal with the rabbit, now skinned by you or a friendly butcher. If you have an open fire, spit roast the rabbit whole (over a roasting tin to catch the drips) with nothing more than a little goose fat and some seasoning. Baste it with the aid of a *flambadou* (see page 15) and the pieces of pork fat at least three times during the cooking. The rabbit will need about ¾ hour to 1 hour, according to size. If you have no *flambadou*, let the pork fat melt in the dripping pan and baste the rabbit with it regularly until cooked. Joint the rabbit at the table.

If you are not cooking the rabbit before the open fire, joint it and flour and sauter the pieces in the goose fat with a little salt and pepper for about half an hour, turning them from time to time so that they cook evenly.

While the rabbit is cooking, you should finish the sauce. Sieve the contents of your cocotte into your serving pot. Sauter the finely chopped liver of the rabbit and add to the pot. Stir in the juices from the cooked rabbit, adding the blood gradually. Allow the mixture to stand for a few minutes at the edge of the heat without boiling. Check for seasoning; the sauce can be made more piquant if you like by adding a little more red wine vinegar. The rabbit can either be served jointed in the *saupiquet*, or the sauce passed separately.

———— ● ————

Other versions of *saupiquet* are useful if it is not possible for you to use the blood of the rabbit. For example, here is a basic interpretation, not for the timid.

LE SAUPIQUET (rustic version)
Piquant sauce

Serves 4

liver of the rabbit	8 tablespoons olive oil
6 cloves garlic, finely chopped	salt, pepper
1 dessertspoon red wine vinegar	

In a pudding bowl crush the liver and the garlic until you have a smooth paste. Stir in the vinegar and mix well. Add the olive oil little by little as for a mayonnaise. Season and serve with the rabbit.

A gentler version of this is to sauter the liver for a few minutes and to cook the garlic cloves in the oven for half an hour before making the sauce.

Wild rabbit has a more gamey taste than the domestic kind, and those coming from the upland *causses* are especially esteemed. Their diet of wild herbs, flowers and grasses makes them particularly savoury, though their energetic life may make them tough. They are on this account eminently suitable for making a terrine.

LA TERRINE DE LAPIN
Terrine of rabbit

Serves 8

a wild rabbit
rosemary, thyme
quatre-épices
2 medium-sized onions, finely sliced
2 cloves garlic, finely chopped
6 hazelnuts

salt, pepper
6 tablespoons *eau-de-vie*
strips of pork back fat to line
  terrine etc.
500 g (1 lb) sausagemeat (page 66)

Bone the rabbit and cut the meat into thickish slices. Put them to marinate overnight with the herbs, onion, garlic, hazelnuts, seasonings and *eau-de-vie*.

Next day, line a terrine with the strips of pork, keeping enough to cover the surface at the end and if possible, to layer the terrine with as you go along. Rabbit has little natural fat so the recipe has to compensate for this if the terrine is to have the right consistency. Lay at the bottom a thin layer of the sausagemeat, cover with a layer of the rabbit mixture, then of pork, sausage, rabbit, pork and so on until the terrine is three-quarters full. Finish with a layer of the sausagemeat and finally a covering of strips of pork fat. Cover the terrine, sealing it with a flour and water paste and cook it for 2 hours in a *bain-marie* in a warm oven (160°C, 325°F, Gas Mark 3).

Allow to cool with the lid on. This *pâté* is better if kept for a few days before eating. Store in a cool place. It can be kept even longer if the surface is sealed with a layer of melted lard.

———— ● ————

A terrine of hare can be made in exactly the same way but you will need to adjust the quantities of the other ingredients according to the size of the animal. The cooking time may also need extending, depending on how coarsely the meat is chopped.

Rabbit, especially if young, can be cooked in many of the ways that are traditional for chicken. If on the other hand it is of *un certain âge*, braising *en cocotte* with *couennes*, onions, garlic, *bouillon* and wine may be safer, but really young animals can be jointed and fried like chicken, pointed with *verjus* in this local manner:

LE LAPIN OU LE LAPEREAU SAUTÉ AU VERJUS
Rabbit or hare with verjuice

Serves 4

a wild rabbit or hare
3 tablespoons goose fat
salt, pepper
2 large cloves garlic, chopped

175 ml (6 fl oz) chicken stock
175 ml (6 fl oz) *verjus* (see page 132)
3 tablespoons chopped parsley
liver of the rabbit or hare

The method is classically simple and designed to show off the quality of the ingredients.

Joint the rabbit or hare into serving pieces and brown them in a thick-bottomed frying pan in the goose fat. When they have attained a golden colour, season them, lower the heat, and add the garlic which you must not allow to brown. After a minute or two, moisten the contents of the pan with the stock and the *verjus*. Add the parsley and the liver of the animal. Continue cooking over a good heat with the lid off. The liquid should be allowed to evaporate until there is only a short and slightly thickened sauce left. All you will need is good country bread, perhaps some *pommes sarladaises* (page 176) and a green salad.

———— ● ————

Another characteristic and famous recipe for hare, but with a great deal more elaboration and expense, is one of the classics of the Périgord: the apotheosis of the hare and one of the most luxurious of all the specialities of South-West France. Variations of this dish were to be found in all the great houses of France. In the Périgord no doubt this dish was confined to the tables of the landowners and the bourgeoisie, but surely there would have been special occasions, a marriage perhaps, when the daughter of a peasant household would bring an echo of this recipe back from the château or the town house where she was working, and the family would put all their spare resources into emulating this classic dish as best they could?

Le Lièvre à la Royale
Rich casserole of boned and stuffed hare

Serves 8

a hare, less than a year old
salt, pepper
700 g (1½ lb) Toulouse sausagemeat
   mixture (page 66)
thin strips of pork back fat
as many truffles as you can afford
one fresh *foie gras* – 'as big as your
   purse'
2 tablespoons goose fat
2 cloves garlic, chopped
3 shallots

1 onion
1 carrot, sliced
60 g (2 oz) fresh belly of pork
1 bottle good, dry white wine, e.g.
   Graves or Bergerac
1 litre (1¾ pt) chicken or duck stock
bouquet garni
quatre-épices
125 ml (4 fl oz) armagnac or
   cognac

Hares should not be hung like pheasants and are best cooked within two or three days of their capture. Unless you are expert at skinning and boning a hare, you had best leave this to your butcher. The art is to get the spine, the ribs and the main bones out without tearing the flesh. Any odd bits of meat which become detached in the process can be added to the sausagemeat stuffing.

The hare, once boned, is laid out on a large flat surface on kitchen paper or towel. Season it generously with salt and pepper. Cover the base of the interior of the animal with a layer of the sausagemeat mixture and cover this with a thin layer of the pork fat. On this surface lay the chopped truffle and cover these in turn with some more fat. Next, place the two lobes of the *foie gras*, which must first be seasoned. Follow with more layers of fat, truffles and sausagemeat. Lay any spare pieces of the meat or other ingredients on the top before sewing the whole creation up like an enormous sausage. If you are using tinned truffle, do not forget to add the juices from the tin. Wrap it in bards of the pork fat and allow the reconstituted animal to rest for at least a day, to take on all the flavours inside.

This will give you plenty of time to start making the sauce. Chop up the bones of the hare and put them into a large pan with the goose fat. Add the garlic, shallots, onion and carrot, plus the chopped belly of pork, wine, *bouillon* and flavourings. Simmer as slowly as possible for at least 3 hours, the longer the better. Pass through a sieve.

When it comes to cooking the hare, you can either roast it in the oven as it is, in which case it will need 2½ hours slow and regular cooking (180°C, 350°F, Gas Mark 4). Remove the bards and serve the hare with the pan juices and your wine sauce as a separate accompaniment.

More traditionally the hare is cooked in a special long *cocotte*, laid on a wide strip of pork skin. The sauce from the bones is added to come three-quarters of the way up the hare. The lid of the cocotte is sealed with a flour and water paste and it is then left to simmer on the stove or in the hot ashes of the fire in the chimney for a good half-day. A glass of armagnac is added 1 hour before serving. All that remains is to remove the string and the bards, and the rest can be eaten with a spoon.

You can serve the finest bottle of red wine from your cellar with this sumptuous dish.

———— • ————

Bigger game scarcely exists in the South-West these days. Venison is either farmed, or protected in the great cultivated forests like Gresigné. The bears in the Pyrenees are, mercifully, protected, if they are not extinct, and the *izard*, a kind of Pyrenean mountain chamois is also not for hunting. From time to time, however, *sanglier* (wild boar) is still to be met, and the experience can be formidable. *Un sanglier* is considerably larger than a domestic pig with a fiercely bristly skin and two elephantine tusks. Although vegetarian, it is a fearful destroyer of crops and its killing is therefore not without justification. Even though not a carnivore, it can and does savage grown men if surprised or menaced. The wild boar is a migratory animal, and several well-known routes of passage link the mountain ranges of the Pyrenees, the Massif Central and the Alps. Sometimes the boars travel in small parties: if the rumour gets abroad that wild boar are about, every *chasseur* in the neighbourhood will be out. A *sanglier* will even venture into the towns if the weather is hard. One was found in the streets of Clermont-Ferrand in December 1975.

The flesh is highly esteemed as butcher's meat, more gamey than pork and lending itself to strongly flavoured sauces and garnishes. Sometimes *un sanglier* can be seen hanging outside a butcher's shop in the winter, if the hunting party has deemed it would prefer some ready cash. It can be roasted, casseroled or made into the most lovely *pâtés*. A young *sanglier* is called *un marcassin* and these small animals are quite enchanting before they acquire the fearsome characteristics of their elders. They are correspondingly more delicate and tender to eat.

If you have a good number of people to sit down to table, the best joint of *sanglier* is the leg. It is delicious roasted, but will need marinating, and the longer the better – even for as long as a fortnight.

Le Sanglier Mariné Rôti
Wild boar marinated and roasted

Serves 10

leg of wild boar, approx 2.5 kg (5½ lb)
60 g (2 oz) goose fat
4 tablespoons armagnac or *eau-de-vie*
salt, pepper

for the marinade:
1 litre country red wine
150 ml (5 fl oz) olive oil
1 tablespoon crushed juniper berries
3 small onions, sliced
1 carrot, sliced
1 stick of celery
thyme, bay leaf, nutmeg
salt
12 peppercorns

Put the meat with the ingredients from the marinade in a cold place for as long as possible in advance. The longer you leave it, the more gamey – and tender – it will be. Turn it often in the juices so that it is evenly impregnated.

When the time comes to cook it, remove from the marinade and wipe dry. Spread the goose fat all over and season well. Put the leg to roast in a baking tin in the oven (190°C, 375°F, Gas Mark 5), allowing 30 minutes to 500 g (1 lb). When it has started to cook, pour the spirit over and flamber it. Add about 300 ml (½ pint) of the marinade and baste frequently.

A purée of potatoes and perhaps a dish of braised chestnuts would be a good accompaniment.

You could practise this dish with an ordinary leg of pork. After three or four days in the marinade, the flavour is not unlike that of *sanglier*.

———— ● ————

The most popular way of preparing *sanglier* is undoubtedly *en civet*. Large quantities can be prepared at one time if a boar happens to be caught and is not sold on. *Le civet* can also be canned and preserved indefinitely. The French are great canners – after all, a Rouergat from Decazeville invented the process. They are just as likely to put up their *conserves* in tins as in glass *bocaux*. Someone in every village has a canning machine and every village ironmonger or general store sells the tins and the lids.

Le Civet de Sanglier
A rich stew of wild boar

1 kg (2¼ lb) lean wild boar meat

for the marinade:
½ bottle red *vin de pays*
150 ml (5 fl oz) olive or sunflower
   oil
2 onions, chopped
pepper

for the *civet*:
60 g (2 oz) goose or pork fat
125 g (4 oz) salt belly of pork, diced
   small
125 g (4 oz) small onions
125 g (4 oz) button mushrooms
60 g (2 oz) flour
salt, pepper
2 carrots, finely chopped
1 large onion, finely chopped
4 cloves garlic, finely chopped
bouquet garni
125 g (4 oz) peeled chestnuts

Cut the meat into small steaks and marinate them overnight in the wine, oil and onions. Season with pepper.

To make the *civet*, brown the diced pork, onions and mushrooms in turn in the fat in a frying pan. Keep them on one side. Dry and flour the pieces of meat and seal them in the fat remaining in the pan, adding a little more lard or goose fat if need be. Transfer the meat to a cocotte and add the marinade, the chopped vegetables and the bouquet garni. Bring to a boil and simmer over a slow fire for 2 hours.

Half an hour before the meat is done, strain a little of the cooking liquid into a small pan and finish cooking the diced pork, onions and mushrooms, also adding the chestnuts. When all is cooked, remove the meat to a serving dish, strain the sauce over it and decorate with the other ingredients.

This dish can be made equally with young goat or venison.

———— ● ————

As far as game birds are concerned, the French have very much the same species as we do, except for grouse. Quail used to be quite common but nowadays is much less so because of the effect of modern farming methods and viticulture. The farmed equivalents are rather dull, suggestive of braised knitting needles. Wild duck may be found in many other areas of France but not so much in the South-West. Snipe are less common than they used to be. Partridge, pheasant and woodcock are the most sought-after birds, and in the open farming lands of the Tarn and the Gers partridge are relatively common. Some of the finest birds are said to come from the Cantal, where cabbage is a traditional accompaniment.

LES PERDRIX AUX CHOUX
Partridges braised on a bed of cabbage

Serves 4

500 g (1 lb) cabbage, Savoy type	250 g (½ lb) pork boiling sausage
1 large piece of fat pork	175 g (6 oz) belly of pork
1 medium-sized onion	1 bouquet garni
2 cloves	salt, pepper
2 carrots	approx 850 ml (1½ pt) stock
2 partridges, weighing 250–350 g	30 g (1 oz) butter
(½–¾ lb) each	2 tablespoons flour

Cut out the hard stalk at the bottom of the cabbage, then separate the leaves. Blanch these for 5 minutes in boiling, salted water. Drain, refresh under the cold tap and drain well again.

Line the bottom of a flameproof casserole, big enough to take the two birds and the vegetables, with the piece of fat pork, cutting it into thin slices if necessary. Cut the onion in half and spike each with a clove. Slice the peeled carrots and place round the sides of the pot; cover with a layer of cabbage leaves. Put the dressed partridges on this bed, surrounded by the sausage, the piece of pork belly and the bouquet garni. Cover completely with the remainder of the cabbage leaves, add seasoning and enough hot stock to come three-quarters of the way up the pot. Seal with a sheet of aluminium foil before putting on the lid. Bring to the boil on the top of the stove, then cook in a cool oven (150°C, 300°F, Gas Mark 2) for 1–1¼ hours for young birds; up to 2 hours for tough older ones.

Lift out the covering of cabbage and drain it into a jug or bowl. Transfer the partridge, sausage and pork pieces to a hot covered casserole and keep warm. Drain off the remainder of the cabbage and the vegetables and return to the pot to dry out over a low heat. The fat pork pieces are discarded.

Melt the butter in a pan, stir in the flour and when it is golden, whisk in 575 ml (1 pt) of the stock. Stir until it has thickened, then allow it to bubble quite fiercely to reduce the sauce, stirring it from time to time.

Spread the cabbage on a heated serving dish, arrange the partridges in the centre, surrounded by slices of sausage and pieces of pork, cut up. Strain the sauce over the top, allowing just enough to coat the dish nicely. Any remaining sauce can be served separately for those who may like more. Serve very hot.

We have seen how useful dried *cèpes* can be in stews and civets. They go particularly well with game birds, both flavours evoking the floor of the chestnut woods where they come from. Chestnuts themselves make up a perfect trinity in the next recipe, which is for pheasant. These birds are rarely to be seen in the wild in France but are readily available in Britain during the season. If possible, choose wild birds; the farmed ones do not have the same gamey taste. This recipe is particularly useful if you are in any doubt as to the age of your birds.

LES FAISANS AUX CÈPES ET AUX CHÂTAIGNES
Pheasant with ceps and chestnuts

Serves 6

a brace of pheasants	300 ml (½ pt) white wine
60 g (2 oz) goose or pork fat	300 ml (½ pt) chicken stock
125 g (4 oz) fresh or salt belly of pork	salt, pepper
1 medium-sized onion	bouquet garni
1 small glass armagnac	250 g (½ lb) fresh chestnuts
	fresh, bottled or dried *cèpes*

Wipe the birds inside and out with a damp cloth and check there are no feathers or ends of quills remaining unplucked.

Heat the fat in a *cocotte* or stew pan with a close-fitting lid, large enough to take both birds. Brown the pheasants all over, one at a time. While they are colouring, dice the pork and chop the onion and put them into a pan – a non-stick pan if you have one – so that they can melt together without colouring or burning. If in doubt, add a little fat.

When the birds are nicely coloured, fit them side by side into the cocotte, heat the brandy in a ladle, pour it over the birds and quickly set fire to it. When the flames have died down, tuck the softened pork and onion under the birds, add the wine and stock, seasonings and bouquet garni. Cover the pan closely with a piece of foil under the lid and bring to a gentle simmer.

If you are using dried chestnuts, these must be soaked overnight first. Parboil them the next day. If fresh chestnuts are used, peel them first before adding to the *cocotte* half-way through the cooking, together with the *cèpes*. The quantities of *cèpes* will probably depend on how many are to hand. If fresh, wipe them with a damp cloth and cut into rough slices before adding them to the pot. If at this stage you are able to turn the birds or to baste them well with the stock, this will help them from drying out. The cooking time will depend on the age of the pheasants and on the fact that the cock is a larger and tougher bird than the hen. Allow a good hour and test them after this time is up.

When cooked, transfer the birds to a heated serving dish and keep warm. Tip the remaining contents of the pot into a sieve placed over a smaller pan. Put the drained chestnuts, *cèpes* and pork pieces into a hot vegetable dish and bubble up the pan juices to reduce slightly. If you like you can thicken the liquor with a little cornflour.

———— • ————

The old marshlands of Les Landes are where you would rightly expect to find *bécasse* (woodcock). As in Britain, the French usually roast these undrawn; when they are cooked, they are gutted and the giblets mashed and spread on to large croûtons. The roasted birds are then served on top. The roasting is best done, of course, before an open wood fire with the aid of the *flambadou*. Woodcock should not be hung for more than three days, especially if they are to be cooked still with their innards inside.

In the Landes they have an even older and more traditional way with woodcock, and that is *en salmis*. English cooks tend to think of a salmi as any old casserole of game or poultry which has a dark sauce reached via a bottle of gravy browning. The Landais do not claim to have invented the *salmis*, which as a cooking method crops up all over France. What they do have is a version which dispenses with pyrotechnics at the table and prefabricated sauces which seem to be the hallmark of more elaborate manifestations of the *salmis*.

LE SALMIS DE BÉCASSE
A salmi of woodcock

Serves 6

for the stock:
2 leeks, chopped
3 carrots, chopped
a veal bone, cut up
bouquet garni
700 ml (1¼ pt) water

2 or 3 woodcock (not dressed)
   according to size
2 tablespoons goose fat

for the wine sauce:
100 g (3½ oz) slice of *jambon de campagne* (or unsmoked gammon)
1 tablespoon goose fat
2 tablespoons tomato purée
1½ tablespoons flour
1 bottle red wine
3 lumps sugar

6 tablespoons armagnac
30 g (1 oz) butter
salt, pepper

Make a stock from the leeks and carrots, the veal bone, the bouquet garni and the water. Bring slowly to the boil and allow to simmer gently until reduced to about 400 ml (¾ pt). Do not season at this stage.

Meanwhile prepare the wine sauce. Cut the ham into dice and soften these with the goose fat. Add the tomato purée and flour and allow all to cook together for a few minutes. Add the wine gradually and finally the sugar lumps. Reduce this mixture to about 400 ml (¾ pt) by gentle boiling.

Mix the stock and the sauce together, reducing it further if desired and seasoning to taste.

Smear the woodcock with goose fat, season and roast them for 15 minutes by a hot fire or in a hot oven (220°C, 425°F, Gas Mark 7). At the end of this time, joint the birds and add them to the sauce, together with any juices which run. Crush all the cooked insides (except the gizzards) of the birds, and add to the sauce. Stir in the armagnac. Allow all to cook together for a few minutes before finishing the dish with the knob of butter – this gives the sauce an attractive sheen.

In the Landes little *miques* (see page 144) are served with this salmis (though they call them locally *escotons* or *cruchades*) together with a green salad.

———— • ————

Pheasant too may be cooked in this way and indeed the method is sometimes applied to poultry. It is important to remember that the essential feature of a real *salmis* is that the birds are only roasted for a fraction of their normal cooking time and are still only partly cooked when added to the sauce. If you try making this dish with fully roasted birds you may end up with a very nice casserole but it will not be a *salmis*.

The recipes for *salmis* of birds other than woodcock follow the same lines but the birds are cleaned before cooking and when larger ones are jointed, the backbone and other pieces which do not go to table can be used to enrich the sauce. This is illustrated in the classic recipe for a *salmis de palombes*, which is included here because the *palombe* is exclusive to the south-west of France, and, even there, only to be found in quantity during its migration from the Black Forest to North Africa in October. It is a kind of pigeon, less commonplace than our own wood-pigeon. Its migration route seems to pass over the southern half of the Landes, where the small town of Sare is a famous centre for shooting *palombes*. *Civets* and *salmis de palombes* are frequently to be found in the better groceries and *charcutiers* of the region. If made in quantity, an older bird which has been hung for ten days or so is roasted and added to the sauce. The flesh is said to disintegrate and to give the sauce an extra something.

Le Salmis de Palombes
A salmi of wild wood pigeon

Serves 4

2 *palombes*
30 g (1 oz) butter
salt, pepper
4 slices belly of pork or unsmoked
    bacon
1 tablespoon armagnac
1 carrot

1 onion
clove of garlic
bouquet garni
300 ml (½ pt) red wine
575 ml (1 pt) stock
beurre manié

Empty and clean the pigeons if this has not already been done. Reserve their livers for the sauce if possible. If they have already been gutted and dressed, just wipe over with a damp cloth. Smear them with the butter, season with salt and pepper, put a rasher of pork or bacon over each breast and tie round. Roast the birds in a pre-heated oven at 200°C, 400°F, Gas Mark 6, for 30 minutes.

When the pigeons are ready, transfer to a plate (they will run juices) and cut off each breast and leg from the carcass, in one piece. Place the four joints in a casserole and keep covered while preparing the sauce.

Using the fat in the roasting tin, pour enough into a casserole or pan to fry the pigeon carcasses. Break these up into several pieces and brown them in the fat. Then warm a ladleful of armagnac, set fire to it and flamber the carcasses. When the flames have died down, add the sliced carrot and onion and chopped garlic and let fry for 5 minutes or so. Deglaze the roasting tin with the red wine and pour it over the bones. Add the stock, seasonings and bouquet garni and allow to simmer together for 15 minutes. Pull off as much as possible of the flesh clinging to the bones; discard the bones. Strain the liquid contents of the pan through a sieve, then rub through as much of the solid contents as possible. Thicken this sauce with 60 g (2 oz) of *beurre manié*; when it has returned to the boil, strain it over the pigeon pieces you have been keeping warm. If the birds are young, you need only reheat them in the sauce before serving. But if there is any doubt about their age, leave them to cook gently in the sauce for another half-hour, then test for tenderness.

Serve with boiled potatoes or fried croûtons.

If you have the birds' livers, you can either use them to thicken the sauce or make them into a *pâté*. Fry them lightly, then chop up with some butter, salt, nutmeg and a dash of armagnac. Spread this *pâté* over some pieces of toast and serve as a garnish for the *salmis*.

LES FROMAGES

FOOD COMMENTATORS AND writers on the South-West seem to give up when they reach the cheese chapter. It is true that in the valleys and plains towards the mouth of the Gironde the only local cheeses you will find will be humble goats' cheeses and occasionally fresh farmhouse cheeses that neither travel nor keep. None of the big-name cheeses come from these lush arable and wine-growing areas. We have seen that one reason for this is that, away from the mountain pastures, cows were working farm animals and were kept almost exclusively for that purpose. If the peasants wanted cheese they made it from sheep or goats' milk. Furthermore one litre of goats' milk makes twice as much cheese as a litre of cows' milk.

Very delicious are the small discs of goats' cheese which you can often buy at market. They vary from the very fresh, often served like ice cream from a bowl, to the hard, well-seasoned kind, matured with *eau-de-vie* or armagnac in chestnut leaves and called Picadou – not a cheese for the faint-hearted. In between, *chèvre* may be bought in all stages of maturity and degrees of pungency. A generic name for these cheeses is Cabécou; particularly well thought of are those which come from the upper valley of the Lot (Le Fel and Entraygues) and from the Causse de Gramat (Rocamadour and Livernon). An average mature Cabécou can be recognized from its blueish rind, often diffused with pinky-orange. Down in the Cévennes they are called Pélardons and are usually eaten fresher and creamier, when they are still white.

On the farms, fresh goats' cheeses are made simply by adding rennet to the milk, draining the resulting curd well, salting and storing them on a slatted shelf. They are sometimes preserved in olive oil to keep their freshness and softness. Goats are fussy about the times of year when they will condescend to mate, so goats' milk cheese is not always available. Similar cheese may be made from ewes' milk. Light, fruity red wines such as Marcillac or Côtes d'Auvergne or other local *vins de pays* go best with all these cheeses. They are eaten, as you might expect, with fresh crusty bread either as a snack on their own or at the end of a meal, and are delicious with walnuts. It should be noted that the French never eat butter with their cheese.

The varieties of this kind of cheese are endless: on the Causse de Larzac, not far from the caves of Roquefort, they produce for sale in the shops of Paris a kind of hybrid Cabécou, based on sheep or goats' milk but mixed with milk or cream, some Roquefort and *eau-de-vie*. This may well be a traditional recipe for stretching Roquefort or adding flavour to Cabécou. Known in patois as *froumatche de santat (fromage de santé)*, perhaps the penicillin in the Roquefort was responsible for its therapeutic qualities.

The South-West does not need to apologize for its cheeses. In the mountains that ring the great Gironde basin are made some of the finest cheeses in France. Le *Grand Sud-Ouest*, taken as a whole, can offer as varied and distinguished a selection as any other region of France. The celebrated Roquefort has already been mentioned. There are the other blue cheeses made from cows' milk – the Bleu d'Auvergne and Bleu des Causses; the pressed hard cheeses from Cantal, including its offspring from Laguiole; the creamy cake-shaped cheeses from the mountain caves of Saint-Nectaire in the Auvergne; and the Pyrenean cheeses in the same style from Bethmale, Moulis and Iraty, plus the hard and very expensive ewes' milk cheeses from the same mountains. Not a bad rollcall, really. A board containing these cheeses in prime condition would be the pride of any restaurant anywhere in the world.

Until fairly recently, all of these cheeses – except Roquefort which is a special case – were made on the farms and many still are. There is a fundamental quality gap between *le fromage fermier* and *le fromage laitier*, i.e. that which is made where the milk is produced and that made from milk sold to the cooperatives and factories. This is not just a question of gourmet snobbery. The distinction is obvious if you taste the two side by side. Try, for example, asking for a sliver of each at one of the itinerant cheese stalls on market day and you will notice the difference straight away. Not that all factory-made cheese is to be despised. Some of the best is that which has been 'invented' so that it does not have to compete with a farmhouse version. For example, the firm Soulié in

Villefranche-de-Rouergue has produced a full, soft creamy white cheese (75 per cent *matière grasse*, which is a lot) called St André which has found ready markets in London and New York. It is made from cows' milk and *crème fraîche*, which is not quite the same as what we mean by fresh cream. *Crème fraîche* is slightly piquant, as if a little sour cream had been added.

Villefranche-de-Rouergue is one of the biggest markets for the sale of an unusual cows' milk cheese called Tomme de Rouergue or Tomme de Cantal. This is made high up in the pastures of the Aubrac and the Cantal and is at its best in the late spring or summer when the cattle enjoy the new season's grass mixed with the wild spring flowers. It is unusual because it is not cured, though it has been pressed. It is sold while still fresh, which means it does not keep for long. It can be eaten like any ordinary cheese, which in a sense it is, being the unfermented first stage of Cantal cheese. But it is principally sold as the main ingredient for *aligot* (see page 148), the favourite potato dish of the region. No other French cheese will really do for this dish, which is why the cheese is sometimes sold by the name of the dish. The raw Tomme has a slightly sour taste, not disagreeable at all, and is very good with some *pain de campagne* and a glass of light Marcillac wine.

Cantal and its sub-variety Laguiole are eaten in various stages of maturity. The summer pastures give the best milk, so the cheese is better in autumn and early winter. Commercially it is made all the year and in large quantities but the finest is still made on the hill farms by traditional methods. It is one of the most widely-consumed of French cheeses, lending itself to all kinds of dishes in which the English might use Cheddar or the Italians Parmesan. The peasants do not seem to cook with cheese to the same extent as the bourgeoisie or town-dwellers, although they eat plenty of it raw, at the appropriate stage in the meal, that is to say *before* the fruit or sweet. Do not be tempted into trying to telescope the salad and the cheese courses by only serving a salad with cheese in it or with a Roquefort dressing. We once did this, having virtually no other cheese in the house. When we then put the dessert on the table we were immediately asked: '*Il n'y a pas de fromage?*' and had to go scurrying for the few old scraps which we had left. A course of cheese on its own will always be expected – *un repas sans fromages est une belle à qui il manque un oeil*, according to one commentator.

The rind of real Cantal is natural and grey with hairline cracks, never fissures. It is dry-cured in humid cellars for three to six months. It is made in huge cylinders as tall as they are broad, weighing between 34–45 kg (75–100 lb). If made in smaller shapes, the cheese is called

Cantalon of which one of the best kinds is Fourme de Rochefort whose production is in the hands of a few farmers and needs active promotion if it is not to be taken over by the *laiteries*. When freshly cut, Cantal smells strongly of milk and the flavour is not unlike that of Cheddar but nuttier. It varies from *doux* (mild), through *entre-deux* (medium) to *vieux* (strong). In its latter stages the rind seems to invade the cheese, the texture hardens and the flavour becomes very strong, hot and mustardy. This is how the true cheese lover likes it. Certainly it is the stage at which Laguiole seems to come into its own. A young Cantal is a perfect foil for just about every kind of wine but when really ripe it calls for a big, fruity red.

There are still in the mountains of the Cantal some of the old *burons*, barns where the old tradition of cheese-making is carried on by local people. Originally *burons* were primitive huts, partly mud-built, roofed with thatch or tufts of grass. Later they were built of stone and roofed with *lauzes*, the same sheets of granite used to roof so many of the local farmhouses. The main door at the end of the *buron* is often decorated externally with a cross, carved in stone, to ward off bad weather and evil spirits, and there is usually stabling for the calves and for pigs round the side. The cellar where the cheese matures in summer is cool and well ventilated.

Cheeses sold as *fermier* are almost invariably made from unpasteurized milk and Cantal fermier is no exception. As the curd thickens, the cheesemaker puts it to drain. After a few days he divides it into pieces, salts them and then moulds them into the final shape, that of a huge cylinder. Watch out for roadside signs for *fromage fermier* – you don't have to buy a whole Cantal cheese.

Farmhouse Cantal from the Plateau de Mauriac is particularly prized, the finest made at over 2,600 feet above sea-level being called Salers Haute Montagne, after the variety of cattle rather than the place. (You can recognise these handsome beasts by their mahogany-coloured hide, long eyelashes and horns curved in the shape of a lyre.)

Laguiole, too, is made on the very highest farms of the Aubrac and is matured for at least four months at a cellar temperature never allowed to rise above 14°C. Factory-made Cantal is brought on with rennet in containers with cavity walls which enable water to be pumped round the curd at a heat of 30°C. This way the cheese needs to mature for only two months and has a much less pronounced flavour.

Cream is also plentiful in the mountains where Cantal is made, and the two are combined in this local recipe for a kind of quiche.

LE FLAN DE L'AUBRAC
Quiche of Cantal cheese

Serves 6

275 g (9½ oz) flour
150 g (5 oz) butter
4 eggs
salt, pepper
water

300 ml (½ pt) double cream
nutmeg
150 g (5 oz) mature Cantal cheese, grated

Prepare a *pâte brisée* for the quiche with 200 g (7 oz) of the flour, 100 g (3½ oz) of the butter, one egg, a pinch of salt and just a little water. Roll it out in the usual way and line a buttered flan tin with it.

Preheat the oven to 200°C, 400°F, Gas Mark 6.

To make the filling, put the cream and remaining butter in a saucepan, adding seasoning and a pinch of nutmeg. When the butter has melted, sift in the remaining 75 g (2½ oz) flour over a low flame, blending and stirring it until the mixture thickens. Separate the yolks from the whites of the remaining three eggs. Remove the pan from the heat, add the yolks and the grated cheese. Beat the whites until they are stiff and fold them delicately into the quiche mixture, which has then to be poured into the pastry case. Bake in the centre of the oven on a metal tray for 35–40 minutes.

A similar quiche may be made with blue cheese: the cheese is mixed with a little cream and spread directly on to the uncooked pastry before being covered with the egg and cream mixture.

———— • ————

The river Dordogne rises in the Monts Dore of the Auvergne. In this region another cheese from the milk of Salers cows is made, called Saint-Nectaire after a small local town where there is a thermal establishment specializing in the treatment of kidney problems and gout. This cheese has probably developed from an older local variety called Vachard which is still occasionally to be seen locally and is somewhat stronger on the palate. Saint-Nectaire is extremely popular as far afield as the Quercy and the Tarn-et-Garonne. Since 1964 an industrialized version has been marketed to meet the demand but one-third of the total production is still in the hands of the farmers. Once again, the *fermier* version is immeasurably superior.

Saint-Nectaire is, like Cantal, at its best when made from milk produced when the mountain pastures are perfumed by the wild spring flowers in June, and again when the grasses shoot again in the early autumn. It is produced in the form of a flat disc 20 cm (8 in) across and 3.5 cm (1½ in) thick. It will weigh about 1.5 kg (3½ lb), and about 15 litres of milk go into the production of each cheese. There is also a smaller version, about half the size, but less commonly seen. The rind is greyish or pinky-grey in colour; the texture is only semi-soft. The cheese should not be allowed to dry out or become excessively firm, when it will become bitter. It should be supple to the feel and have quite a pronounced bouquet when cut. It is fairly mild but with a surprising tang and a back taste of hazelnuts.

Normally the cheese is marketed when fully mature but Saint-Nectaire is sometimes sold freshly made and then requires two or more months' storage. The local farmers use caves in the hillsides which were once used for the storage of wine before the phylloxera scourge a hundred years ago. The cheeses are laid on straw so that they are ventilated from beneath and kept in the dark, under lock and key, in these formidable granite dungeons. Some of the most impressive are at Beaune-le-Froid where local producers will be pleased to show you round. Take a pullover and a powerful torch if you want to see anything and not catch cold. The accumulated aromas of a permanent cheese store are unforgettable!

Saint-Nectaire is made differently from the hard cheeses of the Cantal. The curd is developed from the milk in wooden tubs raised to a temperature of 30°–32°C, (86–90°F) for one hour. The curd is broken up to allow the whey to drain off and then re-assembled. The cheese is then salted and pressed into moulds, where it is allowed to dry for a few days before it is put on its straw mat to mature. If you are in the Auvergne it is hard to resist the temptation to stop at farms advertising *fromage fermier* for sale, and to bring one of these lovely cheeses home.

The one cheese which could never be called a *fromage fermier* is perhaps the greatest of all French cheeses, Roquefort. Some would say this is the finest cheese in the world, though others find it too salty and pungent. Partly to prevent fraud and partly to maintain a high and uniform standard of production, Roquefort cheese has become the subject of complicated rules as to production and storage, benefitting from the fact that there is only one place in the world where it can be made, and that is in the natural caverns under the mountain-plateau called Le Combalou. This is near to the village of Roquefort-sur-Soulzon in the east of the Rouergue, and is on the western fringe of the Causse de Larzac.

The northern face of the *causse* has been broken down by erosion and the weather over a period of thousands of years, causing a landslip. A complex pattern of air penetration into the caves under the limestone plateau has been set up through the gaps – *fleurines* – caused by these falls of rock. The result is a quite dramatic cooling of the air filtering through the caverns so that a cycle of condensation and evaporation maintains the temperature at a steady level between 6 and 8°C (43 and 47°F). A film of mist keeps the atmosphere permanently damp and this in turn produces the perfect setting in which develops a unique microscopic fungus, which has come to be called *penicillium roqueforti*.

It is not known how anyone discovered how suitable these caves were for the storage of cheese or the effect on them of the prevailing atmosphere. There is the charming myth about the local shepherd who took his picnic of bread and cheese into the caves to escape the fierce heat of the summer sun, but was called away in the middle, leaving most of his lunch behind. When he returned to the caves some weeks later he saw to his amazement how his previously fresh ewes' milk cheese had become veined with blue and had acquired a taste like nothing which had been known before.

Whatever the truth of this tale, the caves of Roquefort were certainly known by reputation to Pliny. Casanova claimed for it particularly useful properties, especially taken with a glass of Chambertin. King Charles VI had granted the first letters patent in 1407 and royal recognition followed at regular intervals. Roquefort cheese is protected within France by modern laws which date back to 1925, and on an international level by the Stresa Convention of 1951. The foreign market is huge: the USA alone takes ten per cent of total production.

We seem to be getting a long way away from peasant food production. Not really, because what Roquefort offers is not so much a product but the facility for milk producers from various regions to market their milk for conversion in the Roquefort caves into a cheese that has characteristics like no other. The first rule about Roquefort is that it can be made only from unpasteurized, full-cream sheeps' milk. The milk has to originate either within a fairly wide local area (including large parts of the Tarn and the Rouergue) or in the inland areas of Corsica, or in the Pyrenees or in any other area of France where similar climatic and agricultural conditions prevail. Over three-quarters is in fact made from milk produced in the local area which is called the *rayon*; nearly 90% of that comes from the Rouergue or the Tarn. The finest of all the local milk is thought to come from the herb-strewn Plateau de Larzac on the edge of which the Combalou caves are to be found.

The lambing season starts in December and the young lambs are sacrificed at the age of only one month. They are no doubt very good to eat and, as usual, nothing is wasted – even their tripe goes to make a kind of *tripou* called *les trenels*. The lambs' skins are sent to Millau, the nearest large town to Roquefort. There they are turned into gloves – Millau produces one half of all the kid gloves made in France, and one now sees why. The ewes are available for milking from mid-January onwards although their best milk is in the spring. Roquefort takes three months to mature so it follows that the cheese is at its best from midsummer through to the autumn. The cheese can in fact be bought all the year round because its development mostly stops when it is wrapped in foil. Even so, it loses some of its creamy texture if kept for too long.

The first stage of manufacture may not be carried out in the Roquefort caves at all. Shepherds in many of the permitted areas of milk production set up *fromageries* as Roquefort satellites. They sell their milk to the *fromageries* and from then on the cheese-making process is in the hands of the central organization at Roquefort. The shepherd's function after the lambs have been killed is therefore limited to the production of the raw material. In the areas of the Rouergue and the Tarn, which together account for over two-thirds of the total production of Roquefort, the sheep are pastured in the Aubrac, on the *causses* and in the mountain areas round Lacaune. This town gives its name to the breed of sheep most commonly to be found in the area.

The *causses* are dry and arid in the summer but sheep can go for a long time without drinking water. The *causses* are dotted with man-made watering holes called *lavagnes* where goats as well as sheep can be watered after a storm. There are no natural ponds because the subsoil is mostly limestone which sponges up the rare summer rain. Not all shepherds live locally to the *fromageries*. Many drive their flocks on to the pastures in the spring. They are gone again when the nights begin to draw in at the end of September and the mountain temperatures start to drop dramatically after nightfall.

The *fromagerie* is a local community centre to which lorries and vans daily bring the ewes' milk production of the whole neighbourhood. Once the shepherd has parted with his milk, it is treated with rennet in huge stainless steel baths. As the cheese thickens, it is cut in the tanks into small cubes to encourage effective drainage. It is then transferred and pressed into perforated moulds to complete the process. At this stage some of the penicillin spores are 'sown' in the cheese. The penicillin has been gathered in the caves at Roquefort and then processed in the laboratories of the *fromageries*.

The cheeses, now at the *tomme* stage, are transported to Roquefort itself. Before being buried underground they are lightly salted on every face, brushed, and then needles are pushed through the cheese, making tiny holes for the cheese to breathe. This will protect the cheese against the internal development of undesirable organisms as well as encourage the development of the penicillin. Every cheese is given a distinguishing mark, indicating its origin and the conditions in which it was made. They are now ready for despatch to the bowels of the earth. There are eleven floors of storage space underground. Tourists are allowed down to have a look and the trip is very worthwhile. From their accounts, one gets little idea of the sheer size of the subterranean city of Roquefort. Corridors have been cut in the rock to connect the caves with the *fleurines*, those faults in the mountainside, some of which are 300 feet high. The cellars have gothic arches spanning naves a hundred yards long and in these temples 16,000 tons of cheese are matured each year.

The shape of the Roquefort cylinder is familiar. Each one weighs about 2.5 kg (5½ lb). Its rind will have been scraped and thinned and it is wrapped in foil to preserve its condition. Despite the most careful attention which every cheese should have received up to the point where it leaves the caves, both good and bad Roquefort are to be found in the shops and at the markets, even in France. To start with, no one can predict how well the *penicillium* will affect any given cheese once it has been put away to mature. Every cheese can be different. Cheeses which have been badly handled, perhaps stored at wrong temperatures or in a particularly dry atmosphere, or which have been chilled, will be pale shadows of one which has been well looked after.

A good Roquefort should feel firm, and the rind should be unblemished and quite smooth. There should be a light smell of mould and, when cut, a very pungent bouquet with the characteristic blue-green marbling evenly spread throughout the cheese. The French call this *persillage*. The flesh of the cheese should be an ivory-yellow, the texture buttery and never crumbly. Avoid a cheese with a disintegrating rind, which has a white or greying interior, or which is lacking in *persillage*, or whose *persillage* is not evenly distributed. Unlike most cheeses, *Roquefort* ripens from the inside outwards so the perimeter of the cheese is the last part to mature. Avoid, too, any which the seller is having any difficulty in cutting cleanly, without its crumbling.

The yield of milk from ewes is much smaller than the bountiful quantities supplied by cows or goats. Sheeps' milk cheese is therefore always expensive. Local cooperatives have developed blue cows' milk cheeses which cost the consumer half the price of Roquefort and are good in their own right, even if not a substitute for the real thing. At

Thiézac, under the brow of the mountain called Le Plomb de Cantal, the pioneering version of this cheese is still made from unpasteurized milk on the local farms. Elsewhere it is all factory-made and sold under names like Bleu d'Auvergne, Bleu des Causses (in the Rouergue), Bleu de Laqueville (another Auvergnat variety) and Bleu de Quercy (the best examples of which are made near Figeac in the east, Gourdon in the west and the wetter areas on the northern boundary with the Corrèze).

The factory-made cheeses are made from pasteurized milk and have a strong visual resemblance to Roquefort. Indigo blue is a better description of the *persillage* than the greeny-blue of Roquefort. They are all made in the shape of a shallow cylinder some 18–20 cm (7–8 in) in diameter (Laqueville a little larger) and about 10 cm (4 in) high, though smaller versions are sometimes marketed. Like Roquefort they are wrapped in foil which has the effect of stopping further maturation. The fat content is a little higher than that of Roquefort and they require a much shorter period of curing, usually about a month. These cheeses have a strong smell and are sharp in taste, less subtle than Roquefort.

Roquefort and the other *bleus* can be used in local recipes but, with the high price of Roquefort, it is tempting and quite valid to use one of the other *bleus*. Danish Blue is not, however, recommended: it is vulgar and too salty. Americans love what they call a 'Roke fort' dressing on their salads and they have obviously borrowed this from the *salade aveyronnaise* (see page 203). Recipes for using blue cheese in cookery are not likely to be authentic in the peasant tradition, although some of the local restaurants catering for the bourgeoisie as well as tourists have devised attractive ways of presenting chicken and even sweetbreads with Roquefort. The longest established hotel in Roquefort itself serves a delicious *feuilleté* filled with Roquefort, and this is the way we try to reproduce it. Any of the *bleus* can be used in the same way.

LES FEUILLETÉS AU ROQUEFORT
Roquefort in flaky pastry

Serves 4

125 g (4 oz) Roquefort cheese	a squeeze of lemon juice
125 g (4 oz) cream cheese	250 g (½ lb) flaky pastry
salt, pepper	egg yolk for glazing

Crumble the Roquefort cheese into a bowl and mix the cream cheese into it. Taste this mixture to see if it needs any more salt – it probably won't. Add some freshly-ground black pepper and a squeeze of lemon juice. Form this filling into four or five small sausage shapes and put them to firm up in the refrigerator for 20 minutes if they seem too soft; otherwise the filling may ooze out of the pastry cases as you fill and seal their edges.

Roll out the pastry to an oblong 20 × 15 cm (8 in × 6 in). Turn it over carefully on to its other side and leave it to rest for 10 minutes or so before cutting it into four smaller rectangles. Any trimmings could be rolled out to make a fifth rectangle.

Place the fillings on one half of each piece of pastry, leaving about 1 cm (½ in) round the edges. Moisten these edges with a little egg yolk or milk and fold the other half over. Pinch the edges together and knock them up with the back of a knife. Cut three good-sized slits in the top of each one and brush the tops with the egg yolk, diluted with a few drops of water.

Preheat the oven to 220°C, 425°F, Gas Mark 7. Place the *feuilletés* on a greased and floured baking tray and bake them in the top of the oven for 15 minutes. Serve warm or quite hot, whichever you prefer, though they are most delicious straight from the oven.

A double quantity of half-size *feuilletés* could be served with aperitifs, in which case 10–12 minutes' cooking would be sufficient.

————— ● —————

Blue cheese makes lovely pancakes, combining unusual flavours with a quick and simple method.

LES CRÊPES AU ROQUEFORT
Roquefort pancakes

Serves 4

for the pancake batter:
125 g (4 oz) flour
½ teaspoon salt
1 egg
150 ml (¼ pt) milk mixed with
    150 ml (¼ pt) water
15 g (½ oz) melted butter

for the filling:
25 g (¾ oz) butter
25 g (¾ oz) flour
250 ml (½ pt) milk
salt, pepper, nutmeg
100 g (3½ oz) Roquefort cheese

30 g (1 oz) melted butter

Sift the flour and salt into a basin. Put the egg in a well in the centre and start mixing in the milk and water a little at a time until half has been added. Beat the batter well at this stage until it is smooth and starts making bubbles – an electric whisk is a definite asset. Add the melted butter and whisk in the rest of the liquid. Leave the batter to stand for up to 2 hours at room temperature to allow the flour to absorb the liquid – this gives a lighter and more digestible pancake.

Make a béchamel sauce with the melted butter mixed with the flour to make a roux, then blend in the milk. Reheat, stirring continuously while it thickens. Leave to simmer very gently for 10 minutes to cook the flour. Add the seasoning and, off the heat, stir in the cheese, previously crumbled with a fork, until the sauce is smooth. Keep the filling warm.

Make 8 medium-sized pancakes and keep them hot on a plate over a pan of simmering water. Put a large tablespoonful of the cheese filling in the centre of a pancake, fold the two sides over it, one after the other and then fold down each of the ends so that you have a square packet. Turn it over and put it into a flameproof, warmed serving dish. Stuff the remaining pancakes in the same way, arrange them in the dish and pour some melted butter over them. Flash the pancakes under a hot grill for a minute or two to give them a golden, sizzling coating, and serve immediately.

—— ● ——

More in the country tradition are the cheeses made at monasteries, often Trappist ones where silence is the rule. Trappist monasteries have a reputation all over France for producing interesting cheeses and the South-West has its share. One of the best known is near the small town of Échourgnac in the Forêt de la Double, about half way between Ribérac and Mussidan in the western Périgord. The Abbaye de Notre Dame de l'Espérance produces little cheeses about 10 cm (4 in) across and 2.5 cm (1 in) thick, rather in the style of a Saint-Paulin. The rind is a smooth yellow, sometimes with a tinge of grey, the inside a pale yellow but perforated with tiny holes. This cheese is mild, with little smell, and keeps well, even during summer heat.

Further to the west in Les Landes, sheep-rearing was a traditional way of life for many farmers, who had to master the extraordinary art of going about on stilts if they were not to sink into the swamps or lose sight of their flocks in the flat, desolate marshlands which used to be where the pine forests now are. Little surprise therefore that these tough peasants devised their own sheep's milk cheese called Poustagnacq, which is still made. It is put into *bocaux* or crocks when fresh and allowed to ferment as it matures. It is really at its best in winter but some jars may be kept longer and eaten the following spring.

These traditions still survive, as we found recently on a visit to friends with a vineyard in the Sauternes. They sent us to a local farm where the family, who came from the Béarn end of the Pyrenees, were rearing sheep for cheesemaking. They showed us their flock of 250 ewes which had to be milked by hand twice a day, a task that took three of them 6 hours. Some of the sheep were the white-faced Béarn variety, while others were black-faced and from the Basque area. We were intrigued by their elaborately-shaped horns until it was explained to us that they were twisted into characteristic shapes by the shepherds so that they could identify their own flock when they grazed them on the mountains. The small hard cheese we bought from them was wonderfully nutty and deep in flavour.

On the borders with the Gers, in Armagnac country – where curiously enough there is no cheese named after D'Artagnan or the musketeers – another sheep's milk cheese is made in the neighbourhood of Amou, itself a great gastronomic centre. Amou is prepared in the form of a large disc, over 30 cm (12 in) across and 7.5 cm (3 in) deep. It has a thin, golden rind and its texture is firm even after as little curing as two months. When older it tends to crumble. Mild when young, it can develop a certain sharpness. It goes well with any of the local wines, whatever their colour.

Related to Amou are the Basque cheeses of Etorki, Ardi-Gasna (meaning in the local language simply 'local cheese') and Esbareich. These are mentioned here for completeness even though the food and wines of the Basque country are not dealt with in this book. Nevertheless the traditions of cheese-making are largely the same from one end of the Pyrenean chain to the other – and it would be churlish to exclude the Basque mountain cheeses. We are very much here in ewes' milk country; sheep-rearing has been one of the most important types of farming in the Pyrenees right back to the Middle Ages. Before there was any formal boundary between what are now respectively France and Spain, the young men of the *oustals* used to disappear up into the mountains with their sheep in the spring and spend the whole summer roaming the Pyrenees and often penetrating quite a long way into Spain.

In the valley of Ossau and the surrounding country high in the mountains beyond Lourdes, a ewes' milk cheese called Laruns is made, named after the principal market town. Unusually this cheese is 'cooked', that is to say, the curd when it has been broken up, is heated in the whey before it is wrapped and put into the mould. The cheese is then treated with special ferments and swells as it matures, often developing holes in its texture. The rind is yellow and should be quite thin. Laruns is supple and mild at two months but at six months has really hardened. With age it develops a pronounced sharpness and is useful in cooking.

In the higher ranges of the Pyrenees an uncooked version of a similar cheese is called Iraty, named after a high mountain plateau. This however is made from a mixture of cows' and ewes' milk and is considered to be of lesser quality although no mean cheese in its own right. There is an increasing tendency to blend the two types of milk, especially in commercial manufacture, simply because of the high cost of producing ewes' milk for an unblended cheese.

Delicious pure cows' cheeses are made all along the north side of the Pyrenees. In the Ariège the cows from Bethmale produce a lovely, creamy, semi-hard cheese of the Saint-Nectaire type, and Moulis is another name to watch out for at local markets. Rogallais is another *fromage artisanal* to note in this area. It has a texture rather like *tomme*, with a lot of tiny holes and a lovely, buttery-nutty flavour. The cheese industry seems to be making rapid progress in these regions with the *laiteries* manufacturing more and more *fromages des Pyrénées* for consumption both locally and further afield. Cheese from cows' milk usually has a black plastic rind while the ewes' milk cheeses are given an orange-coloured coat.

LES CHÂTAIGNES

Noix, châtaigne et fille, la robe couvre l'astuce

THE SWEET CHESTNUT is not fussy about soil or terrain. It grows quite happily all over the almost vertical slopes of the river gorge below our farmhouse. The climate is, however, all important; the essential requirement of chestnuts is alternating heat and rain. A scorching August and a wet September make for a bumper harvest in October. The hot sun develops the fruit and the rain swells it. In August chestnuts 'should boil in their shells'.

In most upland areas of the South-West these conditions generally recur from year to year. The chestnut plantations are most extensive where other staple crops will not grow. In the hills of the Cévennes, for example, there is little arable land and therefore little corn or rye. Before the days of modern communications chestnuts were more basic than bread, which was a comparative luxury. To Anglo-Saxons who associate chestnuts with *marrons glacés* and stuffing for the turkey, it is hard to understand that chestnuts were once the most important foodstuff in some country areas and that if the crop failed, total destitution followed. Before the arrival of coffee, peasant families started the day with a dish of boiled chestnuts and nothing more. The housewife's first job in the morning was to prepare this crude but nourishing breakfast.

The chestnut has been indigenous to the South-West since prehistory. Fossilized remains prove that it goes back beyond 14,000 B.C. Since the Middle Ages they have been widely cultivated as food. In the Cévennes they were until this century the basis of the diet; elsewhere, they were almost as vital. Chestnut flour was used to make a type of *mique*, a bread substitute, and it also went into a kind of pancake eaten hot and sprinkled with sugar. Up to the 1914–1918 war it was only during the chestnut season that some people managed to fill their bellies. This is hard to believe when you see how abandoned the chestnut woods are now, the ground covered with dead wood, brambles and undergrowth, which sometimes make it impossible to gather any of the nuts. Nevertheless, areas of the Cantal and Périgord depended on chestnuts until the end of the nineteenth century and in the Limousin they were at least as important as potatoes. The large area of wooded country between Quercy and Cantal is to this day called La Châtaigneraie.

A hundred years ago the chestnut woods were properly husbanded. They were kept meticulously clean, as the walnut orchards are today, so that the fruit did not get lost in the undergrowth. The trees were always grafted. In the picking season, called *Li Castagnàdo* in patois, the nuts were gathered into piles, green prickly shells and all, because the shells would be used later for fertiliser. These shells were either beaten on the spot with sticks or mallets to get the nuts out, or they were taken back to the farm where the nuts were got out of their prickly coats. This was often a family event, an occasion for *une veillée*, an evening gathering round the fire when gossip would be exchanged, old stories told and re-told, or some literate member of the family might be asked to read aloud extracts from some adventure story or spine-chilling tale of the supernatural. Our house is but one among many that still have a small outbuilding (*sécadou* or *clédo*) reserved for the drying of the chestnuts; some of our neighbours still remember the *veillées* in what is now our sitting-room. The nuts were spread out in the upper part of the *sécadou* and a fire of chestnut leaves was lit beneath them and allowed to smoulder gently for three weeks. At the end of this time the nuts were dry and in this form they were called *auriols*. They were put into sacks and then beaten to get their husks off. Chestnuts dried in this way have a quite pronounced smoky taste, and anything made from them will have this flavour. It is quite agreeable really but not altogether expected. Sometimes the nuts are dried off beneath an extension of the roof on a slatted floor (*plancadou*). In the Périgord they were stored in sand, rather than smoked. If the season is warm, they can be laid out to dry in the sun, though it is wise to soak them in water first for a few days to get rid of any insects which may have burrowed into them. Dried smoked chestnuts make a tasty soup if reconstituted in a mixture of half milk and half water and cooked until they have dissolved.

Some of the fresh nuts were set aside to enjoy round the fire in an evening with a glass of wine. These might be roasted over the embers in a kind of long-handled frying pan with holes in it, or perhaps put to cook under the hot ashes of the fire, or they might be boiled in water perfumed with aniseed, fennel or coriander or even gently steamed under a wet tea-towel as we describe.

When the nuts were cooked they were covered with sacking or an old blanket to make them sweat. Nowadays a tea-towel would be more hygienic. This makes the nuts easier to peel. They also peel more easily if they are kept for a few days after being gathered. The first nuts of the season, perhaps because of the temptation to pick them before they are really ripe, are also hard to peel. The type of knife the locals used had a short, curved blade with a hooked point and was known as *une serpette*.

The chestnut harvest used to be celebrated just like *le vendange* or the gathering of the main cereal crops, and this tradition is being kept alive today by various *fêtes de châtaignes* at which quantities of nuts and the new season's sweet cider are consumed while folk orchestras regale those present with musical reminders of the pre-rock era. At Sauveterre-de-Rouergue, the festivities go on for two days and a revolving drum roasts chestnuts over an open wood fire in the main square of this attractive, arcaded village.

There were, and still are, many different varieties of chestnut. Some nuts were elongated, others were almost black in colour, some looked like olives. A chestnut called *saboya*, local to the Tarn, was highly prized for its keeping qualities and for its flavour, though it was very small.

During the last hundred years the cultivation of chestnuts has been in decline. Simultaneously with the onslaught of phylloxera on the vines, the *châtaigneraies* were ravaged by a disease called *l'encre* (ink) which is a vivid description of the effect of the malady; it slowly turns the inside of the fruit black and rotten. Although modern grafts are being produced which are thought to be immune, most of the trees in the old plantations are blighted so that the nuts have to be eaten fresh from the trees and will not keep. Many trees were also killed by the extraction of tannin from the bark. Chestnuts are rich in tannin and factories were set up to extract it commercially for use in the manufacture of leather goods. These processing plants depended on access to railways and in turn the railways opened up areas of land where, as we have seen, crops would not grow before. They also made it easier for a greater variety of foodstuffs to be available to peasant communities that were beginning to struggle out of the appalling conditions of poverty which had been their lot for so long. These factors tended to make the chestnut less vital to these poorer areas and the inhabitants had no motivation to replace the diseased trees.

The decline was further hastened by a need for pit props and telegraph poles: chestnut wood is hard and particularly suitable for outdoor use. It also makes fine furniture and floors. But the trees which were felled were not replaced and those which were left were no longer cut back, the self-seeded striplings were not thinned out and the old way of life, of setting up a sort of winter camp in the woods where the forester – *le feuillardier* – lived an entirely solitary existence during the cold months – almost died out. Some of their primitive huts are still to be seen in the country round St Yrieix, south of Limoges.

Despite this decline in chestnut production, there is still an important trade. During the forty years before 1914, production was halved, but enough commerce remained to keep the reputation of the better grown produce very much alive. The coming of the railway from Brive through the heart of the chestnut country opened up markets all over Europe and to this day the *foires* at the time of *Li Castagnàdo* see huge quantities of nuts changing hands and being bought by wholesalers.

The decline continues today. Prices are still falling and, despite the enthusiasm of some local groups of growers, the quick return to be had from planting conifers is preferred to the long wait for a yield from a tree which is in so many ways obsolete to the peasant economy. Cattle are now bedded on straw, not on chestnut leaves. There is plenty of firewood without chestnut prunings. Barrel hoops are now mostly made from metal, not chestnut sticks, while boxes and most furniture are made from deal which is a soft wood.

This is all rather sad because the sweet chestnut is a beautiful, even exotic tree. At the beginning of summer, its branches are decorated with long greenish-white catkins, which look like huge bouquets of ostrich feathers. These flowers gradually give way to the fruit, prickly and lime-green in colour. As the leaves start to turn golden the nuts ripen in their shells which burst open while still on the branches. You can see the nuts peeping out, three to a shell, bright and shiny and the colour of polished mahogany. Encouraged by the autumn breeze they gradually fall from the trees, bumping off one branch on to another before hitting the ground with a muffled thud, the most characteristic and typical sound to be heard in the woods during October. In his *Cévennes Journal*, Robert Louis Stevenson writes:

> I wish I could catch a notion of how these noble trees grow. They were like the olive in this, that out of the oldest and most riven bole, they

could put out smooth and straight and stalwart shoots, and begin a new tree, as it were, upon the ruins of an old one. Sometimes, again, they grow like oaks in handsome upright shafts, deeply fluted; sometimes vertically, sometimes spirally, sometimes one after the other. But the bunches of great leaves, their palm-like top-knots, the prickly nuts against the sky, that was a thing of their own.

The Cévennes Journal, R.L. Stevenson (Mainstream Publishing, Edinburgh, 1978, p. 95)

The tiresome problem with chestnuts is peeling them. In our part of the Rouergue men wore a special kind of heavy shoe (*soulos*) for treading the heaps of nuts. In other areas peeling was done by heating the nuts slowly in a *toupi*, the almost spherical cooking pot which stood in the ashes, and then thrashing them about in the water with a strange gadget called *un déboiradour*. This was like a large pair of wooden scissors, about 40 cm (16 in) long. The 'blades' were not sharp but all four surfaces were serrated, and these were worked with two hands in a rapid scissor-like movement so as to agitate the chestnuts in the hot water. This got the nuts out of their skins and also removed the inner, second skin, so disagreeably tannic in flavour. Sometimes each nut is *cloisonné* i.e. divided into two sections, separated by a bitter membrane. It is more difficult than ever to get rid of this and the second skin, but the *déboiradour* is said to have achieved even this miracle. Nowadays most are resigned to scoring the nuts with a knife, heating them in the water and getting them out of their jackets as best they can, inevitably burning the fingers.

To prepare the nuts as simply as possible, they can be put in *un oule* or a casserole, first lined with fig or cabbage leaves and accompanied by two or three potatoes or some celeriac or other root vegetable and a very little water. The nuts are covered with a wet tea towel, then with the lid, and cooked slowly by the fire. They can then be eaten exactly as they are, or perhaps with redcurrant jelly or honey or with hot, sweetened milk.

Another way of preparing them with milk – and on most farms it would have been goats' or sheep's milk – is in the following soup, found as its name suggests, all over the region. In the Cévennes it is known as *bajanado* after the local word for a chestnut, *bajanol*. A modern liquidizer produces a smoother finish than an old-fashioned sieve, so this version is to that extent updated.

LE POTAGE D'AQUITAINE
Cream of chestnut soup

Serves 4

500 g (1 lb) chestnuts	1 tablespoon goose fat
1 medium-sized onion, chopped	salt, pepper
stick of celery with leaves, chopped	croûtons
large clove of garlic, chopped	*crème fraîche*, or soured cream

Peel the chestnuts, using whichever method suits you best. Soften the onion, celery and garlic in the goose fat. Add the nuts, 1 litre (1¾ pt) of water, and some salt and pepper. Bring the soup slowly to the boil, cover and simmer for an hour.

Transfer to a liquidizer and blend to a smooth purée. Reheat gently, and serve with fried croûtons and a dob of *crème fraîche*, or soured cream. This is a soup of pinkish hue and delicate flavour; do not serve it too thick.

———— • ————

Another version from the Haut-Languedoc, in which the chestnuts are left whole in the liquid, is further heightened by the addition of bitter chocolate and a little sugar. This is not as exotic as it sounds because chocolate is traditional in Catalan and Basque cookery, both of which have had some influence in the Languedoc.

As a vegetable, mashed chestnuts were undoubtedly the precursor of mashed potatoes. The following purée combines the two, mixing the sweetness of the nuts with the lighter texture of the potato.

LE GRATIN AUVERGNAT
Chestnut and potato purée

Serves 4

500 g (1 lb) chestnuts, peeled	60 g (2 oz) butter
500 g (1 lb) potatoes	salt, pepper
milk, stock or water	

Simmer the chestnuts gently in enough stock and water or milk and water to cover them until they are very tender and most of the liquid has been absorbed. Purée them in a liquidizer or sieve them, and add enough of their cooking liquor to make a thin purée. At the same time, steam or boil the potatoes, with or without their skins as you prefer. Peel them if necessary and mash or sieve them.

Combine the two purées and reheat them gently, stirring in the butter, some salt and plenty of pepper. Be careful to keep the purée as light as possible, adding more milk or stock if necessary; it easily becomes leaden.

An alternative to this mixed purée is one of chestnuts alone but this is only possible if you have plenty of them, and plenty of time to spare for shelling them. Serve with grilled sausage, chicken or roast pork. Any left-over purée can be made into small flat cakes, floured on both sides, then fried.

●

Because chestnuts came to be so much associated with poverty, they tend to have disappeared from country cooking, at least when guests are invited. Indeed many farmers scarcely bother to collect their crop. It is perhaps ironic that the *bourgeoisie* has discovered how delicious chestnuts can be, setting off so well the richness of the local pork and poultry. In the Auvergne, for example, chestnuts are mixed with Brussels sprouts and a few *lardons*. This mixture, (surprising to find Brussels sprouts in the Auvergne!) is good on its own or as a garnish, and is of course traditional in North European cookery as well.

A roast guinea fowl is delicious with chestnuts. Here is a dish where they absorb very effectively the fat and the juices from a spit-roasted duck.

LE CANARD À LA BROCHE AUX CHÂTAIGNES
Spit-roasted duck with chestnuts

Serves 4

1 young duck, approx 1.5 kg (3 lb) dressed weight	1 clove garlic
	bouquet garni
salt, pepper	24–36 sweet chestnuts
1 small onion	1 glass each red wine and stock

Season the interior of the duck, adding the onion, garlic and bouquet garni.

Peel the chestnuts, using your favourite method. Put half of them into the duck and tie it up, tucking in the ends, before placing it on the spit ready for roasting. Ideally this should be before an open fire. Otherwise pre-heat an electric *rôtissoire* or oven. Put the bird to roast for 1¾ hours (in front of an open fire), 1½ hours (*rôtissoire*) or 1¼ hours on a rack in a conventional oven at 220°C, 425° F, Gas Mark 7.

After the first half-hour, when the fat has started to run and is basting the bird, sprinkle the skin all over with salt to make it crisp and flavoursome. Add the remaining chestnuts to the drip tray under the bird for the last half-hour of the spit-roasting (or to the roasting tin if you are using a conventional oven).

Serve the duck surrounded by the chestnuts, together with the pan juices scraped up and deglazed with a little red wine and stock.

———— ● ————

This dish is greatly esteemed in the Périgord. When chestnuts are out of season, the duck can be filled instead with a stuffing made with chopped bacon, garlic, parsley, the duck liver, ham if available, breadcrumbs soaked in milk, all bound together with an egg. This is known as a white stuffing. There is also a black stuffing – *la farce noire* – in which the breadcrumbs are soaked not in milk but in the blood of the bird, which has been collected when it was killed.

Cooks in the South-West are particularly fond of cooking pork in a *cocotte* – braising rather than roasting it. In a covered dish it seems to stay more moist. Rather after the style of an *enchaud* (page 76), a joint of pork can be braised with chestnuts, onions and wine.

LE PORC EN COCOTTE AUX CHÂTAIGNES
Braised pork with chestnuts

Serves 5–6

3 tablespoons pork fat
1 kg (2¼ lb) roasting pork, boned,
  barded, and tied
250 g (½ lb) onions, coarsely
  chopped

2 or 3 cloves garlic, chopped
200 ml (7 fl oz) dry white wine
salt, pepper
40 chestnuts

Preheat your oven to 170°C, 325°F, Gas Mark 3. Melt the cooking fat in a heavy *cocotte* which has a tight-fitting lid. Brown the meat on all sides, add the onions and garlic and allow them to take on a little colour. Add the wine and allow it to bubble fiercely, reduce the heat, season and allow to cook gently for 5 minutes or so. Cover and transfer to the oven. It will need about 1½ hours' cooking time.

Blanch and peel the chestnuts and add them to the *cocotte* for the last 45 minutes of the cooking. To serve, transfer the meat to a carving dish, surround with the onions and chestnuts and pass the pan juices separately.

For a similar but more sophisticated treatment of a shoulder of veal, the chestnuts are joined by their companions of the woods, *girolles, cèpes* or whatever mushrooms happen to be available.

LE RÔTI DE VEAU CÉVENOL
Veal with chestnuts and mushrooms

Serves 6

1.5 kg (3¼ lb) boned and rolled shoulder of veal	salt, pepper
60 g (2 oz) goose or pork fat	500 g (1 lb) chestnuts
30 g (1 oz) flour	250 g (8 oz) fresh *girolles* or other mushrooms or
400 ml (¾ pt) stock	30–60 g (1–2 oz) dried *cèpes* or other
bouquet garni	mushrooms, pre-soaked

Choose a casserole with a lid, large enough to take the joint and the chestnuts and mushrooms. If it is a flameproof one, so much the better otherwise you will need a large frying pan in which to brown the meat before transferring it to the oven in an ovenproof casserole. This is the kind of slowly-cooked dish which is more suited to oven cooking, although originally it would have been cooked in a pot over the fire, or on top of a stove.

In the casserole or frying pan, heat the fat and brown the meat on all sides. While it is taking on colour, preheat the oven to 190°C, 375°F, Gas Mark 5, warming the casserole in it at the same time (if you are starting the cooking in a frying pan). When the veal is nicely golden, season it and transfer it to the casserole. Stir the flour into the fat left in the browning pan, blend in the stock until you have a thin sauce. Bring this to the boil, check the seasoning, then pour it into the casserole. Add a bouquet garni, cover and transfer to the oven.

Peel the chestnuts and chop up the mushrooms and add these to the casserole after the first three-quarters of an hour. Add more seasoning if necessary. After a further 15 minutes, reduce the heat to 160°C, 325°F, Gas Mark 3, and leave to simmer gently for an hour. Check the seasoning at the end, leaving the joint to 'rest' in a low oven for 15 minutes while dishing up the accompaniments.

Either serve the meat surrounded by the chestnuts and mushrooms, strained out of their gravy, passing round the sauce separately, or carve the meat on its own and serve the chestnuts and mushrooms in their sauce.

———— ● ————

There are remarkably few points of contact between English country cooking and the peasant cooking of South-West France but one thing they do have in common is the use of chestnuts for stuffing a turkey. A small turkey is traditional to the end-of-year festivities in both countries, though French cooks tend to prefer a small young bird to the monsters which haunt English butchers' shops in December. A small bird has also the advantage of not needing so much stuffing.

LE DINDONNEAU FARCI AUX CHÂTAIGNES
Turkey stuffed with chestnuts

Serves 8

1 kg (2¼ lb) chestnuts	chives, chervil, sorrel
250 g (½ lb) salt belly of pork	salt, pepper
a young turkey, weighing about	2 eggs
4 kg (9 lb)	2 tablespoons armagnac
2 large shallots, chopped	3 tablespoons goose or duck fat
6 tablespoons chopped parsley	1 teaspoon red wine vinegar

Shell and remove the inner skin of the chestnuts by whatever method you prefer. Then parboil them to enable you to crush them with a fork. If they remain at all hard, crumble them as best you can into small pieces. It is important that they should absorb the juices from the stuffing and they will not do this as successfully if they are left whole.

To the chestnuts add the belly of pork, liver of the bird, both diced small, the shallots, the parsley and any other *fines herbes* you may be able to find in season. Add some black pepper and perhaps a little salt depending on the saltiness of the pork. Bind the mixture with the beaten eggs and stir in the brandy.

Prepare the turkey for roasting and stuff it with the mixture. Sew up the opening. Season the outside of the bird and roast it. A 4 kg (9 lb) bird will need about 2¼ hours in a moderately hot oven (200°C, 400°F, Gas Mark 6) because of the stuffing which must be cooked through. If you are able to roast in front of a fire, the cooking time will depend on the heat of the fire and your skill in keeping it up to the required temperature for as long as may be necessary.

Baste with a little goose or duck fat to start with, then with a stock which you have made from the neck and giblets of the bird. The pan juices will make all the sauce you need but if they dry up, add a little water and in any event, add a dash of wine vinegar before serving.

You can stuff and roast a chicken in the same way: reduce the quantities for the stuffing proportionately.

——— • ———

Apart from their uses as a hot vegetable, chestnuts are also delicious in a salad where their slightly floury texture contrasts with the crispness of a really fresh lettuce, and the sweetness of the flavour is pointed by the vinaigrette dressing. Note that in this recipe the chestnuts are cooked in their shells.

LES CHÂTAIGNES EN SALADE
Chestnut salad

Serves 4

500 g (1 lb) chestnuts
corn or vegetable oil
vinegar
seasoning

2 hard-boiled eggs, sliced
1 small onion, finely chopped
a crisp lettuce

Cut a slit in the shell of each nut, and put them into boiling salted water for a quarter of an hour. They should be just turning floury but should remain whole.

At the end of the cooking time, remove the pan from the heat, taking the chestnuts out a few at a time to peel them, taking care to remove all the inner skin (rubber gloves are useful here). Put them in the bottom of a salad bowl and while they are still tepid, dress them with a well-seasoned vinaigrette.

When ready to serve, add the hard-boiled eggs, onion and lettuce.

—— ● ——

The next recipe is one of the most surprising we have come across. One would not normally think of a mixture of chestnuts and cabbage as constituting a dessert. Try this one out on your gourmet friends and ask them why they bother to go to the expense of buying *marrons glacés*.

LES CHÂTAIGNES BLANCHIES
Poor man's *marrons glacés*

Serves 4

500 g (1 lb) chestnuts
2 or 3 cabbage leaves

white wine

Cut an incision in the outer skins of the chestnuts, and peel them off. Drop them into boiling water and allow to simmer for 10 minutes. Then use a *déboiradour* – or more probably two wooden spoons – to rub off the second, inner skin while they are still in the water. Drain them and refresh them in cold water. Blanch the cabbage leaves for a minute or two to make them pliable. Then wrap the chestnuts in them and tie them up into parcels with some string.

Take a pan with a thick base and a tight-fitting lid, and put in a very little cold water – just enough to cover the base. Add the bundles of nuts, cover the pan and cook very gently for 45 minutes. By the end the water will be entirely absorbed and the nuts will have turned opaque like *marrons glacés*. Empty the parcels, serve them hot, sprinkled with a little sweet white wine and drink the rest with them. A quite delicious dessert.

LES NOIX

Rien n'est perdu dans la noix, sauf le bruit qu'elle fait en se cassant.

IF CHESTNUTS ARE a reminder to the peasant of the former poverty of his ancestors, walnuts are an assurance of prosperity and well-being. Walnut trees are grown all over the South-West, many families having a few trees between them to guarantee a supply from one season to another. The commercial exploitation of walnuts seems to be confined, however, to the Dordogne valley and the countryside which borders it. Walnut trees do not like extreme heat, so will not be seen much south of the Quercy. On the other hand they are susceptible to late frosts so are not much cultivated on the high ground to the east of our region.

The town of Sarlat is not on the river Dordogne nor is it the county-town of the *département*. Nevertheless it seems to be the centre of so much agricultural production; geese, truffles and not least of all walnuts have traditionally centred on the markets of Sarlat. But gradually the distribution of walnuts is taking on a different pattern. Instead of the peasants having to find buyers at market, the merchants and whole-salers know to which farms to go and they buy direct from the property. The reputation of the walnuts of Périgord is such that they account for 60 per cent of all the French walnut trade as well as supplying the export markets of Germany, Spain, Switzerland and Belgium.

Until recently it was common to see the odd walnut tree standing on its own in a field. It may or may not have belonged to the owner of the field, because French law enables you to own a tree on someone else's land. The division of peasants' estates often involved one member of a family being allocated trees in a field allotted to a relative, so that when the field was sold or left to someone else, the new owner did not get the tree. The habit of having these isolated trees is dying out, largely because of modern farming methods which make a tree like that a nuisance. It gets in the way of the tractor.

Walnut trees tend either to be grown close to a farmhouse, or along the sides of a road, or, more and more commonly, in whole orchards devoted exclusively to walnut production. Where isolated trees die, they are seldom replanted, and it is not hard to see why. At least ten years are needed before a walnut tree will produce a decent crop, so only intensive farming with a regular replanting programme makes any commercial sense. More than a hundred years is required before a walnut tree acquires the maturity to provide wood of a quality fit for the finest furniture. This wood was not all sold to Parisian furniture makers. Much of it went into making cupboards, sideboards, tables and chests for the local farms as well as for the rich townspeople. At one time it was common for every barn to have a small reserve of walnut planks being seasoned and held in reserve to make a piece of furniture as part of a girl's dowry.

Every part of a walnut tree makes its contribution to the peasant economy. The leaves, picked before midsummer day, go to make *vin de noyer* (see page 315). The walnut tree is one of the last to come out in spring. Its hard dark buds need two weeks of sun before they will condescend to produce the maroon shoots which turn dark green in time for the high summer. The leaves are quite perfumed if you rub them, but beware the stain on your hands which is very difficult to get rid of. By the time you've made the walnut wine, it's time to make the *crème de noix* or *eau-de-vie de noix* from the young green nuts (see page 313). This is taken as a *digestif* after a good dinner, and acquires a touch of velvet if allowed to age.

Then there are the nuts themselves. They ripen at the same time as the chestnuts in October. If they are to be kept for any length of time they are not picked from the tree but are allowed to fall to the ground of their own accord and in their own time. Only nuts which are fully ripe will keep. They must be dried too, preferably in the autumn sunshine or they will rot. Thereafter they must be kept buried in sand in a cool cellar. In the fridge they will keep for 9 months. Walnuts for immediate consumption need not be dried; they can be eaten as they are, 'wet', and there is nothing more delicious.

The shelling of the walnuts benefits from the same kind of communal co-operative spirit as the chestnut harvest. The Périgourdins call this *l'énoisement* or in patois *enouzdhia*. The process of shelling walnuts is a rather more expert affair, however, because each nut has a slightly different shape and size and requires the individual judgment of the person wielding the mallet designed for the purpose. A skilled sheller will open one a minute without damaging the kernel.

A farmer down the road from us explained to us how, just before the nuts ripen, the ground beneath the tree is scrupulously cleared of leaves or any débris. The hay or grass is cut short, he says, so that the falling nuts do not get lost in the herbage. The nuts will be picked off the ground each morning, like eggs, before the leaves falling from the tree have a chance of smothering them. At least that is what he does. We planted two trees about ten years ago and waited patiently for them to get to a decent size and start yielding. In the last few years we have found quite a number of green 'balls' decorating the branches. But when we come to harvest our crop, we find the green husks empty – the edible dormice have got there first.

Peasants who produce walnuts surplus to their own needs can often be seen on market day making a little pin money from quite modest quantities. These are usually the smaller varieties of nut, but are good value because there is proportionately less shell than in the Franquette variety which is much larger, more oval in shape and the kind which is grown for commercial purposes.

The shells are not despised just because they can't be eaten. They can be pounded to a powder and used to line the floor of your bread-oven, keeping the undersurface of your loaves smooth and free from soot or ash. This powder is also apparently used for soundproofing aeroplane cabins and as an abrasive agent in oil drilling in the Middle East. Any shells which are left over from these bizarre applications burn very well in the *cheminée*. Surplus nuts may be stored in salt or sand for a few months.

The nuts which the peasants keep for themselves have two basic functions. First, to be eaten as dessert, raw as something to nibble before meals, and in a green salad (see page 202); or for the making of walnut oil. This is produced by grinding the nuts to a pulp that is then cooked and pressed. The oil is the extract of this pressing. Such a process requires a lot of pressure, which formerly could only be generated by a water-driven mill. There sprang up, therefore, a number of these artisan-run mills along the banks of streams; these mills processed the greater part of the walnut oil produced in the Périgord. Some of them still exist and carry on a thriving business; for example at St Nathalène near Sarlat, and at Martel, just above the river Dordogne.

The machinery may be primitive but the product is absolutely pure, with no additives whatsoever and for this reason will not go rancid if kept in a cool place. Unfortunately most factory-made walnut oil is of inferior quality by comparison. It is cheaper and keeps less well. The real thing costs so little extra that there is no question as to which is the better value for money. It is a fraction of the price charged by fashionable shops in England, and since it is available in quantities as small as half a litre, it is a sensible souvenir to bring back from a visit to the Périgord. Walnut oil is strong in flavour, and many people prefer to use it diluted in equal quantities with some flavourless oil such as sunflower or ground-nut.

Only peasants who lived close to water and had enough trees to warrant the cost of the plant would make their own oil. Otherwise they would trade their walnuts for a quantity of the finished oil. When you realize that it takes 10 kilos of nuts to make 1 litre of oil, you begin to understand how precious it was. The oil was used to fuel the lamps in the farmhouse, as an antidote to fleas, ants, worms and jaundice, but it was also used in the making of the most exquisite salad dressing (page 202) and in mayonnaise, as in the next recipe. The nuts themselves were pounded into the making of that sublime transformation of garlic, *aillade toulousaine* (page 47) and the hardy people of the Rouergue blended the oil into their *éstofinado* (see page 136).

Apart from these basic uses, walnuts were not much used in cooking, unless it was in the making of a tart or cake. Modern cooks have found all sorts of interesting things to do with them. They make a fine omelette, and it is surprising that such a dish is not traditional; a good change from almonds with trout, and an alternative in macaroons. They are good too in stuffings for poultry and rabbit.

Here is a variation on traditional walnut salads, such as on page 202, using the freshly gathered walnuts that are still juicy or 'wet'.

La Salade Quercynoise
Walnut salad

Serves 4

2 medium-sized potatoes	mayonnaise made with:
3 small apples	2 egg yolks
3 stalks of young celery	150 ml (¼ pt) walnut oil
12 fresh walnuts	150 ml (¼ pt) sunflower oil
salt and pepper	lemon juice

Steam the potatoes in their skins and allow them to cool until they can be handled. Peel and slice them. Peel and quarter the apples and cut them into thin segments. Cut the celery into dice and chop up the nuts. Mix all together and blend with a mayonnaise made from the ingredients indicated. Season well before serving. Such a salad would be more likely to be eaten as an hors d'oeuvre than after meat.

———— • ————

The most frequent use of walnuts in cooking in the traditional repertoire of the South-West is without doubt in the field of *pâtisserie*. Walnut tarts may be bought from local pastry-makers, but many farmers' wives and even restaurateurs pride themselves on the ones they themselves make. Here is our attempt to copy the delicious tart made by Madame Sylvestre in the tiny village of Bouzic just south of the Dordogne.

La Tarte aux Noix
Walnut tart

Serves 6–8

pâte sucrée for a 20 cm (8 in) flan case made with:	125 g (4 oz) walnuts
	100 g (3½ oz) sugar
150 g (5 oz) flour	50 g (1¾ oz) fresh breadcrumbs
2 teaspoons sugar	3 tablespoons cold black coffee
salt	2 egg yolks
85 g (3 oz) butter	75 g (2½ oz) good dessert chocolate,
1 egg yolk	e.g. Chocolat-Menier
1 tablespoon water	knob of butter

Mix together the sifted flour, sugar and salt, and rub the butter into it to form fine breadcrumbs. Add the egg yolk, beaten up with a tablespoon of cold water, and blend with the fingertips to form a soft dough. Stretch it out with the palm of your hand until smooth. Roll into a ball and dust with flour. Wrap in aluminium foil or muslin and chill in the refrigerator until firm.

Line a 20 cm (8 in) flan case with the pastry and bake it 'blind', on a baking sheet, for 10 minutes at 200°C, 400°F, Gas Mark 6.

Pound the walnuts to a fine powder (or grind them in a liquidizer). Soak the breadcrumbs in a little milk and then squeeze them dry.

Add the sugar and the crumbs to the walnuts, mix well, then stir in the coffee and the beaten egg yolks. Fill the pastry case with the mixture and put it back to bake in a moderate oven (180°C, 350°F, Gas Mark 4) for about 20 minutes, or until the filling looks set and firm.

Break up the chocolate, melt it in a pan with a knob of butter, and spread it in a thin smooth layer over the walnut filling.

LES PRUNEAUX

I T IS STRANGE how the French succeed even with those foods which were most hated in childhood and which never get given a second chance. Just as Normandy has a sublimated version of rice pudding – *tergoule* – so the Lot-et-Garonne in the South-West excels in the production of truly beautiful prunes. Its cooks have also developed a whole repertoire of fascinating dishes to show them off.

Prunes are nothing more than dried plums. It is confusing that the French for plum is *prune* while our 'prune' translates as *pruneau*. The French prunes which are marketed commercially are not made from any old plums. They come from a special plum tree called *prunier d'ente*, an old French term signifying simply a grafted tree, but which includes the particular kind of tree which has been used for the production of prunes in South-West France since the time of the Crusades, and is today called *Robe-Sergent*. The monks of Clairac, an abbey near the town of Tonneins on the river Garonne, were astute enough to spot the commercial value of the prune and by the eighteenth century an extensive market had been built up.

Today France is the third largest prune-producing country after the USA and, perhaps strangely, Yugoslavia. They grow particularly well in those parts of the South-West best sheltered from spring frosts and where there are frequent summer showers as well as hot sunshine. This explains why the Lot-et-Garonne, particularly the south-facing banks of the two eponymous rivers, has proved so suitable. Three-quarters of all French prunes come from here, about 16,000 tons a year. The advent of the Common Market has helped French producers to resist competition from overseas. So has the inherent quality of the product.

The local prunes are usually called *pruneaux d'Agen* and the epithet *à l'Agenaise* in cooking will always promise prunes. This is because Agen has become the chief market distribution centre, although most of the prunes themselves come either from other parts of the Garonne valley or from the country round Villeneuve-sur-Lot.

The conversion of plums into prunes is basically simple. The plums are sorted into sizes after picking and then dried on trays, first in the hot sun, then in large modern ovens at just under boiling temperature. Before the industrialization of production and the mass-marketing of the fruit, the locals made their own, not just the inhabitants of the favoured areas but any peasant in the South-West who had more plums then he needed either as fresh fruit or for making into *eau-de-vie*. In an abundant year, one tree could furnish enough to provide a family with *une tarte aux pruneaux* every Sunday of the year.

How to make prunes from plums
Ideally you need a large wickerwork tray but a rectangular wooden frame with close wire-netting will do. The important thing is for air to get at the plums from all sides during the initial drying process. Then there is the question of the plums. Some say you shouldn't pick them but shake the tree and use those which fall. If you need only a few, then by all means go up the tree but pick only those which actually drop into your hand by their own weight. In any event use only those which are completely sound, with unbroken skin and free from insects of any kind.

Lay the plums on your tray or frame in one layer and dry them in the hot sun for several days. Bring them in under cover each night and turn the plums frequently. The fruit then has to face fiercer heat three times. Formerly in the larger farmhouses the bread oven was useful. When the bread was done and the temperature had fallen to about 90°C (200°F), the prunes were left in it overnight. Next day, the plums were turned over and put back into the oven, a bit hotter this time, about 100°C, (212°F). The third and last time the oven was hotter still. Those who do not have bread ovens could experiment either with solid fuel slow-cooking stoves of the Aga type, or with a *diable*, the round earthenware dish in two equal halves which the French use for cooking potatoes and chestnuts entirely without liquid and which retains heat very well. It is important to get the heat right because the quality of the prune at the end of the day depends partially on its humidity content.

Finally the prunes should be packed in layers in boxes with a bed of bay leaves between each layer. It is a good idea to sort them out roughly into sizes first, because it will appear from the recipes which follow that the various sizes have different purposes, the small ones being best for tarts and as an ingredient in stuffings, and the larger ones for preserving in alcohol.

Every recipe requires the prunes eventually to be rehydrated. In the old days this would be done in an infusion of dried lime blossom (*tilleul*). Many recipes now indicate tea because, even in rural France, not everyone has their own lime tree and tea can be bought at every village shop. In practice, it probably makes little difference what you soak the prunes in and even water would do as a last resort. Where a dish calls for wine in the cooking, the prunes can be steeped overnight in the wine so that the flavours can mingle with each other.

Prunes partner the richer poultry very successfully. They also go well with rabbit. Terrines of duck with prunes are to be found generally in all regions where the *charcuterie* is good. Monsieur Vanel, the celebrated restaurateur in Toulouse whose professional style is rooted in the country cooking of his native Quercy, has combined prunes with a kind of *rillettes de lapin*. His recipe has been used to provide a gourmet dish intended for a Russian space flight including a French scientist. This would seem to give a new dimension to the term *goût du terroir*!

The recipe involves a fair amount of work and time to prepare, but for a special occasion, when time can be afforded more easily, it makes a superb first course. The juices of the marinade combine to give a delicious, strongly flavoured aspic.

La Compôte de Lapin aux Pruneaux
Potted rabbit with prunes

Serves 6

1 rabbit, weighing about 900 g–1 kg (2–2¼ lb)	for the marinade:
350 g (12 oz) big prunes	1 large onion, sliced
575 ml (1 pt) weak tea	2 carrots, sliced
125 g (¼ lb) fresh pork fat, cubed	6 tablespoons olive oil
2 teaspoons French mustard	400 ml (¾ pt) of dry white wine
approx 400 ml (¾ pt) chicken stock	3 sprigs parsley
salt, pepper	2 bay leaves
	sprig of thyme and of rosemary
	1 clove garlic, chopped

Wash and dry the rabbit and cut it into pieces. Slice the onion and carrots. Put the meat and vegetables into a bowl with the oil and wine, the herbs tied into a bunch and the garlic. Leave to marinate overnight, or for at least 12 hours.

Soak the prunes in the warm tea for about 3 hours so that they plump up, then bring them to the boil and let them barely simmer for 10 minutes. Leave the prunes to cool in their liquor.

Take a large, flameproof casserole and melt the pork fat in it. While it is melting, take the pieces of rabbit out of the marinade and dry them on a clean cloth or with kitchen paper. Then brown them in the hot fat – in two or three batches if necessary. Put them to one side. Strain the vegetables from the marinade, keeping the liquid, and remove the bouquet garni. Brown the vegetables in the same fat and when they are golden, drain off as much of any remaining fat as possible. Stir the mustard into the pan, then gradually add the marinade, which should amount to about 300 ml (½ pt). Put the rabbit back in, packing it down among the vegetables, add the bouquet garni, and top up with the chicken stock so that the meat is covered. Season, cover and bring to the boil. When all is simmering quite gently, transfer to an oven pre-heated to 140°–150°C, 275°–300°F, Gas Mark 1–2 for 2½ hours. Check during this time that it is not simmering too fast or the rabbit will become tough.

When it is cooked, leave the rabbit to cool in the casserole. Then take out the pieces and carefully pick the meat off the bones, placing the flesh in a bowl. Do a few pieces at a time, then shred the flesh between two forks so that it is broken into strands but is not crushed. Transfer each batch as you do it to a terrine or flat earthenware dish, packing it in quite lightly. Strain the cooking liquor through a muslin and pour most or all of it – 375–400 ml (12–15 fl oz) – over the rabbit which must absorb it completely; the *compôte* must be soft and juicy, well-flavoured with this stock, but not runny.

Chill for several hours before serving, accompanied by the drained prunes and some crisp toast.

———— ● ————

In the river valleys of the South-West, eels are a popular dish to eat. The larger ones are sometimes called *murène* or, in the Landes, *sardiat*. They are closely related to the lamprey, an almost meat-like larger cousin found in the estuary of the Gironde and cooked in the red wine of St Emilion. Lampreys are usually sold in tins in expensive *épiceries*, already cooked in their wine sauce. Eels can be prepared in the same way but in Lot-et-Garonne they are cooked with prunes and in white wine, a dish which is better prepared ahead of time and re-heated.

L'ANGUILLE AUX PRUNEAUX
Eel simmered with prunes and wine

Serves 6

18 large prunes
½–¾ bottle dry white wine
Eel or eels weighing 1.25 kg (2¾ lb)
4 tablespoons cooking oil
8 button onions

125 g (4 oz) lean fresh belly of pork,
  cubed
2 tablespoons flour
salt, pepper
bouquet garni

Soak the prunes in the wine overnight. Heat the oil in a frying pan for which you have a tight-fitting lid. Chop the eel into cutlets about 3 cm (1¼ in) thick and flour them. When the oil is really hot toss the pieces in it to seize them on all sides. Add the button onions and the pork. Cook all together until lightly coloured. Remove all the ingredients from the pan while you make a roux with the flour and the pan-juices. Add the wine gradually until you have a smooth sauce. Put back all the solids into the sauce, season and add the bouquet garni, then the prunes. Bring back to simmering point, cover the pan and cook slowly for 1 hour.

———— ● ————

Perhaps it is surprising to find prunes in the mountains of the Cantal or indeed anywhere in the Auvergne, where spring comes late and frosts are possible into the month of May. There is no shortage of rain to swell the fruit but hot sun for drying the plums is just about as reliable as in North Wales. Even so, the Auvergne has given birth to one of the best prune dishes of France. Undoubtedly the *pounti* is of very humble origin but even the best of the restaurants in the Cantal and the upper Rouergue serve their own version, and sometimes under fancy names such as *Feuilles de saison au fars de pruneaux*: even that title is more informative than the rustic original which gives the uninitiated no clue as to what he might expect. *Pounti* is a sort of crustless quiche, of ham or pork and spinach, as well as prunes. The recipe is given on page 152.

Prunes stuffed with *pâté* are an unusually good accompaniment to all kinds of poultry. If you are serving them hot, be careful not to raise the temperature too much, or the *pâté* will melt. These stuffed prunes can be served cold, with a truffled duck in aspic for instance, or very gently warmed, to have with any roast bird. We always have them with Christmas goose.

LES PRUNEAUX FOURRÉS
Prunes stuffed with pâté

Serves 4

16 large prunes, pre-soaked

200 g (7 oz) smooth *pâté* (ideally *mousse de foie gras*)

Poach the prunes in salt water for 15 minutes. Drain them and allow them to cool, then cut them carefully along one side and remove the stones.

Stuff the cavities with pieces of the *pâté*.

— • —

Prunes also make an interesting addition to all kinds of stews and slow-simmered meat and game dishes, *plats mitonnés* as the French call them to distinguish them from dishes quickly prepared in a *sauteuse*. Try, for example, adding them (allowing 3 or 4 per person and remembering to rehydrate them first) to a *civet* of rabbit or hare, or to any of the *daubes* of beef described earlier in this book. Do not forget that they need to cook for about an hour in order that their texture be soft enough not to be chewy. Do not overcook them or they will fall to pieces in your stew.

So far the use of prunes has been considered only in relation to *pâtés* or main dishes where their natural sweetness serves to set off the richness of the other ingredients. Prunes do, however, have their uses throughout the repertoire, and no more so than in the delicious desserts in which they feature. A prune tart is a Sunday treat all over the South-West (see the recipe on page 301) and there is no more Lucullan ice-cream than that which is made from prunes and armagnac. This may not be a traditional peasant recipe, but the ingredients and final result are certainly typical of the region.

LA GLACE AUX PRUNEAUX ET À L'ARMAGNAC
Prune and armagnac ice-cream

Serves 4

20–24 prunes, preferably preserved in armagnac
3 egg yolks
150 ml (¼ pt) single cream

100 g (3½ oz) vanilla sugar
2 tablespoons armagnac
150 ml (¼ pt) double cream

If you are not using prunes preserved in armagnac, soak them until they have softened, then stew them in their soaking water. Drain and remove the stones. Chop the flesh roughly, but do not purée it. Leave to cool. Put the egg yolks into a double boiler or bowl set over simmering water. Heat the single cream nearly to boiling point then beat it into the yolks. Add the vanilla sugar and continue stirring until the mixture thickens. Leave to cool. Mix the chopped prunes and the armagnac into the custard cream. Whip the double cream lightly and fold it in. Pour into a metal mould and freeze in a deep freeze or in the icemaking compartment of the refrigerator, previously turned to its coldest setting.

———— ● ————

While on the subject of prunes and armagnac, the pickling of this fruit in spirit is one of the most popular of all *conserves* in the South-West. In the poorest peasant homes there used to be no dessert other than fresh fruit except on special occasions when a tart or cake might be produced. To finish a meal when there had been no visit to the local *pâtisserie*, perhaps because there was no spare money to spend there, the peasant would draw on his own supply of home-made prunes preserved in his home-made *eau-de-vie*. This is still one of the most popular sweets of the region.

LES PRUNEAUX À L'ALCOOL
Prunes preserved in alcohol

The spirit used depends on what is to hand. In the old days it would have been *eau-de-vie* from the plums in the garden. Depending on its strength this might be diluted with flavourless spirit. Alternatively, armagnac can be used, either on its own, or diluted with the spirit. The two kinds of brandy should not be mixed together. This recipe is adapted from the advice given by M. Lalbie from Penne d'Agenais who travels in prunes from one market town to another. He sells nothing else and his stall, piled high with a glistening assortment of prunes of different sizes, and of varying degrees of humidity, is worthy of the most serious study.

1 kg (2¼ lb) prunes
175 g (6 oz) sugar

1 litre (35 fl oz) alcohol (*alcool de fruits, eau-de-vie, armagnac* etc)

Soak the prunes in tepid weak tea until they have plumped up. Sterilize a glass jar or jars in boiling water, drain and dry them. Fill the jars three-quarters full with the prunes, keeping the liquid in which they have been soaked.

Use 400 ml (16 fl oz) of this to make a syrup; boil it up with the sugar. (If you use one large jar, you will need less syrup so dissolve the sugar in 300 ml (½ pt) of the tea.) After the syrup has cooled a little (or it will crack the glass), pour enough into each jar to come about one third up the jar. Top up with the alcohol and screw on the lid. Shake up the jars every few days to begin with and if there is room for a top-up of more alcohol, add a little.

Keep for at least six to eight weeks before consuming.

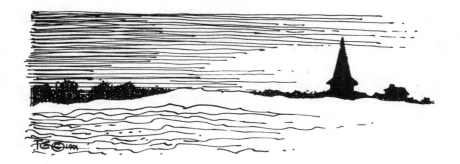

LES DESSERTS

T HE SIMPLICITY, the monotony and the meagreness of the diet for many of the poorer peasants until this century are difficult for us to realize. When you do reach the point of accepting the hard realities of their lives, the last idea which comes to mind is 'desserts'. The word nowadays conjures up an image of a sweet, creamy and rich concoction, totally inappropriate for a peasant community.

What was there by way of a sweetener anyway? For those who kept their own bees honey was a possibility or there was the pulp and juice of sweet grapes, figs or melons but apart from that, until cheap sugar was imported from the colonies and until the development of the sugar beet industry in the north at the end of the last century, sugar was very scarce. In fact before then it was sold only by chemists and so was regarded with some distrust.

When sugar did appear in more quantity there was the problem for the peasant that it had to be purchased. It was therefore a luxury, reserved for feast days and not to be used with abandon. Everyday meals ended with the main course or after the salad or the chestnuts. When sugar was bought this was in *un pain*, a loaf to be broken up as required. It might be needed for making jam from any fruit growing on the property so this was its most important use.

When there was some kind of festive meal to prepare, what was there in the larder which was home-produced and might contribute to a dessert on that special day? Well, there would usually be flour, eggs, milk, perhaps nuts, with fruit, honey and jam to give some sweetness.

At a pretty basic level there was *le millas*, the maize flour 'bun' which often replaced bread in the meal but which could also be spread with jam or sprinkled with sugar. *Le millas* (page 143) is not at all sophisticated and can be cooked in a pot over the open fire, as can pancakes and *galettes*, made with whatever kind of flour is available, and again, eaten with home-made jam or honey. There are several types of simple, plain biscuit which as the word implies, are twice cooked. These *échaudés* or *chaudels* made from flour, egg and a raising agent, are first poached in boiling water, then dried off in the oven. Again, over a fire you could fry *beignets* – usually *beignets de pommes* (apple fritters) – while for a very special occasion country cooks devised a most lengthy, skilled and unusual cake which can only be made on a spit revolving in front of a hot wood fire. This is the famous *gâteau à la broche*, said to come from Villecomtal in the Rouergue. By dripping batter rich in eggs, butter and sugar round a conical mould as it turns on a spit, layers of cooked, crisp biscuit are slowly built up to form a spectacular cone-shaped cake which when finished, looks like a golden fir tree.

Where there was an oven, either the family's own bread oven or the communal one in a village, the scope became wider. Fruit tarts and pastries, baked fruit in custard like *clafoutis* and *flaugnarde* and cakes like *la fouace* were put to cook after the bread-making was finished.

Chestnuts and walnuts were eaten in place of dessert, as we have seen, and plums played an important role at this end of the meal. Farms would have a small orchard containing a few fruit trees – plum, cherry, pear, apple and perhaps a quince too. Or, more commonly, various fruit trees were planted along the farm's boundary or by the side of the road bordering the property. This way the trees did not occupy or overshadow scarce arable or grazing land. Great store was set by the plum trees because the fruit dried so well, turning into really sweet nuggets which would keep, always an added asset. Peaches and nectarines, apricots, melons and soft fruit like strawberries and raspberries have become popular crops only more recently and they will not grow everywhere. The river valleys, sheltered from damaging winds and frosts or the more Mediterranean climate in the south favour them best. The Tarn, the Tarn-et-Garonne, the Lot-et-Garonne and the Haute-Garonne now have extensive orchards and are important producers of 40% of the country's total fruit production.

As in Great Britain, the pancake was traditionally a dish for festive occasions, especially Mardi Gras (our Shrove Tuesday). It was not difficult or expensive to make but was nevertheless reserved for religious or special family occasions. At Candlemas the making of pancakes was hoped to guarantee the presence of money in the house for the rest of the year – you held the frying pan in one hand and clutched a louis d'or coin in the other – while at Mardi Gras, together with *gaufres* (waffles) and *beignets*, they formed part of the final celebrations of Carnival before eggs were given up for Lent. There was even a meal known as *une crespérade* which consisted solely of pancakes (*crespères*) washed down with *le vin nouveau*. They were also a treat at family gatherings, on the local Saint's day or at the end of haymaking and harvesting.

As the pancakes had to be cooked over the wood fire, this was done in a special frying pan which had an extra long handle. The pan rested on *le trépied*, a tripod set over the hot embers, and the handle could either be attached by a piece of wire to the hook of *la crémaillère* which hung in the chimney, or slipped through the ring of *le landier* (the fire dog). This then held the pan in position while it was heating up or during the frying, so saving the cook from being fried herself. The art of tossing the pancakes was part of the housewife's skills and you can easily imagine that at a special festival meal, there would be plenty of fun got out of the process. To ensure a good harvest and some money in the house, everyone had to take a turn and the head of the family had to toss his pancake especially high in the air.

The batter for *les crêpes* is often flavoured with *anis* (aniseed) – a favourite from the Périgord down to Gascony – or else with *eau-de-vie*, rum or orange-flower water. *Les Jacques* are another Périgord favourite – rounds of apple set between two layers of pancake batter.

LES CRÊPES À L'ANIS
Pancakes flavoured with aniseed

Serves 4

for the batter:
125 g (4 oz) flour
2 large eggs
2 tablespoons sugar
pinch of salt
1 teaspoon *graines d'anis*
eau-de-vie (optional)
150 ml (¼ pt) milk
150 ml (¼ pt) water

castor sugar

Make the batter by putting all its ingredients except the milk and water in a bowl and mixing well together. Start adding the milk and water a little at a time until half has been used. Beat the batter very well at this stage until it is smooth and forming bubbles. Whisk in the rest of the liquid. Leave the batter to stand for at least 2 hours.

Heat your frying pan until it is really hot and then grease it lightly. (The traditional way was to tie a piece of cloth round the end of a stick or fork, then dip it into melted goose fat and paint the pan with it.) Make the pancakes with a tablespoonful of batter for each one, running the batter round the pan to make a thin covering. When the underside is coloured, flip the pancake over and cook the other side. Sprinkle with sugar and roll up. Serve with jam or honey.

———— • ————

A fun variation, particularly for the benefit of the children, are *les crêpes frisées* or *les crêpes à l'entonnoir*. With the aid of a funnel filled with the batter, you employ whatever *tour de main* you possess to trickle the batter into the pan in a sort of spiral so as to make a haphazard pattern, leaving the pancake with holes and irregularities whose edges all go *frisées* and crisp.

LES JACQUES
Apple pancakes

Serves 4

300 ml (½ pt) pancake batter (as above)
4 dessert apples, peeled, cored and cut into rings

castor sugar

Make the pancake batter and leave it to rest for a couple of hours. When the time comes to cook the pancakes, pour a layer of batter into a well-greased hot frying pan, spreading it round in the usual way. As soon as the pancake is formed, put pieces of apple on top and then cover these with a further thin layer of batter. Continue the cooking and then turn the pancake carefully – it will be rather fragile – to cook the other side.

To serve, sprinkle with sugar but do not roll up.

———— • ————

While *les jacques* are associated mainly with the Périgord, *les pescajouns aux fruits* are fruit-filled soufflé pancakes from the Quercy. A mixture of whatever fruit is to hand, peaches, pears and prunes, for example, are diced and then soaked in *eau-de-vie*. Another pan-fried sweet is *la galette*. This is a sort of scone made from a flour, sugar and egg paste which also contains a raising agent. The paste is rolled out and cut into scone-sized rounds which are then fried. *Gaufres* or *curbelets* (waffles), made with a batter flavoured with aniseed, lemon or orange-flower water, are cooked over the fire in an iron *gaufrier*. These waffle irons were often elaborately made with ornate decorations.

All these are resourceful products of the frying pan and the open fire but the housewife also made biscuits long before industrial biscuit-making arrived. In fact they are said to go back as far as ancient Egyptian times. A raised dough was prepared, then small pieces of it were poached in boiling water before being dried by baking them in the oven – twice cooked therefore. These plump little biscuits were used to decorate the laurel branches carried to church by the children on Palm Sunday, and they were given various names – *échaudés*, *chaudels*, or in the Rouergue *tchaoudals*. Albi in the Tarn has its own, called *gimblettes*, flavoured with pieces of crystallized fruit or aniseed and often shaped in a ring, while the *échaudés* of Marcillac, in the wine-growing area of the Aveyron, were a speciality on days of the fair, to be eaten with the local wine.

It has to be admitted that these crisp, dry biscuits were a very basic treat; so is another, equally simple, which is particularly associated with the Rouergue and the Auvergne – *la pompe à l'huile*. Just as boiled or roasted chestnuts were eaten as a sweet, so walnuts or in this case walnut oil is the touch of gourmandise. *La pompe* is a thin round of white bread dough, well sprinkled with walnut oil before being baked and afterwards sugared. It was a robust treat, one for Lent when the strict diet did not always assuage hunger. The name is said to derive from the word for the handful of dough which was payment to the village baker for using the communal oven for a batch of loaves. In the Périgord they stuffed this risen bread dough with sugar crystals and pieces of fresh fruit as well, calling them *pain de fruits* or *tourtes aux fruits* – in the latter case because if there was no oven available, they were cooked in *la tourtière*, the primitive 'oven' which was set on the hot ashes in the fire with more ashes placed in its lid.

A more refined relative of *la pompe* is the traditional festive cake of the Aveyron which exists to this day, *la fouace* or *la fougasse*. This has been described as *un pain aux oeufs sucré* – the connection with bread comes from the use of baker's yeast as a raising agent and the fact that the cake is put to rise like bread before being baked in the bread oven. *La fouace* has a long history. Gastronome historians trace the name back to the Latin *panis focacius*, deriving from *focus* meaning the hearth. References to it are found in the works of Rabelais and it evidently became the ceremonial cake, offered with wine, on the feast days of Epiphany, Palm Sunday or the local Saint's day. Later it was, and still is, eaten on family occasions, including marriages and christenings. At marriages it was offered to a newly-wedded couple as they did the traditional round on their wedding night, calling on their neighbours; nowadays it is quite often part of the wedding 'breakfast'. Each year in August when the local fête is held in the picturesque village of Najac, which stands with its ruined castle high above the river Aveyron, an enormous beribboned *fouace*, oval in shape and more than a metre in length, is paraded through the streets during the three-day festivities before being broken up and served to all comers. This tradition has managed to survive two world wars. A *fouace* is not only a speciality of the Rouergue, although they particularly claim it for their own. Francois Mauriac in his novel *Thérèse Desqueyroux*, which is set in Les Landes, tells how Thérèse's aunt 'brought me treats which I had loved as a child and which she thought I still liked, those grey buns of rye and honey called *miques*; the cake known as *fougasse* or *roumadjade*'.

LA FOUACE
Hearth cake

Serves 4

15 g (½ oz) fresh yeast
60 ml (2 fl oz) milk
500 g (1 lb) white flour
175 g (6 oz) sugar
pinch of salt
3 large eggs
125 g (4 oz) butter, melted
125 g (4 oz) crystallized fruits
   (optional)

for the decoration:
1 tablespoon orange-flower water
1 egg
sugar, crystals or granulated

Dissolve the yeast in the warm milk. In a bowl mix together the flour, sugar, salt and the yeast mixture, and the beaten eggs, one by one. Knead this dough very well, working the melted butter into it.

Roll the dough into a ball on a floured surface and form it into a ring by making a hole in the centre with your finger, moving the dough round it so as to enlarge the hole. When it is big enough, insert more fingers and then both hands and keep turning the dough until you have a large ring, about 30 cm (12 in) in diameter. Place it on a buttered baking sheet and decorate, if wished, with pieces of crystallized fruit.

Cover with a clean cloth and leave to rise for 3–4 hours, to double in volume. Paint with beaten egg yolk and bake in a preheated moderately hot oven (190°C, 375°F, Gas Mark 5) for about 45 minutes.

Remove the *fouace* from the oven and paint its top with egg white, whipped up with a tablespoonful of orange-flower water. Sprinkle with sugar – if possible crystals otherwise granulated sugar will do.

———— ● ————

When it is the season for fruit, this can be incorporated into a dough or a batter, or a pastry case in various ways. *Beignets* are the simplest example. But with access to an oven instead of only *la tourtière* a housewife could not only put her *tourte aux salsifis* to bake after breadmaking but she could bake fruit batters and fruit tarts. The most famous of the traditional *pâtisseries campagnardes* of the South-West is probably *le clafoutis*. This is said to have originated in the Limousin where cherries abound, but so they do in the Lot and further south towards Toulouse or over in the Cévennes, so you will find this pudding on many restaurant menus. In the Auvergne, however, it is called *millard*.

In days gone by *clafoutis* was often made with small, wild black cherries known as *les merises* but nowadays the sharp *griottes* are used. The fruit is baked in a sweetened batter of eggs and milk and the result will vary according to the generosity of the cook so far as the proportion of fruit and eggs to flour is concerned. It is usually served warm rather than hot, sometimes cold, and can be either juicy and fruity or rather stodgy and slightly boring.

LE CLAFOUTIS
Sweetened cherry batter

Serves 4

a knob of butter
350 g (¾ lb) ripe black cherries,
  eg *griottes*
2 eggs
2 tablespoons flour

2 tablespoons vanilla sugar
300 ml (½ pt) milk
1 dessertspoon *eau-de-vie*
vanilla sugar

Butter generously a shallow baking dish, approximately 18 × 25 cm (7 × 10 in), and put it to heat in a moderately hot oven, 190°C, 375°F, Gas Mark 5, while you de-stalk the cherries and wash them and dry them.

Beat up the eggs and mix into the flour, add the sugar, milk and *eau-de-vie* (or put all the ingredients into a liquidizer or food processor for a couple of minutes). Cover the heated dish with a layer of cherries and pour the batter over. Return quickly to the oven and bake for between 30–45 minutes until the *clafoutis* has risen and set.

Sprinkle with a little vanilla sugar and serve lukewarm. This recipe uses a minimum of flour and so you may find it difficult to serve neatly. If more flour is added, it will hold together better but will become more stodgy.

———— • ————

According to La Mazille, in his illuminating book *La Bonne Cuisine du Périgord*, other fruit such as plums, cherry plums, grapes or a mixture of several often replace the cherries in the Périgord, though this is not so traditional. And in fact in the Périgord when other fruit is used, the dish is more often known as *une flaugnarde*.

In autumn and winter what is really very traditional all over the South-West is the *tarte aux pruneaux*. The windows of the *boulangeries* and *pâtisseries* are crowded with large open tarts, their almost black filling of baked prunes covered with a lattice work of pale pastry, and on Sunday mornings after church the trade in them is phenomenal.

LA TARTE AUX PRUNEAUX
Prune tart

Serves 4

350 g (¾ lb) prunes (pre-soaked)	for the *pâte sucrée* (sweet shortcrust
300 ml (½ pt) red wine	pastry):
300 ml (½ pt) water	125 g (4 oz) sifted flour
60 g (2 oz) sugar	¼ teaspoon salt
1 egg white	60 g (2 oz) sugar
	60 g (2 oz) softened butter
	1 egg yolk

Sift the flour and salt into a bowl, make a well in the centre and add the butter, sugar and egg yolk. Mix together with the fingertips, gradually drawing in the flour until all is incorporated. Knead the pastry lightly until it is smooth, then flour and wrap it and leave to rest in a cool place for an hour or more.

Cook the prunes in the wine diluted with the water and sugar for 10 minutes. When they have cooled, cut them in half and remove the stones. Reduce the wine syrup they have been cooked in.

Line a 20 cm (8 in) greased flan case with the pastry and prick it all over with a fork. Brush the base with the lightly-beaten egg white before filling the case with the prunes. Pour over some of the reduced syrup – enough to moisten the prunes but not too much. Roll out the pastry trimmings, cut ribbons of pastry and lay these in a lattice over the top, pressing the ends to seal them to the rim. Bake on a baking sheet in a pre-heated oven set at 200°C, 400°F, Gas Mark 6, for 30–40 minutes.

———— ● ————

The fat for pastry making in this part of France depends largely on individual taste – goose fat, butter and oil all have their supporters. Open tarts are filled not only with prunes but with all the other fruits as they come into season. Plums, especially the green-yellow *reines-claude* or greengages, apricots, apples, pears all make fine tarts, and sometimes the fruit is given an extra lift by being first macerated in alcohol. In August in the hills of the Auvergne and the Pyrenees a harvest of the wild *airelles* or *myrtilles* (bilberries) is gathered off the scrubby bushes which grow wild on the moorland. The tiny, acidic, nearly black berries are combed off the bushes with a special wooden sieve called *un peigne* and then made into tarts or individual tartlets. We first found them at a simple wayside café perched nearly 6,000 feet up on the top of Puy Mary. On a clear summer's day we ate them with a cup of coffee while looking at the breath-taking view of the mountains of the Auvergne lying below us, carpeted with wild yellow anemones.

LA TARTE AUX MYRTILLES
Bilberry tart

Serves 4

pâte sucrée (as for previous recipe)
500 g (1 lb) bilberries
juice of ½ lemon
60 g (2 oz) sugar

for the *crème pâtissière*:
30 g (1 oz) flour
90 g (3 oz) sugar
pinch of salt
2 eggs
250 ml (9 fl oz) milk
piece of vanilla pod
8 g (¼ oz) butter

Make the pastry as in previous recipe, and after leaving it to rest, line a buttered flan case. Prick the bottom all over with a fork.

Make the *crème pâtissière* by mixing together in a pan the flour, sugar, salt and eggs. Add the hot milk in which the vanilla pod has been infused, and, after mixing, stir this cream over the heat for a few minutes. Remove from the heat and blend in the butter. Leave to cool.

Wash and drain the bilberries and put them to macerate in the lemon juice and sugar.

Preheat the oven to 200°C, 400°F, Gas Mark 6. Line the pastry case with a piece of foil or greaseproof paper weighted with dried beans and bake it on a baking sheet for 10 minutes. Remove the paper and return the case to the oven for another 10 minutes or until the pastry is lightly browned. Turn it out of its tin on to a rack to cool.

When it is cold, fill the case with a layer of the *crème pâtissière* and garnish the top with the bilberries.

As an alternative, small bilberry tartlets can be made by the same method.

——— • ———

In the realm of *pâtisserie* into which we have now moved the queen is a featherlight kind of tart going under various names and shapes. The most spectacular to look at is *le pastis*, as it is called in the Quercy and the Périgord. The genre is said to have come to the region from the Arabs and to be related to the North African Bstilla pastry and the Middle Eastern filo pastry with which baklava is made. The pastry is prepared like filo pastry, then brushed with goose fat or oil as it is built up in layers and filled with fruit – usually apple – or sometimes just flavoured with rum or orange-flower water. It is then topped with a mass of curling petals of the sugared, wafer-thin pastry.

It is a skilled operation to make *un pastis* and one which in some families is still handed down from mother to daughter. Making and stretching out the pastry into paper-thin sheets is time-consuming and tricky and not everyone may have the patience when they can buy other delicious *gâteaux* from the *pâtisseries en ville*. This tart exists also in Gascony where it is known as *une croustade* and in Les Landes as *une tourtière*. Sometimes the pastry is rolled up into a log which then earns it the title of *l'anguille* (the eel). Cahors, the attractive town on the river Lot, used to be famous for its pastry *à l'huile* – the oil or fat was painted over the thin pastry by means of a goose feather – and it is still possible to find these home-made *pastis* for sale at market there and in other towns in the area.

LE PASTIS QUERCYNOIS
Apples in filo pastry

Serves 8–10

for the pastry:
2 eggs
125 ml (4 fl oz) milk, slightly heated
125 ml (4 fl oz) water, slightly
    heated
pinch of salt
600 g (1 lb 5 oz) plain flour
1 tablespoon cooking oil

for the filling:
2 dessert apples, peeled and
    quartered
150 ml (5 fl oz) cooking oil
6 tablespoons *eau-de-vie*
250 g (8 oz) sugar

for the syrup:
4 tablespoons sugar
2 tablespoons water

1 tablespoon *eau-de-vie*

The pastry must be prepared in advance and then put to rest for 2½–3 hours before it is pulled out. In a large bowl mix the eggs, the warmed milk and water mixture, and the salt, before tipping in all the flour and blending it with a fork. When it is well blended, turn in the oil and then start to knead the paste very thoroughly with the fingers, working it round the bowl, folding and turning it until it is very supple and smooth. This will take up to 10 minutes. Then take a smaller bowl, oil it generously and roll the ball of paste in it to coat it with oil. Put a layer of greaseproof paper or clingwrap over the bowl and leave it to rest for at least 2½–3 hours. Do no more kneading after this resting time.

The next stage is the stretching of the pastry. For this you need a large table, about 1.8 × 1.35 metres (6 × 4½ ft). Cover it first with a thick protective material and then with an old sheet or tablecloth. Flour this cloth well all over, then place the ball of pastry in the centre and start pulling and lifting it outwards by its edge from the centre, working round and round, circling the table as you go until the pastry is stretched paper thin to cover the whole table. Trim off an inch or two from the very edge which tends to be thicker than the rest of the pastry. (You can use this for another *pastis* or to make *merveilles*, which are deep-fried biscuits.) The pastry is then left to dry for 1½ hours or more, depending on the temperature of the room. It should not become completely dry but still contain enough moisture to enable you to mould it into the flan case.

While waiting for the pastry to dry, prepare the ingredients for the filling. Peel and quarter the apples, and mix together in a separate bowl the oil and the *eau-de-vie*. Take a round cake tin or flan case which is 25 cm (10 in) in diameter and 5 cm (2 in) deep and oil it well. Cut a rough round out of the centre of the pastry, big enough to cover the base and the sides and place it in the bottom of the tin. Then cut a rough fan shape three-quarters the size of the tin and lay it on top with the straight edges hanging slightly over the side. Dip your fingers into the oil and brandy mixture and sprinkle this over the layer as if dampening linen before ironing it. Add a sprinkling of sugar and then cut out another fan-shaped piece of pastry. Lay this in, moisten and sugar it, then another adding at this stage two quarters of the apple, cut up into small pieces. Continue with two layers of pastry, then two more apple quarters, sprinkling every layer with the oil, brandy and sugar. The pieces of pastry should not be arranged too carefully but lightly dropped into the tin so that they are slightly crumpled and '*en l'air*' – with plenty of air between the folds. The final layer should be really crumpled and upstanding, with the overhang lifted up round the edge, to form the top, crisp layer of 'petals', making the finished gâteau look like one large over-blown rose. Do not moisten the top layer at this stage.

Bake the *pastis* in an oven pre-heated to 180°C, 350°F, Gas Mark 4, for an hour. Just before it is cooked, make a hot syrup with the sugar, water and *eau-de-vie*, and when the pastry is ready and still hot, sprinkle it all over to glaze the top.

The *pastis* is eaten warm and can be reheated if necessary. It will keep for 5–6 days in a cool place.

———— • ————

Since the Second World War the Garonne basin has become an important producer of fruit; more than a dozen co-operatives produce some 100,000 tons of fruit a year. Apples head the list, followed by pears, peaches, plums, also nectarines – including a local clingstone variety known as *brugnons* – then grapes, melons and cherries. Nowadays the markets during the summer and autumn contain an abundance of fresh fruit, most of it commercially grown. At the same time there is clear evidence of 'home-grown' fruit to be seen, growing on the tree or on the vine, and sometimes brought to market. In former days and often still, apples and pears, if they were not consumed straight away, were stored through the winter in the *grenier*, that is, if they were not dried in the bread oven or bottled in syrup.

As far as apples are concerned, there is now a preponderance of *la golden*, that insipid variety which unfortunately seems to grow only too well. But *les reinettes* are still about and are always recommended either for eating fresh or for cooking in tarts. Sometimes you come across one of the older varieties of apple by the side of the road, perhaps the *pommes de l'Estre* or *la coujonne* or *la pomme d'anis* which keep well right through the winter. There are also the old cider apple trees, surviving from the end of the last century when their existence was reluctantly appreciated by many at the time of the phylloxera disaster. Robert Louis Stevenson records in his *Travels with a Donkey*:

> Phylloxera has ravaged the vineyards in this [St. Jean de Gard] neighbourhood and in the morning . . . I found a party of men working with a cider press [and] asked one fellow to explain.
> 'Making cider. *Oui, c'est comme ça, comme dans le nord!*' There was a ring of sarcasm in his voice; the country was doing to the devil.

These apple trees still yield and local cider or apple juice is bottled and sold in food stores alongside wine, while cider and roast chestnut *fêtes* are part of the local scene in autumn.

Two varieties of pears appear to be the market leaders – the soft-textured *poire William* and the crisper, more rustic *beurré Hardy* which is yellow-skinned as its name suggests.

Montauban is the peach-growing centre. Most of those grown commercially are the yellow-fleshed variety, *les pêches jaunes* and in high season these are sold not only by the kilo but more advantageously, by *le plateau*, a trayful containing about 4 kilos of fruit. If there are *les pêches blanches* to be had, these will be more expensive but their finer flavour will justify this to a peach lover. And if by luck there should be the smaller *pêches de vignes* with their grey, fuzzy skin and yellow flesh, these have an even better taste despite their less luscious appearance. Nectarines with their smooth, plum-like skin do not bruise as easily as peaches. Their flesh is juicier and they now seem to be taking a larger share of the market.

At the same time as the peaches and nectarines, the high season for melons arrives. These are the delicious, orange-fleshed melons which, although developed in the Charente, are now grown in the Quercy and the Gers. For many this is the best of all the varieties. Melons may start selling at a price which means serving them as a treat – a slice sprinkled with salt to bring out its flavour or eaten with a piece of salty *jambon de campagne* as an hors d'oeuvre. But when the prices fall low enough to allow a half-melon each, *melons à l'estagel* make a delicious end to a summer meal. As a guide to buying, a ripe melon will give slightly beneath the thumb when pressed gently at the stalk end, and must smell quite definitely of melon. If there is no perfume or only a very slight one, a melon needs putting to ripen in the sun for however long it takes to soften and for it to give off its characteristic odour.

LES MELONS À L'ESTAGEL
Melon filled with fruit and brandy

Serves 4

2 Charentais melons
4 tablespoons Muscat de Rivesaltes,
   port or other fortified wine
half a pineapple
250 g (½ lb) of another fruit –
   strawberries, raspberries etc.

4 tablespoons armagnac or other
   brandy
castor sugar to taste

Cut the melons in half horizontally, remove the seeds and then with a grapefruit knife, cut out most of the flesh and dice this into a bowl. Put a tablespoonful of Muscat into each half.

Cut the pineapple into 1 cm (½ in) slices, cut off the spines and remove the core and cut the flesh into dice. Add to some of the cubed melon, together with whatever other fruit you are using. Sprinkle with the brandy and sugar to taste and put to chill with the melon halves until required.

Just before serving, fill the scooped-out melons with the mixed fruit.

———— ● ————

Strawberries can be used to fill the melon; the smaller, darker-coloured variety which comes from the Lot has a sweetness and depth of flavour vastly superior to the large, woodier kind we seem to favour in Great Britain. The story of the arrival, at the end of the last century, of the strawberry which has since made St Geniez d'Olt in the Lot its fortune, is a delightful example of peasant perseverance.

As a reward for climbing a neighbour's particularly awkwardly placed cherry tree to pick the fruit for him, a young boy from St Geniez was given a handful of strawberries. Never having seen such fruit before, he did not eat them but dried the berries and then planted their seeds. After three years of persevering, he picked his first crop and went on from there to start a big strawberry cultivation, using as beds the abandoned terraces where vines had grown until they were devastated by phylloxera. By the turn of the century the strawberries of St Geniez d'Olt were famous and they now export tens of thousands of kilos daily in high season.

By far the most delicious strawberries of all must be *les fraises des bois* which grow wild on the edges of woodland in many parts of the South-West. These tiny fruit have a concentration of flavour which is remarkable since they seem to need little nourishment or sun. They can be traced by their heart-shaped leaf, a smaller version of the cultivated strawberry leaf. Picking is a slow, back-breaking job but given enough plants, a handsome crop can be served, either *nature* with no sweetening or liquor, or else with a generous helping of *crème fraîche* or *fromage frais* (unripened fresh cheese). French *crème fraîche* has a slightly fermented taste due to its lactic acid content. This, and other fermenting bacteria, are normally killed by pasteurization but the French wisely replace these. It is possible to make an approximation by mixing two parts of double cream with one part buttermilk or soured cream. Heat these gently to just below body temperature (about 24°C/ 75°F) and then store, partly covered, in a warm place overnight or until the cream thickens and tastes slightly acid. It will thicken more as it matures and will keep for a week or so in the refrigerator. (French *crème fraîche* has a high butterfat content, up to 60%, which makes it a better thickener and enricher of cooked sauces since it does not easily curdle.)

Other fruits to enjoy during the summer are cherries, figs and grapes. Some of the earliest cherries come from the far south of the Languedoc close to the Spanish border in the east of the Pyrenees. They can also be seen growing in neglected profusion on the southern slopes of the Cévennes. Varieties to look for are *les griottes* – small, sharp-tasting and black, *les bigarreaux* which have firm dryish flesh and the sweet *guignes* which have a pointed end. Fig trees are quite a common sight and will grow at quite high altitudes as well as in the valleys, although recent severe winter frosts have done considerable damage to some, just as they have to the olive trees further south. There are one- and two-crop varieties, for picking in early summer and then in August-September. The green-skinned fruit is more common in the region than the blue-black kind.

Finally at the end of the fruit harvest come *les raisins*, grapes. Although wine grapes play such a large part in those areas of the region where they like the soil and the climate, there is, as well, a thriving production of sweet dessert grapes, mainly in the Garonne valley. Here they grow the juicy, large white and black *muscat* grapes and the smaller, green-gold *chasselas*, all providing a cheap and refreshing dessert.

In the wine-growing areas before the advent of sugar, the sweetening agent for jam-making was grapes. A popular Languedocian jam is *le raisiné* for which the grape pulp and juice is boiled down until it thickens and then pieces of fruit – pears, apples, figs, carrots or whatever is available – are added. Since all these fruits arrive in such abundance – in a good year that is – converting them to jam is not the only way to save them so they can do duty at a later date. Drying or bottling are other solutions but preserving fruit in alcohol seems to achieve the best of all possible worlds. Grapes and cherries are treated in this way and a description of the method for prunes is to be found on page 292. Earlier in the season fresh plums are also treated in this way. To be more exact it is the first plums to arrive, *les reines-claude* (greengages) which get 'bottled'.

LES REINES-CLAUDE À L'EAU-DE-VIE
Greengages bottled in plum brandy

Serves 4

1 kg (2¼ lb) greengages	*eau-de-vie* (equal quantity with the
500 g (1 lb) sugar	syrup)
300 ml (½ pt) water	

Buy or pick slightly under-ripe fruit and discard any bruised or blemished ones. Leave their stalks on. Prick them several times with a needle through to the stone.

Bring a pan of water barely to simmering point. Put a small quantity of the plums into a piece of muslin and plunge them into the hot water while you count up to 15. Transfer them immediately into a bowl of cold water. When they are cool, drain them. Repeat these operations with the rest of the fruit.

Sterilize two large, wide-necked jars. Make a syrup with the sugar and water, allowing it to bubble for 5 minutes. Plunge half of the fruit into this syrup, bring the pan gently back to a bare simmer and lift out the fruit. Repeat with the second lot of fruit; care should be taken not to heat the fruit too quickly or too much or their skins may burst.

Put the drained plums into the jars and boil up the syrup again. Leave it to cool slightly, otherwise the jars could crack, before pouring it over the fruit. Before doing so, however, measure the quantity of syrup you have – it should be about 400 ml (15 fl oz) – and pour half into each jar. Top up with an equal quantity of *eau-de-vie*, making sure that the fruit is entirely immersed. Seal and leave for 6 to 8 weeks before using. The sugar in the syrup may crystallize on cooling but it will slowly re-dissolve in time, so do not worry about this.

———— • ————

Although these are originally peasant recipes for preparation at home, like so many others they are now being prepared on a commercial basis and it is possible to buy attractive jars filled with all kinds of fruit, macerated in alcohol. These make most acceptable gifts or are a useful addition to the store cupboard for those unable to prepare their own. In France they are shared with family and friends at the end of a festive meal, or perhaps offered to a visitor making an impromptu call. This is a part of the innate hospitality and generosity of the country people, however modest their circumstances.

LE VIN

T HE ROLL-CALL of the wines of the South-West is one of the
most resplendent in the world. The red wines of Bordeaux are
the finest made anywhere, and there are commercial producers
all over the area making wines which enjoy an international market:
Cahors, Madiran, Tursan, Buzet, Duras, Fronton, Bergerac and
Marcillac among the reds; Gaillac, Monbazillac, Jurançon and
Montravel among the whites.

At first sight it is surprising that the quality divide between these
famous growths and the wines which the peasant farmers make for
their own consumption should be so dramatic. You might think that in
an area where so much good wine is made even the most basic wine
would be of high quality. This is not so, however, and the reasons are
not hard to find.

Good wine results from the right combination of grape-variety,
climate and soil, brought to fruition by the skill of the wine-maker.
From the Middle Ages onwards men learnt that certain areas were
capable of producing good wine from certain grapes. Such was the
demand for wine for blending that soon whole wine-growing areas
developed as clusters of monocultures in contrast to the normal peasant
tradition of growing a bit of everything on the farm.

Nor did the peasants have any need or appreciation of these better
wines, which were made largely for overseas markets. Wine was
simply what you made yourself to accompany meals on the farm. It was
the symbolic counterpart of bread. Water contains no nourishment, but
wine represents all the goodness to be had in liquid rather than solid

form. It is neither an extravagance nor a luxury and is healthy – a natural food.

It is used with what seems to us wanton abandon in *daubes* and braised dishes, but it costs less to buy in its basic form than mineral water at the village shop. Not that the peasant buys water, relying as he does on his own spring or well if it is a good one – or the village pump. When mains water came to our house, we were thought real townies for buying a long hose to water the *potager*. Some peasants will watch their produce crumple in the summer heat rather then ruin it with 'chemicals'.

In an effort to reduce alcohol consumption in France, peasant farmers in the South-West are being persuaded to dig up their vines, except in areas of quality production, and the tradition of having a few rows of their own may one day die out. The French Government could however be aiming at the wrong targets. Alcoholism may be a problem in some of the larger towns, but it is seldom seen in the countryside.

Certainly it has been traditional for every *oustal* to have its own vines, sometimes at some distance from the farmhouse. They may have been inherited or have come to the *oustal* through marriage, and, if they face the right way and the soil is right, they will be a much prized possession. Even peasants who have moved into the towns have cherished plots of vines within easy reach of their homes.

Our farmhouse used to belong to the local *notaire* and records show that he made quite a lot of wine which had a good reputation (relatively) in the district. Although we have no vines ourselves, we are always struck by the sense of busyness and excitement locally at the time of *la vendange*, when the grapes are picked and the wine is made. The work is very hard: it has to be done quickly if the wine is not to spoil through too much exposure to the air, but the satisfaction is evident as you watch teams of pickers at work. Different plots of vines ripen at different times, so it is common for families to collaborate in harvesting each other's grapes. It is the accomplishment of a seasonal cycle, bringing the same sense of fulfilment as the corn harvest or the killing of a pig. Work takes on for the peasant its true meaning on such occasions, an end or beginning of life, or its perpetuation from year to year.

The old mystical link between the peasant and his vines is still strong. The bourgeois may look down his nose at much of this locally made stuff, which is fairly basic. But that is not the point. It is the produce of one's own labour, and acquires more quality as a result than is afforded by all the skills of the modern wine-maker. You only have to watch Paul Mader's cousin bringing in his crop of grapes in an old cart towed behind his tractor to feel his sense of pride and satisfaction.

Just as there is a contrast in style and quality between the world-famous wines of the region and the home-made peasant wine, so there is a corresponding difference in the standards of brandy and other spirits. The South-West is famous for its armagnac brandy, some of the finest made anywhere in the world. But the same kind of 'still' (locally called *alambic*) which is used to make armagnac is also used in country districts to make *eaux-de-vie* from all kinds of fruit as well as grapes. One of the most picturesque sights in the autumn is the travelling *alambic* which goes from village to village so that the peasants can bring their plums or, after *la vendange*, the debris of the grapes, to turn them into a potent brandy or a fiery *marc*. The machine looks rather like a primitive steam-engine and huffs and puffs huge quantities of steam in the same way. From somewhere in its lower recesses the brandy emerges in a thin trickle, a tiny amount in relation to the quantity of skins and pulp which went into the making of it.

The village *eau-de-vie de prunes* can be either a fierce, colourless dose of fire-water far above the alcoholic strength of what you can buy in the shops, or a normal-strength liqueur, tinted by the addition of caramel, refined for the bourgeois market. The nearly neat variety will be more often used to lace coffee than taken on its own.

Eau-de-vie may be made only for holders of a licence. The amount which each is allowed to have made is in theory controlled by the law, but the winter climate is a good excuse to stretch the system to its utmost. Sadly, home-distillation is said by the powers-that-be to encourage alcoholism, so the days when the travelling still comes to the village are slowly coming to an end. The licences held by the peasants will die with them; the law will not allow them to be passed on to the next generation.

Eau-de-vie de noix cannot be made in this way, because of the hardness of the walnuts. So you don't need a 'still' and you can make it at home. The green walnuts are picked in summer and macerated in flavourless alcohol, which is produced industrially and available at most grocers.

L'EAU-DE-VIE DE NOIX
Walnut liqueur

20 to 25 green walnuts	small piece of cinnamon stick
575 ml (1 pt) 40° alcohol for	125 g (4 oz) sugar
preserving fruit	100 ml (3 fl oz) water
1 clove	

Crush the nuts with a mallet. The young nuts are wonderfully juicy but you will find that they stain your hands dark brown, so use rubber gloves.

Put the pieces of crushed nut into a large glass jar which you have cleansed thoroughly, and pour in the alcohol. Add the clove and cinnamon, cover the jar and leave it in the sun for at least two weeks, preferably longer.

Then strain the liquid through a muslin into a clean bottle. Dissolve the sugar in the water, bringing it gently to the boil, then simmer for a minute or two. Remove this syrup from the heat and add a little more alcohol. Leave to cool and when barely lukewarm pour it on to the liquor in the bottle. Cork and leave it to mature for as long as you can – two months at least. These quantities should be enough to fill a normal 75cl wine bottle.

———— ● ————

In country farms there is no apéritif tradition as such, although visitors will always be offered something to drink, irrespective of the time of day. This surprised us in our early days in France, particularly when we called on the local carpenter who was making some windows and shutters for us. We had to contend with rather large glasses of sweet red Martini at eight in the morning.

Sometimes the offering will be home-made; sometimes it will be a sweet brown wine from the Midi, the universal pastis, or a simple glass of wine. It is not done to refuse offers of this kind unless you know your host really well.

When they are on their own, country people will take their midday meal immediately they get back at lunchtime. They will have wine with their meal but nothing before it. Similarly in the evening it is straight to supper. The following recipe is nevertheless still typical of the sort of drink that is made to offer visitors, inexpensive and easy to prepare, quite distinctive and most refreshing. The dried, bitter orange skin is obtainable from chemists in even quite small villages.

L'Apéritif de Villevayre
Orange peel apéritif

This is named after a tiny village in the Rouergue where the recipe was given to us by the schoolmistress.

1 litre (1¾ pt) *vin rosé*
1 coffee cup (100 cl) *eau-de-vie*

50 g (1¾ oz) dried bitter orange peel
250 g (8 oz) sugar

Put all the ingredients into a thoroughly cleaned bowl and leave to macerate for two days. Strain the liquid through a fine muslin and bottle. It can be drunk straight away.

———— • ————

Walnut leaves are used to produce an apéritif, particularly in areas which do not produce much wine. Tradition requires the young leaves to be picked before midsummer's day, and this should be observed since the leaves which must be used are the very young ones, still a very fresh green in colour, tinged with crimson and slightly translucent. When handled they give off a strong aromatic scent.

LE VIN DE NOYER
Walnut leaf wine

45 g (1½ oz) fresh walnut leaves   200 g (7 oz) sugar
300 ml (½ pt) *eau-de-vie*   1 litre (1¾ pt) young red wine

Steep the walnut leaves in the *eau-de-vie* in a covered jar for two weeks. Strain off the *eau-de-vie* at the end of this time and discard the leaves.

Dissolve the sugar in the red wine by shaking or stirring, then add this to the liquor and mix well together. Pour into sterilized bottles, cork them and leave for a week or two before using.

———— • ————

In the Cévennes they steep chopped walnuts in wine for forty days, strain off the liquid and sweeten it with sugar. It is then stored for as long as possible before use. They also make their own instant version of *Pineau des Charentes* which they call *Cartagène*. They mix one part of brandy with three of grape-juice and this is said to be something of a carpet-slipper drink.

On cold winter nights, or indeed at any time when internal warmth is required to eke out the supplies of fire-wood, *vin chaud* is prepared around the fire – not as elaborate a concoction as our mulled wine, but serving the same purpose and just as effective.

Le Vin Chaud
Mulled wine

1 litre (1¾ pt) good red wine
300 ml (½ pt) water
250 g (½ lb) sugar

juice of 2 oranges or 1 lemon
a small piece of cinnamon stick

Put all the ingredients into a casserole (enamelled not metal) and bring almost to boiling point. Leave to cool slightly before pouring into heat-resistant glasses.

———— ● ————

In the Ariège a variation on this theme is called *Hypocras*. This can be made from any wine, or from beer or cider, and can be flavoured with angelica, juniper berries, walnuts, orange, vanilla or whatever flavours you choose to infuse in it. Here is a typical example:

Hypocras
Hippocras

500 ml (16 fl oz) sweet white wine
125 ml (4 fl oz) white port
125 ml (4 fl oz) medium sherry
250 ml (8 fl oz) *eau-de-vie* or
  armagnac

small piece of cinnamon stick
1 clove
pinch of nutmeg and of pepper

Put all the ingredients into a bowl or jug to macerate for 24 hours. Strain into clean bottles and serve, either as an aperitif or after a meal.

———— ● ————

Country districts have various local recipes for drinks and infusions, often medicinal in origin. Sometimes they even taste good too, and are enjoyed for their own merits. For example, *Le Vespreto* calls for coriander, angelica, anise and fennel seeds to be steeped for a week in *eau-de-vie* with sugar and lemon. The country people are able to make their own versions of commercial aperitifs – anything better than buying a branded version.

Crème de cassis is also easy to make, for use as an ingredient in a *kir* or as a flavouring for desserts, especially ice-cream. Our local postmaster's wife managed to lose for five years some blackcurrants she had set aside macerating in *eau-de-vie* and the result was sensational.

LA CRÈME DE CASSIS
Blackcurrant liqueur

250 g (½ lb) blackcurrants, and a few leaves
500 ml (16 fl oz) *eau-de-vie*
pinch of cinnamon

1 clove
175 g (6 oz) sugar
100 ml (3 fl oz) water

De-stalk the currants and crush them roughly – with a fork or in a liquidizer. Transfer the pulp to a jar, add the leaves, *eau-de-vie* and spices, and cover. Leave for at least two months, longer if possible, and exposed to sunlight.

Strain the crushed fruit and liquid through fine muslin into a sterilized bottle. Make a syrup with the sugar and water, allowing it to simmer for a minute or two. Remove from the heat, add a good extra dash of *eau-de-vie* and leave to cool before adding it to the currant juice in the bottle. Cork it and leave to mature. These quantities make a good half litre (1 pint) of liqueur.

•

In the Périgord a special kind of *eau-de-vie* is made from the tiny dark blue fruit of a species of wild plum. Here is a translation of a local farmer's recipe:

LA GNOLE (LIQUEUR DE PRUNELLE)
Wild plum brandy

'I gather the fruits of the prunellier when they are really ripe, after the first frosts when the blackbirds are after them. I crush them and put them in a barrel. I add a bouquet of fresh wild mint. I then leave the fruit to ferment, not forgetting to leave the cork out of the barrel, or it will explode. In January or February I distil the juice. Once made *la gnole* should be stored in an oak or chestnut barrel, well corked, and kept for preference in a cellar hewn out of rock and well-aerated, where the temperature does not change much from 12 degrees (C) winter and summer. A good *gnole* should be at least five years old.

When ready it can be bottled and it will stop developing. It has this slightly russet colour, warm to look at and lively, like well-waxed wood.'

—— ● ——

We end, appropriately, with these old country drinks and customs. It is sad that the peasants see their traditional habits disappearing one by one, with the regimentation of animal food-production, the industrialization of poultry-rearing and egg-raising, the mass production in northern France of vast surpluses of grain, and gradually the conversion of wine-making into an industry created for the benefit of those living in the towns and abroad. The peasant has always had enough to complain about. It is remarkable that in reality his daily life still provides a fair amount of philosophical satisfaction and the knowledge that his ways of doing things are still often the best.

ENVOI

Looking back over the recipes in this book, one is astonished at their invention and variety, when, as recently as one hundred years ago, much of South-West France was so desperately poor and backward. The improvement in living standards which has occurred in the meantime has not been accompanied by an erosion of the regional character to the same extent as in Britain. Each area of the South-West has been able to create with the ingredients it can produce best an astonishing range of dishes, which all share the unmistakeable imprint of the South-West.

One is astonished, too, at the extent to which culinary tradition and local taste in food have survived, despite the competition from mass-production, globalization and the power of media-marketing. In this respect so little has changed since the first edition of this book. *Manger Sud-ouest* is now the chic thing to do in Paris and scores of restaurants have sprung up to cash in on the trend. Those which boast *cassoulet* or *confit* as a speciality far outnumber those from any other region, according to the Michelin *Guide Rouge*. Many Parisians have their roots in the South-West and come back to stay with relations for holidays. This helps to keep the traditions alive. Home food to them is South-West cooking, not that of the mainstream Parisian restaurant menus. It may even be that sympathy with those who have vandalized fast-food establishments springs not so much from a desire to make a political statement as from a resistance to what José Bové calls *la malbouffe* (a surfeit of trashy food).

Holidays are also the times when *fêtes* are held and enterprising village committees run local events round dishes that can be cooked in bulk and that are typical of the *terroir*, dishes too which may be hard to find outside the region. *Soirées aligot* or *soirées estofinado* are frequently held in the villages local to us, like the *fêtes de châtaignes* already described. Restaurants which offer a choice of fixed-price menus often include one which is exclusively regional, proposing specialities such as *foie gras*, *confits* and *cèpes*. The increasing number of British expatriates and holiday-makers have helped popularize these South-West staples in restaurants back home, in dishes which until recently would have been widely regarded as bizarre.

The South-West is not, however, immune from change. The tradition is always undergoing mutation, sometimes as a result of the introduction of new crops or ingredients. Notable, for example, is the rapid spread of sunflower cultivation, the oil from which is taking over part of the role played by the traditional cooking fats. It may be tasteless, but it is light and healthier than many other cooking oils. Increased prosperity means that families are eating much more meat than they did. Thrift and economy remain the order of the day, however; nothing is thrown away if it can possibly be put to use, as many of the recipes show.

The mechanization of farming has come late to the South-West. When we bought our house in 1961, oxen were still in use as beasts of burden and for ploughing: tractors were a relative novelty. Today even the smallest units own or have access to combine harvesters and the latest mechanical aids. Machines for pruning the vines in summer and for harvesting the grapes in autumn are widely used in the more serious wine-making areas, and the French love of gadgetry in general ensures a steady stream of mechanical novelties at country fairs and markets.

Farming units are tending to get bigger and fewer, reversing a trend that was set in motion by the Napoleonic laws of inheritance. A village near to us has four farms today, compared with over forty when we bought our house. The state has intervened to encourage the increase in the size of farms. Under a policy known as *remembrement* a farmer sometimes has the right of first refusal over land adjoining his own which is up for sale.

Mechanization and inheritance laws have also accelerated the movement of people away from the land. This does not necessarily mean that they go to live and work in Paris or Toulouse: some stay on in the country, adapting traditional trades to new markets, or, like Alain, the *gardien* of our house, who does not work the land as his father did but has a job in the local town. Nevertheless Alain is a fanatical grower of fruit and vegetables, and arranges for a neighbour to rear the family pig for him in the traditional way. Alain will also take his own fruit to the travelling still in November for conversion into fiery *eau-de-vie*.

The inbred passion for *la chasse*, whether for game or mushrooms, persists and shows no sign of abating, and the countryside still flocks to the local town on market-day, whether to do serious business with livestock, or to make some pocket-money with vegetables from the garden – or just for a chance to meet old friends and relations for a good gossip. As the older peasants die, fewer youngsters are taking their place in the local markets with modest offerings from their *potagers*. But there are still the large number of itinerant market-stallholders who go from one town to another as a regular full-time way of life, sometimes offering some exotic imports – remember that oranges were once regarded as exotic – as well as the usual display of local produce. The markets themselves have lost none of their appeal to the local population, and some towns and villages have developed evening markets which specialize in local produce from small growers, often biological ones.

The semi-industrial manufacture of *charcuterie* and other products for sale at the larger markets is a thriving industry. Some country artisans have established sales outlets in the shops and market-stalls of local towns, and they even sell by mail-order. Many offer hams, either whole or in joints, vacuum-packed, while a wide range of *pâtés* are sold in tins. Pork, chicken-liver, rabbit, hare, wild boar and even the poor little thrush all appear in this guise. *Cassoulet* is sold in jars or tins and *confits* of all kinds are put up into cans. Goose and duck fat – or sometimes a mixture of the two – clarified for use in cooking can also be bought in large tins. Mushrooms, especially *cèpes*, are canned or dried on a large scale and aimed at overseas markets. It is noticeable how many of the dishes in this book can now be bought in some form or another, tinned or bottled, vacuum-packed or frozen. These replace the home-made versions which today's families cherish, but often no longer have the skill or the time to prepare in their own kitchens.

Also increasingly geared to international trade is the cheese industry; Roquefort has had its world-wide market for some time but is no longer unique. Pyrenean farmers who once sent their ewes' milk to Roquefort now find it more profitable to make their own hard cheeses which today enjoy an international reputation. What was once a family cheese-business in our local town achieved such an international reputation that it was taken over by big business.

Another old tradition lately given a new push is the keeping of goats for cheese-making. Whereas thirty years ago you might have found a peasant, his wife, or even a child or two sitting in the shade of a tree at the edge of a field while their cows grazed their way through the meadow, you are more likely today to find a farmer's wife minding her herd of goats. And then she will be seen at the local market with a tray of small, round cheeses, some of a creamy mildness, others more mature and with a hefty tang and aroma.

Old culinary traditions are being resuscitated, and marketed along lines which were unheard of twenty-five years ago. Since walnut oil was taken up again by some of the more enterprising chefs for use in their salads, it is now being produced on a larger scale. Big firms have moved into this market, but the best oil is still made by the artisan-millers. Then there are the experiments being made in the Périgord and the Gers to see if truffles can be persuaded to grow on a commercial scale: young truffle orchards are being planted in the hope if not the faith that, if the growers have got things right, there will be good truffle-harvests in ten or fifteen years' time. Wine-making in once lesser-known wine areas has developed tremendously over the last few years with exports all over the world, whereas to most people outside the region, South-West wine used to mean exclusively Bordeaux. Who in England ten years ago would have heard of Cahors or Madiran, for example? As a sideline for the wine-industry, there is a thriving trade in some of the local *apéritifs* and liqueurs, such as *liqueur de noix, pétillant de raisin, vin paillé*, as well as a whole range of fruits bottled in armagnac or *eaux-de-vie*.

In the richer, more fertile areas of the valleys, fruit is cultivated in huge quantities, small farming units having given way to immense, highly industrialized farms, where peaches, apricots, nectarines and pears are grown for sale all over Europe. There are, too, the ubiquitous Golden Delicious orchards, but some smaller growers are concentrating on preserving and reproducing the older, more indigenous species of fruits. Some farmers in the Périgord and the Lot are specializing in strawberry-growing ; they have produced a new variety, a cross between the wild strawberry and the cultivated kind: called *mara des bois,* it manages to combine the perfume of the one with the commercial size of the other.

But, despite this growth in production, there has been little drop in quality, control of which is something the French encourage. At the markets, boxes of fruit and vegetables nearly always indicate the name and home-town of the producer, and in the butchers' shops, the identity of the farmer-producer is proudly proclaimed as a guarantee of regional origin and quality. The system of *appellation contrôlée* has been extended to cover foodstuffs as well as wines and the parallel *Label Rouge* is a certificate of quality given to poultry and other products. There are strict regulations for food-manufacture and classifications for food-retailing. The French also stimulate the maintenance of quality through national and regional exhibitions and competitions where awards are given for excellence. All these factors help to counteract the influence that the fast foods and mass-produced raw materials inevitably have. Add to this the innate conservatism of the countryman, hitherto regarded as a misfortune, and his love of local traditions, and these now become a precious asset.

For those who want to see the character of regional cooking maintained and not swept away by the tide of convenience, the French peasant's resistance to change may yet turn out to be a virtue. It must be remembered that his traditional fear of novelty was based on the fact that peasant diet reflected the fruit of peasant labour, so that anything which was not capable of production by the *oustal* was, by definition, foreign.

Perhaps the greatest irony is that the best chance for the preservation of the peasant repertoire of cookery lies with the bourgeoisie, who seem to be turning away from the more weird manifestations of fancy restaurant preparations, and rediscovering the *goût du terroir*. The cuisine of the South-West is enjoying a fashion in both France and Great Britain: restaurants in the South-West itself no longer assume that their customers want to move up-market from peasant to bourgeois styles. Could it be that when *mousse au chocolat* and *tournedos Rossini* are long forgotten, we may yet be pulling out the pastry for a traditional *pastis quercynois* and simmering aromatic *daubes* over a wood fire?

APPENDIX

REGULATIONS CONTROLLING CONTENTS OF TINNED FOIE GRAS PRODUCTS

CATEGORY I : PRODUCTS BEARING WORDS "FOIE GRAS"*

a) *Foie gras d'oie entier* — 1 or more lobes of liver per tin. A small piece of lobe is permitted as make-weight if necessary.

Foie gras de canard entier — The same but only 1 piece of lobe of liver per tin if capacity of tin is less than 250g. A small piece of lobe is permitted as make-weight if necessary.

b) *Foie gras d'oie*
Foie gras de canard — Pieces of lobes of liver assembled together. Each piece must weigh at least 20g.

c) *Bloc de foie gras d'oie*
Bloc de foie gras de canard — *Foie gras* reconstituted by machine. The words "*avec morceaux*" require that these pieces of *foie gras* must weigh at least 10g each and constitute not less than 30% of the contents.

CATEGORY II : PRODUCTS CONTAINING A MINIMUM OF 75% FOIE GRAS

Parfait de foie d'oie
Parfait de foie de canard — Processed *foie gras* (75% minimum). Can be a blend of the two livers. May have up to 25% added liver from unfattened goose or duck.

---

*AUTHOR'S NOTE: ONLY PRODUCTS BEARING THE DESCRIPTION "*FOIE GRAS*" AS IN THIS CATEGORY ARE 100% *FOIE GRAS*. IN ALL OTHER CATEGORIES THE PERCENTAGE OF FOIE GRAS MUST BE STATED ON THE LABEL.

CATEGORY III : PRODUCTS CONTAINING A MINIMUM OF 50% FOIE GRAS

a) *Médaillon* or *pâté de foie d'oie* *Médaillon* or *pâté de foie de canard*

Foie gras or *bloc de foie gras* (50% minimum) surrounded by forcemeat. Can also be a blend of the two livers.

b) *Galantine de foie d'oie* *Galantine de foie de canard*

Foie gras mixed with forcemeat, 35% of which must be visible pieces of liver. Can also be a blend of the two livers.

c) *Mousse de foie d'oieFoie gras* *Mousse de foie de canard*

(50% minimum) and forcemeat mixed to produce a mousse. Can also be a blend of the two livers.

CATEGORY IV : PRODUCTS CONTAINING A MINIMUM OF 20% FOIE GRAS

All products described as '*au foie d'oie*' '*au foie de canard*' (x% de *foie gras*)

Foie gras and forcemeat mixed or assembled according to its description.

Permitted use of term *truffé*

If the guaranteed percentage of truffles is at least 3%. This applies only to Categories I and II.

Permitted use of term *truffé à x%*

If the percentage is between 1 and 3% (Categories III and IV).

Forcemeat

Can be made from pork meat and fat, veal, chicken, pork and chicken liver.

Decree no. 93-999, approved by the French Ministers of State, of the Economy, of Agriculture & Fisheries, 9 August 1993.

GLOSSARY

abattis. Giblets of poultry.

alambic. Travelling 'still' for making local brandies.

basse-cour. The parts of the farm where the family poultry and rabbits are reared.

batterie de cuisine. A collection of cooking utensils.

bocal (pl. *bocaux*). Glass preserving jar with rubber seal.

bouillon. Meat, fish or vegetable stock.

braise. Glowing embers, hence slow cooking on a gentle fire (*braiser*).

buron. Primitive house where herdsmen live and make cheese in summer.

cantou, lou (patois). The fireside.

capucin (patois: *lou flambadou*). Cone-shaped implement for basting spit roasts.

cassole. Glazed earthenware pot for cassoulet.

causses. The arid, limestone plateaux between valleys.

chabrol (faire). To add wine to the last spoonfuls of soup in the bowl.

chapon (patois: *lou capou*). Garlic and oil impregnated piece of bread or toast.

châtaigneraie. Chestnut woods.

cheminée. Chimney above open hearth, sometimes occupying the whole wall of a room.

civet. Stew, usually enriched with wine and giblets.

cocotte, en. Cooked in a heavy-bottomed pot with a tight-fitting lid.

confit. Meat cooked and preserved in its own fat.

couenne. Pork rind.

crémaillère. Pot hook, to hang over the fire.

crépine. Caul, the stomach lining of a pig.

daube (patois: *estouffat*). Slowly-cooked meat stew.

daubière. Formerly a copper casserole, sometimes on feet, with indented lid which held hot ashes. For braising. Modern equivalents include enamel-lined Le Creuset range, and unlined cast-iron casseroles.

déboiradour. wooden 'scissors' for shelling chestnuts.

demi-sec. Partially-dried (pulses).

eau-de-vie. Distillation of wine or fruits into brandy.

fête. Local celebrations, usually village-based.

foie gras. Liver of the specially fattened goose or duck.

foire. Fair, usually monthly. A more important version of a weekly market (*marché*).

fonte. Cast-iron.

flageolet. Green bean, the size and shape of a white haricot bean.

flambadou (patois). Cone-shaped implement for basting spit roasts.

flamber. To ignite with alcohol as a means of burning off surplus fat.

fromage, doux, entre-deux, vieux. Cheese, mild, medium, strong.

gavage. Force-feeding of geese and ducks with maize.

gousse d'ail. Clove of garlic.

graisse. Rendered fat. Formerly referred mainly to goose fat.

grès. Earthenware.

hachoir. Two-handled chopper with crescent-shaped blade.

jambon de campagne. Country-cured ham, usually eaten raw.

julienne. Thin strips, usually of vegetables.

jus, au. With its juices.

landier. Fire-dog.

lard. Pork hard back fat.

lard maigre de poitrine salée. Lean salt belly of pork.

lardons. Small strips of salt belly of pork (*poitrine salée*).

lèchefrite. Rectangular iron or copper dish placed under roasting spit to collect meat juices.

livre, une. Half a kilo or just over 1 lb.

manteau. Fattened goose or duck, boned in preparation for making *confit*, and without its liver. Also known as *paletot*.

marché, Market for sale of foodstuffs, clothing etc.

marmite. Tall pot for soup and *pot-au-feu*.

miche. Large, round country loaf, weighing up to 2 kilos.

mi-cuit. Lightly cooked (of *foie gras*). Not for long-keeping.

mouli-légumes. Vegetable mill.

oeufs fermier. Free-range eggs.

oule. Bulbous shaped *marmite* (q.v.) in cast-iron or earthenware, sometimes on feet, and in varying sizes.

oustal. The farm as a continuing family unit.

pain de campagne. Country-style bread made from unrefined flour.

pain de seigle. Rye bread.

paletot. See *manteau*.

persillade. Chopped garlic and parsley usually added to a dish at the end.

pétrin. Wooden, lidded trough for mixing bread dough.

pigeonnier. Pigeon house or dove-cot.

poêle. Frying pan, formerly often with a long handle (*à longue queue*)

poitrine salée. Salt belly of pork (also known as *ventrèche*).

potager. Vegetable garden.

poulet fermier. Free-range chicken.

primeur, en. Early in the season.

prune. Plum.

pruneau. Prune.

quatre-épices. A ground mixture of pepper, cloves, nutmeg, ginger or cinnamon, sold ready-made.

roux. Thickening agent made from flour and fat.

saignant. Underdone or 'rare', of meat.

saloir. Crock in which pieces of meat are preserved in dry salt or brine.

sarments de vigne. Prunings from a vine.

saucisse sèche. Dried pure pork sausage.

saucisson sec. Salami-type country sausage.

sauter. To fry in shallow fat.

sauteuse. Straight-sided frying pan with lid.

sécadou, clédo (patois). Out-building for drying chestnuts.

seigle. Rye.

sel, gros sel. Coarse sea salt.

souillarde. Scullery-cum-larder.

tête d'ail. A head of garlic.

tisane. Herbal tea, usually made of dried lime blossom (*tilleul*).

toupine. Stoneware jar for preserving *confit* or storing fat.

tourtière. Shallow cast-iron or copper pot with indented lid for hot ashes, used mostly for baking pastry dishes before introduction of domestic oven.

tremper. To cook or soak pieces of country bread in soup.

trépied. A trivet.

veillées. Fireside working evenings.

vendange. Harvesting the grapes (*les raisins*) to make wine.

ventrèche. see *poitrine salée.*

verjus. Unfermented juice of unripe grapes, used as a seasoning, before the arrival of the lemon.

vinaigrier. A barrel-shaped container for making and storing vinegar.

vin de rancio. A sweet wine which has maderized, i.e. oxydized, taking on the taste of madeira.

BIBLIOGRAPHY

FRENCH TITLES

Béteille, Roger, *Souvenirs d'un Enfant du Rouergue*, Hachette, 1984.

Béteille, Roger, *La Vie Quotidienne en Rouergue avant 1914*, Hachette, 1973.

Blanc. Pierre S.J., *Au Pays de mes Aïeux (en Bas-Rouergue)*, Imp. Jeanne d'Arc, Le-Puy-en-Velay, 1936.

Chapelle, Max, *Pour que vive la truffe noire*, Comp. J-J. Pauvert, 1981.

Costes, Fernande, *Bonaguil ou le château fou*, Editions du Seuil, Paris, 1976.

Delmas, Jean, *Autour de la Table, (Recettes traditionelles du Rouergue)*, Ed. Française d'Arts Graphiques, Rodez, 1983.

De Rivoyre, E. et J., *La Cuisine Landaise*, Editions Denoël, Paris, 1980.

Dufour, Henri, *Armagnac (Eau-de-vie et Terroir)*, Privat, Toulouse, 1982.

Fromage, M et Sabourin, L., *Des Légumes Toute l'Année*, Flammarion, Paris, 1964.

Gauchy, Marcel, *Najac en Rouergue* – 1000 ans d'histoire et de vie économique, Imp. Grapho 12, Villefranche-de Rouergue, 1982.

Guide des Champignons, Readers' Digest, Paris, 1982.

Guinandeau-Franc, Zette, *Les Secrets des Fermes en Périgord Noir*, Editions Serg, Paris, 1978.

Hugues, Robert, *Le Grand Livre du Foie Gras*, Briand-Laffont, Toulouse, 1982.

Mazille, La, *La Bonne Cuisine du Périgord*, Flammarion, 1929.

Merlin, A. & Beaujour, A.Y., *Les Mangeurs de Rouergue*, Editions Duculot, Paris, 1978.

Molinier, Fernand, *Promenade Culinaire en Occitanie*, Imp. Coop. du Sud-Ouest, Albi, 1975.

Philippon, Henri, *Cuisine du Quercy et du Périgord*, Denoël, Paris, 1979.

Poueigh, Jean, *Le Folklore des Pays d'Oc*, Eds. Payot, 1976.
Poulain, M., *Le Livre de L'Apprenti Charcutier*, Eds. J. Lanore, Malakoff, 1983.
Pourrat, Annette, *Traditions d'Auvergne*, Marabout, Belgium, 1976.

ENGLISH TITLES

Androuet, *Guide du Fromage*, (Eng. Edition). Aidan Ellis, 1973.
Beck, S., Bertholle, L. & Child, J., *Mastering the Art of French Cooking*, Vol. 1, Penguin, 1966.
Beck, S., Bertholle, L. & Child, J., *Mastering the Art of French Cooking*, Vol. 2, Michael Joseph, 1977.
David, Elizabeth, *French Provincial Cooking*, Michael Joseph, London, 1960.
David, Elizabeth, *French Country Cooking*, Penguin, 1959.
Grigson, Jane, *Charcuterie & French Pork Cookery*, Michael Joseph, London, 1967.
Grigson Jane, *The Mushroom Feast*, Michael Joseph, London, 1975.
Gordon, Jan & Gordon, Cora J., *Two Vagabonds in Languedoc*, Bodley Head, London, 1925.
Le Roy Ladurie, Emmanuel, *Montaillou*, Penguin, 1980.
Le Roy Ladurie, Emmanuel, *Death and Money in the Pays d'Oc*, Penguin, 1984.
Oyler, Philip, *The Generous Earth*, Penguin, 1961.
Oyler, Philip, *Sons of the Generous Earth*, Hodder & Stoughton, 1963.
Segalen, Martine, *Love & Power in the Peasant Family*, (Eng. Transl.) Blackwell, Oxford, 1983.
Stevenson, R.L., *Travels with a Donkey in the Cevennes*, Th. Nelson, Edinburgh.
Stevenson R.L., *The Cevennes Journal*, Mainstream Publishing, Edinburgh, 1978.
Weber, Eugen, *Peasants into Frenchmen. Modernisation of Rural France, 1870–1914*, Chatto & Windus, London, 1977.
White, Freda, *Three Rivers of France*, Faber & Faber, London, 1972.
White, Freda, *West of the Rhone*, Faber & Faber, London 1964.
White, Freda, *Way of Aquitaine*, Faber & Faber, London, 1968.
Willings, Heather, *A Village in the Cevennes*, Gollancz, London, 1979.

INDEX

Recipe titles, in French and English, have page references in bold type.

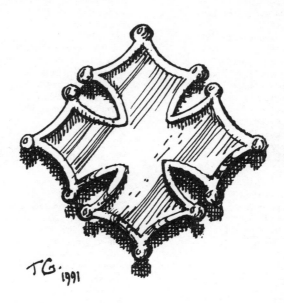

TG. 1991